murach's
MySQL

Joel Murach

TRAINING & REFERENCE

murach's MySQL

Joel Murach

MIKE MURACH & ASSOCIATES, INC.

4340 N. Knoll Ave. • Fresno, CA 93722
www.murach.com • murachbooks@murach.com

Editorial team

Author: Joel Murach

Editors: Ray Halliday
Anne Boehm

Cover design: Zylka Design

Production: Maria Pedroza David

Books for web developers

Murach's HTML5 and CSS3
Murach's JavaScript and DOM Scripting

Murach's PHP and MySQL
Murach's Java Servlets and JSP (2nd Edition)
Murach's ASP.NET 4 Web Programming with VB 2010
Murach's ASP.NET 4 Web Programming with C# 2010

Books on Java, Visual Basic, and C#

Murach's Java Programming (4th Edition)
Murach's Visual Basic 2010
Murach's C# 2010

Books for database programmers

Murach's Oracle SQL and PL/SQL
Murach's SQL Server 2008 for Developers

For more on Murach books, please visit us at www.murach.com

© 2012, Mike Murach & Associates, Inc.

Printed in the United States of America

10 9 8 7 6 5 4 3 2 1
ISBN: 978-1-890774-68-4

Content

Section 1 An introduction to MySQL

Chapter 1	An introduction to relational databases and SQL	3
Chapter 2	How to use MySQL Workbench and other development tools	41

Section 2 The essential SQL skills

Chapter 3	How to retrieve data from a single table	75
Chapter 4	How to retrieve data from two or more tables	115
Chapter 5	How to code summary queries	151
Chapter 6	How to code subqueries	169
Chapter 7	How to insert, update, and delete data	197
Chapter 8	How to work with data types	215
Chapter 9	How to use functions	241

Section 3 Database design and implementation

Chapter 10	How to design a database	277
Chapter 11	How to create databases, tables, and indexes	313
Chapter 12	How to create views	353

Section 4 Stored program development

Chapter 13	Language skills for writing stored programs	373
Chapter 14	How to use transactions and locking	401
Chapter 15	How to create stored procedures and functions	415
Chapter 16	How to create triggers and events	445

Section 5 Database administration

Chapter 17	An introduction to database administration	461
Chapter 18	How to secure a database	491
Chapter 19	How to back up and restore a database	525

Appendixes

Appendix A	How to install the software for this book on Windows	557
Appendix B	How to install the software for this book on Mac OS X	565

Expanded contents

Section 1   An introduction to MySQL

Chapter 1   An introduction to relational databases and SQL

An introduction to client/server systems **4**
The hardware components of a client/server system 4
The software components of a client/server system 6
Other client/server architectures 8

An introduction to the relational database model **10**
How a table is organized 10
How tables are related 12
How columns are defined 14
How to read a database diagram 16

An introduction to SQL and SQL-based systems **18**
A brief history of SQL 18
A comparison of Oracle, DB2, Microsoft SQL Server, and MySQL 20

The SQL statements **22**
An introduction to the SQL statements 22
How to work with database objects 24
How to query a single table 26
How to join data from two or more tables 28
How to add, update, and delete data in a table 30
SQL coding guidelines 32

How to use SQL from an application program **34**
Common options for accessing MySQL data 34
PHP code that retrieves data from MySQL 36
Java code that retrieves data from MySQL 38

Perspective **40**

Chapter 2   How to use MySQL Workbench and other development tools

An introduction to MySQL Workbench **42**
The Home tab of MySQL Workbench 42
How to start and stop the database server 44

How to use MySQL Workbench to work with a database **46**
How to open a database connection 46
How to navigate through the database objects 48
How to view and edit the data for a table 50
How to view and edit the column definitions for a table 52

How to use MySQL Workbench to run SQL statements **54**
How to enter and execute a SQL statement 54
How to use the Snippets tab 56
How to handle syntax errors 58
How to open and save SQL scripts 60
How to enter and execute SQL scripts 62

How to use the MySQL Reference Manual **64**
How to view the manual 64
How to look up information 64

How to use the the MySQL monitor **66**
How to start and stop the MySQL monitor 66
How to use the MySQL monitor to work with a database 68

Perspective **70**

Section 2 The essential SQL skills

Chapter 3 **How to retrieve data from a single table**

An introduction to the SELECT statement **76**
The basic syntax of the SELECT statement 76
SELECT statement examples 78

How to code the SELECT clause **80**
How to code column specifications 80
How to name the columns in a result set using aliases 82
How to code arithmetic expressions 84
How to use the CONCAT function to join strings 86
How to use functions with strings, dates, and numbers 88
How to test expressions by coding statements without FROM clauses 90
How to eliminate duplicate rows 92

How to code the WHERE clause **94**
How to use the comparison operators 94
How to use the AND, OR, and NOT logical operators 96
How to use the IN operator 98
How to use the BETWEEN operator 100
How to use the LIKE and REGEXP operators 102
How to use the IS NULL clause 104

How to code the ORDER BY clause **106**
How to sort by a column name 106
How to sort by an alias, expression, or column number 108

How to code the LIMIT clause **110**
How to limit the number of rows 110
How to return a range of rows 110

Perspective **112**

Chapter 4 **How to retrieve data from two or more tables**

How to work with inner joins **116**
How to code an inner join 116
How to use table aliases 118
How to join to a table in another database 120
How to use compound join conditions 122
How to use a self-join 124
How to join more than two tables 126
How to use the implicit inner join syntax 128

How to work with outer joins **130**
How to code an outer join 130
Outer join examples 132

Other skills for working with joins **136**
How to join tables with the USING keyword 136
How to join tables with the NATURAL keyword 138
How to use cross joins 140

How to work with unions **142**
How to code a union 142
A union that combines results sets from different tables 142
A union that combines result sets from the same tables 144
A union that simulates a full outer join 146

Perspective **148**

Chapter 5   How to code summary queries

How to work with aggregate functions **152**
How to code aggregate functions 152
Queries that use aggregate functions 154

How to group and summarize data **156**
How to code the GROUP BY and HAVING clauses 156
Queries that use the GROUP BY and HAVING clauses 158
How the HAVING clause compares to the WHERE clause 160
How to code compound search conditions 162
How to use the WITH ROLLUP operator 164

Perspective **166**

Chapter 6   How to code subqueries

An introduction to subqueries **170**
Where to code subqueries 170
When to use subqueries 172

How to code subqueries in the WHERE clause **174**
How to use the IN operator 174
How to use the comparison operators 176
How to use the ALL keyword 178
How to use the ANY and SOME keywords 180
How to code correlated subqueries 182
How to use the EXISTS operator 184

How to code subqueries in other clauses **186**
How to code subqueries in the HAVING clause 186
How to code subqueries in the SELECT clause 186
How to code subqueries in the FROM clause 188

How to work with complex queries **190**
A complex query that uses three subqueries 190
A procedure for building complex queries 192

Perspective **194**

Chapter 7   How to insert, update, and delete data

How to create test tables **198**
How to create the tables for this book 198
How to create a copy of a table 198

How to insert new rows **200**
How to insert a single row 200
How to insert multiple rows 200
How to insert default values and null values 202
How to use a subquery in an INSERT statement 204

How to update existing rows **206**
How to update rows 206
How to use a subquery in an UPDATE statement 208

How to delete existing rows **210**
How to delete rows 210
How to use a subquery in a DELETE statement 210

Perspective **212**

Chapter 8   How to work with data types

The data types **216**
Overview 216
The character types 218
The integer types 220
The fixed-point and floating-point types 222
The date and time types 224
The ENUM and SET types 228
The large object types 230

How to convert data **232**
How implicit data conversion works 232
How to convert data using the CAST and CONVERT functions 234
How to convert data using the FORMAT and CHAR functions 236

Perspective **238**

Chapter 9   How to use functions

How to work with string data **242**
A summary of the string functions 242
Examples that use string functions 244
How to sort by a string column that contains numbers 246
How to parse a string 248

How to work with numeric data **250**
How to use the numeric functions 250
How to search for floating-point numbers 252

How to work with date/time data **254**
How to get the current date and time 254
How to parse dates and times with date/time functions 256
How to parse dates and times with the EXTRACT function 258
How to format dates and times 260
How to perform calculations on dates and times 262
How to search for a date 264
How to search for a time 266

Other functions you should know about **268**
How to use the CASE function 268
How to use the IF, IFNULL, and COALESCE functions 270

Perspective **272**

Section 3   Database design and implementation

Chapter 10   How to design a database

How to design a data structure **278**
The basic steps for designing a data structure 278
How to identify the data elements 280
How to subdivide the data elements 282
How to identify the tables and assign columns 284
How to identify the primary and foreign keys 286

How to enforce the relationships between tables 288
How normalization works 290
How to identify the columns to be indexed 292

How to normalize a data structure **294**
The seven normal forms 294
How to apply the first normal form 296
How to apply the second normal form 298
How to apply the third normal form 300
When and how to denormalize a data structure 302

How to use MySQL Workbench for database design **304**
How to open an existing EER model 304
How to create a new EER model 304
How to work with an EER model 306
How to work with an EER diagram 308

Perspective **310**

Chapter 11   How to create databases, tables, and indexes

How to work with databases **314**
How to create and drop a database 314
How to select a database 314

How to work with tables **316**
How to create a table 316
How to code a primary key constraint 318
How to code a foreign key constraint 320
How to alter the columns of a table 322
How to alter the constraints of a table 324
How to rename, truncate, and drop a table 326

How to work with indexes **328**
How to create an index 328
How to drop an index 328

A script that creates a database **330**

How to use MySQL Workbench **334**
How to work with the columns of a table 334
How to work with the indexes of a table 336
How to work with the foreign keys of a table 338

How to work with character sets and collations **340**
An introduction to character sets and collations 340
How to view character sets and collations 342
How to specify a character set and a collation 344

How to work with storage engines **346**
An introduction to storage engines 346
How to view storage engines 346
How to specify a storage engine 348

Perspective **350**

Chapter 12   How to create views

An introduction to views **354**
How views work 354
Benefits of using views 356

How to work with views **358**
How to create a view 358
How to create an updatable view 362
How to use the WITH CHECK OPTION clause 364
How to insert or delete rows through a view 366
How to alter or drop a view 368

Perspective **370**

Section 4 Stored program development

Chapter 13 Language skills for writing stored programs

An introduction to stored programs **374**
Four types of stored programs 374
A script that creates and calls a stored procedure 374
A summary of statements for coding stored programs 376

How to write procedural code **378**
How to display data 378
How to declare and set variables 380
How to code IF statements 382
How to code CASE statements 384
How to code loops 386
How to use a cursor 388
How to declare a condition handler 390
How to use a condition handler 392
How to use multiple condition handlers 396

Perspective **398**

Chapter 14 How to use transactions and locking

How to work with transactions **402**
How to commit and rollback transactions 402
How to work with save points 404

How to work with concurrency and locking **406**
How concurrency and locking are related 406
The four concurrency problems that locks can prevent 408
How to set the transaction isolation level 410
How to prevent deadlocks 412

Perspective **414**

Chapter 15 How to create stored procedures and functions

How to code stored procedures **416**
How to create and call a stored procedure 416
How to code input and output parameters 418
How to set a default value for a parameter 420
How to validate parameters and raise errors 422
A stored procedure that inserts a row 424
How to work with user variables 428
How to work with dynamic SQL 430
How to drop a stored procedure 432

How to code stored functions **434**
How to create and call a function 434
A function that calculates balance due 436
How to drop a function 438

How to use MySQL Workbench with stored routines **440**
How to view stored routines 440
How to create stored routines 440
How to drop stored routines 440

Perspective **442**

Chapter 16   How to create triggers and events

How to work with triggers **446**
How to create a BEFORE trigger 446
How to use a trigger to enforce data consistency 448
How to create an AFTER trigger 450
How to view or drop triggers 452

How to work with events **454**
How to turn on the event scheduler 454
How to create an event 454
How to view, alter, or drop events 456

Perspective **458**

Section 4   Database administration

Chapter 17   An introduction to database administration

Database administration concepts **462**
Database administrator responsibilities 462
Types of database files 464
Types of log files 464

How to monitor the server **466**
How to view and kill processes 466
How to view the status variables 468
How to view the system variables 470

How to configure the server **472**
How to set system variables using MySQL Workbench 472
How to set system variables using a text editor 474
How to set system variables using the SET statement 476

How to work with logging **478**
How to enable and disable logging 478
How to configure logging 480
How to view text-based logs 482
How to view the binary log 484
How to manage logs 486

Perspective **488**

Chapter 18   How to secure a database

An introduction to user accounts **492**
An introduction to SQL statements for user accounts 492
A summary of privileges 494
The four privilege levels 498
The grant tables in the mysql database 498

How to work with users and privileges **500**
How to create, rename, and drop users 500
How to specify user account names 502

How to grant privileges 504
How to view privileges 506
How to revoke privileges 508
How to change passwords 510
A script that creates users 512

How to use MySQL Workbench **514**
How to use the Admin tab to work with users 514
How to use the SQL Editor tab to connect as a user for testing 518

Perspective **522**

Chapter 19   How to back up and restore a database

Strategies for backing up and restoring a database **526**
A backup strategy 526
A restore strategy 526

How to back up a database **528**
How use mysqldump to back up a database 528
A SQL script file for a database backup 530
How to set advanced options for a database backup 534

How to restore a database **536**
How to use a SQL script file to restore a full backup 536
How to execute statements in the binary log 538
How to view and edit statements in the binary log 540

How to import and export data **542**
How to export data to a file 542
How to import data from a file 544

How to check and repair tables **546**
How to use the CHECK TABLE statement 546
How to use the REPAIR TABLE statement 548
How to repair an InnoDB table 548
How to use the mysqlcheck program 550
How to use the myisamchk program 552

Perspective **554**

Introduction

Since its release in 2000, MySQL has become the world's most popular open-source database. It has been used by everyone from hobbyists to the world's largest companies to deliver cost-effective, high-performance, scalable database applications...the type of applications that the web is built on. In fact, MySQL has been used as the database for many high-profile web sites, including Wikipedia, Facebook, and Twitter. So knowing MySQL is a plus for any developer today.

Who this book is for

This book is designed for developers who are new to MySQL, as well as developers who have been using MySQL for years but who still aren't getting the most from it. It shows how to code all the SQL statements that developers need for their applications, and it shows how to code these statements so they run efficiently.

This book is also a good choice for anyone who wants to learn standard SQL. Since SQL is a standard language for accessing database data, most of the SQL code in this book will work with any database management system. As a result, once you use this book to learn how to use SQL to work with a MySQL database, you can transfer most of what you have learned to another database management system, such as Oracle, SQL Server, or DB2.

This book is also the right *first* book for anyone who wants to become a database administrator. Although this book doesn't present all of the advanced skills that are needed by a DBA, it will get you started. Then, when you complete this book, you'll be prepared for more advanced books on the subject.

5 reasons why you'll learn faster with this book

- Unlike most MySQL books, this one starts by showing you how to query an existing database rather than how to create a new database. Why? Because that's what you're most likely to need to do first on the job. Once you master those skills, you can learn how to design and implement a database if you need to do that. Or, you can learn how to work with other database features like transactions or stored procedures if you need to do that.

- Unlike most MySQL books, this one shows you how to use MySQL Workbench to enter and run your SQL statements. MySQL Workbench is a graphical tool that's an intuitive and user-friendly replacement for MySQL Monitor, a command-line program that has been around since the beginning of MySQL. In our experience, using MySQL Workbench instead of the command line helps you learn more quickly.

- Like all of our books, this one includes hundreds of examples that range from the simple to the complex. That way, you can quickly get the idea of how a feature works from the simple examples, but you'll also see how the feature is used in the real world from the complex examples.

- Like most of our books, this one has exercises at the end of each chapter that give you hands-on experience by letting you practice what you've learned. These exercises also encourage you to experiment and to apply what you've learned in new ways.

- If you page through this book, you'll see that all of the information is presented in "paired pages," with the essential syntax, examples, and guidelines on the right page and the perspective and extra explanation on the left page. This helps you learn more with less reading, and it is the ideal reference format when you need to refresh your memory about how to do something.

What you'll learn in this book

- In section 1, you'll learn the concepts and terms you need for working with any database. You'll also learn how to use MySQL Workbench to work with a database and run SQL statements.

- In section 2, you'll learn all the SQL skills for retrieving data from a database and for adding, updating, and deleting that data. These skills move from the simple to the complex, so you won't have any trouble if you're new to SQL. But these skills are also sure to raise your expertise even if you already have SQL experience.

- In section 3, you'll learn how to design a database. This includes learning how to use MySQL Workbench to create an EER (enhanced entity-relationship) model for your database. Then, you'll learn how to implement that design by using the DDL (Data Definition Language) statements that are a part of SQL. When you're done, you'll be able to design and implement your own database. In addition, you'll gain valuable perspective that will make you a better SQL programmer, even if you never have to design a database.

- In section 4, you'll learn how to use MySQL to create stored procedures, functions, triggers, and events. In addition, you'll learn how to manage transactions and locking. These features allow you to create stored programs made up of multiple SQL statements that can be stored in the database and accessed as needed, either to run on their own or to use in application programs…a great productivity booster! So once you master these features, you'll have a powerful set of MySQL skills.

- In section 5, you'll learn a starting set of skills for becoming a database administrator (DBA). These skills include how to secure a database, how to back up a database, and how to restore a database.

What software you need for this book

Although you should be able to use this book with most versions of MySQL, we recommend that you use:

- MySQL Community Edition 5.5 or higher
- MySQL Workbench 5.2 or higher

Both of these products can be downloaded for free from MySQL's web site. And appendixes A (for Windows) and B (for Mac OS X) provide complete instructions for installing them.

Since the MySQL server is backwards compatible, all of the SQL statements presented in this book should also work with future versions of MySQL. In addition, most statements presented in this book work with earlier versions of MySQL, and we have done our best to identify any statements that don't.

If you use MySQL Workbench 5.2.38, all of the skills presented in this book should work exactly as described. However, MySQL Workbench is being actively developed, so its functionality is improving all the time. As a result, you may want to use a later version of MySQL Workbench. If you do, the skills presented in this book may not work exactly as described, but they'll be similar enough that you shouldn't have any trouble with them.

What you can download from our web site

You can download all the source code for this book from our web site. That includes:

- A script file that creates the three databases used by this book.
- The source code for all examples in this book.
- The solutions to the exercises that are at the end of each chapter.

Again, appendixes A (Windows) and B (Mac OS X) provide complete instructions for installing these items on your computer.

Support materials for trainers and instructors

If you're a corporate trainer or a college instructor who would like to use this book for a course, we offer an Instructor's CD that includes: (1) a complete set of PowerPoint slides that you can use to review and reinforce the content of the book; (2) instructional objectives that describe the skills a student should have upon completion of each chapter; (3) test banks that measure mastery of those skills; (4) additional chapter exercises that aren't in this book; and (5) solutions to those exercises.

To learn more about this Instructor's CD and to find out how to get it, please go to our web site at www.murach.com and click on the Trainers link or the Instructors link. Or, if you prefer, you can call Kelly at 1-800-221-5528 or send an email to kelly@murach.com.

Please let me know how this book works for you

When I started this book, I had two goals. First, I wanted to get you started with MySQL as quickly and easily as possible. Second, I wanted to raise your database development skills to a professional level.

Now, I thank you for buying this book. I wish you all the best with your MySQL development. And if you have any comments about this book, I'd love to hear from you.

Joel Murach, Author
joel@murach.com

Section 1

An introduction to MySQL

Before you begin to learn the fundamentals of programming in MySQL, you need to understand some concepts and terms related to SQL and relational databases. That's what you'll learn in chapter 1. Then, in chapter 2, you'll learn about some of the tools you can use to work with a MySQL database. At that point, you'll have all of the background and skills that you need to work with the rest of this book.

1

An introduction to relational databases and SQL

This chapter presents the concepts and terms that you should understand before you begin learning how to work with a SQL database such as MySQL. Although this chapter doesn't present the coding details, it does present an overview of the most important types of SQL statements that are presented in this book.

An introduction to client/server systems 4
The hardware components of a client/server system 4
The software components of a client/server system 6
Other client/server architectures 8
An introduction to the relational database model 10
How a table is organized 10
How tables are related 12
How columns are defined 14
How to read a database diagram 16
An introduction to SQL and SQL-based systems 18
A brief history of SQL 18
A comparison of Oracle, DB2, Microsoft SQL Server, and MySQL 20
The SQL statements 22
An introduction to the SQL statements 22
How to work with database objects 24
How to query a single table 26
How to join data from two or more tables 28
How to add, update, and delete data in a table 30
SQL coding guidelines 32
How to use SQL from an application program 34
Common options for accessing MySQL data 34
PHP code that retrieves data from MySQL 36
Java code that retrieves data from MySQL 38
Perspective 40

An introduction to client/server systems

In case you aren't familiar with client/server systems, the topics that follow introduce you to their essential hardware and software components. When you use SQL to access a MySQL database, that system is often a client/server system.

The hardware components of a client/server system

Figure 1-1 presents the three hardware components of a client/server system: the clients, the network, and the server. The *clients* are usually the PCs that are already available on the desktops throughout a company. Clients can also be mobile devices like laptops, tablets, and smartphones. And the *network* is the cabling, communication lines, network interface cards, hubs, routers, and other components that connect the clients and the server.

The *server*, commonly referred to as a *database server*, is a computer that has enough processor speed, internal memory (RAM), and disk storage to store the files and databases of the system and provide services to the clients of the system. This computer can be a high-powered PC, a midrange system like an IBM System x or Unix system, or even a mainframe system. When a system consists of networks, midrange systems, and mainframe systems, often spread throughout the country or world, it is commonly referred to as an *enterprise system*.

To back up the files of a client/server system, a server usually has a backup disk drive or some other form of offline storage. It often has one or more printers or specialized devices that can be shared by the users of the system. And it can provide programs or services like e-mail that can be accessed by all the users of the system.

In a simple client/server system, the clients and the server are part of a *local area network* (*LAN*). However, two or more LANs that reside at separate geographical locations can be connected as part of a larger network such as a *wide area network* (*WAN*). In addition, individual systems or networks can be connected over the Internet.

A simple client/server system

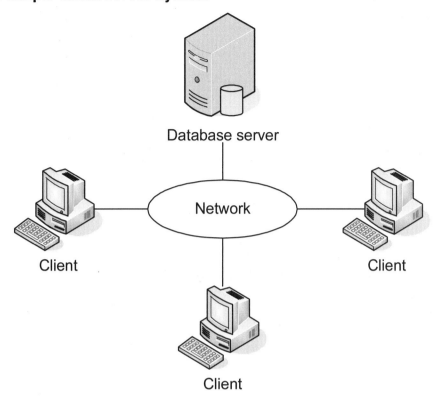

The three hardware components of a client/server system

- The *clients* are the PCs, Macs, or workstations of the system. They can also be mobile devices like laptops, tablets, and smartphones.
- The *server* is a computer that stores the files and databases of the system and provides services to the clients. When it stores databases, it's often referred to as a *database server*.
- The *network* consists of the cabling, communication lines, and other components that connect the clients and the servers of the system.

Client/server system implementations

- In a simple *client/server system* like the one above, the server is typically a high-powered PC that communicates with the clients over a *local area network* (*LAN*).
- The server can also be a midrange system, like an IBM System x or a Unix system, or it can be a mainframe system.
- A client/server system can also consist of one or more PC-based systems, one or more midrange systems, and a mainframe system in dispersed geographical locations. This type of system is commonly referred to as an *enterprise system*.
- Individual systems and LANs can be connected and share data over larger private networks, such as a *wide area network* (*WAN*), or a public network like the Internet.

Figure 1-1   The hardware components of a client/server system

The software components
of a client/server system

Figure 1-2 presents the software components of a typical client/server system. Here, the server requires a *database management system* (*DBMS*) like MySQL or Microsoft SQL Server. This DBMS manages the databases that are stored on the server.

In contrast to a server, each client requires *application software* to perform useful work. This can be a purchased software package like a financial accounting package, or it can be custom software that's developed for a specific application.

Although the application software is run on the client, it uses data that's stored on the server. To do that, it uses a *data access API* (*application programming interface*). Since the technique you use to work with an API depends on the programming language and API you're using, you won't learn those techniques in this book. Instead, you'll learn about a standard language called *SQL* (*Structured Query Language*) that lets any application communicate with any DBMS. (In conversation, SQL is pronounced as either *S-Q-L* or *sequel*.)

Once the software for both client and server is installed, the client communicates with the server via *SQL queries* (or just *queries*) that are passed to the DBMS through the API. After the client sends a query to the DBMS, the DBMS interprets the query and sends the results back to the client.

In a client/server system, the processing is divided between the clients and the server. In this figure, for example, the DBMS on the server processes the requests that are made by the application running on the client. Theoretically, at least, this balances the workload between the clients and the server so the system works more efficiently.

Client software, server software, and the SQL interface

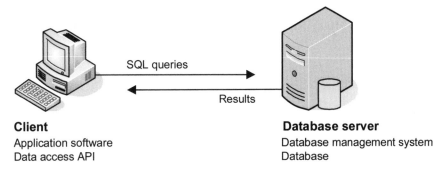

Client
Application software
Data access API

Database server
Database management system
Database

Server software

- To store and manage the databases of the client/server system, each server requires a *database management system* (*DBMS*) like MySQL.
- The processing that's done by the DBMS is typically referred to as *back-end processing*, and the database server is referred to as the *back end*.

Client software

- The *application software* does the work that the user wants to do. This type of software can be purchased or developed.
- The *data access API* (*application programming interface*) provides the interface between the application program and the DBMS. For example, for Java applications, the most common data access API for MySQL is *JDBC* (*Java Database Connectivity*).
- The processing that's done by the client software is typically referred to as *front-end processing*, and the client is typically referred to as the *front end*.

The SQL interface

- The application software communicates with the DBMS by sending *SQL queries* through the data access API. When the DBMS receives a query, it provides a service like returning the requested data (the *query results*) to the client.
- *SQL* stands for *Structured Query Language*, which is the standard language for working with a relational database.

Client/server versus file-handling systems

- In a client/server system, the processing done by an application is typically divided between the client and the server.
- In a file-handling system, all of the processing is done on the clients. Although the clients may access data that's stored in files on the server, none of the processing is done by the server. As a result, a file-handling system isn't a client/server system.

Figure 1-2   The software components of a client/server system

Other client/server architectures

In its simplest form, a client/server system consists of a single database server and one or more clients. Many client/server systems today, though, include additional servers. For example, figure 1-3 shows two client/server systems that include an additional server between the clients and the database server.

The first illustration is for a simple networked system. With this system, only the user interface for an application runs on the client. The rest of the processing that's done by the application is stored in one or more *business components* on the *application server*. Then, the client sends requests to the application server for processing. If the request involves accessing data in a database, the application server formulates the appropriate query and passes it on to the database server. The results of the query are then sent back to the application server, which processes the results and sends the appropriate response back to the client.

Similar processing is done by a web-based system, as illustrated by the second example in this figure. In this case, though, a *web browser* running on the client is used to send requests to a *web application* running on a *web server* somewhere on the Internet. The web application, in turn, can use *web services* to perform some of its processing. Then, the web application or web service can pass requests for data on to the database server.

Although this figure should give you an idea of how client/server systems can be configured, you should realize that they can be much more complicated than what's shown here. For example, business components can be distributed over any number of application servers, and those components can communicate with databases on any number of database servers. Similarly, the web applications and services in a web-based system can be distributed over numerous web servers that access numerous database servers. In most cases, though, you don't need to know how a system is configured to use SQL.

Before I go on, you should know that client/server systems aren't the only systems that support SQL. For example, traditional mainframe systems and newer *thin client* systems also use SQL. Unlike client/server systems, though, most of the processing for these types of systems is done by a mainframe or another high-powered machine. The terminals or PCs that are connected to the system do little or no work.

A networked system that uses an application server

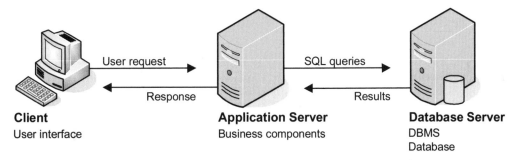

Client
User interface

Application Server
Business components

Database Server
DBMS
Database

A simple web-based system

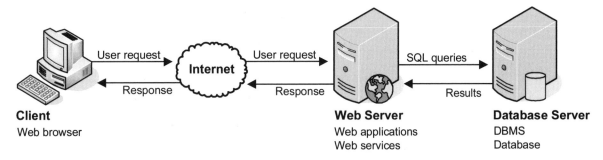

Client
Web browser

Web Server
Web applications
Web services

Database Server
DBMS
Database

Description

- In addition to a database server and clients, a client/server system can include additional servers, such as *application servers* and *web servers*.

- Application servers are typically used to store *business components* that do part of the processing of the application. In particular, these components are used to process database requests from the user interface running on the client.

- Web servers are typically used to store *web applications* and *web services*. Web applications are applications that are designed to run on a web server. Web services are like business components, except that, like web applications, they are designed to run on a web server.

- In a web-based system, a *web browser* running on a client sends a request to a web server over the Internet. Then, the web server processes the request and passes any requests for data on to the database server.

- More complex system architectures can include two or more application servers, web servers, and database servers.

Figure 1-3   Other client/server architectures

An introduction to the relational database model

In 1970, Dr. E. F. Codd developed a model for a new type of database called a *relational database*. This type of database eliminated some of the problems that were associated with standard files and other database designs. By using the relational model, you can reduce data redundancy, which saves disk storage and leads to efficient data retrieval. You can also view and manipulate data in a way that is both intuitive and efficient. Today, relational databases are the de facto standard for database applications.

How a table is organized

The model for a relational database states that data is stored in one or more *tables*. It also states that each table can be viewed as a two-dimensional matrix consisting of *rows* and *columns*. This is illustrated by the relational table in figure 1-4. Each row in this table contains information about a single vendor.

In practice, the rows and columns of a relational database table are often referred to by the more traditional terms, *records* and *fields*. In fact, some software packages use one set of terms, some use the other, and some use a combination. In this book, I use the terms *rows* and *columns* because those are the terms used by MySQL.

In general, each table is modeled after a real-world entity such as a vendor or an invoice. Then, the columns of the table represent the attributes of the entity such as name, address, and phone number. And each row of the table represents one instance of the entity. A *value* is stored at the intersection of each row and column, sometimes called a *cell*.

If a table contains one or more columns that uniquely identify each row in the table, you can define these columns as the *primary key* of the table. For instance, the primary key of the Vendors table in this figure is the vendor_id column. In this example, the primary key consists of a single column. However, a primary key can also consist of two or more columns, in which case it's called a *composite primary key*.

In addition to primary keys, some database management systems let you define additional keys that uniquely identify each row in a table. If, for example, the vendor_name column in the Vendors table contains unique data, it can be defined as a *non-primary key*. In MySQL, this is called a *unique key*.

Indexes provide an efficient way of accessing the rows in a table based on the values in one or more columns. Because applications typically access the rows in a table by referring to their key values, an index is automatically created for each key you define. However, you can define indexes for other columns as well. If, for example, you frequently need to sort the Vendor rows by zip code, you can set up an index for that column. Like a key, an index can include one or more columns.

The Vendors table in an Accounts Payable database

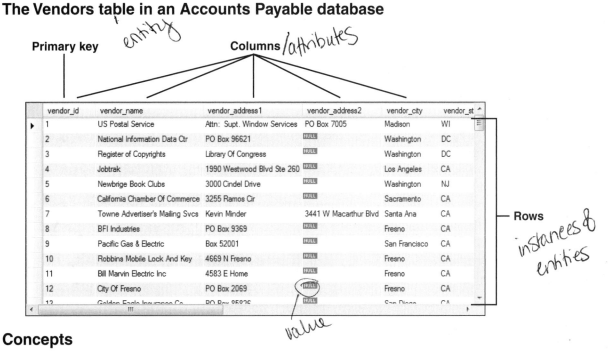

Concepts

- A *relational database* consists of *tables*. Tables consist of *rows* and *columns*, which can also be referred to as *records* and *fields*.

- A table is typically modeled after a real-world entity, such as an invoice or a vendor.

- A column represents some attribute of the entity, such as the amount of an invoice or a vendor's address.

- A row contains a set of values for a single instance of the entity, such as one invoice or one vendor.

- The intersection of a row and a column is sometimes called a *cell*. A cell stores a single *value*.

- Most tables have a *primary key* that uniquely identifies each row in the table. The primary key is usually a single column, but it can also consist of two or more columns. If a primary key uses two or more columns, it's called a *composite primary key*.

- In addition to primary keys, some database management systems let you define one or more *non-primary keys*. In MySQL, these keys are called *unique keys*. Like a primary key, a non-primary key uniquely identifies each row in the table.

- A table can also be defined with one or more *indexes*. An index provides an efficient way to access data from a table based on the values in specific columns. An index is automatically created for a table's primary and non-primary keys.

Figure 1-4   How a database table is organized

How tables are related

The tables in a database can be related to other tables by values in specific columns. The two tables shown in figure 1-5 illustrate this concept. Here, each row in the Vendors table is related to one or more rows in the Invoices table. This is called a *one-to-many relationship*.

Typically, relationships exist between the primary key in one table and the *foreign key* in another table. The foreign key is simply one or more columns in a table that refer to a primary key in another table. In this figure, for example, the vendor_id column is the foreign key in the Invoices table and is used to create the relationship between the Vendors table and the Invoices table.

Although one-to-many relationships are the most common, two tables can also have a one-to-one or many-to-many relationship. If a table has a *one-to-one relationship* with another table, the data in the two tables could be stored in a single table. Because of that, one-to-one relationships are used infrequently.

In contrast, a *many-to-many relationship* is usually implemented by using an intermediate table that has a one-to-many relationship with the two tables in the many-to-many relationship. In other words, a many-to-many relationship can usually be broken down into two one-to-many relationships.

If you define a foreign key for a table in MySQL, you can have the foreign key enforce *referential integrity*. When MySQL enforces referential integrity, it makes sure that any changes to the data in the database don't create invalid relationships between tables. For example, if you try to add a row to the Invoices table with a vendor_id value that doesn't exist in the Vendors table, MySQL won't add the row and will display an error. This helps to maintain the integrity of the data that's stored in the database.

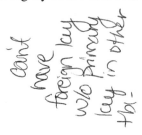

The relationship between the Vendors and Invoices tables in the database

Primary key

vendor_id	vendor_name	vendor_address1	vendor_address2	vendor_city	vendor_:
114	Postmaster	Postage Due Technician	1900 E Street	Fresno	CA
115	Roadway Package System, Inc	Dept La 21095	NULL	Pasadena	CA
116	State of California	Employment Development ...	PO Box 826276	Sacramento	CA
117	Suburban Propane	2874 S Cherry Ave	NULL	Fresno	CA
118	Unocal	P.O. Box 860070	NULL	Pasadena	CA
119	Yesmed, Inc	PO Box 2061	NULL	Fresno	CA
120	Dataforms/West	1617 W. Shaw Avenue	Suite F	Fresno	CA
121	Zylka Design	3467 W Shaw Ave #103	NULL	Fresno	CA
122	United Parcel Service	P.O. Box 505820	NULL	Reno	NV
123	Federal Express Corporation	P.O. Box 1140	Dept A	Memphis	TN

one-to-many

invoice_id	vendor_id	invoice_number	invoice_date	invoice_total	payment_total	credit_total	
55	123	963253245	2011-06-10	40.75	40.75	0.00	:
56	86	367447	2011-06-11	2433.00	2433.00	0.00	1
57	103	75C-90227	2011-06-11	1367.50	1367.50	0.00	E
58	123	963253256	2011-06-11	53.25	53.25	0.00	:
59	123	4-314-3057	2011-06-11	13.75	13.75	0.00	:
60	122	989319-497	2011-06-12	2312.20	2312.20	0.00	:
61	115	24946731	2011-06-15	25.67	25.67	0.00	4
62	123	963253269	2011-06-15	26.75	26.75	0.00	:
63	122	989319-427	2011-06-16	2115.81	2115.81	0.00	:
64	123	963253267	2011-06-17	23.50	23.50	0.00	:

Foreign key

Concepts

- The vendor_id column in the Invoices table is called a *foreign key* because it identifies a related row in the Vendors table. A table may contain one or more foreign keys.

- When you define a foreign key for a table in MySQL, you can have that foreign key enforce *referential integrity*. Then, MySQL makes sure that any changes to the data in the database don't create invalid relationships between tables.

- The most common type of relationship is a *one-to-many relationship* as illustrated by the Vendors and Invoices tables. A table can also have a *one-to-one relationship* or a *many-to-many relationship* with another table.

Figure 1-5   How tables are related

How columns are defined

When you define a column in a table, you assign properties to it as indicated by the design of the Invoices table in figure 1-6. The most critical property for a column is its data type, which determines the type of information that can be stored in the column. With MySQL, you can choose from the *data types* listed in this figure as well as several other data types that are described in chapter 8. As you define each column in a table, you generally try to assign the data type that minimizes the use of disk storage because that improves the performance of the queries later.

In addition to a data type, you must identify whether the column can store a *null value* (or just *null*). A null represents a value that's unknown, unavailable, or not applicable. In this figure, the columns that have the NN (not null) box checked don't allow null values. If you don't allow null values for a column, you must provide a value for that column when you store a new row in the table.

You can also assign a *default value* to each column. Then, that value is assigned to the column if another value isn't provided. As you can see, three of the columns of the Invoices table have a default value. You'll learn more about how to work with null and default values later in this book.

Each table can also contain a numeric column whose value is generated automatically by the DBMS. In MySQL, a column like this is called an *auto increment column*. You'll learn more about defining auto increment columns in chapter 11. For now, just note that the primary key of both the Vendors and Invoices tables—vendor_id and invoice _id—are auto increment columns.

The columns of the Invoices table

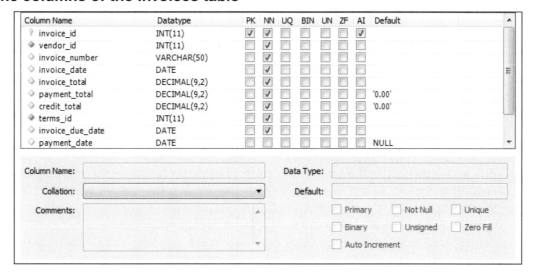

Common MySQL data types

Type	Description
CHAR, VARCHAR	A string of letters, symbols, and numbers.
INT, DECIMAL	Integer and decimal numbers that contain an exact value.
FLOAT	Floating-point numbers that contain an approximate value.
DATE	Dates and times.

Description

- The *data type* that's assigned to a column determines the type of information that can be stored in the column.

- Each column definition also indicates whether or not it can contain *null values*. A null value indicates that the value of the column is unknown.

- A column can also be defined with a *default value*. Then, that value is used if another value isn't provided when a row is added to the table.

- A column can also be defined as an *auto increment column*. An auto increment column is a numeric column whose value is generated automatically when a row is added to the table.

Figure 1-6   How columns are defined

How to read a database diagram

When working with relational databases, you can use an *entity-relationship (ER) diagram* to show how the tables in a database are defined and related. Or, you can use a newer version of an ER diagram known as an *enhanced entity-relationship (EER) diagram*. In figure 1-7, for example, you can see an EER diagram for the AP (Accounts Payable) database that's used throughout this book. This diagram shows that the database contains five related tables: Vendors, Terms, Invoices, Invoice_Line_Items, and General_Ledger_Accounts.

For each table, this diagram shows how the columns are defined. For example, it shows that the Vendors table has 12 columns. It shows the name and data type for each column. It uses a key icon to show that the primary key for this table is the vendor_id column. And it uses a dark diamond icon to show that the table has two columns that are foreign keys: default_terms_id and default_account_number.

This diagram also shows how the tables are related. To do that, it places a connector symbol between the tables. For example, the connector between the Vendors and Invoices table shows that these tables have a one-to-many relationship. On this connector, the symbol closest to the Invoices table indicates that many invoices can exist for each vendor, and the symbol closest to the Vendors table shows that only one vendor can exist for each invoice. If you study the primary and foreign keys for these tables, you can deduce that these tables are designed to be joined on the vendor_id column that's in both tables.

Similarly, this diagram shows that there's a one-to-many relationship between the Terms and Vendors table. In other words, each terms of payment can have many vendors, but each vendor can only have one default terms of payment. If you study the primary and foreign keys for these tables, you can deduce that these tables are designed to be joined on the terms_id column of the Terms table and the default_terms_id column of the Vendors table.

Most of the tables in this diagram begin with a single column that defines the primary key for the table. However, the Invoice_Line_Items table begins with two columns (invoice_id and invoice_sequence) that define the primary key for this table. In other words, since the invoice_id column doesn't uniquely identify the line item, the primary key must include the invoice_sequence column so it can uniquely identify each row.

In chapter 10, you'll learn how to use MySQL Workbench to create and work with EER diagrams. For now, you just need to understand how to read the diagram presented in this figure so you can understand the relationships between the tables in the AP database.

An EER diagram for the AP (Accounts Payable) database

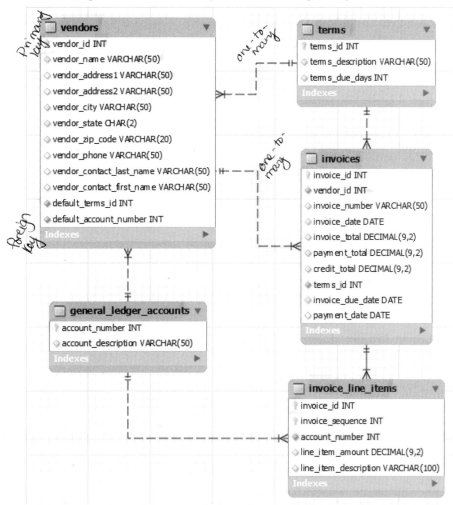

Description

- An *entity-relationship* (*ER*) *diagram* or *enhanced entity-relationship* (*EER*) *diagram* can be used to show how the tables in a database are defined and related.

Figure 1-7   How to read a database diagram

An introduction to SQL and SQL-based systems

In the topics that follow, you'll learn how SQL and SQL-based database management systems evolved. In addition, you'll learn how some of the most popular SQL-based systems compare.

A brief history of SQL

Prior to the release of the first relational database management system, each database had a unique physical structure and a unique programming language that the programmer had to understand. That all changed with the advent of SQL and the relational database management system.

Figure 1-8 lists the important events in the history of SQL. In 1970, Dr. E. F. Codd published an article that described the relational database model he had been working on with a research team at IBM. Then, in 1979, Relational Software, Inc. released the first *relational database management system*, called *Oracle*. This *RDBMS* ran on a minicomputer and used SQL as its query language. This product was widely successful, and the company later changed its name to Oracle to reflect that success.

In 1982, IBM released its first commercial SQL-based RDBMS, called *SQL/DS* (*SQL/Data System*). This was followed in 1985 by *DB2* (*Database 2*). Both systems ran only on IBM mainframe computers. Later, DB2 was ported to other operating systems, including Unix and Windows. Today, it continues to be IBM's premier database system.

During the 1980s, other SQL-based database systems, including SQL Server, were developed. Although each of these systems used SQL as its query language, each implementation was unique. That began to change in 1989, when the *American National Standards Institute* (*ANSI*) published its first set of standards for a database query language. As each database manufacturer has attempted to comply with these standards, their implementations of SQL have become more similar. However, each still has its own *dialect* of SQL that includes additions, or *extensions*, to the standards.

Although you should be aware of the SQL standards, they will have little effect on your job as a MySQL programmer. The main benefit of the standards is that the basic SQL statements are the same in each dialect. As a result, once you've learned one dialect, it's relatively easy to learn another. On the other hand, porting applications that use SQL from one type of database to another often requires substantial changes.

1995 saw the first release of MySQL, which was used internally by the company that developed it, MySQL AB. In 2000, MySQL became an open-source database. Since then, MySQL has become one of the most popular databases, especially for web applications. In 2008, MySQL was acquired by Sun Microsystems, and in 2010, Oracle acquired Sun.

Important events in the history of SQL

Year	Event
1970	Dr. E. F. Codd developed the relational database model.
1979	Relational Software, Inc. (later renamed Oracle) released the first relational DBMS, Oracle.
1982	IBM released their first relational database system, SQL/DS (SQL/Data System).
1985	IBM released DB2 (Database 2).
1987	Microsoft released SQL Server.
1989	The American National Standards Institute (ANSI) published the first set of standards for a database query language, called ANSI/ISO SQL-89, or SQL1. These standards were similar to IBM's DB2 SQL dialect. Because they were not stringent standards, most commercial products could claim adherence.
1992	ANSI published revised standards (ANSI/ISO SQL-92, or SQL2) that were more stringent than SQL1 and incorporated many new features. These standards introduced levels of compliance, or levels of conformance, that indicated the extent to which a dialect met the standards.
1995	MySQL AB released MySQL for internal use.
1999	ANSI published SQL3 (ANSI/ISO SQL:1999). These standards incorporated new features, including support for objects. Levels of compliance were dropped and were replaced by a core specification that defined the essential elements for compliance, plus nine packages. Each package is designed to serve a specific market niche.
2000	MySQL became an open-source database.
2003	ANSI published SQL4 (ANSI/ISO SQL:2003). These standards introduced XML-related features, standardized sequences, and identity columns.
2008	Sun Microsystems acquired MySQL.
2010	Oracle acquired Sun Microsystems and MySQL.

Description

- Although SQL is a standard language, each vendor has its own *SQL dialect*, or *variant*, that may include extensions to the standards.

How knowing "standard SQL" helps you

- The most basic SQL statements are the same for all SQL dialects.
- Once you have learned one SQL dialect, you can easily learn other dialects.

How knowing "standard SQL" does not help you

- Any non-trivial application will require modification when moved from one SQL database to another.

Figure 1-8   A brief history of SQL

A comparison of Oracle, DB2, Microsoft SQL Server, and MySQL

Although this book is about MySQL, you may want to know about some of the other SQL-based relational database management systems. Figure 1-9 compares MySQL with three other popular databases: Oracle, DB2, and Microsoft (MS) SQL Server.

Oracle has a huge installed base of customers and continues to dominate the marketplace, especially for servers running the Unix operating system. Oracle works well for large systems and has a reputation for being extremely reliable. However, it also has a reputation for being expensive and difficult to use.

DB2 was originally designed to run on IBM mainframe systems and continues to be the premier database for those systems. It also dominates in hybrid environments where IBM mainframes and newer servers must coexist. Although it has a reputation for being expensive, it also has a reputation for being reliable and easy to use.

SQL Server was designed by Microsoft to run on Windows and is widely used for small- to medium-sized departmental systems. It has a reputation for being inexpensive and easy to use. However, it also has a reputation for not scaling well for systems with a large number of users.

MySQL runs on all major operating systems and is widely used for web applications. MySQL is an *open-source database*, which means that any developer can view and improve its source code. In addition, the MySQL Community Server is free for most users, though Oracle also sells an Enterprise Edition of MySQL that has advanced features.

One of the main differences between MySQL and SQL Server is that MySQL runs under most operating systems including Unix, Windows, Mac OS, and IBM's z/OS. In contrast, SQL Server only runs under the Windows operating system. Since many developers consider z/OS and Unix to be more stable and secure than Windows, most large companies use z/OS or Unix as the operating system for the servers that store the databases for mission-critical applications. As a result, they can't use SQL Server and must use Oracle, DB2, or MySQL.

If you search the Internet, you'll find that dozens of other relational database products are also available. These include proprietary databases like Informix, Sybase, and Teradata. And they include open-source databases like PostgreSQL.

A comparison of Oracle, DB2, SQL Server, and MySQL

	Oracle	DB2	SQL Server	MySQL
Release year	1979	1985	1987	2000
Platforms	Unix	OS/390, z/OS	Windows	Unix
	OS/390, z/OS	Unix		Windows
	Windows	Windows		Mac OS
	Mac OS	Mac OS		z/OS

Description

- Oracle is typically used for large, mission-critical systems that run on one or more Unix servers.

- DB2 is typically used for large, mission-critical systems that run on legacy IBM mainframe systems using the z/OS or OS/390 operating system.

- Microsoft (MS) SQL Server is typically used for small- to medium-sized systems that run on one or more Windows servers.

- MySQL is a popular *open-source database* that runs on all major operating systems and is commonly used for web applications.

Figure 1-9   A comparison of Oracle, DB2, SQL Server, and MySQL

The SQL statements

In the topics that follow, you'll learn about some of the SQL statements provided by MySQL. You can use some of these statements to manipulate the data in a database, and you can use others to work with database objects. Although you may not be able to code these statements after reading these topics, you should have a good idea of how they work. Then, you'll be better prepared to learn the details of coding these statements when they're presented in the rest of this book.

An introduction to the SQL statements

Figure 1-10 summarizes some of the most common SQL statements. These statements can be divided into two categories. The statements that work with the data in a database are called the *data manipulation language (DML)*. These statements are presented in the first group in this figure, and these are the statements that application programmers use the most.

The statements that create databases and work with the objects within a database are called the *data definition language (DDL)*. On large systems, these statements are used exclusively by *database administrators (DBAs)*. It's the DBA's job to maintain existing databases, tune them for faster performance, and create new databases. On smaller systems, though, the SQL programmer may fill the role of the DBA.

SQL statements used to work with data (DML)

Statement	Description
SELECT	Retrieves data from one or more tables.
INSERT	Adds new rows to a table.
UPDATE	Changes existing rows in a table.
DELETE	Deletes existing rows from a table.

SQL statements used to work with database objects (DDL)

Statement	Description
CREATE DATABASE	Creates a new database on the server.
CREATE TABLE	Creates a new table in a database.
CREATE INDEX	Creates a new index for a table.
ALTER TABLE	Changes the definition of an existing table.
ALTER INDEX	Changes the structure of an existing index.
DROP DATABASE	Deletes an existing database and all of its tables.
DROP TABLE	Deletes an existing table.
DROP INDEX	Deletes an existing index.

Description

- The SQL statements can be divided into two categories: the *data manipulation language (DML)* that lets you work with the data in the database and the *data definition language (DDL)* that lets you work with the objects in the database.

- MySQL programmers typically work with the DML statements, while *database administrators (DBAs)* use the DDL statements.

Figure 1-10   An introduction to the SQL statements

How to work with database objects

To give you an idea of how you use the DDL statements shown in the previous figure, figure 1-11 presents some examples. Here, the first example creates a database named AP. Then, the second example selects that database. As a result, the rest of the statements in this figure are run against the AP database.

The third example creates the Invoices table that's used throughout this chapter. If you don't understand all of this code right now, don't worry. You'll learn how to code statements like this in chapter 11. For now, just realize that this statement defines each column in the table, including its data type, whether or not it allows null values, and its default value if it has one.

In addition, the third example defines the primary and foreign key columns for the table. These definitions are one type of *constraint*. Since the Invoices table includes foreign keys to the Vendors and Terms tables, these tables must be created before the Invoices table. Conversely, before you can delete the Vendors and Terms tables, you must delete the Invoices table.

The fourth example in this figure changes the Invoices table by adding a column to it. Like the statement that created the table, this statement specifies the attributes of the new column. Then, the fifth example deletes the column that was just added.

The sixth example creates an index on the Invoices table. In this case, the index is for the vendor_id column, which is used frequently to access the table. Then, the last example deletes the index that was just added.

A statement that creates a new database

```
CREATE DATABASE ap
```

A statement that selects the current database

```
USE ap
```

A statement that creates a new table

```
CREATE TABLE invoices
(
  invoice_id            INT             PRIMARY KEY    AUTO_INCREMENT,
  vendor_id             INT             NOT NULL,
  invoice_number        VARCHAR(50)     NOT NULL,
  invoice_date          DATE            NOT NULL,
  invoice_total         DECIMAL(9,2)    NOT NULL,
  payment_total         DECIMAL(9,2)                   DEFAULT 0,
  credit_total          DECIMAL(9,2)                   DEFAULT 0,
  terms_id              INT             NOT NULL,
  invoice_due_date      DATE            NOT NULL,
  payment_date          DATE,
  CONSTRAINT invoices_fk_vendors
    FOREIGN KEY (vendor_id)
    REFERENCES vendors (vendor_id),
  CONSTRAINT invoices_fk_terms
    FOREIGN KEY (terms_id)
    REFERENCES terms (terms_id)
)
```

A statement that adds a new column to a table

```
ALTER TABLE invoices
ADD balance_due DECIMAL(9,2)
```

A statement that deletes the new column

```
ALTER TABLE invoices
DROP COLUMN balance_due
```

A statement that creates an index on the table

```
CREATE INDEX invoices_vendor_id_index
ON invoices (vendor_id)
```

A statement that deletes the new index

```
DROP INDEX invoices_vendor_id_index
```

Figure 1-11   Typical statements for working with database objects

How to query a single table

Figure 1-12 shows how to use a SELECT statement to query a single table in a database. To start, this figure shows some of the columns and rows of the Invoices table. Then, in the SELECT statement that follows, the SELECT clause names the columns to be retrieved, and the FROM clause names the table that contains the columns, called the *base table*. In this case, six columns will be retrieved from the Invoices table.

Note that the last column, balance_due, is calculated from three other columns in the table. In other words, a column by the name of balance_due doesn't actually exist in the database. This type of column is called a *calculated value*, and it exists only in the results of the query.

In addition to the SELECT and FROM clauses, this SELECT statement includes a WHERE clause and an ORDER BY clause. The WHERE clause gives the criteria for the rows to be selected. In this case, a row is selected only if it has a balance due that's greater than zero. Finally, the returned rows are sorted by the invoice_date column.

This figure also shows the *result set* (or *result table*) that's returned by the SELECT statement. A result set is a logical table that's created temporarily within the database. When an application requests data from a database, it receives a result set.

The Invoices base table

invoice_id	vendor_id	invoice_number	invoice_date	invoice_total	payment_total	credit_total	terms_id
1	122	989319-457	2011-04-08	3813.33	3813.33	0.00	3
2	123	263253241	2011-04-10	40.20	40.20	0.00	3
3	123	963253234	2011-04-13	138.75	138.75	0.00	3
4	123	2-000-2993	2011-04-16	144.70	144.70	0.00	3
5	123	963253251	2011-04-16	15.50	15.50	0.00	3

A SELECT statement that retrieves and sorts selected columns and rows from the Invoices table

```
SELECT invoice_number, invoice_date, invoice_total,
    payment_total, credit_total,
    invoice_total - payment_total - credit_total AS balance_due
FROM invoices
WHERE invoice_total - payment_total - credit_total > 0
ORDER BY invoice_date
```

The result set defined by the SELECT statement

invoice_number	invoice_date	invoice_total	payment_total	credit_total	balance_due
39104	2011-07-10	85.31	0.00	0.00	85.31
963253264	2011-07-18	52.25	0.00	0.00	52.25
31361833	2011-07-21	579.42	0.00	0.00	579.42
263253268	2011-07-21	59.97	0.00	0.00	59.97
263253273	2011-07-22	30.75	0.00	0.00	30.75

Concepts

- You use the SELECT statement to retrieve selected columns and rows from a *base table*. The result of a SELECT statement is a *result table*, or *result set*, like the one shown above.

- A result set can include *calculated values* that are calculated from columns in the table.

- A SELECT statement is commonly referred to as a *query*.

Figure 1-12   How to query a single table

How to join data from two or more tables

Figure 1-13 presents a SELECT statement that retrieves data from two tables. This type of operation is called a *join* because the data from the two tables is joined together into a single result set. For example, the SELECT statement in this figure joins data from the Invoices and Vendors tables.

An *inner join* is the most common type of join. When you use an inner join, rows from the two tables in the join are included in the result table only if their related columns match. These matching columns are specified in the FROM clause of the SELECT statement. In the SELECT statement in this figure, for example, rows from the Invoices and Vendors tables are included only if the value of the vendor_id column in the Vendors table matches the value of the vendor_id column in one or more rows in the Invoices table. If there aren't any invoices for a particular vendor, that vendor won't be included in the result set.

Although this figure shows only how to join data from two tables, you can extend this syntax to join data from three or more tables. If, for example, you want to include line item data from a table named Invoice_Line_Items in the results shown in this figure, you can code the FROM clause of the SELECT statement like this:

```
FROM vendors
    INNER JOIN invoices
        ON vendors.vendor_id = invoices.vendor_id
    INNER JOIN invoice_line_items
        ON invoices.invoice_id = invoice_line_items.invoice_id
```

Then, in the SELECT clause, you can include any of the columns in the Invoice_Line_Items table.

In addition to inner joins, most relational databases including MySQL support other types of joins such as *outer joins*. An outer join lets you include all rows from a table even if the other table doesn't have a matching row. You'll learn more about the different types of joins in chapter 4.

A SELECT statement that joins data from the Vendors and Invoices tables

```
SELECT vendor_name, invoice_number, invoice_date, invoice_total
FROM vendors INNER JOIN invoices
    ON vendors.vendor_id = invoices.vendor_id
WHERE invoice_total >= 500
ORDER BY vendor_name, invoice_total DESC
```

The result set defined by the SELECT statement

vendor_name	invoice_number	invoice_date	invoice_total
Federal Express Corporation	963253230	2011-07-07	739.20
Ford Motor Credit Company	9982771	2011-07-24	503.20
Franchise Tax Board	RTR-72-3662-X	2011-05-25	1600.00
Fresno County Tax Collector	P02-88D77S7	2011-05-03	856.92
IBM	Q545443	2011-06-09	1083.58
Ingram	31359783	2011-06-03	1575.00
Ingram	31361833	2011-07-21	579.42
Malloy Lithographing Inc	0-2058	2011-05-28	37966.19

Concepts

- A *join* lets you combine data from two or more tables into a single result set.
- The most common type of join is an *inner join*. This type of join returns rows from both tables only if their related columns match.
- An *outer join* returns rows from one table in the join even if the other table doesn't contain a matching row.

Figure 1-13   How to join data from two or more tables

How to add, update, and delete data in a table

Figure 1-14 shows how you can use the INSERT, UPDATE, and DELETE statements to modify the data in a table. In this figure, for example, the first statement is an INSERT statement that adds a row to the Invoices table. To do that, the INSERT clause names the columns whose values are supplied in the VALUES clause.

In chapter 7, you'll learn more about specifying column names and values. For now, just note that you have to specify a value for a column unless it's a column that allows null values or a column that's defined with a default value.

The two UPDATE statements in this figure show how to change the data in one or more rows of a table. The first statement, for example, assigns a value of 35.89 to the credit_total column of the invoice in the Invoices table with invoice number 367447. The second statement adds 30 days to the invoice due date for each row in the Invoices table whose terms_id column has a value of 4.

To delete rows from a table, you use the DELETE statement. For example, the first DELETE statement in this figure deletes the invoice with invoice number 4-342-8069 from the Invoices table. The second DELETE statement deletes all invoices with a balance due of zero. However, since the Invoices table has a foreign key that references the Invoice_Line_Items table, these DELETE statements won't work unless the invoice doesn't contain any line items. One way to get these DELETE statements to work is to delete the corresponding rows from the Invoice_Line_Items table first.

A statement that adds a row to the Invoices table

```
INSERT INTO invoices
    (vendor_id, invoice_number, invoice_date,
     invoice_total, terms_id, invoice_due_date)
VALUES
    (12, '3289175', '2011-07-18', 165, 3, '2011-08-17')
```

A statement that changes the value of the credit_total column for a selected row in the Invoices table

```
UPDATE invoices
SET credit_total = 35.89
WHERE invoice_number = '367447'
```

A statement that changes the values in the invoice_due_date column for all invoices with the specified terms_id

```
UPDATE invoices
SET invoice_due_date = DATE_ADD(invoice_due_date, INTERVAL 30 DAY)
WHERE terms_id = 4
```

A statement that deletes a selected invoice from the Invoices table

```
DELETE FROM invoices
WHERE invoice_number = '4-342-8069'
```

A statement that deletes all paid invoices from the Invoices table

```
DELETE FROM invoices
WHERE invoice_total - payment_total - credit_total = 0
```

Concepts

- You use the INSERT statement to add rows to a table.
- You use the UPDATE statement to change the values in one or more rows of a table based on the condition you specify.
- You use the DELETE statement to delete one or more rows from a table based on the condition you specify.

Warning

- If you're new to SQL statements, please don't execute the statements above until you read chapter 7 and understand the effect that these statements can have on the database.

Figure 1-14   How to add, update, and delete data in a table

SQL coding guidelines

SQL is a freeform language. That means that you can include line breaks, spaces, and indentation without affecting the way the database interprets the code. In addition, SQL isn't case-sensitive like some languages. That means that you can use uppercase or lowercase letters or a combination of the two without affecting the way the database interprets the code.

Although you can code SQL statements with a freeform style, we suggest that you follow the coding recommendations presented in figure 1-15. The examples in this figure illustrate the value of these coding recommendations. The first example presents an unformatted SELECT statement that's difficult to read. In contrast, this statement is much easier to read after our coding recommendations are applied as shown in the second example.

The third example illustrates how to code a *block comment*. This type of comment is typically coded at the beginning of a group of statements and is used to document the entire group. Block comments can also be used within a statement to describe blocks of code, but that's not common.

The fourth example in this figure includes a *single-line comment*. This type of comment is typically used to document a single statement or line of code. A single-line comment can be coded on a separate line as shown in this example, or it can be coded at the end of a line of code. In either case, the comment is delimited by the end of the line.

Although many programmers sprinkle their code with comments, that shouldn't be necessary if you write your code so it's easy to read and understand. Instead, you should use comments only to clarify sections of code that are difficult to understand. Then, if you change the code, you should be sure to change the comments too. Otherwise, the comments won't accurately represent what the code does, which will make the code even more difficult to understand.

A SELECT statement that's difficult to read

```
select invoice_number, invoice_date, invoice_total,
payment_total, credit_total, invoice_total - payment_total -
credit_total as balance_due from invoices where invoice_total -
payment_total - credit_total > 0 order by invoice_date
```

A SELECT statement that's coded with a readable style

```
SELECT invoice_number, invoice_date, invoice_total,
    payment_total, credit_total,
    invoice_total - payment_total - credit_total AS balance_due
FROM invoices
WHERE invoice_total - payment_total - credit_total > 0
ORDER BY invoice_date
```

SELECT statement with a block comment

```
/*
Author: Joel Murach
Date: 8/22/2011
*/
SELECT invoice_number, invoice_date, invoice_total,
    invoice_total - payment_total - credit_total AS balance_due
FROM invoices
```

A SELECT statement with a single-line comment

```
-- The fourth column calculates the balance due
SELECT invoice_number, invoice_date, invoice_total,
    invoice_total - payment_total - credit_total AS balance_due
FROM invoices
```

Coding recommendations

- Capitalize all keywords, and use lowercase for the other code in a SQL statement.
- Separate the words in names with underscores, as in invoice_number.
- Start each clause on a new line.
- Break long clauses into multiple lines and indent continued lines.
- Use *comments* only for portions of code that are difficult to understand. Then, make sure that the comments are correct and up-to-date.

How to code a comment

- To code a *block comment*, type /* at the start of the block and */ at the end.
- To code a *single-line comment*, type -- followed by the comment.

Description

- Line breaks, white space, indentation, and capitalization have no effect on the operation of a statement.
- Comments can be used to document what a statement does or what specific parts of the code do. They are not executed by the system.

Figure 1-15   SQL coding guidelines

How to use SQL from an application program

This book teaches you how to use SQL from within the MySQL environment. As you learned in the last chapter, though, SQL is commonly used from application programs too. So in the topics that follow, you'll get a general idea of how that works.

As you'll see, there's a lot involved in accessing a MySQL database from an application program. That's why most application programmers use a framework that makes it easier to execute SQL statements against a database. In some cases, application programmers create their own framework by writing utility classes and data access classes. In other cases, application programmers use an existing framework that provides the classes they need.

Common options for accessing MySQL data

Figure 1-16 shows three ways to access a MySQL database when you use a programming language to write a custom application. The technique that's used varies depending on the language that's used to develop the application. However, most modern languages provide an API that allows you to connect to a MySQL database.

An API uses a piece of software known as a *database driver* to communicate with the database. For some languages, the database driver is built in. For others, you need to download and install a database driver.

To access a MySQL database from a PHP application, for example, you typically choose from two APIs. Some programmers prefer to use the *mysqli* (*MySQL Improved Extension*) API. Other programmers prefer to use the newer *PDO* (*PHP Data Objects*) API. Neither of these APIs requires a database driver, since that driver is typically included as part of the PHP language.

On the other hand, to access a MySQL database from a Java application, you typically use the *JDBC* (*Java Database Connectivity*) API. This API requires a driver to communicate with MySQL. In most cases, you can use the Connector/J driver that's available from the MySQL web site to connect a Java application to a MySQL database.

Although it's more common to use MySQL with non-Microsoft languages such as PHP and Java, it's possible to use MySQL with Microsoft .NET languages such as C# and Visual Basic.NET. However, the .NET platform doesn't include a database driver by default, so you typically need to download and install the Connector/Net driver that's available from the MySQL web site. Then, you can use the *ADO.NET* API to access a MySQL database.

Common options for accessing MySQL data

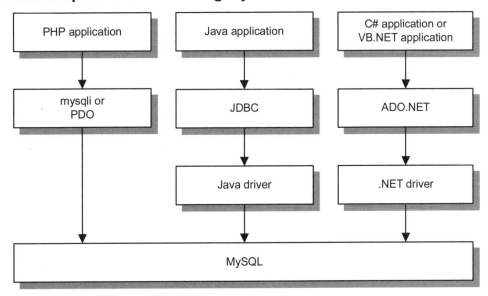

Two commonly used MySQL drivers

Name	Description
Connector/J	Connects Java applications to a MySQL database.
Connector/Net	Connects .NET applications to a MySQL database.

Description

- To work with a MySQL database, an application uses a data access API. For example, PHP uses the *mysqli* API or the *PDO* API, Java uses the *JDBC* API, and .NET languages like C# and Visual Basic.NET use the *ADO.NET* API.

- Most modern programming languages provide an API that you can use to access MySQL.

- Some programming languages include a piece of software known as a *database driver* for the API that it uses to access MySQL. For example, PHP includes a MySQL driver for both the mysqli and PDO APIs. As a result, you typically don't need to install a database driver when you use PHP.

- Some programming languages don't provide a database driver to communicate with a MySQL database. For example, Java doesn't include a MySQL driver for the JDBC API. As a result, you typically need to install a database driver such as the Connector/J driver before you can use Java to access MySQL.

Figure 1-16   Common options for accessing MySQL data

PHP code that retrieves data from MySQL

Figure 1-17 presents PHP code that uses the PDO API to execute a SQL statement against a MySQL database. This code displays information from the Vendors and Invoices tables. It creates the PDO objects used by the application and then uses them to display the data that's retrieved.

If you have some PHP programming experience, you shouldn't have much trouble understanding this code. If you don't have PHP experience, that's fine too. In that case, focus on how this code uses the PDO API to execute SQL against a MySQL database. If you want to learn more about using PHP to work with a database, we recommend *Murach's PHP and MySQL*.

The code in this figure begins by defining a PHP script. Within this script, the first statement stores a SELECT statement in a variable named $query. Then, the next three statements create variables that store the information that's needed to connect to a MySQL database named AP that's running on the same computer as the PHP application. That includes variables that specify a username of "root" and a password of "sesame".

After specifying the connection information, this code uses these variables to create a PDO object that represents a connection to the database. If this code isn't able to create a PDO object, an error known as a PDOException occurs, and the application displays an error message and ends. Otherwise, this code uses the PDO object to execute the SELECT statement, and it stores the result set in a variable named $rows.

At this point, the HTML tags begin displaying an HTML page. Within the <body> tag, a PHP script loops through each row in the result set and displays that data on the HTML page. In particular, it displays the vendor_name, invoice_number, and invoice_total columns. Here, the PHP function named number_format is used to apply formatting to the invoice_total column.

Although this code may seem complicated, there's only one statement in this figure that uses SQL. That's the statement that specifies the SELECT statement to be executed. Of course, if an application updates data, it can execute INSERT, UPDATE, and DELETE statements as well. With the skills that you'll learn in this book, though, you won't have any trouble coding the SQL statements you need for your PHP applications.

PHP code that retrieves data from MySQL

```php
<?php
    $query =
        "SELECT vendor_name, invoice_number, invoice_total
        FROM vendors INNER JOIN invoices
            ON vendors.vendor_id = invoices.vendor_id
        WHERE invoice_total >= 500
        ORDER BY vendor_name, invoice_total DESC";

    $dsn = 'mysql:host=localhost;dbname=ap';
    $username = 'root';
    $password = 'sesame';

    try {
        $db = new PDO($dsn, $username, $password);
    } catch (PDOException $e) {
        $error_message = $e->getMessage();
        echo $error_message;
        exit();
    }

    $rows = $db->query($query);
?>
<!DOCTYPE html>
<html lang = "en">
    <head>
        <title>DB Test</title>
    </head>
    <body>
        <h1>Invoices with totals over 500:</h1>

        <?php foreach ($rows as $row) : ?>
        <p>
            Vendor: <?php echo $row['vendor_name']; ?><br/>
            Invoice No: <?php echo $row['invoice_number']; ?><br/>
            Total: $<?php echo number_format($row['invoice_total'], 2); ?>
        </p>
        <?php endforeach; ?>

    </body>
</html>
```

> statement

Figure 1-17   PHP code that retrieves data from MySQL

Java code that retrieves data from MySQL

Figure 1-18 presents Java code that uses the JDBC API to execute a SQL statement against a MySQL database. This code displays information from the Vendors and Invoices tables.

If you have some Java programming experience, you shouldn't have much trouble understanding this code. If you don't have Java experience, that's fine too. In that case, focus on how this code uses an API to execute SQL against a MySQL database. If you want to learn more about using Java to work with a database, we recommend *Murach's Java Programming* and *Murach's Java Servlets and JSP*.

Before this code can be executed, a database driver must be installed. To do that, you can download the Connector/J database driver from the MySQL web site. Then, you can add the JAR file for that driver to the libraries that are available to your application.

The code in this figure begins by importing all classes in the java.sql package. These classes define JDBC objects like the Connection object that are used to access a MySQL database.

Within the main method, the first statement stores a SQL SELECT statement in a variable named query. Then, the next three statements create variables that store the information that's needed to connect to a MySQL database named AP that's running on the same computer as the Java application on port 3306. That includes variables that specify a username of "root" and a password of "sesame".

After specifying the connection information, this code uses a try-with-resources statement to create the Connection, Statement, and ResultSet objects that are needed to display the data. Since the try-with-resources statement was introduced with Java SE 7, it won't work with earlier versions of Java. If this statement isn't able to create these objects, an error known as a SQLException occurs, and the application prints an error message and ends. Otherwise, this code uses the Connection and Statement objects to execute the SELECT statement, and it stores the result set in a ResultSet object.

Next, this code uses the get methods of the ResultSet object to retrieve the values that are stored in the vendor_name, invoice_number, and invoice_total columns. Here, the getString method is used to get the VARCHAR data and the getDouble method is used to get the DECIMAL data. Finally, the NumberFormat class is used to apply currency formatting to the invoice_total column, and the values are printed to the console.

Java code that retrieves data from MySQL

```java
import java.sql.*;
import java.text.NumberFormat;

public class DBTestApp
{
    public static void main(String args[])
    {
        String query =
            "SELECT vendor_name, invoice_number, invoice_total " +
            "FROM vendors INNER JOIN invoices " +
            "    ON vendors.vendor_id = invoices.vendor_id " +
            "WHERE invoice_total >= 500 " +
            "ORDER BY vendor_name, invoice_total DESC";

        String dbUrl = "jdbc:mysql://localhost:3306/ap";
        String username = "root";
        String password = "sesame";

        try (Connection connection = DriverManager.getConnection(
                dbUrl, username, password);
            Statement statement = connection.createStatement();
            ResultSet rs = statement.executeQuery(query))
        {
            System.out.println("Invoices with totals over 500:\n");
            while(rs.next())
            {
                String vendorName = rs.getString("vendor_name");
                String invoiceNumber = rs.getString("invoice_number");
                double invoiceTotal = rs.getDouble("invoice_total");

                NumberFormat currency = NumberFormat.getCurrencyInstance();
                String invoiceTotalString = currency.format(invoiceTotal);

                System.out.println(
                    "Vendor:     " + vendorName + "\n" +
                    "Invoice No: " + invoiceNumber + "\n" +
                    "Total:      " + invoiceTotalString + "\n");
            }
        }
        catch(SQLException e)
        {
            System.out.println(e.getMessage());
        }
    }
}
```

Description

- Before you can use Java to work with MySQL, you must install a database driver. To do that, you can download the JAR file for the driver and add it to the libraries that are available to your Java application.

- To execute a SQL statement from a Java application, you can use JDBC objects such as the Connection, Statement, and ResultSet objects.

Figure 1-18   Java code that retrieves data from MySQL

Perspective

To help you understand how SQL is used from an application program, this chapter has introduced you to the hardware and software components of a client/server system. It has also described how relational databases are organized and how you use some of the SQL statements to work with the data in a relational database. With that as background, you're now ready to start using MySQL. In the next chapter, then, you'll learn how to use some of the tools for working with a MySQL database.

Terms

client	column	database administrator
server	record	(DBA)
database server	field	constraint
network	cell	base table
client/server system	value	result set
local area network	primary key	calculated value
(LAN)	composite primary key	join
enterprise system	non-primary key	inner join
wide area network (WAN)	unique key	outer join
database management	index	comment
system (DBMS)	foreign key	block comment
back end	one-to-many relationship	single-line comment
application software	one-to-one relationship	database driver
API (application	many-to-many relationship	mysqli
programming interface)	referential integrity	PDO
data access API	data type	ADO.NET
JDBC (Java Database	null value	
Connectivity)	default value	
front end	auto increment column	
SQL (Structured Query	entity-relationship (ER)	
Language)	diagram	
query	enhanced entity-relationship	
query results	(EER) diagram	
application server	relational database	
web server	managment system	
business component	(RDBMS)	
web application	SQL dialect	
web service	SQL extension	
web browser	open-source database	
thin client	data manipulation language	
relational database	(DML)	
table	data definition language	
row	(DDL)	

2

How to use
MySQL Workbench
and other development tools

In the last chapter, you learned about some of the SQL statements that you can use to work with the data in a relational database. Before you learn the details of coding these statements, however, you need to learn how to use MySQL Workbench to enter and execute SQL statements. In addition, you should learn how to use the MySQL Reference Manual, and you should at least be familiar with an older tool, called the MySQL monitor.

An introduction to MySQL Workbench **42**
The Home tab of MySQL Workbench 42
How to start and stop the database server 44
How to use MySQL Workbench to work with a database . **46**
How to open a database connection 46
How to navigate through the database objects 48
How to view and edit the data for a table 50
How to view and edit the column definitions for a table 52
How to use MySQL Workbench to run SQL statements ... **54**
How to enter and execute a SQL statement 54
How to use the Snippets tab 56
How to handle syntax errors 58
How to open and save SQL scripts 60
How to enter and execute SQL scripts 62
How to use the MySQL Reference Manual **64**
How to view the manual 64
How to look up information 64
How to use the MySQL monitor **66**
How to start and stop the MySQL monitor 66
How to use the MySQL monitor to work with a database 68
Perspective **70**

An introduction to MySQL Workbench

MySQL Workbench is a free graphical tool that makes it easy to work with MySQL. We recommend using this tool as you work through this book. As of press time for this book, the current version of MySQL Workbench is version 5.2, so that's the version presented in this chapter. However, with some minor variations, the skills presented in this chapter should work for later versions as well.

The Home tab of MySQL Workbench

When you start MySQL Workbench, it displays its Home tab as shown in figure 2-1. This tab is divided into three sections: SQL Development, Data Modeling, and Server Administration.

The SQL Development section contains links that you can use to open a connection to a MySQL server. Then, you can use that connection to code and run SQL statements. If you're using Windows, this section contains one connection by default that allows you to connect to a MySQL server that's running on the local computer as the root user. If you're using Mac OS X, you can create a connection like this using the New Connection link as described in appendix B.

The Data Modeling section contains links that let you create a database diagram from a type of data model known as an EER model. You can also use this section to open existing EER models or to create new ones. Then, you can work with EER diagrams that correspond with these models. To learn more about this, you can read chapter 10.

The Server Administration section contains links that let you manage the database server. In chapters 17 and 18, you can learn more about this. For now, you just need to be able to start and stop the database server as described in the next figure. Before you can do that on a Mac, though, you need to create a connection for managing the local server. You can learn how to do that in appendix B. This connection is automatically created for Windows when you install Workbench.

As you work with MySQL Workbench, the Home tab may become hidden by other tabs. Then, you can return to the Home tab by clicking on the tab with the house icon on it near the top left corner of the Workbench window. In this figure, the Home tab is the only tab that's shown, but you'll see some other tabs in the next few figures.

The Home tab of MySQL Workbench

How to start MySQL Workbench

Start→All Programs→MySQL→MySQL Workbench

Description

- The Home tab of *MySQL Workbench* is divided into three main sections: SQL Development, Data Modeling, and Server Administration.
- You can use the SQL Development section to code and run SQL statements.
- You can use the Data Modeling section to design databases. You'll learn more about that in chapter 10.
- You can use the Server Administration section to stop and start the database server.
- If the Home tab becomes hidden by other tabs, you can display it again by clicking the tab that has the house icon on it. This tab is always displayed in the top left corner of the Workbench window.

Figure 2-1   The Home tab of MySQL Workbench

How to start and stop the database server

If you installed MySQL on your computer as described in appendix A (PC) or B (Mac), the *database server* starts automatically when you start your computer. This piece of software is sometimes referred to as the *database service* or *database engine*. It receives SQL statements that are passed to it, processes them, and returns the results.

Before you can work with a MySQL database, the database server must be started. To check whether the MySQL database server is running on your computer, you can use the Admin tab of MySQL Workbench as shown in figure 2-2. Then, if the server isn't already running, you can start it by clicking on the Start Server button. When you do that, MySQL Workbench displays a message that indicates the status of the MySQL server, and it displays the Stop Server button.

You may also want to stop the database server from time to time. For example, you can stop the server if you aren't going to be using it and you want to free the resources on your computer. Or, you can stop the server if the port that is being used by the MySQL database server conflicts with another program. Then, when you want to work with the database server again, you can start it.

The easiest way to stop the database server is to use the Stop Server button that's available from the Admin tab of the MySQL Workbench as described in this figure. When you click this button, MySQL Workbench displays a message when the MySQL server has successfully stopped, and it displays the Start Server button.

When you're running the MySQL database server on your own computer for training purposes, you can stop the database server whenever you want. However, if a database server is running in a production environment, you should make sure that all users are logged off and that no applications are using the database server before you stop it.

In some cases, you might not be able to use MySQL Workbench to start and stop the MySQL server. For example, when you display the Startup/Shutdown category, it might not be able to determine whether the server has been started or stopped. In that case, you can attempt to use your operating system to start or stop the server. On Windows, for example, you can use the View Local Services icon in the Administrative Tools section of the Control Panel to launch a dialog box that lets you start or stop the MySQL service. On Mac OS X, you can use the MySQL preference pane to start or stop MySQL as described in appendix B.

The Admin tab of MySQL Workbench

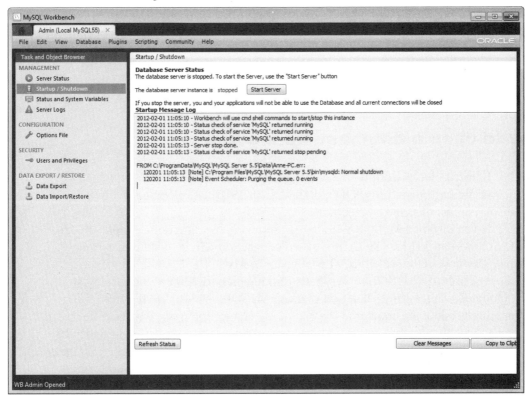

How to stop and start the database server

1. Display the Home tab of MySQL Workbench.

2. In the Server Administration section, double-click on the Local MySQL55 item. This should connect you to the local MySQL server as the root user. If necessary, enter the password for the root user. This displays an Admin tab.

3. In the Task and Object Browser section of the Admin tab, select the Startup/Shutdown category.

4. Click on the Stop Server button to stop the database server, or click on the Start Server button to start it.

Description

- After you install the MySQL Community Server, the *database server* usually starts automatically each time you start your computer. If it doesn't, you can use the Admin tab of MySQL Workbench to start it.

- The database server can also be referred to as the *database service* or the *database engine*.

- If you can't use MySQL Workbench to start and stop the server on Mac OS X, you can use the MySQL preference pane as described in appendix B.

Figure 2-2   How to start and stop the database server

How to use MySQL Workbench to work with a database

Now that you know how to start the database server, you're ready to use MySQL Workbench to connect to that server. Then, you can use MySQL Workbench to work with the databases that are running on that server.

How to open a database connection

Before you can work with a database, you need to connect to the database server. When you start MySQL Workbench, the SQL Development section displays a list of saved connections.

If you installed MySQL Workbench following the directions in appendix A (Windows) or B (Mac OS X), one saved connection will be displayed in this list. This connection is named "Local instance MySQL55", and it connects as the root user to a MySQL server that's running on port 3306 of the local host computer. (This assumes that you're using MySQL version 5.5. If you're using another version, the number at the end of the connection name will be different.) Since this is what you want when you're first getting started, you typically use this connection to connect to the server. To do that, you double-click on the connection and enter the password for the root user if you're prompted for it.

If you're using Windows, the password for the root user is "sesame." If you're using Mac OS X, the root user doesn't have a password. If you want to assign a password to the root user using MySQL Workbench, you can refer to figure 18-11 in chapter 18 to learn how to do that. In most cases, though, you don't need to do that unless other users have access to your system.

In figure 2-3, you can see the dialog box that MySQL Workbench displays to prompt for a password. This dialog box shows that it's attempting to use the root user to connect to a MySQL server running on port 3306 of the local host. In addition to entering a password in this dialog box, you can select the "Save password in vault" option to save the password so you don't have to enter it every time you connect to this server. Then, if you ever want to clear the password from the vault, you can click on the "Manage Connections" link, select the connection, and click the Clear button.

If you need to connect as another user, or if you need to connect to a MySQL server running on a different computer, you can use MySQL Workbench to specify custom connection parameters. To do that, click the "Open Connection to Start Querying" link. This displays a dialog box that lets you specify the connection parameters, such as the username, the host address, and the port number.

If you want to save a custom connection, you can click the "New Connection" link and enter the parameters for the connection. Then, this connection appears in the list of connections, and you can double-click it to use it.

The dialog box for opening database connections

Description

- To connect as the root user to an instance of MySQL that's running on the local host computer, double-click on the stored connection named "Local instance MySQL55", and enter the password for the root user if prompted.

- To specify your own connection parameters, click the "Open Connection to Start Querying" link, enter the connection parameters, click the OK button, and enter the password for the specified user if prompted. This lets you specify the username, the host address, the port number, and other connection parameters.

- To save a connection and add it to the Home tab, click the "New Connection" link and enter the connection parameters. Then, the connection appears in the list of connections.

- To save the password for a connection so you don't have to enter it every time, check the "Save password in vault" option when you're prompted for your password.

- To clear the password from the vault so you are prompted for your password, click on the "Manage Connections" link, select the connection, and click the Clear button.

Figure 2-3   How to open a database connection for querying

How to navigate through the database objects

After you connect to a database server, a SQL Editor tab for that server is displayed as shown in figure 2-4. You can use the Object Browser window in that tab to navigate through the *database objects* in the databases on the server. As you can see, these objects include tables, views, and routines. For this chapter, however, you can focus on the tables. Later in this book, you'll learn more about views and routines.

In this figure, I double-clicked the node for the AP database (or *schema*) in the Object Browser window to select it and view the database objects it contains (tables, views, and routines). Then I expanded the Tables node to view all of the tables in the AP database.

To work with a node or an object, you can right-click on it to display a context-sensitive menu. Then, you can select a command from that menu. For example, you can right-click on the node for the AP database to display a list of commands for working with that database.

The tables available for the AP database

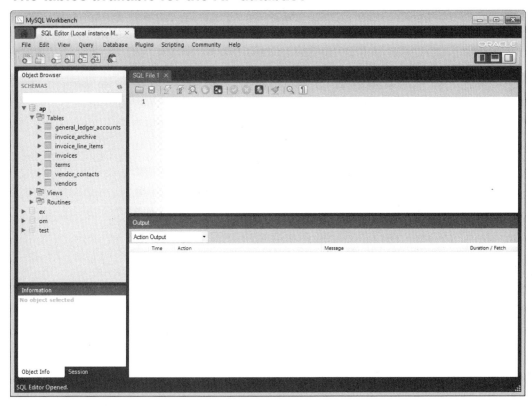

Description

- Each database (or *schema*) provides access to the *database objects* that are available. These database objects include tables, views, and routines.

- To navigate through the database objects for a database, click on the arrows to the left of the nodes in the Object Browser window to expand or collapse the node.

- To work with a node or an object, right-click on the node or object and select a command from the resulting menu.

Figure 2-4   How to navigate through the database objects

How to view and edit the data for a table

To view the data for a table, you can right-click on the table name and select the Edit Table Data command from the menu that's displayed. In figure 2-5, for example, I selected this command for the Invoices table. This displayed the data for the table in a Result tab. In addition, it displayed information about the SELECT statement that was used to retrieve the data in the Output tab.

To insert, edit, and delete the rows in the table, you can use the buttons at the top of the Result tab. Then, to apply the changes to the table, you can click on the Apply button at the bottom of the Result tab. Or, if you want to cancel the changes, you can click on the Cancel button.

The data for the Invoices table displayed in a Result tab

Result tab

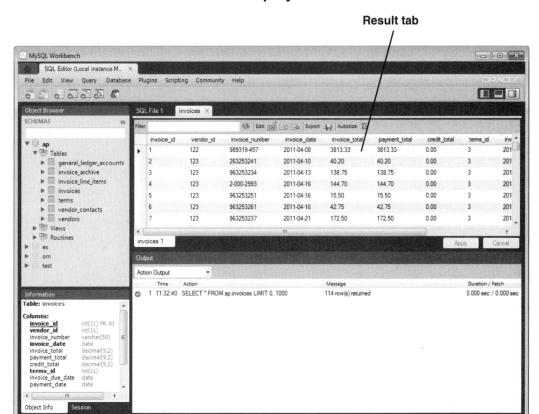

Description

- To view the data for a table, right-click on the table in the Object Browser window and select the Edit Table Data command to display it in a Result tab.

- To edit the data for a table, view the data. Then, you can use the buttons at the top of the Result tab to insert, update, and delete rows.

- To apply the changes to the table, click the Apply button at the bottom of the tab. To cancel the changes, click the Cancel button.

Figure 2-5   How to view and edit the data for a table

How to view and edit the column definitions for a table

If you want to edit a column definition for a table, you can use the technique described in figure 2-6 to display the column definitions for the table. In this figure, for example, the column definitions for the Vendors table are displayed. At this point, you can view information about each column of the table such as its name and data type.

Once you display the column definitions for a table, you can use the Columns tab to add a column, delete a column, or modify a column. For example, you can add a new column by entering it at the bottom of the list. You can delete a column by right-clicking on it and selecting the Delete command. You can change the name of a column by selecting the column and then clicking on the name and editing it. You can change the data type of a column by selecting the column and then clicking on its data type and selecting another data type from the drop-down list that appears. And so on.

Most of the time, you won't want to use MySQL Workbench to edit the column definitions for a table. Instead, you'll want to edit the scripts that create the database so you can easily recreate the database later. In chapter 11, you'll learn more about creating and modifying the column definitions for a table using both techniques.

The column definitions for the Vendors table

Description

- To view the column definitions for a table, right-click on the table name in the Object Browser window and select the Alter Table command. Then, select the Columns tab at the bottom of the window that's displayed to view the column definitions for the table.

- To edit the column definitions for a table, view the column definitions. Then, you can use the resulting window to add new columns and modify and delete existing columns.

- For more information about creating and modifying tables, see chapter 11.

Figure 2-6   How to view and edit the column definitions

How to use MySQL Workbench to run SQL statements

Besides letting you review the design of a database, MySQL Workbench is a great tool for entering and running SQL statements. That's what you'll learn how to do next.

How to enter and execute a SQL statement

When you first connect to a MySQL server in MySQL Workbench, a code editor tab is automatically opened. Figure 2-7 shows how to use the code editor to enter and execute a SQL statement. Note that you can open several code editor tabs at a time. The easiest way to open a code editor tab is to click on the Create New SQL Tab button in the SQL Editor toolbar or press the Ctrl+T keys.

Once you open a code editor tab, you can use standard techniques to enter or edit a SQL statement. As you enter statements, you'll notice that MySQL Workbench automatically applies colors to various elements. For example, it displays keywords in green. This makes your statements easier to read and understand and can help you identify coding errors.

To execute a single SQL statement like the one in this figure, you can press Ctrl+Enter or click the Execute Current Statement button in the code editor toolbar. If the statement returns data, that data is displayed below the code editor tab in a corresponding Result tab. In this figure, for example, the result set returned by the SELECT statement is displayed. If necessary, you can adjust the height of the Result tab by dragging the bar that separates the code editor tab from the Result tab.

Before you execute a SQL statement, make sure you've selected a database by double-clicking the database in the Object Browser window. Otherwise, you'll get an error message like this:

`Error Code: 1046. No database selected`

Similarly, if you haven't selected the correct database, you'll get an error message that says the table doesn't exist. For example, if a database other than the AP database is selected when you attempt to retrieve data from the Vendors table, you'll get an error message like this:

`Error Code: 1146. Table 'ex.vendors' doesn't exist`

To fix this, you can double-click on the AP database to select it.

A SELECT statement and its results

Create New SQL Tab button   **Execute Current Statement button**   **Code editor tab**   **Result tab**

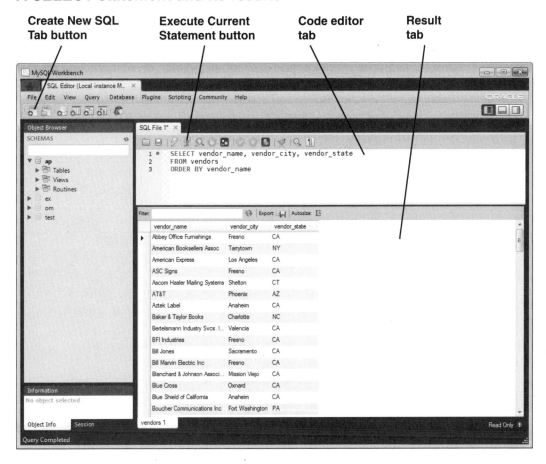

Description

- To open a new code editor tab, press the Ctrl+T keys or click the Create New SQL Tab button in the SQL Editor toolbar.

- To select the current database, double-click it in the Object Browser window. The selected database is displayed in bold.

- To enter a SQL statement, type it into the code editor tab.

- As you enter the text for a statement, the code editor tab applies color to various elements, such as SQL keywords, to make them easy to identify.

- To execute a SQL statement, select the Query→Execute Current Statement command, press the Ctrl+Enter keys, or click the Execute Current Statement button in the code editor toolbar. If the statement retrieves data, the data is displayed in a Result tab below the code editor tab.

Figure 2-7   How to enter and execute a SQL statement

How to use the Snippets tab

You can think of the *snippets* that come with MySQL Workbench as a library of SQL syntax. This library is divided into statements that you can use to manage a database, define objects in a database, and manipulate the data in a database. You can also create your own snippets that provide custom code. In fact, you're more likely to create your own snippets than you are to use the built-in snippets. That's because the syntax that's provided for the built-in snippets is much more complex than what you typically need.

Figure 2-8 shows how to use snippets. To start, if the Snippets tab isn't displayed, you can display it by clicking on the rightmost button at the right side of the SQL Editor tab. Then, you can use the drop-down list at the top of the Snippets tab to select a category of snippets. In this figure, for example, the My Snippets category is displayed. From here, you can select a snippet and then click the Insert Snippet button to enter the snippet into the code editor tab. Finally, you can edit the snippet code so it's appropriate for your SQL statement.

In this figure, the snippet contains code that I wrote for joining the vendors, invoices, and invoice_line_items tables. To create this snippet, I entered it into a code editor tab and then clicked the Add New Snippet button. By saving this statement as a snippet, I can now use it anytime I want to join these three tables instead of having to type it each time.

For now, don't worry if you don't understand the SQL statement presented in this figure. The main point is that you can use the Snippets tab to save and retrieve a variety of SQL code. As you learn more about SQL statements, you'll see how useful this can be.

The Snippets tab with a snippet created by a user

Description

- The *snippets* contain the syntax for many common SQL statements. You can use the snippets to guide you as you create a SQL statement. You can also create your own snippets and save them for later use.

- The Snippets tab is displayed to the right of the code editor tab by default. If this tab isn't displayed, you can click the rightmost button at the right side of the SQL Editor toolbar to display it.

- The snippets are organized into four categories: My Snippets, DB Mgmt, SQL DDL, and SQL DML. To display any category of snippets, select the category from the drop-down list at the top of the Snippets tab.

- To enter a snippet into a code editor tab, select the snippet and then click the Insert Snippet button at the top of the Snippets tab. Then, edit the snippet code so it's appropriate for your SQL statement.

- To replace code in the code editor tab with a snippet, select the code, select the snippet you want to replace it with, and then click the Replace Current Text button.

- To create your own snippet, enter the code for the snippet into a code editor tab. Then, select the category where you want to save the snippet, click the Add New Snippet button, and enter a name for the snippet.

- To delete a snippet, select it in the Snippets tab and then click the Delete Snippet button.

Figure 2-8   How to use the Snippets tab

How to handle syntax errors

If an error occurs during the execution of a SQL statement, MySQL Workbench displays a message that includes the error number and a brief description of the error. In figure 2-9, for example, the message displays an error number of 1146 and a brief description that says "Table ap.vendor doesn't exist."

In this example, the problem is that the Vendor table doesn't exist in the database. To fix the problem, you need to edit the SQL statement so the table is Vendors instead of Vendor. Then, you should be able to successfully run the SQL statement.

This figure also lists some other common causes of errors. As you can see, most errors are caused by incorrect syntax. However, it's also common to get an error if you have selected the wrong database. If, for example, you have selected the EX database and you try to run a statement that refers to tables in the AP database, you will get an error. Regardless of what's causing the problem, you can usually identify and correct the problem without much trouble. In some cases, though, it may be difficult to figure out the cause of an error. Then, you can usually get more information about the error by searching the Internet or by searching the MySQL Reference Manual as described later in this chapter.

How to handle syntax errors

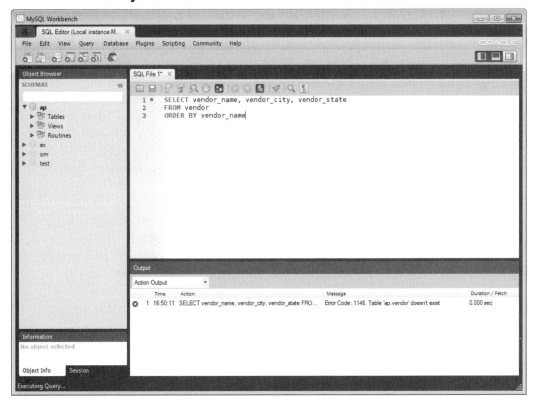

Common causes of errors

- Having the wrong database selected
- Misspelling the name of a table or column
- Misspelling a keyword
- Omitting the closing quotation mark for a character string

Description

- If an error occurs during the execution of a SQL statement, MySQL Workbench displays a message in the Output tab that includes an error code and a brief description of the error.
- Most errors are caused by incorrect syntax and can be corrected without any additional assistance. Otherwise, you can usually get more information about an error by searching for the error code or description in the MySQL Reference Manual or on the Internet.

Figure 2-9   How to handle syntax errors

How to open and save SQL scripts

In MySQL, a *script* is a file that contains one or more SQL statements. To create a script, you enter the statements you want it to include into a code editor tab. You'll learn more about that in the next figure. Then, you can click the Save button or press Ctrl+S to save the script as described in figure 2-10.

Once you've saved a script, you can open it later. To do that, you can click the Open SQL Script File button in the SQL Editor toolbar, or you can press Ctrl+Shift+O. In this figure, the dialog box that's displayed shows the script files that have been saved for chapter 2. These files are created when you download and install the source code for this book. Note that the names of these files have the .sql extension.

Once you open a script, you can run it as shown in the next figure. You can also use it as the basis for a new SQL script. To do that, just modify it any way you want. Then, you can save it as a new script by pressing the Ctrl+Shift+S keys or selecting the File→Save Script As command.

The screen in this figure shows the tabs for two script files that have been opened. After you open two or more scripts, you can switch between them by clicking on the appropriate tab. Then, you can cut, copy, and paste code from one script to another.

The Open SQL Script dialog box

Open SQL Script File button

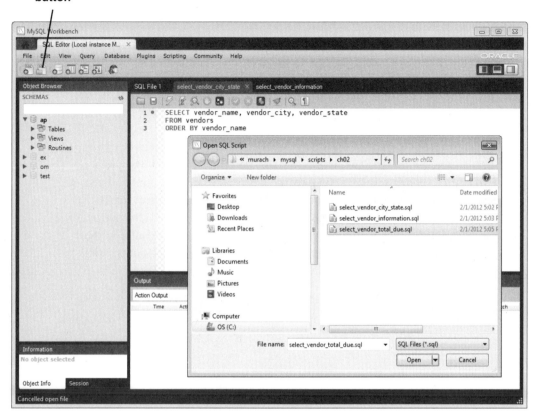

Description

- A *SQL script* is a file that contains one or more SQL statements.
- To a open file that contains a SQL script, click the Open SQL Script File button in the SQL Editor toolbar or press the Ctrl+Shift+O keys. Then, use the Open SQL Script dialog box to locate and open the SQL script.
- When you open a SQL script, MySQL Workbench displays it in its own code editor tab. To switch between open scripts, select the appropriate tab.
- To cut, copy, and paste code from one SQL script to another, use the standard techniques.
- To save a SQL statement to a script file, click the Save button in the code editor toolbar or press Ctrl+S. Then, use the Save SQL Script dialog box to specify a location and name for the file.
- To save a script you've modified to a new file, press the Ctrl+Shift+S keys or select the File→Save Script As command.

Figure 2-10   How to open and save SQL scripts

How to enter and execute SQL scripts

In the last topic, you saw a SQL script that contained a single SQL statement. However, a SQL script typically contains multiple statements. Figure 2-11 shows how to enter and execute scripts like that.

When you code multiple SQL statements within a script, you must code a semicolon at the end of each statement. For example, this figure shows a script that contains two SELECT statements. To execute both of these statements, you can press the Ctrl+Shift+Enter keys, or you can click the Execute SQL Script button in the code editor toolbar. When you do, the results of each statement are displayed in a separate Result tab.

If you want to execute a single SQL statement that's stored within a script, you can do that by moving the insertion point into the statement and pressing the Ctrl+Enter keys or clicking the Execute Current Statement button. Then, if the statement retrieves data, the data is displayed in a single Result tab.

If you need to, you can also execute two or more statements in a script. To do that, you select the statements and then press the Ctrl+Shift+Enter keys or click the Execute SQL Script button. This is useful if a script contains many statements and you just want to execute some of them.

A SQL script and its results

Execute SQL Script
button

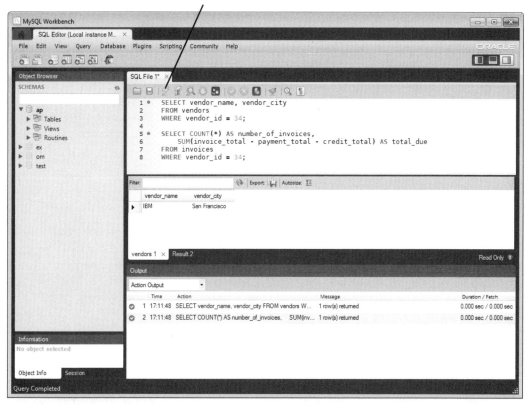

Description

- When you code a script that contains more than one statement, you must code a semicolon at the end of each statement.

- To run an entire SQL script, press the Ctrl+Shift+Enter keys or click the Execute SQL Script button that's located just to the left of the Execute Current Statement button in the code editor toolbar.

- When you run a SQL script, the results of each statement that returns data are displayed in a separate Result tab.

- To execute one SQL statement within a script, move the insertion point into that statement and press the Ctrl+Enter keys or click the Execute Current Statement button. If the statement retrieves data, the data is displayed in a Result tab.

- To execute two or more statements within a script, select them in the editor and then press the Ctrl+Shift+Enter keys or click the Execute SQL Script button.

Figure 2-11   How to enter and execute SQL scripts

How to use
the MySQL Reference Manual

Figure 2-12 shows how to use another useful tool for working with the MySQL database: the *MySQL Reference Manual*. In most cases, you'll use a web browser to view this manual directly from the Internet. That way, you can be sure that the information is always up-to-date. However, you can also download this manual and save it on your hard drive. Either way, you can use the MySQL Reference Manual to quickly look up detailed technical information about the MySQL database, including information about SQL statements and functions.

How to view the manual

You can view the MySQL Reference Manual by using a web browser to go to the web address shown at the top of this figure. Here, the Reference Manual for version 5.5 of MySQL is displayed. However, you can easily select another version by clicking on the links in the left column of the page.

How to look up information

Once you've navigated to the correct version of the MySQL Reference Manual, it's easy to look up information. To do that, you can use the links in the right column to drill down to the information that you're looking for. When you find the topic you want, you can click on it to display it in the middle column. Then, if you want to navigate back up the hierarchy of information, you can use the breadcrumb links across the top of the page. In this figure, for example, you can click on the "MySQL 5.5 Reference Manual" link to return to the Home page for the manual. Or, you can click on the "General Information" link to navigate to that page.

Another easy way to look up information is to search for a specific word or phrase. To do that, type the word or phrase in the "Search manual" text box located at the left side of the page and click the Go button. Then, you can click on the links in the search results to view information about the search terms.

The web address for the MySQL 5.5 Reference Manual

`http://dev.mysql.com/doc/refman/5.5/en/`

A web page from the MySQL Reference Manual

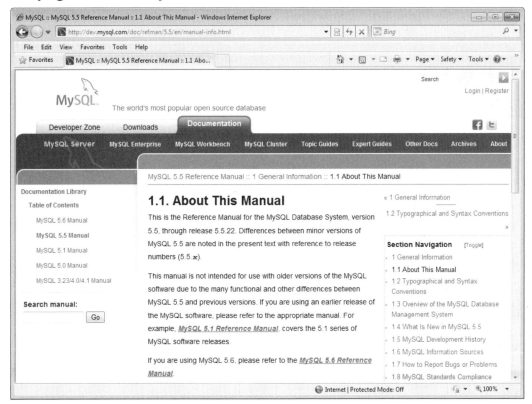

Description

- To view the *MySQL Reference Manual*, go to the MySQL web site and select the correct version of the manual.

- To view a chapter, click the link for the chapter in the table of contents on the right side of the page.

- To return to the Home page for the manual, click the link for the manual that's displayed across the top of the current page.

- To search for a particular word or phrase, type the word or phrase in the "Search manual" text box on the left side of the page and click the Go button. Then, you can scroll through the results and click on links to get more information.

- You can also download the MySQL Reference Manual in several different formats. However, it typically makes sense to use it online.

Figure 2-12   How to use the MySQL Reference Manual

How to use the MySQL monitor

Before MySQL Workbench was available, programmers used a command-line tool known as the *MySQL monitor* to connect to a MySQL server and work with it. This tool is also referred to as the *MySQL command line*. Although you may never need this tool, you should at least be aware that it exists. This tool comes with MySQL, and it can be useful if MySQL Workbench isn't installed on the system that you're using.

How to start and stop the MySQL monitor

Figure 2-13 shows how to start and stop the MySQL monitor. Although this figure shows the Command Prompt window that's available from Windows, you can use a command prompt to start the MySQL monitor on other operating systems too. In particular, on Mac OS X, you can use the Terminal window.

When you use a PC, there's an easy way to start the MySQL monitor if you want to log in as the root user for the database server that's running on the local computer. To do that, you just select the MySQL Command Line Client command from the Start menu. Then, MySQL will prompt you for a password. If you enter the password correctly, you will be logged on to the database server as the root user.

In some cases, you'll need to use a command prompt to start the MySQL monitor instead of using the Start menu. For example, you may need to do that if you want to log into a database that's running on a different computer, if you want to log in as a user other than the root user, or if you're using another operating system such as Mac OS X. In those cases, you can open a command prompt and change the directory to the bin directory for the MySQL installation. Then, you can execute the mysql command and supply the parameters that are needed to connect to the database server.

If the MySQL server is located on a remote computer, you can specify -h followed by the host name of the computer, and -u followed by a valid username. In addition, you specify -p so MySQL prompts you for a valid password. Although it can take some experimentation to get these connection parameters right, you only need to figure this out once.

Once you enter a valid password for the specified username, the MySQL monitor displays a welcome message and a command prompt that looks like this:

```
mysql>
```

From this prompt, you can enter any statement that works with MySQL. To exit from the MySQL monitor, for example, you can enter "exit" or "quit" followed by a semicolon.

The MySQL monitor from a Windows command prompt

```
Command Prompt - mysql -u root -p                              _ □ ✕

Microsoft Windows XP [Version 5.1.2600]
(C) Copyright 1985-2001 Microsoft Corp.

C:\Documents and Settings\Ray Halliday>cd \Program Files\MySQL\MySQL Server 5.5\
bin

C:\Program Files\MySQL\MySQL Server 5.5\bin>mysql -u root -p
Enter password: ******
Welcome to the MySQL monitor.  Commands end with ; or \g.
Your MySQL connection id is 58
Server version: 5.5.14 MySQL Community Server (GPL)

Copyright (c) 2000, 2010, Oracle and/or its affiliates. All rights reserved.

Oracle is a registered trademark of Oracle Corporation and/or its
affiliates. Other names may be trademarks of their respective
owners.

Type 'help;' or '\h' for help. Type '\c' to clear the current input statement.

mysql>
```

How to start the MySQL monitor from the Windows Start menu

Start→All Programs→MySQL→MySQL Server→MySQL Command Line Client

How to start the MySQL monitor from the command line

On a PC

```
cd \Program Files\MySQL\MySQL Server 5.5\bin
mysql -u root -p
```

On a Mac

```
cd /usr/local/mysql/bin
./mysql -u root -p
```

How the mysql command works

The syntax

```
mysql -h hostname -u username -p
```

Examples

```
mysql -u jmurach -p
mysql -h localhost -u root -p
mysql -h murach.com -u jmurach -p
```

How to exit from the MySQL monitor

```
mysql>exit;
```

Description

- MySQL provides a command-line client program called the *MySQL monitor*, or *MySQL command line*, that lets you enter SQL statements that work with MySQL databases.
- On a PC, you can use a Command Prompt window to start the MySQL monitor.
- On a Mac, you can use a Terminal window to start the MySQL monitor.
- To stop the MySQL monitor, enter "exit" or "quit" at the command prompt, followed by a semicolon.

Figure 2-13   How to start and stop the MySQL monitor

How to use the MySQL monitor
to work with a database

Once the MySQL monitor is connected to a database server, you can use it to run SQL statements that work with the databases that are available from that server. When you enter a statement, you must end it with a semicolon. Otherwise, the mysql prompt displays a second line when you press the Enter key like this:

```
mysql> show databases
    ->
```

This shows that the MySQL monitor is waiting for you to finish your statement. To finish a statement and execute it, you just type a semicolon and press the Enter key.

Figure 2-14 shows how to execute three SQL statements. Notice that I entered all three of these statements in lowercase letters. That's because SQL isn't case-sensitive, and lowercase letters are easier to type.

To list the names of the databases stored on a server, you use the SHOW DATABASES statement as illustrated by the first example. Here, the "ap", "ex", and "om" databases are the databases that are created when you install our downloadable databases as described in appendixes A and B. The "information_schema", "performance_schema", and "mysql" databases are internal databases that are used by the MySQL server. And the "test" database is a test database that comes with MySQL.

To select the database that you want to work with, you can enter a USE statement as illustrated by the second example. Here, the AP database is selected, and the message after this command says "Database changed" to indicate that the statement was successful. After you select a database, the commands and statements that you enter will work with that database.

To retrieve data from the database, you use a SELECT statement as illustrated in the third example. Here, the vendor_name column from the Vendors table is displayed. Note, however that the result set is limited to only the first five rows. When you successfully execute a SELECT statement, the MySQL monitor displays a message giving the number of rows that are included in the result set and the amount of time it took to run the query.

How to list the names of all databases managed by the server

```
mysql> show databases;
+--------------------+
| Database           |
+--------------------+
| information_schema |
| ap                 |
| ex                 |
| mysql              |
| om                 |
| performance_schema |
| test               |
+--------------------+
7 rows in set (0.05 sec)
```

How to select a database for use

```
mysql> use ap;
Database changed
```

How to select data from a database

```
mysql> select vendor_name from vendors limit 5;
+------------------------------+
| vendor_name                  |
+------------------------------+
| Abbey Office Furnishings     |
| American Booksellers Assoc   |
| American Express             |
| ASC Signs                    |
| Ascom Hasler Mailing Systems |
+------------------------------+
5 rows in set (0.09 sec)
```

Description

- You can use the MySQL monitor to work with any of the databases running on the database server. To do that, you can use any SQL statement that works with a MySQL database.

- To execute a SQL statement, type the statement after the prompt, followed by a semicolon. Then, press the Enter key.

- To show a list of all available databases, you can use the SHOW DATABASES statement.

- To select the database that you want to work with, you can use the USE statement.

- SQL statements aren't case-sensitive. As a result, when using the MySQL monitor, most programmers enter their statements in lowercase letters because they're easier to type.

Figure 2-14   How to use the MySQL monitor to work with a database

Perspective

In this chapter, you learned how to use MySQL Workbench to start and stop a MySQL server and to enter and execute SQL statements. With that as background, you're ready to go on to the next chapter, where you'll start learning the details of coding your own SQL statements. To start, you'll learn how to code a SELECT statement that retrieves data from a single table.

Terms

MySQL Workbench
database server
database service
database engine
database object
schema
snippet
SQL script
MySQL Reference manual
MySQL monitor
MySQL command line

Before you start the exercises...

Before you start the exercises for this chapter, you need to install MySQL Server and MySQL Workbench. In addition, you need to download and install the source files for this book, and you need to create the databases and tables for this book. The procedures for doing all of these tasks are provided in appendix A (PC) and B (Mac).

Exercises

In these exercises, you'll use MySQL Workbench to review the tables in the AP database. In addition, you'll use MySQL Workbench to enter SQL statements and run them against these tables.

Make sure the MySQL server is running

1. Start MySQL Workbench and open a connection for managing the server.

2. Check whether the MySQL server is running. If it isn't, start it. When you're done, close the Admin tab.

Use MySQL Workbench to review the Accounts Payable (AP) database

3. Open a connection to start querying.

4. In the Object Browser window, expand the node for the AP database so you can see all of the database objects it contains.

5. View the data for the Vendors and Invoices tables.

6. Navigate through the database objects and view the column definitions for at least the Vendors and Invoices tables.

Use MySQL Workbench to enter and run SQL statements

7. Double-click on the AP database to set it as the default database. When you do that, MySQL Workbench should display the database in bold.

8. Open a code editor tab. Then, enter and run this SQL statement:

    ```
    SELECT vendor_name FROM vendors
    ```

9. Delete the *e* at the end of vendor_name and run the statement again. Note the error number and the description of the error.

10. Open another code editor tab. Then, enter and run this statement:

    ```
    SELECT COUNT(*) AS number_of_invoices,
        SUM(invoice_total) AS grand_invoice_total
    FROM invoices
    ```

Use MySQL Workbench to open and run scripts

11. Open the select_vendor_city_state script that's in the c:\murach\mysql\book_scripts\ch02 directory. Note that this script contains just one SQL statement. Then, run the statement.

12. Open the select_vendor_total_due script that's in the ch02 directory. Note that this opens another code editor tab.

13. Open the select_vendor_information script that's in the ch02 directory. Notice that this script contains two SQL statements that end with semicolons (scroll down if you need to).

14. Press the Ctrl+Shift+Enter keys or click the Execute SQL Script button to run both of the statements in this script. Note that this displays the results in two Result tabs. Make sure to view the results of both SELECT statements.

15. Move the insertion point into the first statement and press Ctrl+Enter to run just that statement.

16. Move the insertion point into the second statement and press Ctrl+Enter to run just that statement.

17. Exit from MySQL Workbench.

Section 2

The essential SQL skills

This section presents the essential SQL coding skills for working with the data in an existing MySQL database. The first four chapters in this section show you how to retrieve data using the SELECT statement. In chapter 3, you'll learn how to retrieve data from a single table. In chapter 4, you'll learn how to retrieve data from two or more tables. In chapter 5, you'll learn how to summarize the data that you retrieve. And in chapter 6, you'll learn how to code subqueries, which are SELECT statements coded within other statements.

In chapter 7, you'll learn how to use the INSERT, UPDATE, and DELETE statements to add, update, and delete rows in a table. In chapter 8, you'll learn more about the types of data that MySQL supports. Finally, in chapter 9, you'll learn how to use MySQL functions in your SQL statements. When you complete these chapters, you'll have the skills you need for coding SELECT, INSERT, UPDATE, and DELETE statements.

3

How to retrieve data from a single table

In this chapter, you'll learn how to code SELECT statements that retrieve data from a single table. The skills covered here are the essential ones that apply to any SELECT statement you code…no matter how many tables it operates on, no matter how complex the retrieval. So you'll want to be sure you have a good understanding of the material in this chapter before you go on to the chapters that follow.

An introduction to the SELECT statement **76**
The basic syntax of the SELECT statement 76
SELECT statement examples 78
How to code the SELECT clause **80**
How to code column specifications 80
How to name the columns in a result set using aliases 82
How to code arithmetic expressions 84
How to use the CONCAT function to join strings 86
How to use functions with strings, dates, and numbers 88
How to test expressions by coding statements without FROM clauses 90
How to eliminate duplicate rows 92
How to code the WHERE clause **94**
How to use the comparison operators 94
How to use the AND, OR, and NOT logical operators 96
How to use the IN operator 98
How to use the BETWEEN operator 100
How to use the LIKE and REGEXP operators 102
How to use the IS NULL clause 104
How to code the ORDER BY clause **106**
How to sort by a column name 106
How to sort by an alias, expression, or column number 108
How to code the LIMIT clause **110**
How to limit the number of rows 110
How to return a range of rows 110
Perspective **112**

An introduction
to the SELECT statement

To get you started quickly, this chapter begins by presenting the basic syntax of the SELECT statement. Then, it presents several examples that should give you an overview of how this statement works.

The basic syntax of the SELECT statement

Figure 3-1 presents the basic syntax of the SELECT statement. The syntax summary at the top of this figure uses conventions that are similar to those used in other programming manuals. Capitalized words are *keywords* that you have to type exactly as shown. In contrast, you have to provide replacements for the lowercase words. For example, you can enter a list of columns in place of *select_list*, and you can enter a table name in place of *table_source*.

Beyond that, you can omit the clauses enclosed in brackets ([ ]). If you compare the syntax in this figure with the coding examples in the next figure, you should easily see how the two are related.

This syntax summary has been simplified so that you can focus on the five main clauses of the SELECT statement: SELECT, FROM, WHERE, ORDER BY, and LIMIT. Most SELECT statements contain the first four of these clauses. However, only the SELECT clause is required.

The SELECT clause is always the first clause in a SELECT statement. It identifies the columns in the result set. These columns are retrieved from the *base tables* named in the FROM clause. Since this chapter focuses on retrieving data from a single table, the examples in this chapter use FROM clauses that name a single base table. In the next chapter, though, you'll learn how to retrieve data from two or more tables.

The WHERE, ORDER BY, and LIMIT clauses are optional. The ORDER BY clause determines how the rows in the result set are sorted, and the WHERE clause determines which rows in the base table are included in the result set. The WHERE clause specifies a *search condition* that's used to *filter* the rows in the base table. When this condition is true, the row is included in the result set.

The LIMIT clause limits the number of rows in the result set. In contrast to the WHERE clause, which uses a search condition, the LIMIT clause simply returns a specified number of rows, regardless of the size of the full result set. Of course, if the result set has fewer rows than are specified by the LIMIT clause, all the rows in the result set are returned.

The basic syntax of the SELECT statement

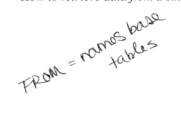

```
SELECT select_list
[FROM table_source]
[WHERE search_condition]
[ORDER BY order_by_list]
[LIMIT row_limit]
```

keyword *change* *FROM = names base tables*

The five clauses of the SELECT statement

Clause	Description
SELECT	Describes the columns in the result set.
FROM	Names the base table from which the query retrieves the data.
WHERE	Specifies the conditions that must be met for a row to be included in the result set.
ORDER BY	Specifies how to sort the rows in the result set.
LIMIT	Specifies the number of rows to return.

Description

- You use the basic SELECT statement shown above to retrieve the columns specified in the SELECT clause from the *base table* specified in the FROM clause and store them in a result set.

- The WHERE clause is used to *filter* the rows in the base table so that only those rows that match the search condition are included in the result set. If you omit the WHERE clause, all of the rows in the base table are included.

- The search condition of a WHERE clause consists of one or more *Boolean expressions* that result in a true, false, or null value. If the combination of all the expressions is a true value, the row being tested is included in the result set. Otherwise, it's not.

- If you include the ORDER BY clause, the rows in the result set are sorted in the specified sequence. Otherwise, the rows are returned in the same sequence as they appear in the base table. In most cases, that means that they're returned in primary key sequence.

- If you include the LIMIT clause, the result set that's retrieved is limited to a specified number of rows. If you omit this clause, all rows that match are returned.

- You must code the clauses in the order shown or you'll get a syntax error.

Note

- The syntax shown above does not include all of the clauses of the SELECT statement. You'll learn about the other clauses later in this book.

Figure 3-1   The basic syntax of the SELECT statement

SELECT statement examples

Figure 3-2 presents five SELECT statement examples. All of these statements retrieve data from the Invoices table that you experimented with in the last chapter. After each statement, you can see its result set as displayed by MySQL Workbench. In these examples, a horizontal or vertical scroll bar indicates that the result set contains more rows or columns than can be displayed at one time.

The first statement in this figure retrieves all of the rows and columns from the Invoices table. Here, an asterisk (*) is used as a shorthand to indicate that all of the columns should be retrieved, and the WHERE and LIMIT clauses are omitted so all of the rows in the table are retrieved. In addition, this statement doesn't include an ORDER BY clause, so the rows are in primary key sequence.

The second statement retrieves selected columns from the Invoices table. These columns are listed in the SELECT clause. Like the first statement, this statement doesn't include a WHERE or a LIMIT clause, so all the rows are retrieved. Then, the ORDER BY clause causes the rows to be sorted by the invoice_total column in descending order, from largest to smallest.

The third statement also lists the columns to be retrieved. In this case, though, the last column is calculated from two columns in the base table, credit_total and payment_total, and the resulting column is given the name total_credits. In addition, the WHERE clause specifies that only the invoice whose invoice_id column has a value of 17 should be retrieved.

The fourth SELECT statement includes a WHERE clause whose condition specifies a range of values. In this case, only invoices with invoice dates between 06/01/2011 and 06/30/2011 are retrieved. In addition, the rows in the result set are sorted by invoice date.

The last statement in this figure shows another example of the WHERE clause. In this case, only those rows with invoice totals greater than 50,000 are retrieved. Since none of the rows in the Invoices table satisfy this condition, the result set is empty.

A SELECT statement that retrieves all the data from the Invoices table

```
SELECT * FROM invoices
```

invoice_id	vendor_id	invoice_number	invoice_date	invoice_total	payment_total	credit_total	terms_id
1	122	989319-457	2011-04-08	3813.33	3813.33	0.00	3
2	123	263253241	2011-04-10	40.20	40.20	0.00	3
3	123	963253234	2011-04-13	138.75	138.75	0.00	3

(114 rows)

A SELECT statement that retrieves three columns from each row, sorted in descending sequence by invoice total

```
SELECT invoice_number, invoice_date, invoice_total
FROM invoices
ORDER BY invoice_total DESC
```

invoice_number	invoice_date	invoice_total
0-2058	2011-05-28	37966.19
P-0259	2011-07-19	26881.40
0-2060	2011-07-24	23517.58

(114 rows)

A SELECT statement that retrieves two columns and a calculated value for a specific invoice

```
SELECT invoice_id, invoice_total,
       credit_total + payment_total AS total_credits
FROM invoices
WHERE invoice_id = 17
```

invoice_id	invoice_total	total_credits
17	10.00	10.00

result 6?

A SELECT statement that retrieves all invoices between given dates

```
SELECT invoice_number, invoice_date, invoice_total
FROM invoices
WHERE invoice_date BETWEEN '2011-06-01' AND '2011-06-30'
ORDER BY invoice_date
```

invoice_number	invoice_date	invoice_total
111-92R-10094	2011-06-01	19.67
989319-437	2011-06-01	2765.36
1-202-2978	2011-06-03	33.00

(37 rows)

A SELECT statement that returns an empty result set

```
SELECT invoice_number, invoice_date, invoice_total
FROM invoices
WHERE invoice_total > 50000
```

invoice_number	invoice_date	invoice_total

Figure 3-2 SELECT statement examples

How to code the SELECT clause

Now that you have a general idea of how the main clauses of a SELECT statement work, you're ready to learn the details for coding the first clause, the SELECT clause. You can use this clause to specify the columns for a result set.

How to code column specifications

Figure 3-3 begins by presenting a more detailed syntax for the SELECT clause. In this syntax, you can choose between the items in a syntax summary that are separated by pipes (|), and you can omit items enclosed in brackets ([ ]). If you have a choice between two or more optional items, the default item is underlined. And if an element can be coded multiple times in a statement, it's followed by an ellipsis (…).

This figure continues by summarizing four techniques you can use to specify the columns for a result set. First, you can code an asterisk in the SELECT clause to retrieve all of the columns in the base table. When you use this technique, MySQL returns the columns in the order that they are defined in the base table.

Second, you can code a list of column names from the base table separated by commas. In this figure, for instance, the second example specifies three columns that are in the Vendors table.

Third, you can code an *expression* that uses arithmetic operators. The result of an expression is a single value. In this figure, for instance, the third example uses an expression to subtract the payment_total and credit_total columns from the invoice_total column and return the balance due.

Fourth, you can code an expression that uses functions. In this figure, for instance, the fourth example uses the CONCAT function to join a column named first_name, a space, and a column named last_name. Here, two single quotes are used to identify the literal value for the space.

When you code the SELECT clause, you should include only the columns you need. For example, you shouldn't code an asterisk to retrieve all the columns unless you need all the columns. That's because the amount of data that's retrieved can affect system performance. This is particularly important if you're developing SQL statements that will be used by application programs.

For now, don't worry if you don't completely understand all four techniques. In the next four figures, you'll learn more about how they work.

The expanded syntax of the SELECT clause

```
SELECT [ALL|DISTINCT]
        column_specification [[AS] result_column]
   [, column_specification [[AS] result_column]] ...
```

Four ways to code column specifications

Source	Option	Syntax
Base table value	All columns	*
	Column name	column_name
Calculated value	Result of a calculation	Arithmetic expressions (see figure 3-5)
	Result of a function	Functions (see figures 3-6 and 3-7)

Column specifications that use base table values

The * is used to retrieve all columns

```
SELECT *
```

Column names are used to retrieve specific columns

```
SELECT vendor_name, vendor_city, vendor_state
```

Column specifications that use calculated values

An arithmetic expression that calculates the balance due

```
SELECT invoice_total - payment_total - credit_total AS balance_due
```
3 columns from base ⟶ new table calculated & displayed in result tbl

A function that returns the full name

```
SELECT CONCAT(first_name, ' ', last_name) AS full_name
```
2 indiv columns from base + ' ' = new column   full-name in results

Description

- Use SELECT * only when you need to retrieve all of the columns from a table. Otherwise, list the names of the columns you need.

- An *expression* is a combination of column names and operators that evaluate to a single value. In the SELECT clause, you can code expressions that include one or more arithmetic operators and expressions that include one or more functions.

- After each column specification, you can code an AS clause to specify the name for the column in the result set. See figure 3-4 for details.

Note

- The ALL and DISTINCT keywords specify whether or not duplicate rows are returned. See figure 3-9 for details.

Figure 3-3   How to code column specifications

How to name the columns in a result set using aliases

By default, MySQL gives a column in a result set the same name as the column in the base table. If the column is based on a calculated value, it's assigned a name based on the expression for the value. However, whenever you want, you can specify a different name known as a *column alias* as shown in figure 3-4.

To assign a column alias, you code the column specification followed by the AS keyword and the new name as shown by the first example in this figure. Here, the statement creates an alias of "Invoice Number" for the invoice_number column, "Date" for the invoice_date column, and "Total" for the invoice_total column. To include a space in the alias for the first column, this statement encloses that alias in double quotes (").

The second example in this figure shows what happens when you don't assign an alias to a calculated column. In that case, MySQL automatically assigns the column an alias that's the same as the column's expression. Since the expressions for many calculated values are cumbersome, you typically assign a shorter alias for calculated values as shown throughout the rest of this chapter.

A SELECT statement that renames the columns in the result set

```
SELECT invoice_number AS "Invoice Number", invoice_date AS Date,
       invoice_total AS Total
FROM invoices
```
be includes space?

Invoice Number	Date	Total
▶ 989319-457	2011-04-08	3813.33
263253241	2011-04-10	40.20
963253234	2011-04-13	138.75
2-000-2993	2011-04-16	144.70
963253251	2011-04-16	15.50
963253261	2011-04-16	42.75

(114 rows)

A SELECT statement that doesn't name a calculated column

```
SELECT invoice_number, invoice_date, invoice_total,
       invoice_total - payment_total - credit_total
FROM invoices
```

invoice_number	invoice_date	invoice_total	invoice_total - payment_total - credit_total
▶ 989319-457	2011-04-08	3813.33	0.00
263253241	2011-04-10	40.20	0.00
963253234	2011-04-13	138.75	0.00
2-000-2993	2011-04-16	144.70	0.00
963253251	2011-04-16	15.50	0.00
963253261	2011-04-16	42.75	0.00

(114 rows)

Description

- By default, a column in the result set is given the same name as the column in the base table. If that's not what you want, you can specify a substitute name, or *column alias*, for the column.

- To specify an alias for a column, use the AS phrase. Although the AS keyword is optional, I recommend you code it for readability.

- If you don't specify an alias for a column that's based on a calculated value, MySQL uses the expression for the calculated value as the column name.

- To include spaces or special characters in an alias, enclose the alias in double quotes (") or single quotes (').

Figure 3-4   How to name the columns in a result set using aliases

How to code arithmetic expressions

Figure 3-5 shows how to code *arithmetic expressions*. To start, it summarizes the *arithmetic operators* you can use in this type of expression. Then, it presents three examples that show how you use these operators.

The SELECT statement in the first example includes an arithmetic expression that calculates the balance due for an invoice. This expression subtracts the payment_total and credit_total columns from the invoice_total column. The resulting column is given an alias of balance_due.

When MySQL evaluates an arithmetic expression, it performs the operations from left to right based on the *order of precedence*. To start, MySQL performs multiplication, division, and modulo operations. Then, it performs addition and subtraction operations.

If that's not what you want, you can use parentheses to specify how an expression is evaluated. Then, MySQL evaluates the expressions in the innermost sets of parentheses first, followed by the expressions in outer sets of parentheses. Within each set of parentheses, MySQL evaluates the expression from left to right in the order of precedence.

If you want, you can also use parentheses to clarify an expression even if they're not needed for the expression to be evaluated properly. However, you should avoid cluttering your SQL statements with unnecessary parentheses.

To show how parentheses and the order of precedence affect the evaluation of an expression, consider the second example in this figure. Here, the expressions in the second and third columns both perform the same operations. These expressions use one column name (invoice_id) that returns a number and two *literal values* for numbers (7 and 3). When you code a literal value for a number, you don't need to enclose it in quotes.

When MySQL evaluates the expression in the second column, it performs the multiplication operation before the addition operation because multiplication comes before addition in the order of precedence. When MySQL evaluates the expression in the third column, though, it performs the addition operation first because it's enclosed in parentheses. Because of this, these two expressions return different values as shown in the result set.

Although you're probably familiar with the addition, subtraction, multiplication, and division operators, you may not be familiar with the MOD (%) or DIV operators. MOD returns the remainder of a division of two integers, and DIV returns the integer quotient of two numbers. These are shown in the third example in this figure. Here, the second column contains the quotient of the two numbers, which MySQL automatically converts from an integer value to a decimal value. Then, the third column uses the DIV operator to return the integer quotient of the same division operation. The fourth column uses the modulo operator to return the remainder of the division operation.

The arithmetic operators in order of precedence

Operator	Name	Order of precedence
*	Multiplication	1
/	Division	1
DIV	Integer division	1
% (MOD)	Modulo (remainder)	1
+	Addition	2
-	Subtraction	2

A SELECT statement that calculates the balance due

```
SELECT invoice_total, payment_total, credit_total,
       invoice_total - payment_total - credit_total AS balance_due
FROM invoices
```

invoice_total	payment_total	credit_total	balance_due
3813.33	3813.33	0.00	0.00
40.20	40.20	0.00	0.00
138.75	138.75	0.00	0.00

Use parentheses to control the sequence of operations

```
SELECT invoice_id,
       invoice_id + 7 * 3 AS multiply_first,
       (invoice_id + 7) * 3 AS add_first
FROM invoices
```

invoice_id	multiply_first	add_first
1	22	24
2	23	27
3	24	30

Use the DIV and modulo operators

```
SELECT invoice_id,
       invoice_id / 3 AS decimal_quotient,
       invoice_id DIV 3 AS integer_quotient,
       invoice_id % 3 AS remainder
FROM invoices
```

invoice_id	decimal_quotient	integer_quotient	remainder
1	0.3333	0	1
2	0.6667	0	2
3	1.0000	1	0

Description

- Unless parentheses are used, the operations in an expression take place from left to right in the *order of precedence*. For arithmetic expressions, MySQL performs multiplication, division, and modulo operations first. Then, it performs addition and subtraction operations.

- Whenever necessary, you can use parentheses to override or clarify the sequence of operations.

Figure 3-5   How to code arithmetic expressions

How to use the CONCAT function to join strings

Figure 3-6 presents the CONCAT function and shows you how to use it to join, or *concatenate*, strings. In MySQL, a *string* can contain any combination of characters, and a *function* performs an operation and returns a value. To code a function, you begin by entering its name followed by a set of parentheses. If the function requires an *argument*, or *parameter*, you enter it within the parentheses. If the function takes more than one argument, you separate them with commas.

In this figure, the first example shows how to use the CONCAT function to join the vendor_city and vendor_state columns in the Vendors table. Since this example doesn't assign an alias to this column, MySQL automatically assigns the expression formula as the column name. In addition, there isn't a space between the vendor_state and the vendor_city in the result set. Since this makes the data difficult to read, this string should be formatted as shown in the second or third example.

The second example shows how to format a string expression by adding spaces and punctuation. Here, the vendor_city column is concatenated with a literal value for a string that contains a comma and a space. Then, the vendor_state column is concatenated with that result, followed by a literal value for a string that contains a single space and the vendor_zip_code column.

To code a string literal, you can enclose the value in either single quotes (') or double quotes ("). Occasionally, you may need to include a single quote as an apostrophe within a literal value for a string. If you're using single quotes around the literal, however, MySQL will misinterpret the apostrophe as the end of the string. To solve this, you can code two single quotation marks in a row as shown by the third example. Or, you can use double quotes like this:

```
CONCAT(vendor_name, "'s Address: ") AS vendor
```

The syntax of the CONCAT function

```
CONCAT(string1[, string2]...)
```

How to concatenate string data

```
SELECT vendor_city, vendor_state, CONCAT(vendor_city, vendor_state)
FROM vendors
```

vendor_city	vendor_state	CONCAT(vendor_city, vendor_state)
Madison	WI	MadisonWI
Washington	DC	WashingtonDC

(122 rows)

How to format string data using literal values

```
SELECT vendor_name,
       CONCAT(vendor_city, ', ', vendor_state, ' ', vendor_zip_code)
           AS address
FROM vendors
```

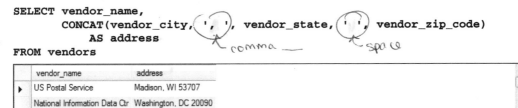
comma   space

vendor_name	address
US Postal Service	Madison, WI 53707
National Information Data Ctr	Washington, DC 20090

(122 rows)

How to include apostrophes in literal values

```
SELECT CONCAT(vendor_name, '''s Address: ') AS Vendor,
       CONCAT(vendor_city, ', ', vendor_state, ' ', vendor_zip_code)
           AS Address
FROM vendors
```

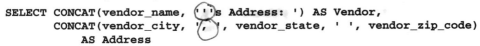

Vendor	Address
US Postal Service's Address:	Madison, WI 53707
National Information Data Ctr's Address:	Washington, DC 20090

(122 rows)

Description

- An expression can include any of the *functions* that are supported by MySQL. A function performs an operation and returns a value.

- To code a function, code the function name followed by a set of parentheses. Within the parentheses, code any *parameters*, or *arguments*, required by the function. If a function requires two or more arguments, separate them with commas.

- To code a literal value for a string, enclose one or more characters within single quotes (') or double quotes (").

- To include a single quote within a literal value for a string, code two single quotes. Or, use double quotes instead of single quotes to start and end the literal value.

- To join, or *concatenate*, two or more string columns or literal values, use the CONCAT function.

Figure 3-6   How to use the CONCAT function to join strings

How to use functions
with strings, dates, and numbers

Figure 3-7 shows how to work with three more functions. The LEFT function operates on strings, the DATE_FORMAT function operates on dates, and the ROUND function operates on numbers. For now, don't worry about the details of how the functions shown here work, because you'll learn more about all of these functions in chapter 9. Instead, just focus on how they're used in column specifications.

The first example in this figure shows how to use the LEFT function to extract the first character of the vendor_contact_first_name and vendor_contact_last_name columns. The first parameter of this function specifies the string value, and the second parameter specifies the number of characters to return. Then, this statement concatenates the results of the two LEFT functions to form initials as shown in the result set.

The second example shows how to use the DATE_FORMAT function to change the format used to display date values. This function requires two parameters. The first parameter is the date value to be formatted and the second is a format string that uses specific values as placeholders for the various parts of the date. The first column in this example returns the invoice_date column in the default MySQL date format, "yyyy-mm-dd". Since this format isn't used as often in the USA, the second column is formatted in the more typical "mm/dd/yy" format. In the third column, the invoice date is in another format that's commonly used. In chapter 9, you'll learn more about specifying the format string for the DATE_FORMAT function.

The third example uses the ROUND function to round the value of the invoice_total column to the nearest dollar and nearest dime. This function can accept either one or two parameters. The first parameter specifies the number to be rounded and the optional second parameter specifies the number of decimal places to keep. If the second parameter is omitted, the function rounds to the nearest integer.

The syntax of the LEFT, DATE_FORMAT, and ROUND functions

```
LEFT(string, number_of_characters)
DATE_FORMAT(date, format_string)
ROUND(number[, number_of_decimal_places])
```

A SELECT statement that uses the LEFT function

```
SELECT vendor_contact_first_name, vendor_contact_last_name,
       CONCAT(LEFT(vendor_contact_first_name, 1),
              LEFT(vendor_contact_last_name, 1)) AS initials
FROM vendors
```

vendor_contact_first_name	vendor_contact_last_name	initials
Francesco	Alberto	FA
Ania	Irvin	AI
Lukas	Liana	LL

(122 rows)

A SELECT statement that uses the DATE_FORMAT function

```
SELECT invoice_date,
       DATE_FORMAT(invoice_date, '%m/%d/%y') AS 'MM/DD/YY',
       DATE_FORMAT(invoice_date, '%e-%b-%Y') AS 'DD-Mon-YYYY'
FROM invoices
```

invoice_date	MM/DD/YY	DD-Mon-YYYY
2011-04-08	04/08/11	8-Apr-2011
2011-04-10	04/10/11	10-Apr-2011
2011-04-13	04/13/11	13-Apr-2011

(114 rows)

A SELECT statement that uses the ROUND function

```
SELECT invoice_date, invoice_total,
       ROUND(invoice_total) AS nearest_dollar,
       ROUND(invoice_total, 1) AS nearest_dime
FROM invoices
```

invoice_date	invoice_total	nearest_dollar	nearest_dime
2011-04-08	3813.33	3813	3813.3
2011-04-10	40.20	40	40.2
2011-04-13	138.75	139	138.8

(114 rows)

Description

- When using the DATE_FORMAT function to specify the format of a date, you use the percent sign (%) to identify a format code. For example, a format code of *m* returns the month number with a leading zero if necessary. For more information about these codes, see chapter 9.

- For more information about using functions, see chapter 9.

Figure 3-7   How to use functions with strings, dates, and numbers

How to test expressions by coding statements without FROM clauses

When you use MySQL, you don't have to code FROM clauses in SELECT statements. This makes it easy for you to code SELECT statements that test expressions and functions like those that you've seen in this chapter. Instead of coding column specifications in the SELECT clause, you use literals or functions to supply the test values you need. And you code column aliases to display the results. Then, once you're sure that the code works as you intend it to, you can add the FROM clause and replace the literals or functions with the correct column specifications.

Figure 3-8 shows how to test expressions. Here, the first example tests an arithmetic expression using numeric literals that make it easy to verify the results. The remaining examples test the functions that you saw in figure 3-7. If you compare these statements, you'll see that the second and fourth examples simply replace the column specifications in figure 3-7 with literal values. The third example uses another function, CURRENT_DATE, to supply a date value in place of the invoice_date column that's coded in figure 3-7.

Four SELECT statements without FROM clauses

Example 1: Testing a calculation

```
SELECT 1000 * (1 + .1) AS "10% More Than 1000"
```

10% More Than 1000
1100.0

Example 2: Testing the CONCAT function

```
SELECT "Ed" AS first_name, "Williams" AS last_name,
    CONCAT(LEFT("Ed", 1), LEFT("Williams", 1)) AS initials
```

first_name	last_name	initials
Ed	Williams	EW

Example 3: Testing the DATE_FORMAT function

```
SELECT CURRENT_DATE,
       DATE_FORMAT(CURRENT_DATE, '%m/%d/%y') AS 'MM/DD/YY',
       DATE_FORMAT(CURRENT_DATE, '%e-%b-%Y') AS 'DD-Mon-YYYY'
```

CURRENT_DATE	MM/DD/YY	DD-Mon-YYYY
2012-02-24	02/24/12	24-Feb-2012

Example 4: Testing the ROUND function

```
SELECT 12345.6789 AS value,
       ROUND(12345.6789) AS nearest_dollar,
       ROUND(12345.6789, 1) AS nearest_dime
```

value	nearest_dollar	nearest_dime
12345.6789	12346	12345.7

Description

- With MySQL, you don't have to code a FROM clause. This makes it easy to test expressions that include arithmetic operators and functions.

- The CURRENT_DATE function returns the current date. The parentheses are optional for this function.

Figure 3-8   How to test expressions

How to eliminate duplicate rows

By default, all of the rows in the base table that satisfy the search condition in the WHERE clause are included in the result set. In some cases, though, that means that the result set will contain duplicate rows, or rows whose column values are identical. If that's not what you want, you can include the DISTINCT keyword in the SELECT clause to eliminate the duplicate rows.

Figure 3-9 shows how this works. Here, both SELECT statements retrieve the vendor_city and vendor_state columns from the Vendors table. The first statement doesn't include the DISTINCT keyword. Because of that, the same city and state can appear in the result set more than once. In the results shown in this figure, for example, you can see that Anaheim CA occurs twice and Boston MA occurs three times. In contrast, the second statement includes the DISTINCT keyword, so each city and state combination is included only once.

A SELECT statement that returns all rows

```
SELECT vendor_city, vendor_state
FROM vendors
ORDER BY vendor_city
```

(122 rows)

A SELECT statement that eliminates duplicate rows

```
SELECT DISTINCT vendor_city, vendor_state
FROM vendors
ORDER BY vendor_city
```

(53 rows)

Description

- The DISTINCT keyword prevents duplicate (identical) rows from being included in the result set. DISTINCTROW is a synonym for DISTINCT.
- The ALL keyword causes all rows matching the search condition to be included in the result set, regardless of whether rows are duplicated. Since this is the default, you'll usually omit the ALL keyword.
- To use the DISTINCT or ALL keyword, code it immediately after the SELECT keyword as shown above.

Figure 3-9   How to eliminate duplicate rows

How to code the WHERE clause

Earlier in this chapter, I mentioned that to improve performance, you should code your SELECT statements so they retrieve only the columns you need. That goes for retrieving rows too: The fewer rows you retrieve, the more efficient the statement will be. Because of that, you typically include a WHERE clause on your SELECT statements with a search condition that filters the rows in the base table so only the rows you need are retrieved. In the topics that follow, you'll learn a variety of ways to code this clause.

How to use the comparison operators

Figure 3-10 shows you how to use the *comparison operators* in the search condition of a WHERE clause to compare two expressions. If the result of the comparison is true, the row being tested is included in the query results.

The examples in this figure show how to use the comparison operators. The first WHERE clause, for example, uses the equal operator (=) to retrieve only those rows whose vendor_state column has a value of 'IA'. Here, the state code is a string literal so it must be enclosed in single or double quotes. In contrast, the second WHERE clause uses the greater than (>) operator to retrieve only those rows that have a balance greater than zero. In this case, zero (0) is a numeric literal so it isn't enclosed in quotes.

The third WHERE clause shows another way to retrieve all the invoices with a balance due by rearranging the comparison expression. Like the second clause, it uses the greater than operator. Instead of comparing the balance due to a value of zero, however, it compares the invoice total to the total of the payments and credits that have been applied to the invoice.

The fourth WHERE clause shows how you can use comparison operators other than equal with string data. In this example, the less than operator (<) is used to compare the value of the vendor_name column to a literal string that contains the letter M. That causes the query to return all vendors with names that begin with the letters A through L.

You can also use the comparison operators with date literals, as shown by the fifth and sixth WHERE clauses. The fifth clause retrieves rows with invoice dates on or before July 31, 2011, and the sixth clause retrieves rows with invoice dates on or after July 1, 2011. Like literal values for strings, literal values for dates must be enclosed in single or double quotes. Also, literal values for dates must use this format: YYYY-MM-DD. This is the default date format used by MySQL.

The last two WHERE clauses show how you can test for a not-equal condition. In both cases, only rows with a credit total that isn't equal to zero are retrieved.

Whenever possible, you should compare expressions that have similar data types. If you compare expressions that have different data types, MySQL implicitly converts the data type for you. Generally, this implicit conversion is acceptable. However, implicit conversions can occasionally yield unexpected

The syntax of the WHERE clause with comparison operators

```
WHERE expression_1 operator expression_2
```

The comparison operators

=	Equal
<	Less than
>	Greater than
<=	Less than or equal to
>=	Greater than or equal to
<>	Not equal
!=	Not equal

Examples of WHERE clauses that retrieve...

Vendors located in Iowa

```
WHERE vendor_state = 'IA'
```

[handwritten: mean it prints exactly]

Invoices with a balance due (two variations)

```
WHERE invoice_total - payment_total - credit_total > 0
WHERE invoice_total > payment_total + credit_total
```

Vendors with names from A to L

```
WHERE vendor_name < 'M'
```

Invoices on or before a specified date

```
WHERE invoice_date <= '2011-07-31'
```

Invoices on or after a specified date

```
WHERE invoice_date >= '2011-07-01'
```

Invoices with credits that don't equal zero (two variations)

```
WHERE credit_total <> 0
WHERE credit_total != 0
```

Description

- You can use a *comparison operator* to compare any two expressions. Since MySQL automatically converts the data for comparison, the expressions may be of unlike data types. However, the comparison may sometimes produce unexpected results.

- If the result of a comparison is a true value, the row being tested is included in the result set. If it's a false or null value, the row isn't included.

- To use a string literal or a date literal in a comparison, enclose it in quotes. To use a numeric literal, enter the number without quotes.

- Character comparisons performed on MySQL databases are not case-sensitive. So, for example, 'CA' and 'ca' are considered equivalent.

- If you compare a null value using one of these comparison operators, the result is always a null value. To test for null values, use the IS NULL clause presented in figure 3-15.

Figure 3-10   How to use the comparison operators

results. To prevent this, you can explicitly convert the data type by using the CAST or CONVERT functions, which you'll learn about in chapter 8.

How to use the AND, OR, and NOT logical operators

Figure 3-11 shows how to use *logical operators* in a WHERE clause. You can use the AND and OR operators to combine two or more search conditions into a *compound condition*. And you can use the NOT operator to negate a search condition. The examples in this figure show how these operators work.

The first two examples show the AND and OR operators. When you use the AND operator, both conditions must be true. So, in the first example, only those vendors in the state of New Jersey and the city of Springfield are retrieved from the Vendors table. When you use the OR operator, though, only one of the conditions must be true. So, in the second example, all the vendors in the state of New Jersey and all the vendors in the city of Pittsburg (no matter what state) are retrieved.

The third example shows how to use the NOT operator to negate a condition. Here, vendors that are not in the state of California are returned. The fourth example shows a compound condition that uses two NOT operators. This condition is difficult to understand. To make it easier to understand, you can rewrite this condition to remove the NOT operators as shown in the fifth example.

The last two examples in this figure show how the order of precedence for the logical operators and the use of parentheses affect the result of a search condition. By default, the NOT operator is evaluated first, followed by AND, and then by OR. However, you can use parentheses to override the order of precedence or to clarify a logical expression, just as you can with arithmetic expressions.

In the next to last example, for instance, no parentheses are used, so the two conditions connected by the AND operator are evaluated first. In the last example, though, parentheses are used so the two conditions connected by the OR operator are evaluated first. If you take a minute to review the results in this figure, you should quickly see how these two conditions differ.

The syntax of the WHERE clause with logical operators

```
WHERE [NOT] search_condition_1 {AND|OR} [NOT] search_condition_2 ...
```

Examples of WHERE clauses that use logical operators

The AND operator
```
WHERE vendor_state = 'NJ' AND vendor_city = 'Springfield'
```

only Springfield, NJ returned

The OR operator
```
WHERE vendor_state = 'NJ' OR vendor_city = 'Pittsburg'
```

Pittsburg, PA or all cities in NJ

The NOT operator
```
WHERE NOT vendor_state = 'CA'
```

The NOT operator in a complex search condition
```
WHERE NOT (invoice_total >= 5000 OR NOT invoice_date <= '2011-08-01')
```

The same condition rephrased to eliminate the NOT operator
```
WHERE invoice_total < 5000 AND invoice_date <= '2011-08-01'
```

A compound condition without parentheses
```
WHERE invoice_date > '2011-07-03' OR invoice_total > 500
    AND invoice_total - payment_total - credit_total > 0
```

invoice_number	invoice_date	invoice_total	balance_due
203339-13	2011-07-05	17.50	0.00
111-92R-10093	2011-07-06	39.77	0.00
963253258	2011-07-06	111.00	0.00

```
(33 rows)
```

The same compound condition with parentheses
```
WHERE (invoice_date > '2011-07-03' OR invoice_total > 500)
    AND invoice_total - payment_total - credit_total > 0
```

invoice_number	invoice_date	invoice_total	balance_due
39104	2011-07-10	85.31	85.31
963253264	2011-07-18	52.25	52.25
31361833	2011-07-21	579.42	579.42

```
(11 rows)
```

Description

- You can use the AND and OR *logical operators* to create *compound conditions* that consist of two or more conditions. You use the AND operator to specify that the search must satisfy both of the conditions, and you use the OR operator to specify that the search must satisfy at least one of the conditions.

- You can use the NOT operator to negate a condition. Because this can make the search condition unclear, you should rephrase the condition if possible so it doesn't use NOT.

- When MySQL evaluates a compound condition, it evaluates the operators in this sequence: (1) NOT, (2) AND, and (3) OR. You can use parentheses to override this order of precedence or to clarify the sequence in which the operations are evaluated.

Figure 3-11   How to use the AND, OR, and NOT logical operators

How to use the IN operator

Figure 3-12 shows how to code a WHERE clause that uses the IN operator. When you use this operator, the value of the test expression is compared with the list of expressions in the IN phrase. If the test expression is equal to one of the expressions in the list, the row is included in the query results. This is shown by the first example in this figure, which returns all rows whose terms_id column is equal to 1, 3, or 4.

You can also use the NOT operator with the IN phrase to test for a value that's not in a list of expressions. This is shown by the second example. Here, only those vendors that aren't in California, Nevada, or Oregon are retrieved.

At the top of this figure, the syntax of the IN phrase shows that you can code a *subquery* in place of a list of expressions. As you'll learn in chapter 6, subqueries are a powerful feature. For now, though, you should know that a subquery is simply a SELECT statement within another statement.

In the third example, for instance, a subquery is used to return a list of vendor_id values for vendors who have invoices dated July 18, 2011. Then, the WHERE clause retrieves a row only if the vendor_id is in that list. Note that for this to work, the subquery must return a single column, in this case, vendor_id.

The syntax of the WHERE clause with an IN phrase

```
WHERE test_expression [NOT] IN
      ({subquery|expression_1 [, expression_2]...})
```

Examples of the IN phrase

An IN phrase with a list of numeric literals

```
WHERE terms_id IN (1, 3, 4)
```

An IN phrase preceded by NOT

```
WHERE vendor_state NOT IN ('CA', 'NV', 'OR')
```

An IN phrase with a subquery

```
WHERE vendor_id IN
    (SELECT vendor_id
     FROM invoices
     WHERE invoice_date = '2011-07-18')
```

Description

- You can use the IN phrase to test whether an expression is equal to a value in a list of expressions. Each of the expressions in the list is automatically converted to the same type of data as the test expression.

- The list of expressions can be coded in any order without affecting the order of the rows in the result set.

- You can use the NOT operator to test for an expression that's not in the list of expressions.

- If you're using MySQL version 4.1 or later, you can also compare the test expression to the items in a list returned by a *subquery*. You'll learn more about coding subqueries in chapter 6.

Figure 3-12   How to use the IN operator

How to use the BETWEEN operator

Figure 3-13 shows how to use the BETWEEN operator in a WHERE clause. When you use this operator, the value of a test expression is compared to the range of values specified in the BETWEEN phrase. If the value falls within this range, the row is included in the query results.

The first example in this figure shows a simple WHERE clause that uses the BETWEEN operator. It retrieves invoices with invoice dates between June 1, 2011 and June 30, 2011. Note that the range is inclusive, so invoices with invoice dates of June 1 and June 30 are included in the results.

The second example shows how to use the NOT operator to select rows that aren't within a given range. In this case, vendors with zip codes that aren't between 93600 and 93799 are included in the results.

The third example shows how you can use a calculated value in the test expression. Here, the payment_total and credit_total columns are subtracted from the invoice_total column to give the balance due. Then, this value is compared to the range specified in the BETWEEN phrase.

The last example shows how you can use calculated values in the BETWEEN phrase. Here, the first value is the credit_total column and the second value is the credit_total column plus 500. So the results include all those invoices where the amount paid is between the credit amount and $500 more than the credit amount.

The syntax of the WHERE clause with a BETWEEN phrase

```
WHERE test_expression [NOT] BETWEEN begin_expression AND end_expression
```

Examples of the BETWEEN phrase

A BETWEEN phrase with literal values

```
WHERE invoice_date BETWEEN '2011-06-01' AND '2011-06-30'
```

A BETWEEN phrase preceded by NOT

≤ 93600 AND > 93799

```
WHERE vendor_zip_code NOT BETWEEN 93600 AND 93799
```

A BETWEEN phrase with a test expression coded as a calculated value

```
WHERE invoice_total - payment_total - credit_total BETWEEN 200 AND 500
```

A BETWEEN phrase with the upper and lower limits coded as calculated values

```
WHERE payment_total BETWEEN credit_total AND credit_total + 500
```

Description

- You can use the BETWEEN phrase to test whether an expression falls within a range of values. The lower limit must be coded as the first expression, and the upper limit must be coded as the second expression. Otherwise, MySQL returns an empty result set.

- The two expressions used in the BETWEEN phrase for the range of values are inclusive. That is, the result set includes values that are equal to the upper or lower limit.

- You can use the NOT operator to test for an expression that's not within the given range.

Figure 3-13   How to use the BETWEEN operator

How to use the LIKE and REGEXP operators

To retrieve rows that match a specific *string pattern*, or *mask*, you can use the LIKE or REGEXP operators as shown in figure 3-14. The LIKE operator is an older operator that lets you search for simple string patterns. When you use this operator, the mask can contain one or both of the *wildcard* symbols shown in the first table in this figure.

In contrast to the LIKE operator, the REGEXP operator allows you to create complex string patterns known as *regular expressions*. To do that, you can use the special characters and constructs shown in the second table in this figure. Although creating regular expressions can be tricky at first, they allow you to search for virtually any string pattern.

In the first example in this figure, the LIKE phrase specifies that all vendors in cities that start with the letters SAN should be included in the query results. Here, the percent sign (%) indicates that any character or characters can follow these three letters. So San Diego and Santa Ana are both included in the results.

The second example selects all vendors whose vendor name starts with the letters COMPU, followed by any one character, the letters ER, and any characters after that. The vendor names Compuserve and Computerworld both match that pattern.

In the third example, the REGEXP phrase searches for the letters SA within the vendor_city column. Since the letters can be in any position within the string, both Pasadena and Santa Ana are included in the results.

The next two examples demonstrate how to use REGEXP to match a pattern to the beginning or end of the string being tested. In the fourth example, the mask ^SA matches the letters SA at the beginning of vendor_city, as in Santa Ana and Sacramento. In contrast, the mask NA$ matches the letters NA at the end of vendor_city, as shown in the fifth example.

The sixth example uses the pipe (|) character to search for either of two string patterns: RS or SN. In this case, the first pattern would match Traverse City and the second would match Fresno, so both are included in the result set.

The last four examples use brackets to specify multiple values. In the seventh example, the vendor_state column is searched for values that contain the letter N followed by either C or V. That excludes NJ and NY. In contrast, the eighth example searches for states that contain the letter N followed by any letter from A to J. This excludes NV and NY.

The ninth example searches the values in the vendor_contact_last_name column for a name that can be spelled two different ways: Damien or Damion. To do that, the mask specifies the two possible characters in the fifth position, E and O, within brackets. In the final example, the REGEXP phrase searches for a vendor_city that ends with any letter, a vowel, and then the letter N.

Both the LIKE and REGEXP operators provide powerful functionality for finding information in a database that can't be found any other way. However, searches that use these operators sometimes run slowly since they can't use a table's indexes. As a result, you should only use these operators when necessary.

For the sake of brevity, this chapter only presents the most common symbols that are used in regular expressions. However, MySQL supports most of

The syntax of the WHERE clause with a LIKE phrase

```
WHERE match_expression [NOT] LIKE pattern
```

The syntax of the WHERE clause with a REGEXP phrase

```
WHERE match_expression [NOT] REGEXP pattern
```

LIKE wildcards

Symbol	Description
%	Matches any string of zero or more characters.
_	Matches any single character.

REGEXP special characters and constructs

Character/Construct	Description
^	Matches the pattern to the beginning of the value being tested.
$	Matches the pattern to the end of the value being tested.
.	Matches any single character.
[charlist]	Matches any single character listed within the brackets. OR
[char1-char2]	Matches any single character within the given range. Between
		Separates two string patterns and matches either one.

WHERE clauses that use the LIKE and REGEXP operators

Example	Results that match the mask
`WHERE vendor_city LIKE 'SAN%'`	"San Diego", "Santa Ana"
`WHERE vendor_name LIKE 'COMPU_ER%'`	"Compuserve", "Computerworld"
`WHERE vendor_city REGEXP 'SA'`	"Pasadena", "Santa Ana"
`WHERE vendor_city REGEXP '^SA'`	"Santa Ana", "Sacramento"
`WHERE vendor_city REGEXP 'NA$'`	"Gardena", "Pasadena", "Santa Ana"
`WHERE vendor_city REGEXP 'RS|SN'`	"Traverse City", "Fresno"
`WHERE vendor_state REGEXP 'N[CV]'`	"NC" and "NV" but not "NJ" or "NY"
`WHERE vendor_state REGEXP 'N[A-J]'`	"NC" and "NJ" but not "NV" or "NY"
`WHERE vendor_contact_last_name REGEXP 'DAMI[EO]N'`	"Damien" and "Damion"
`WHERE vendor_city REGEXP '[A-Z][AEIOU]N$'`	"Boston", "Mclean", "Oberlin"

Description

- You use the LIKE and REGEXP operators to retrieve rows that match a *string pattern*, called a *mask*. The mask determines which values in the column satisfy the condition.

- The mask for a LIKE phrase can contain special symbols, called *wildcards*. The mask for a REGEXP phrase can contain special characters and constructs. Masks aren't case-sensitive.

- If you use the NOT keyword, only those rows with values that don't match the string pattern are included in the result set.

- Most LIKE and REGEXP phrases significantly degrade performance compared to other types of searches, so use them only when necessary.

Figure 3-14   How to use the LIKE and REGEXP operators

the symbols that are standard for creating regular expressions. For more information about creating regular expressions, please consult the online MySQL Reference Manual. If you're familiar with using regular expressions in other programming languages such as PHP, you'll find that they work similarly in MySQL.

How to use the IS NULL clause

In chapter 1, you learned that a column can contain a *null value*. A null value is typically used to indicate that a value is not known. A null value is not the same as an empty string (' '). An empty string is typically used to indicate that the value is known, and it doesn't exist.

If you're working with a database that allows null values, you need to know how to test for them in search conditions. To do that, you use the IS NULL clause as shown in figure 3-15.

This figure uses a table named Null_Sample to show how to search for null values. This table contains two columns: invoice_id and invoice_total. The values in this table are displayed in the first example.

The second example shows what happens when you retrieve all the rows with invoice_total equal to zero. In this case, the row that has a null value isn't included in the result set. As the third example shows, this row isn't included in the result set when invoice_total isn't equal to zero either. Instead, you have to use the IS NULL clause to retrieve rows with null values, as shown in the fourth example.

You can also use the NOT operator with the IS NULL clause, as shown in the last example. When you use this operator, all of the rows that don't contain null values are included in the query results.

The syntax of the WHERE clause with the IS NULL clause

```
WHERE expression IS [NOT] NULL
```

The contents of the Null_Sample table

```
SELECT * FROM null_sample
```

invoice_id	invoice_total
1	125.00
2	0.00
3	NULL
4	2199.99
5	0.00

A SELECT statement that retrieves rows with zero values

```
SELECT * FROM null_sample
WHERE invoice_total = 0
```

invoice_id	invoice_total
2	0.00
5	0.00

A SELECT statement that retrieves rows with non-zero values

```
SELECT * FROM null_sample
WHERE invoice_total <> 0
```

invoice_id	invoice_total
1	125.00
4	2199.99

A SELECT statement that retrieves rows with null values

```
SELECT * FROM null_sample
WHERE invoice_total IS NULL
```

invoice_id	invoice_total
3	NULL

A SELECT statement that retrieves rows without null values

```
SELECT *
FROM null_sample
WHERE invoice_total IS NOT NULL
```

invoice_id	invoice_total
1	125.00
2	0.00
4	2199.99
5	0.00

Description

- A *null value* represents a value that's unknown, unavailable, or not applicable. It isn't the same as a zero or an empty string (").

Figure 3-15   How to use the IS NULL clause

How to code the ORDER BY clause

The ORDER BY clause specifies the sort order for the rows in a result set. In most cases, you'll use column names from the base table to specify the sort order as you saw in some of the examples earlier in this chapter. However, you can also use other techniques to sort the rows in a result set, as described in the topics that follow.

How to sort by a column name

Figure 3-16 presents the expanded syntax of the ORDER BY clause. This syntax shows that you can sort by one or more expressions in either ascending or descending sequence. The three examples in this figure show how to code this clause for expressions that involve column names.

The first two examples show how to sort the rows in a result set by a single column. In the first example, the rows in the Vendors table are sorted in ascending sequence by the vendor_name column. Since ascending is the default sequence, the ASC keyword can be omitted. In the second example, the rows are sorted by the vendor_name column in descending sequence.

To sort by more than one column, you simply list the names in the ORDER BY clause separated by commas as shown in the third example. This can be referred to as a *nested sort* because one sort is nested within another. Here, the rows in the Vendors table are first sorted by the vendor_state column in ascending sequence. Then, within each state, the rows are sorted by the vendor_city column in ascending sequence. Finally, within each city, the rows are sorted by the vendor_name column in ascending sequence.

The expanded syntax of the ORDER BY clause

```
ORDER BY expression [ASC|DESC][, expression [ASC|DESC]] ...
```

An ORDER BY clause that sorts by one column in ascending sequence

```
SELECT vendor_name,
    CONCAT(vendor_city, ', ', vendor_state, ' ', vendor_zip_code) AS address
FROM vendors
ORDER BY vendor_name
```

vendor_name	address
Abbey Office Furnishings	Fresno, CA 93722
American Booksellers Assoc	Tarrytown, NY 10591
American Express	Los Angeles, CA 90096
ASC Signs	Fresno, CA 93703

An ORDER BY clause that sorts by one column in descending sequence

```
SELECT vendor_name,
    CONCAT(vendor_city, ', ', vendor_state, ' ', vendor_zip_code) AS address
FROM vendors
ORDER BY vendor_name DESC
```

vendor_name	address
Zylka Design	Fresno, CA 93711
Zip Print & Copy Center	Fresno, CA 93777
Zee Medical Service Co	Washington, IA 52353
Yesmed, Inc	Fresno, CA 93718

An ORDER BY clause that sorts by three columns

```
SELECT vendor_name,
    CONCAT(vendor_city, ', ', vendor_state, ' ', vendor_zip_code) AS address
FROM vendors
ORDER BY vendor_state, vendor_city, vendor_name
```

vendor_name	address
AT&T	Phoenix, AZ 85062
Computer Library	Phoenix, AZ 85023
Wells Fargo Bank	Phoenix, AZ 85038
Aztek Label	Anaheim, CA 92807

Description

- The ORDER BY clause specifies how you want the rows in the result set sorted. You can sort by one or more columns, and you can sort each column in either ascending (ASC) or descending (DESC) sequence. ASC is the default.

- By default, in an ascending sort, special characters appear first in the sort sequence, followed by numbers, then letters. This sort order is determined by the character set used by the server, which you can change when you start the server.

- Null values appear first in the sort sequence, even if you're using DESC.

- You can sort by any column in the base table regardless of whether it's included in the SELECT clause.

Figure 3-16   How to sort by a column name

How to sort by an alias, expression, or column number

Figure 3-17 presents three more techniques that you can use to specify sort columns. First, you can use a column alias that's defined in the SELECT clause. The first SELECT statement in this figure, for example, sorts by a column named Address, which is an alias for the concatenation of the vendor_city, vendor_state, and vendor_zip_code columns. Notice that within the Address column, the result set is also sorted by the vendor_name column.

You can also use an arithmetic or string expression in the ORDER BY clause, as shown by the second example in this figure. Here, the expression consists of the vendor_contact_last_name column concatenated with the vendor_contact_first_name column. Notice that neither of these columns is included in the SELECT clause. Although MySQL allows this coding technique, many other SQL dialects don't.

The last example in this figure shows how you can use column numbers to specify a sort order. To use this technique, you code the number that corresponds to the column of the result set, where 1 is the first column, 2 is the second column, and so on. In this example, the ORDER BY clause sorts the result set by the second column, which contains the concatenated address, then by the first column, which contains the vendor name. As a result, this statement returns the same result set that's returned by the first statement.

However, the statement that uses column numbers is more difficult to read because you have to look at the SELECT clause to see what columns the numbers refer to. In addition, if you add or remove columns from the SELECT clause, you may also have to change the ORDER BY clause to reflect the new column positions. As a result, you should avoid using this technique in most situations.

An ORDER BY clause that uses an alias

```
SELECT vendor_name,
    CONCAT(vendor_city, ', ', vendor_state, ' ', vendor_zip_code) AS address
FROM vendors
ORDER BY address, vendor_name
```

vendor_name	address
Aztek Label	Anaheim, CA 92807
Blue Shield of California	Anaheim, CA 92850
Malloy Lithographing Inc	Ann Arbor, MI 48106
Data Reproductions Corp	Auburn Hills, MI 48326

An ORDER BY clause that uses an expression

```
SELECT vendor_name,
    CONCAT(vendor_city, ', ', vendor_state, ' ', vendor_zip_code) AS address
FROM vendors
ORDER BY CONCAT(vendor_contact_last_name, vendor_contact_first_name)
```

vendor_name	address
Dristas Groom & McCormick	Fresno, CA 93720
Internal Revenue Service	Fresno, CA 93888
US Postal Service	Madison, WI 53707
Yale Industrial Trucks-Fresno	Fresno, CA 93706

An ORDER BY clause that uses column positions

```
SELECT vendor_name,
    CONCAT(vendor_city, ', ', vendor_state, ' ', vendor_zip_code) AS address
FROM vendors
ORDER BY 2, 1
```

vendor_name	address
Aztek Label	Anaheim, CA 92807
Blue Shield of California	Anaheim, CA 92850
Malloy Lithographing Inc	Ann Arbor, MI 48106
Data Reproductions Corp	Auburn Hills, MI 48326

Description

- The ORDER BY clause can include a column alias that's specified in the SELECT clause if the column alias does not include spaces.

- The ORDER BY clause can include any valid expression. The expression can refer to any column in the base table, even if it isn't included in the result set.

- The ORDER BY clause can use numbers to specify the columns to use for sorting. In that case, 1 represents the first column in the result set, 2 represents the second column, and so on.

Figure 3-17   How to sort by an alias, expression, or column number

How to code the LIMIT clause

The LIMIT clause specifies the maximum number of rows that are returned in the result set. For most queries, you want to see the entire result set so you won't use this clause. However, there may be times when you want to retrieve just a subset of a larger result set.

Figure 3-18 presents the expanded syntax of the LIMIT clause. This clause can take one or two arguments as shown by the three examples in this figure.

How to limit the number of rows

In its simplest form, you code the LIMIT clause with a single numeric argument. Then, the number of rows in the result set is, at most, the number you specify. But if the result set is smaller than the number you specify, the LIMIT clause has no effect.

In the first example, the SELECT statement includes the LIMIT 5 clause, so the entire result set is five rows. Without the LIMIT clause, this statement would return 114 rows. Because the result set is sorted by invoice_total in descending order, this result set represents the five largest invoices.

How to return a range of rows

If you code the optional offset argument of the LIMIT clause, it represents an *offset*, or starting point for the result set. This offset starts from a value of 0, which refers to the first row in the result set. In the second example, then, the offset is 2 so the result set starts with the third invoice. Then, since the row count is 3, the result set contains just 3 rows.

Similarly, the third example has an offset of 100, so the result set starts with row 101. Note that the row count for the LIMIT clause in this example is 1000. Since the table contains only 114 rows, though, the result set contains just the last 14 rows in the table.

The expanded syntax of the LIMIT clause

```
LIMIT [offset,] row_count
```

A SELECT statement with a LIMIT clause that starts with the first row

```
SELECT vendor_id, invoice_total
FROM invoices
ORDER BY invoice_total DESC
LIMIT 5
```

vendor_id	invoice_total
▸ 110	37966.19
110	26881.40
110	23517.58
72	21842.00
110	20551.18

A SELECT statement with a LIMIT clause that starts with the third row

```
SELECT invoice_id, vendor_id, invoice_total
FROM invoices
ORDER BY invoice_id
LIMIT 2, 3
```

offset

invoice_id	vendor_id	invoice_total
▸ 3	123	138.75
4	123	144.70
5	123	15.50

A SELECT statement with a LIMIT clause that starts with the 101st row

```
SELECT invoice_id, vendor_id, invoice_total
FROM invoices
ORDER BY invoice_id
LIMIT 100, 1000
```

invoice_id	vendor_id	invoice_total
▸ 101	123	30.75
102	110	20551.18
103	122	2051.59
104	123	44.44

```
(14 rows)
```

Description

- You can use the LIMIT clause to limit the number of rows returned by the SELECT statement. This clause takes one or two integer arguments.

- If you code a single argument, it specifies the maximum row count, beginning with the first row. If you code both arguments, the *offset* specifies the first row to return, where the offset of the first row is 0.

- If you want to retrieve all of the rows from a certain offset to the end of the result set, code -1 for the row count.

- Typically, you'll use an ORDER BY clause whenever you use the LIMIT clause.

Figure 3-18   How to code the LIMIT clause

Perspective

The goal of this chapter has been to teach you the basic skills for coding SELECT statements. As a result, you'll use these skills in almost every SELECT statement you code.

As you'll see in the chapters that follow, though, there's a lot more to coding SELECT statements than what's presented here. In the next three chapters, then, you'll learn additional skills for coding SELECT statements. When you complete those chapters, you'll know everything you need to know about retrieving data from a MySQL database.

Terms

keyword	parameter
base table	concatenate
search condition	comparison operator
filter	logical operator
Boolean expression	compound condition
expression	subquery
column alias	string pattern
arithmetic expression	mask
arithmetic operator	wildcard
order of precedence	regular expression
literal value	null value
string	nested sort
function	offset
argument	

Exercises

Run some of the examples in this chapter

In these exercises, you'll use MySQL Workbench to run some of the scripts for the examples in this chapter. This assumes that you already know how to use MySQL Workbench, as described in chapter 2.

1. Start MySQL Workbench.

2. Open the query named 3-02.sql that you should find in this directory: c:\murach\mysql\book_scripts\ch03. When it opens, you should see all of the queries for figure 3-2. Note that each of these queries has a semicolon at the end of it.

3. Move the insertion point into the first query and press Ctrl+Enter or click on the Execute Current Statement button to run the query. This shows you the data that's in the Invoices table that you'll be working with in this chapter.

4. Move the insertion point into the second query and run it.

5. Open and run the queries for any of the other examples in this chapter that you're interested in reviewing.

Enter and run your own SELECT statements

In these exercises, you'll enter and run your own SELECT statements. To do that, you can open the query for an example that is similar to the statement you need to write, copy the statement into a new SQL tab, and modify the statement. That can save you both time and syntax errors.

6. Write a SELECT statement that returns three columns from the Vendors table: vendor_name, vendor_contact_last_name, and vendor_contact_first_name. Then, run this statement to make sure it works correctly.

   Add an ORDER BY clause to this statement that sorts the result set by last name and then first name, both in ascending sequence. Then, run this statement again to make sure it works correctly. This is a good way to build and test a statement, one clause at a time.

7. Write a SELECT statement that returns one column from the Vendors table named full_name that joins the vendor_contact_last_name and vendor_contact_first_name columns.

   Format this column with the last name, a comma, a space, and the first name like this:

   `Doe, John`

   Sort the result set by last name and then first name in ascending sequence.

   Return only the contacts whose last name begins with the letter A, B, C, or E. This should retrieve 41 rows.

8. Write a SELECT statement that returns these column names and data from the Invoices table:

Due Date	The invoice_due_date column
Invoice Total	The invoice_total column
10%	10% of the value of invoice_total
Plus 10%	The value of invoice_total plus 10%

   Return only the rows with an invoice total that's greater than or equal to 500 and less than or equal to 1000. This should retrieve 12 rows.

   Sort the result set in descending sequence by invoice_due_date.

9. Write a SELECT statement that returns these columns from the Invoices table:

invoice_number	The invoice_number column
invoice_total	The invoice_total column
payment_credit_total	Sum of the payment_total and credit_total columns
balance_due	The invoice_total column minus the payment_total and credit_total columns

   Return only invoices that have a balance due that's greater than $50.

Sort the result set by balance due in descending sequence.

Use the LIMIT clause so the result set contains only the rows with the 5 largest balances.

Work with nulls and test expressions

10. Write a SELECT statement that returns these columns from the Invoices table:

invoice_number	The invoice_number column
invoice_date	The invoice_date column
balance_due	The invoice_total column minus the payment_total and credit_total columns
payment_date	The payment_date column

Return only the rows where the payment_date column contains a null value. This should retrieve 11 rows.

11. Write a SELECT statement without a FROM clause that uses the CURRENT_DATE function to return the current date in its default format.

Use the DATE_FORMAT function to format the current date in this format:

`mm-dd-yyyy`

This displays the month, day, and four-digit year of the current date.

Give this column an alias of current_date. To do that, you must enclose the alias in quotes since that name is already used by the CURRENT_DATE function.

12. Write a SELECT statement without a FROM clause that creates a row with these columns:

starting_principal	Starting principal of $50,000
interest	6.5% of the principal
principal_plus_interest	The principal plus the interest

To calculate the third column, add the expressions you used for the first two columns.

4

How to retrieve data from two or more tables

In the last chapter, you learned how to create result sets that contain data from a single table. Now, this chapter shows you how to create result sets that contain data from two or more tables. To do that, you can use an inner join, an outer join, or a union.

How to work with inner joins 116
How to code an inner join 116
How to use table aliases 118
How to join to a table in another database 120
How to use compound join conditions 122
How to use a self-join 124
How to join more than two tables 126
How to use the implicit inner join syntax 128

How to work with outer joins 130
How to code an outer join 130
Outer join examples 132

Other skills for working with joins 136
How to join tables with the USING keyword 136
How to join tables with the NATURAL keyword 138
How to use cross joins 140

How to work with unions 142
How to code a union 142
A union that combines result sets from different tables 142
A union that combines result sets from the same tables 144
A union that simulates a full outer join 146

Perspective 148

How to work with inner joins

A *join* lets you combine columns from two or more tables into a single result set. To start, this chapter shows how to code the most common type of join, an *inner join*.

How to code an inner join

Figure 4-1 shows how to use the *explicit syntax* to code an inner join. This syntax is also called the *SQL-92 syntax* because it was introduced by the SQL-92 standards. It's generally considered a best practice to use this syntax.

To join data from two tables, you code the names of the two tables in the FROM clause along with the JOIN keyword and an ON phrase that specifies the *join condition*. The join condition indicates how the two tables should be compared. In most cases, they're compared based on the relationship between the primary key of the first table and a foreign key of the second table.

In this figure, for example, the SELECT statement joins data from the Vendors and Invoices tables based on the vendor_id column in each table. Since the join condition uses the equal operator, the value of the vendor_id column in a row in the Vendors table must match the vendor_id in a row in the Invoices table for that row to be included in the result set. In other words, only vendors with one or more invoices are included. Although you code most inner joins using the equal operator, you can compare two tables based on other conditions too. For example, you can use the greater than or less than operators for an inner join condition.

In this figure, the Vendors table is joined with the Invoices table using a column that has the same name in both tables: vendor_id. As a result, the columns must be qualified so MySQL can tell which table they come from. To code a *qualified column name*, you can enter the table name and a period in front of the column name. In this figure, the SELECT statement only uses qualified column names in the join condition. However, you must qualify a column name anywhere it appears in the statement if the same name occurs in both tables. If you don't, MySQL returns an error indicating that the column name is ambiguous.

The explicit syntax for an inner join

```
SELECT select_list
FROM table_1
    [INNER] JOIN table_2
        ON join_condition_1
    [[INNER] JOIN table_3
        ON join_condition_2]...
```

An inner join of the Vendors and Invoices tables

```
SELECT invoice_number, vendor_name
FROM vendors INNER JOIN invoices
    ON vendors.vendor_id = invoices.vendor_id
ORDER BY invoice_number
```

invoice_number	vendor_name
0-2058	Malloy Lithographing Inc
0-2060	Malloy Lithographing Inc
0-2436	Malloy Lithographing Inc
1-200-5164	Federal Express Corporation
1-202-2978	Federal Express Corporation
10843	Yesmed, Inc

(114 rows)

Description

- A *join* combines columns from two or more tables into a result set based on the *join conditions* you specify. For an *inner join*, only those rows that satisfy the join condition are included in the result set.

- A join condition names a column in each of the two tables involved in the join and indicates how the two columns should be compared. In most cases, you use the equal operator to retrieve rows with matching columns. However, you can also use any of the other comparison operators in a join condition.

- Tables are typically joined on the relationship between the primary key in one table and a foreign key in the other table. However, you can also join tables based on relationships not defined in the database. These are called *ad hoc relationships*.

- If the two columns in a join condition have the same name, you must qualify them with the table name so MySQL can distinguish between them. To code a *qualified column name*, type the table name, followed by a period, followed by the column name.

Note

- The INNER keyword is optional and is seldom used.

table . column_name

Figure 4-1   How to code an inner join

How to use table aliases

When you name a table to be joined in the FROM clause, you can refer to the table by an alias as shown in figure 4-2. A *table alias* is an alternative table name that's typically just a letter or two. This makes it easier to qualify the column names in the rest of the statement, and it makes the query easier to code and read, especially when the table names are long.

The first example in this figure joins data from the Vendors and Invoices tables. Here, both tables have been assigned aliases that consist of a single letter.

The second example only assigns an alias to the second table, not the first. Here, the alias shortens the name of the Invoice_Line_Items table to just Line_Items. As a result, the shorter name can be used to refer to the invoice_id column of the table in the join condition. Although you can use this technique when you code a query, most programmers use abbreviations of the table names as shown in the first example and throughout the rest of this chapter.

After you assign a table alias, you must use the alias in place of the original table name throughout the query. Otherwise, MySQL returns an error message instead of a result set.

The syntax for an inner join that uses table aliases

```
SELECT select_list
FROM table_1 a1
    [INNER] JOIN table_2 a2
        ON a1.column_name operator a2.column_name
    [[INNER] JOIN table_3 a3
        ON a2.column_name operator a3.column_name]...
```

Aliases for all tables

```
SELECT invoice_number, vendor_name, invoice_due_date,
    invoice_total - payment_total - credit_total AS balance_due
FROM vendors v JOIN invoices i
    ON v.vendor_id = i.vendor_id
WHERE invoice_total - payment_total - credit_total > 0
ORDER BY invoice_due_date DESC
```

invoice_number	vendor_name	invoice_due_date	balance_due
547480102	Blue Cross	2011-08-31	224.00
0-2436	Malloy Lithographing Inc	2011-08-30	10976.06
9982771	Ford Motor Credit Company	2011-08-23	503.20
P-0608	Malloy Lithographing Inc	2011-08-22	19351.18

(11 rows)

An alias for only one table

```
SELECT invoice_number, line_item_amount, line_item_description
FROM invoices JOIN invoice_line_items line_items
    ON invoices.invoice_id = line_items.invoice_id
WHERE account_number = 540
ORDER BY invoice_date
```

invoice_number	line_item_amount	line_item_description
I77271-001	478.00	Publishers Marketing
972110	207.78	Prospect list
133560	175.00	Card deck advertising
97/522	765.13	Catalog design

(6 rows)

Description

- A *table alias* is an alternative table name assigned in the FROM clause. You can use an alias, which is typically just a letter or two, to make a SQL statement easier to code and read.

- If you assign an alias to a table, you must use that alias to refer to the table throughout your query. You can't use the original table name.

- You can use an alias for one table in a join without using an alias for another table.

Figure 4-2   How to use table aliases

How to join to a table in another database

If you use the procedure described in appendix A (Windows) or appendix B (Mac) of this book to create the databases for this book, all of the tables are organized into three databases, which are also known as *schemas*. First, all tables pertaining to accounts payable such as the Vendors and Invoices tables are stored in the database, or schema, named AP. Then, all tables pertaining to order management are stored in a database named OM. Finally, all tables that are used by the smaller examples presented in this book are stored in a database named EX.

When you use MySQL Workbench to run a query against a database, you don't need to qualify any table name with its database name. For example, when you run a query against the AP database, you don't need to qualify the Vendors table with the name of the database.

However, you may occasionally need to join to a table that's in another database. To do that, you must qualify the table name in the other database by prefixing the table name with the database name. For example, let's say you need to join the Vendors table in the AP database with the Customers table in the OM database. To do that, you need to qualify the Customers table with the name of the database as shown in figure 4-3.

The syntax of a table name that's qualified with a database name

```
database_name.table_name
```

Join to a table in another database

```
SELECT vendor_name, customer_last_name, customer_first_name,
    vendor_state AS state, vendor_city AS city
FROM vendors v
    JOIN om.customers c
    ON v.vendor_zip_code = c.customer_zip
ORDER BY state, city
```

vendor_name	customer_last_name	customer_first_name	state	city
Wells Fargo Bank	Marissa	Kyle	AZ	Phoenix
Aztek Label	Irvin	Ania	CA	Anaheim
Costco	Neftaly	Thalia	CA	Fresno
Zylka Design	Holbrooke	Rashad	CA	Fresno
Gary McKeighan...	Holbrooke	Rashad	CA	Fresno
Digital Dreamwor...	Holbrooke	Rashad	CA	Fresno
Dataforms/West	Holbrooke	Rashad	CA	Fresno
Lou Gentile's Flo...	Damien	Deborah	CA	Fresno
Wakefield Co	Neftaly	Thalia	CA	Fresno

```
(37 rows)
```

Description

- A MySQL server can store tables in multiple databases. These databases are sometimes referred to as *schemas*.

- When you run a SELECT statement against one database, you can join to a table in another database if you have appropriate permissions. To do that, you must prefix the table name in the other database with the name of that database.

Figure 4-3   How to join to a table in another database

How to use compound join conditions

Although a join condition typically consists of a single comparison, you can include two or more comparisons in a join condition using the AND and OR operators. Figure 4-4 shows how this works.

The query in this figure uses the AND operator to return the first and last names of all customers in the Customers table whose first and last names also exist in the Employees table. Since Thomas Hardy is the only name that exists in both tables, this is the only row that's returned in the result set for this query.

The Customers table

customer_id	customer_last_name	customer_first_name	customer_address	customer_city	customer_state	cust
1	Anders	Maria	345 Winchell Pl	Anderson	IN	4601
2	Trujillo	Ana	1298 E Smathers St	Benton	AR	7201
3	Moreno	Antonio	6925 N Parkland Ave	Puyallup	WA	9837
4	Hardy	Thomas	83 d'Urberville Ln	Casterbridge	GA	3120
5	Berglund	Christina	22717 E 73rd Ave	Dubuque	IA	5200
6	Moos	Hanna	1778 N Bovine Ave	Peoria	IL	6163

(24 rows)

The Employees table

employee_id	last_name	first_name	department_number	manager_id
1	Smith	Cindy	2	NULL
2	Jones	Elmer	4	1
3	Simonian	Ralph	2	2
4	Hernandez	Olivia	1	9
5	Aaronsen	Robert	2	4
6	Watson	Denise	6	8

(9 rows)

An inner join with two conditions

```
SELECT customer_first_name, customer_last_name
FROM customers c JOIN employees e
    ON c.customer_first_name = e.first_name
    AND c.customer_last_name = e.last_name
```

customer_first_name	customer_last_name
Thomas	Hardy

(1 row)

Description

- A join condition can include two or more conditions connected by AND or OR operators.

Figure 4-4   How to use compound join conditions

How to use a self-join

A *self-join* joins a table to itself. Although self-joins are rare, they are sometimes useful for retrieving data that can't be retrieved any other way. For example, figure 4-5 presents a self-join that returns rows from the Vendors table where the vendor is in a city and state that has at least one other vendor. In other words, it does not return a vendor if that vendor is the only vendor in that city and state.

Since this example uses the same table twice, it must use aliases to distinguish one occurrence of the table from the other. In addition, this query must qualify each column name with a table alias since every column occurs in both tables.

Then, the join condition uses three comparisons. The first two match the vendor_city and vendor_state columns in the two tables. As a result, the query returns rows for vendors that are in the same city and state as another vendor. However, since a vendor resides in the same city and state as itself, a third comparison is included to exclude rows that match a vendor with itself. To do that, this condition uses the not-equal operator to compare the vendor_name columns in the two tables.

In addition, this statement includes the DISTINCT keyword. That way, a vendor appears only once in the result set. Otherwise, a vendor would appear once for every other row with a matching city and state. For example, if a vendor is in a city and state that has nine other vendors in that city and state, this query would return nine rows for that vendor.

This example also shows how you can use columns other than key columns in a join condition. Keep in mind, however, that this is an unusual situation and you're not likely to code joins like this often.

A self-join that returns vendors from cities in common with other vendors

```
SELECT DISTINCT v1.vendor_name, v1.vendor_city,
    v1.vendor_state
FROM vendors v1 JOIN vendors v2
    ON v1.vendor_city = v2.vendor_city AND
        v1.vendor_state = v2.vendor_state AND
        v1.vendor_name <> v2.vendor_name
ORDER BY v1.vendor_state, v1.vendor_city
```

vendor_name	vendor_city	vendor_state
Computer Library	Phoenix	AZ
AT&T	Phoenix	AZ
Wells Fargo Bank	Phoenix	AZ
Aztek Label	Anaheim	CA
Blue Shield of C...	Anaheim	CA
Dristas Groom & ...	Fresno	CA
Retirement Plan ...	Fresno	CA
Fresno County T...	Fresno	CA

(84 rows)

Description

- A *self-join* is a join that joins a table with itself.
- When you code a self-join, you must use aliases for the tables, and you must qualify each column name with the alias.

Figure 4-5   How to use a self-join

How to join more than two tables

So far, this chapter has only showed how to join data from two tables. However, it's common for programmers to need to join data from more than two tables. For example, it's not unheard of to need to join 10 or more tables. Fortunately, once you code the join condition correctly, you can often reuse it.

The SELECT statement in figure 4-6 joins data from four tables: Vendors, Invoices, Invoice_Line_Items, and General_Ledger_Accounts. Each of the joins is based on the relationship between the primary key of one table and a foreign key of the other table. For example, the account_number column is the primary key of the General_Ledger_Accounts table and a foreign key of the Invoice_Line_Items table.

This SELECT statement also begins to show how table aliases make a statement easier to code and read. Here, the one-letter and two-letter aliases that are used for the tables allow you to code the ON clause more concisely.

A statement that joins four tables

```
SELECT vendor_name, invoice_number, invoice_date,
    line_item_amount, account_description
FROM vendors v
    JOIN invoices i
        ON v.vendor_id = i.vendor_id
    JOIN invoice_line_items li
        ON i.invoice_id = li.invoice_id
    JOIN general_ledger_accounts gl
        ON li.account_number = gl.account_number
WHERE invoice_total - payment_total - credit_total > 0
ORDER BY vendor_name, line_item_amount DESC
```

vendor_name	invoice_number	invoice_date	line_item_amount	account_description
Blue Cross	547480102	2011-08-01	224.00	Group Insurance
Cardinal Business Media, Inc.	134116	2011-07-28	90.36	Direct Mail Advertising
Data Reproductions Corp	39104	2011-07-10	85.31	Book Printing Costs
Federal Express Corporation	263253270	2011-07-22	67.92	Freight
Federal Express Corporation	263253268	2011-07-21	59.97	Freight
Federal Express Corporation	963253264	2011-07-18	52.25	Freight
Federal Express Corporation	263253273	2011-07-22	30.75	Freight
Ford Motor Credit Company	9982771	2011-07-24	503.20	Travel and Accomodations

(11 rows)

Description

- You can think of a multi-table join as a series of two-table joins proceeding from left to right.

Figure 4-6   How to join more than two tables

How to use the implicit inner join syntax

Although it's generally considered a best practice to use the explicit inner join syntax described earlier in this chapter, MySQL also provides the *implicit inner join syntax* shown in figure 4-7. This syntax was widely used prior to the introduction of the explicit syntax. You should be familiar with the older implicit syntax mainly because you may need to maintain existing SQL statements that use it.

When you use the implicit syntax for an inner join, you code the tables in the FROM clause separated by commas. Then, you code the join conditions in the WHERE clause.

The first SELECT statement joins data from the Vendors and Invoices tables. Like the SELECT statement shown in figure 4-1, this statement joins these tables on an equal comparison between the vendor_id columns in the two tables. In this case, though, the comparison is coded as the search condition of the WHERE clause. However, both of these statements return the same result set.

The second SELECT statement uses the implicit syntax to join data from four tables. This is the same join you saw in figure 4-6. In this example, the three join conditions are combined in the WHERE clause using the AND operator. In addition, an AND operator is used to combine the join conditions with the search condition.

Because the explicit syntax for joins lets you separate join conditions from search conditions, statements that use the explicit syntax are typically easier to read than those that use the implicit syntax. In addition, the explicit syntax helps you avoid a common coding mistake with the implicit syntax: omitting the join condition. As you'll learn later in this chapter, an implicit join without a join condition results in a cross join, which can return a large number of rows. For these reasons, we recommend that you use the explicit syntax in all your new SQL code.

The implicit syntax for an inner join

```
SELECT select_list
FROM table_1, table_2 [, table_3]...
WHERE table_1.column_name operator table_2.column_name
    [AND table_2.column_name operator table_3.column_name]...
```

Join the Vendors and Invoices tables

```
SELECT invoice_number, vendor_name
FROM vendors v, invoices i
WHERE v.vendor_id = i.vendor_id
ORDER BY invoice_number
```

invoice_number	vendor_name
▶ 0-2058	Malloy Lithographing Inc
0-2060	Malloy Lithographing Inc
0-2436	Malloy Lithographing Inc
1-200-5164	Federal Express Corporation
1-202-2978	Federal Express Corporation

(114 rows)

Join four tables

```
SELECT vendor_name, invoice_number, invoice_date,
    line_item_amount, account_description
FROM  vendors v, invoices i, invoice_line_items li,
    general_ledger_accounts gl
WHERE v.vendor_id = i.vendor_id
  AND i.invoice_id = li.invoice_id
  AND li.account_number = gl.account_number
  AND invoice_total - payment_total - credit_total > 0
ORDER BY vendor_name, line_item_amount DESC
```

vendor_name	invoice_number	invoice_date	line_item_amount	account_description
▶ Blue Cross	547480102	2011-08-01	224.00	Group Insurance
Cardinal Business Media, Inc.	134116	2011-07-28	90.36	Direct Mail Advertising
Data Reproductions Corp	39104	2011-07-10	85.31	Book Printing Costs
Federal Express Corporation	263253270	2011-07-22	67.92	Freight
Federal Express Corporation	263253268	2011-07-21	59.97	Freight

(11 rows)

Description

- Instead of coding a join condition in the FROM clause, you can code it in the WHERE clause along with any search conditions. In that case, you list the tables in the FROM clause separated by commas.

- This syntax for coding joins is referred to as the *implicit syntax*. It was used prior to the SQL-92 standards, which introduced the explicit syntax.

Figure 4-7   How to use the implicit inner join syntax

How to work with outer joins

Although inner joins are the most common type of join, MySQL also supports *outer joins*. Unlike an inner join, an outer join returns all of the rows from one of the tables involved in the join, regardless of whether the join condition is true.

How to code an outer join

Figure 4-8 presents the explicit syntax for coding an outer join. Because this syntax is similar to the explicit syntax for inner joins, you shouldn't have any trouble understanding how it works. The main difference is that you include the LEFT or RIGHT keyword to specify the type of outer join you want to perform. You can also include the OUTER keyword, but it's optional and is usually omitted.

When you use a *left outer join*, the result set includes all the rows from the first, or left, table. Similarly, when you use a *right outer join*, the result set includes all the rows from the second, or right, table.

The example in this figure illustrates a left outer join. Here, the Vendors table is joined with the Invoices table. In addition, the result set includes vendor rows even if no matching invoices are found. In that case, null values are returned for the columns in the Invoices table.

The explicit syntax for an outer join

```
SELECT select_list
FROM table_1
    {LEFT|RIGHT} [OUTER] JOIN table_2
        ON join_condition_1
    [{LEFT|RIGHT} [OUTER] JOIN table_3
        ON join_condition_2]...
```

What outer joins do

Joins of this type	Retrieve unmatched rows from
Left outer join	The first (left) table
Right outer join	The second (right) table

A left outer join

```
SELECT vendor_name, invoice_number, invoice_total
FROM vendors LEFT JOIN invoices
    ON vendors.vendor_id = invoices.vendor_id
ORDER BY vendor_name
```

	vendor_name	invoice_number	invoice_total
▶	Abbey Office Furnishings	203339-13	17.50
	American Booksellers Assoc	NULL	NULL
	American Express	NULL	NULL
	ASC Signs	NULL	NULL
	Ascom Hasler Mailing Systems	NULL	NULL

(202 rows)

Description

- An *outer join* retrieves all rows that satisfy the join condition, plus unmatched rows in the left or right table.

- In most cases, you use the equal operator to retrieve rows with matching columns. However, you can also use any of the other comparison operators.

- When a row with unmatched columns is retrieved, any columns from the other table that are included in the result set are given null values.

Note

- The OUTER keyword is optional and typically omitted.

Figure 4-8   How to code an outer join

Outer join examples

To give you a better understanding of how outer joins work, figure 4-9 shows four more examples. To start, part 1 of this figure shows the Departments table, the Employees table, and the Projects table from the EX database. These tables are used by the examples shown in parts 2 and 3 of this figure. In addition, they're used in other examples later in this chapter.

The first example performs a left outer join on the Departments and Employees tables. Here, the join condition joins the tables based on the values in their department_number columns. Then, the result set produced by this statement, shows that department number 3 (Operations) is included in the result set even though none of the employees in the Employees table work in that department. As a result, MySQL assigns a null value to the last_name column from that table.

The second example uses a right outer join to join the Departments and Employees table. In this case, all of the rows from the Employees table are included in the result set. However, two of the employees, Locario and Watson, are assigned to a department that doesn't exist in the Departments table. If the department_number column in the Employees table had been defined as a foreign key to the Departments table, this would not have been allowed by MySQL. In this case, though, a foreign key wasn't defined, so null values are returned for the department_name column in these two rows.

When coding outer joins, it's a common practice to avoid using right joins. To do that, you can substitute a left outer join for a right outer join by reversing the order of the tables in the FROM clause and using the LEFT keyword instead of RIGHT. This often makes it easier to read statements that join more than two tables.

The third example shows that you can use outer joins to work with more than two tables. To do that, you use skills similar to those that you use to work with inner joins with more than two tables. In this example, the statement uses left outer joins to join all three tables: Departments, Employees, and Projects. Because of this, the result set uses a null value to show that none of the employees are assigned to the Operations department. In addition, the result set uses null values to show that two employees, Hardy and Jones, aren't assigned to a project.

The fourth example shows that you can combine inner joins and outer joins in the same query. Here, the query works like the third example, but it uses an inner join for the first join instead of a left outer join. Because of this, the result set doesn't include a row for the Operations department. However, it still displays the rows for the two employees, Hardy and Jones, that aren't assigned to a project.

The Departments table

department_number	department_name
1	Accounting
2	Payroll
3	Operations
4	Personnel
5	Maintenance

The Employees table

employee_id	last_name	first_name	department_number	manager_id
1	Smith	Cindy	2	NULL
2	Jones	Elmer	4	1
3	Simonian	Ralph	2	2
4	Hernandez	Olivia	1	9
5	Aaronsen	Robert	2	4
6	Watson	Denise	6	8
7	Hardy	Thomas	5	2
8	O'Leary	Rhea	4	9
9	Locario	Paulo	6	1

The Projects table

project_number	employee_id
P1011	8
P1011	4
P1012	3
P1012	1
P1012	5
P1013	6
P1013	9
P1014	10

Description

- The examples in this figure use the Departments, Employees, and Projects tables from the EX database.

Figure 4-9   Outer join examples (part 1 of 3)

A left outer join

```
SELECT department_name, d.department_number, last_name
FROM departments d
    LEFT JOIN employees e
    ON d.department_number = e.department_number
ORDER BY department_name
```

department_name	department_number	last_name
Accounting	1	Hernandez
Maintenance	5	Hardy
Operations	3	NULL
Payroll	2	Smith
Payroll	2	Simonian
Payroll	2	Aaronsen
Personnel	4	Jones
Personnel	4	O'Leary

(8 rows)

A right outer join

```
SELECT department_name, e.department_number, last_name
FROM departments d
    RIGHT JOIN employees e
    ON d.department_number = e.department_number
ORDER BY department_name
```

department_name	department_number	last_name
NULL	6	Watson
NULL	6	Locario
Accounting	1	Hernandez
Maintenance	5	Hardy
Payroll	2	Aaronsen
Payroll	2	Simonian
Payroll	2	Smith
Personnel	4	Jones
Personnel	4	O'Leary

(9 rows)

Description

- A left outer join returns unmatched rows from the first (left) table.
- A right outer join returns unmatched rows from the second (right) table.

Figure 4-9   Outer join examples (part 2 of 3)

Join three tables using left outer joins

```
SELECT department_name, last_name, project_number
FROM departments d
    LEFT JOIN employees e
        ON d.department_number = e.department_number
    LEFT JOIN projects p
        ON e.employee_id = p.employee_id
ORDER BY department_name, last_name
```

department_name	last_name	project_number
Accounting	Hernandez	P1011
Maintenance	Hardy	NULL
Operations	NULL	NULL
Payroll	Aaronsen	P1012
Payroll	Simonian	P1012
Payroll	Smith	P1012
Personnel	Jones	NULL
Personnel	O'Leary	P1011

(8 rows)

Combine an outer and an inner join

```
SELECT department_name, last_name, project_number
FROM departments d
    JOIN employees e
        ON d.department_number = e.department_number
    LEFT JOIN projects p
        ON e.employee_id = p.employee_id
ORDER BY department_name, last_name
```

department_name	last_name	project_number
Accounting	Hernandez	P1011
Maintenance	Hardy	NULL
Payroll	Aaronsen	P1012
Payroll	Simonian	P1012
Payroll	Smith	P1012
Personnel	Jones	NULL
Personnel	O'Leary	P1011

(7 rows)

Description

- You can use outer joins to join multiple tables.
- You can combine inner and outer joins within a single SELECT statement.

Figure 4-9   Outer join examples (part 3 of 3)

Other skills for working with joins

Now that you know how to work with inner and outer joins, you're ready to learn how to join tables with the USING and NATURAL keywords. In addition, you're ready to learn about another type of join, called a cross join.

How to join tables with the USING keyword

When you use the equal operator to join two tables on a common column, the join can be referred to as an *equijoin* (or an *equi-join*). When you code an equijoin, it's common for the columns that are being compared to have the same name. For joins like these, you can simplify the query with the USING keyword. To do that, you code a USING clause instead of an ON clause to specify the join as shown in figure 4-10.

The first example in this figure shows how to join the Vendors and Invoices tables on the vendor_id column with a USING clause. This returns the same results as the query shown in figure 4-1 that uses the ON clause. However, the USING clause only works because the vendor_id column exists in both the Vendors and Invoices tables.

The second example shows how to join the Departments, Employees, and Projects tables with the USING keyword. Here, the first USING clause uses an inner join to join the Departments table to the Employees table on the department_number column. Then, the second USING clause uses a left join to join the Employees table to the Projects table on the employee_id column. This shows that you can use a USING clause for both inner and outer joins, and this query returns the same result as the last query shown in figure 4-9.

In some rare cases, you may want to join tables by multiple columns. To do that with a USING clause, you can code multiple column names within the parentheses, separating the column names with commas. This yields the same result as coding two equijoins connected with the AND operator.

Since the USING clause is more concise than the ON clause, it can make your code easier to read and maintain. As a result, it often makes sense to use the USING clause when you're developing new statements. However, if you can't get the USING clause to work correctly because of the way your database is structured, you can always use the ON clause instead.

The syntax for a join that uses the USING keyword

```
SELECT select_list
FROM table_1
    [{LEFT|RIGHT} [OUTER]] JOIN table_2
        USING (join_column_1[, join_column_2]...)
    [[{LEFT|RIGHT} [OUTER]] JOIN table_3
        USING (join_column_1[, join_column_2]...)]...
```

Use the USING keyword to join two tables

```
SELECT invoice_number, vendor_name
FROM vendors
    JOIN invoices USING (vendor_id)
ORDER BY invoice_number
```

invoice_number	vendor_name
0-2058	Malloy Lithographing Inc
0-2060	Malloy Lithographing Inc
0-2436	Malloy Lithographing Inc
1-200-5164	Federal Express Corporation

(114 rows)

Use the USING keyword to join three tables

```
SELECT department_name, last_name, project_number
FROM departments
    JOIN employees USING (department_number)
    LEFT JOIN projects USING (employee_id)
ORDER BY department_name
```

department_name	last_name	project_number
Accounting	Hernandez	P1011
Maintenance	Hardy	NULL
Payroll	Simonian	P1012
Payroll	Aaronsen	P1012
Payroll	Smith	P1012
Personnel	O'Leary	P1011
Personnel	Jones	NULL

(7 rows)

Description

- You can use the USING keyword to simplify the syntax for joining tables.
- The join can be an inner join or an outer join.
- The tables must be joined by a column that has the same name in both tables.
- To include multiple columns, separate them with commas.
- The join must be an *equijoin*, which means that the equals operator is used to compare the two columns.

Figure 4-10   How to join tables with the USING keyword

How to join tables with the NATURAL keyword

Figure 4-11 shows how to use the NATURAL keyword to code a *natural join*. When you code a natural join, you don't specify the column that's used to join the two tables. Instead, the database automatically joins the two tables based on all columns in the two tables that have the same name. As a result, this type of join only works correctly if the database is designed in a certain way.

For instance, if you use a natural join to join the Vendors and Invoices tables as shown in the first example, the join works correctly because these tables only have one column in common: the vendor_id column. As a result, the database joins these two tables on the vendor_id column. However, if these tables had another column in common, this query would attempt to join these tables on both columns and would yield unexpected results.

In addition, you may get unexpected results if you use natural joins for complex queries. In that case, you can use the USING or ON clause to explicitly specify the join since these clauses give you more control over the join. If necessary, you can mix a natural join with the USING or ON clause within a single SELECT statement. In this figure, for example, the second SELECT statement uses a natural join for the first join and a USING clause for the second join. The result is the same as the result for the second statement in figure 4-10.

Finally, since natural joins don't explicitly specify the join column, they may not work correctly if the structure of the database changes later. So although natural joins are easy to code, you'll usually want to avoid using them for production code.

The syntax for a join that uses the NATURAL keyword

```
SELECT select_list
FROM table_1
    NATURAL JOIN table_2
    [NATURAL JOIN table_3]...
```

Use the NATURAL keyword to join tables

```
SELECT invoice_number, vendor_name
FROM vendors
    NATURAL JOIN invoices
ORDER BY invoice_number
```

invoice_number	vendor_name
0-2058	Malloy Lithographing Inc
0-2060	Malloy Lithographing Inc
0-2436	Malloy Lithographing Inc
1-200-5164	Federal Express Corporation

(114 rows)

Use the NATURAL keyword in a statement that joins three tables

```
SELECT department_name AS dept_name, last_name, project_number
FROM departments
    NATURAL JOIN employees
    LEFT JOIN projects USING (employee_id)
ORDER BY department_name
```

dept_name	last_name	project_number
Accounting	Hernandez	P1011
Maintenance	Hardy	NULL
Payroll	Smith	P1012
Payroll	Simonian	P1012
Payroll	Aaronsen	P1012
Personnel	Jones	NULL
Personnel	O'Leary	P1011

(7 rows)

Description

- You can use the NATURAL keyword to create a *natural join* that joins two tables based on all columns in the two tables that have the same name.

- Although the code for a natural join is shorter than the code for joins that use the ON or USING clause, a natural join only works correctly for certain types of database structures. In addition, a natural join often yields unexpected results for complex queries. As a result, it's more common to use the ON or USING clause to join tables.

Figure 4-11   How to join tables with the NATURAL keyword

How to use cross joins

A *cross join* produces a result set that includes each row from the first table joined with each row from the second table. The result set is known as the *Cartesian product* of the tables. Figure 4-12 shows how to code a cross join using either the explicit or implicit syntax.

To use the explicit syntax, you include the CROSS JOIN keywords between the two tables in the FROM clause. Because of the way a cross join works, you don't code an ON clause that includes a join condition. The same is true when you use the implicit syntax. In that case, you simply list the tables in the FROM clause and omit the join condition from the WHERE clause.

The two SELECT statements in this figure illustrate how cross joins work. Both of these statements combine data from the Departments and Employees tables. For both statements, the result is a table that includes 45 rows. That's each of the five rows in the Departments table combined with each of the nine rows in the Employees table. Although this result set is relatively small, you can imagine how large it would be if the tables included hundreds or thousands of rows.

As you study these examples, you should realize that cross joins have few practical uses. As a result, you'll rarely, if ever, need to use one. In fact, you're most likely to code a cross join by accident if you use the implicit join syntax and forget to code the join condition in the WHERE clause. That's one of the reasons why it's generally considered a good practice to use the explicit join syntax.

How to code a cross join using the explicit syntax

The explicit syntax for a cross join

```
SELECT select_list
FROM table_1 CROSS JOIN table_2
```

A cross join that uses the explicit syntax

```
SELECT departments.department_number, department_name, employee_id,
    last_name
FROM departments CROSS JOIN employees
ORDER BY departments.department_number
```

department_number	department_name	employee_id	last_name
1	Accounting	3	Simonian
1	Accounting	7	Hardy
1	Accounting	4	Hernandez
1	Accounting	1	Smith
1	Accounting	8	O'Leary

(45 rows)

How to code a cross join using the implicit syntax

The implicit syntax for a cross join

```
SELECT select_list
FROM table_1, table_2
```

A cross join that uses the implicit syntax

```
SELECT departments.department_number, department_name, employee_id,
    last_name
FROM departments, employees
ORDER BY departments.department_number
```

department_number	department_name	employee_id	last_name
1	Accounting	3	Simonian
1	Accounting	7	Hardy
1	Accounting	4	Hernandez
1	Accounting	1	Smith
1	Accounting	8	O'Leary

(45 rows)

Description

- A *cross join* joins each row from the first table with each row from the second table. The result set returned by a cross join is known as a *Cartesian product*.

Figure 4-12   How to use cross joins

How to work with unions

Like a join, a *union* combines data from two or more tables. Instead of combining columns from base tables, however, a union combines rows from two or more result sets.

How to code a union

Figure 4-13 shows how to code a union. To start, you use the UNION keyword to connect two or more SELECT statements. For this to work, the result of each SELECT statement must have the same number of columns, and the data types of the corresponding columns in each table must be compatible.

In this figure, we have indented all of the SELECT statements that are connected by the UNION operator to make it easier to see how this statement works. However, in a production environment, it's common to see the SELECT statements and the UNION operator coded at the same level of indentation.

If you want to sort the result of a union operation, you can code an ORDER BY clause after the last SELECT statement. In an ORDER BY clause, you must use the column names that are specified in the first SELECT statement. That's because the column names in the first SELECT statement are the ones that are used in the final result set.

By default, a union operation removes duplicate rows from the result set. If that's not what you want, you can include the ALL keyword. In most cases, though, you'll omit this keyword.

A union that combines result sets from different tables

The example in this figure shows how to use a union to combine data from two different tables. In this case, the Active_Invoices table contains invoices with outstanding balances, and the Paid_Invoices table contains invoices that have been paid in full. Both of these tables have the same structure as the Invoices table that's been used in this book so far.

This union operation combines the rows in both tables that have an invoice date on or after June 1, 2011. Here, the first SELECT statement includes a column named source that contains a literal value of "Active." Then, the second SELECT statement includes a column by the same name, but it contains a literal value of "Paid." This column is used to indicate which table each row in the result set came from.

Although this column is assigned the same name in both SELECT statements, you don't have to use the same name for corresponding columns. That's because the corresponding relationships are determined by the order in which the columns are coded in the SELECT clauses, not by their names. When you use column aliases, though, you'll typically assign the same name to corresponding columns so the statement is easier to understand.

The syntax for a union operation

```
    SELECT_statement_1
UNION [ALL]
    SELECT_statement_2
[UNION [ALL]
    SELECT_statement_3]...
[ORDER BY order_by_list]
```

A union that combines result sets from two different tables

```
    SELECT 'Active' AS source, invoice_number, invoice_date, invoice_total
    FROM active_invoices
    WHERE invoice_date >= '2011-06-01'
UNION
    SELECT 'Paid' AS source, invoice_number, invoice_date, invoice_total
    FROM paid_invoices
    WHERE invoice_date >= '2011-06-01'
ORDER BY invoice_total DESC
```

source	invoice_number	invoice_date	invoice_total
Active	40318	2011-07-18	21842.00
Paid	P02-3772	2011-06-03	7125.34
Paid	10843	2011-06-04	4901.26
Paid	77290	2011-06-04	1750.00
Paid	RTR-72-3662-X	2011-06-04	1600.00
Paid	75C-90227	2011-06-06	1367.50
Paid	P02-88D77S7	2011-06-06	856.92
Active	I77271-O01	2011-06-05	662.00
Active	9982771	2011-06-03	503.20

(22 rows)

Description

- A *union* combines the result sets of two or more SELECT statements into one result set.

- Each result set must return the same number of columns, and the corresponding columns in each result set must have compatible data types.

- By default, a union eliminates duplicate rows. If you want to include duplicate rows, code the ALL keyword.

- The column names in the final result set are taken from the first SELECT clause. Column aliases assigned by the other SELECT clauses have no effect on the final result set.

- To sort the rows in the final result set, code an ORDER BY clause after the last SELECT statement. This clause must refer to the column names assigned in the first SELECT clause.

Figure 4-13   How to combine result sets from different tables

A union that combines result sets from the same tables

The first example in figure 4-14 shows how to use unions to combine result sets created from a single table. In this example, rows from the Invoices table that have a balance due are combined with rows from the same table that are paid in full. As in the previous figure, a column named source is added at the beginning of each result set. That way, the final result set indicates whether each invoice is active or paid.

The second example shows how to use unions to combine result sets created from the same two tables after they have been joined. Here, each SELECT statement joins data from the Invoices and Vendors tables. The first SELECT statement retrieves invoices with totals greater than $10,000. Then, it calculates a payment of 33% of the invoice total. The two other SELECT statements are similar. The second one retrieves invoices with totals between $500 and $10,000 and calculates a 50% payment. And the third one retrieves invoices with totals less than $500 and sets the payment amount at 100% of the total. Although this isn't the most practical example, it helps illustrate the flexibility of union operations.

In both of these examples, the same column aliases are assigned in each SELECT statement. Although the aliases in the second and third SELECT statements are optional, they make the query easier to read. In particular, they make it easy to see that the three SELECT statements have the same number and types of columns.

A union that combines result sets from a single table

```
SELECT 'Active' AS source, invoice_number, invoice_date, invoice_total
FROM invoices
WHERE invoice_total - payment_total - credit_total > 0
UNION
SELECT 'Paid' AS source, invoice_number, invoice_date, invoice_total
FROM invoices
WHERE invoice_total - payment_total - credit_total <= 0
ORDER BY invoice_total DESC
```

source	invoice_number	invoice_date	invoice_total
Paid	0-2058	2011-05-28	37966.19
Paid	P-0259	2011-07-19	26881.40
Paid	0-2060	2011-07-24	23517.58
Paid	40318	2011-06-01	21842.00
Active	P-0608	2011-07-23	20551.18
Active	0-2436	2011-07-31	10976.06

(114 rows)

A union that combines result sets from the same two tables

```
SELECT invoice_number, vendor_name, '33% Payment' AS payment_type,
    invoice_total AS total, invoice_total * 0.333 AS payment
FROM invoices JOIN vendors
    ON invoices.vendor_id = vendors.vendor_id
WHERE invoice_total > 10000
UNION
SELECT invoice_number, vendor_name, '50% Payment' AS payment_type,
    invoice_total AS total, invoice_total * 0.5 AS payment
FROM invoices JOIN vendors
    ON invoices.vendor_id = vendors.vendor_id
WHERE invoice_total BETWEEN 500 AND 10000
UNION
SELECT invoice_number, vendor_name, 'Full amount' AS payment_type,
    invoice_total AS total, invoice_total AS payment
FROM invoices JOIN vendors
    ON invoices.vendor_id = vendors.vendor_id
WHERE invoice_total < 500
ORDER BY payment_type, vendor_name, invoice_number
```

invoice_number	vendor_name	payment_type	total	payment
40318	Data Reproductions Corp	33% Payment	21842.00	7273.38600
0-2058	Malloy Lithographing Inc	33% Payment	37966.19	12642.74127
0-2060	Malloy Lithographing Inc	33% Payment	23517.58	7831.35414
0-2436	Malloy Lithographing Inc	33% Payment	10976.06	3655.02798
P-0259	Malloy Lithographing Inc	33% Payment	26881.40	8951.50620
P-0608	Malloy Lithographing Inc	33% Payment	20551.18	6843.54294
509786	Bertelsmann Industry S...	50% Payment	6940.25	3470.12500

(114 rows)

Figure 4-14   How to combine result sets from the same tables

A union that simulates a full outer join

A *full outer join* returns unmatched rows from both the left and right tables. Although MySQL doesn't provide language for coding a full outer join, you can simulate a full outer join by coding a union that combines the result sets for a left outer join and a right outer join as shown in figure 4-15.

The example in this figure uses the UNION keyword to combine the result sets for the left and right outer joins shown in figure 4-9. As a result, this example returns all the rows from the Departments and Employees tables even if these rows don't have matching columns in the other table.

To make it easier to identify the unmatched rows, this statement includes the department_number column from both tables. This shows that two rows in the Employees table don't have matching rows in the Departments table, and it shows that one row in the Departments table doesn't have a matching row in the Employees table. In other words, two employees haven't been assigned to a department, and one department doesn't have any employees.

A union that simulates a full outer join

```
SELECT department_name AS dept_name, d.department_number AS d_dept_no,
       e.department_number AS e_dept_no, last_name
FROM departments d
    LEFT JOIN employees e
    ON d.department_number = e.department_number
UNION
SELECT department_name AS dept_name, d.department_number AS d_dept_no,
       e.department_number AS e_dept_no, last_name
FROM departments d
    RIGHT JOIN employees e
    ON d.department_number = e.department_number
ORDER BY dept_name
```

dept_name	d_dept_no	e_dept_no	last_name
NULL	NULL	6	Watson
NULL	NULL	6	Locario
Accounting	1	1	Hernandez
Maintenance	5	5	Hardy
Operations	3	NULL	NULL
Payroll	2	2	Smith
Payroll	2	2	Simonian
Payroll	2	2	Aaronsen
Personnel	4	4	Jones
Personnel	4	4	O'Leary

```
(10 rows)
```

Description

- When you use a *full outer join*, the result set includes all the rows from both tables.
- MySQL doesn't provide language keywords for full outer joins, but you can simulate a full outer join by using the UNION keyword to combine the results from a left outer join and a right outer join.

Figure 4-15   How to simulate a full outer join

Perspective

In this chapter, you learned a variety of techniques for combining data from two or more tables into a single result set. In particular, you learned how to use the explicit syntax to code inner joins. Of all the techniques presented in this chapter, this is the one you'll use most often. So you'll want to be sure you understand it thoroughly before you go on.

Terms

join	implicit syntax
join condition	outer join
inner join	left outer join
ad hoc relationship	right outer join
qualified column name	equijoin
explicit syntax	natural join
SQL-92 syntax	cross join
table alias	Cartesian product
schema	union
self-join	full outer join

Exercises

1. Write a SELECT statement that returns all columns from the Vendors table inner-joined with all columns from the Invoices table. This should return 114 rows. *Hint: You can use an asterisk (*) to select the columns from both tables.*

2. Write a SELECT statement that returns these four columns:

vendor_name	The vendor_name column from the Vendors table
invoice_number	The invoice_number column from the Invoices table
invoice_date	The invoice_date column from the Invoices table
balance_due	The invoice_total column minus the payment_total and credit_total columns from the Invoices table

    Use these aliases for the tables: v for Vendors and i for Invoices.

    Return one row for each invoice with a non-zero balance. This should return 11 rows.

    Sort the result set by vendor_name in ascending order.

3. Write a SELECT statement that returns these three columns:

DISTINCT

vendor_name	The vendor_name column from the Vendors table
default_account	The default_account_number column from the Vendors table
description	The account_description column from the General_Ledger_Accounts table

Return one row for each vendor. This should return 122 rows.

Sort the result set by account_description and then by vendor_name.

4. Write a SELECT statement that returns these five columns:

vendor_name	The vendor_name column from the Vendors table
invoice_date	The invoice_date column from the Invoices table
invoice_number	The invoice_number column from the Invoices table
li_sequence	The invoice_sequence column from the Invoice_Line_Items table
li_amount	The line_item_amount column from the Invoice_Line_Items table

Use aliases for the tables. This should return 118 rows.

Sort the final result set by vendor_name, invoice_date, invoice_number, and invoice_sequence.

5. Write a SELECT statement that returns three columns:

vendor_id	The vendor_id column from the Vendors table
vendor_name	The vendor_name column from the Vendors table
contact_name	A concatenation of the vendor_contact_first_name and vendor_contact_last_name columns with a space between

WHERE

Return one row for each vendor whose contact has the same last name as another vendor's contact. This should return 2 rows. *Hint: Use a self-join to check that the vendor_id columns aren't equal but the vendor_contact_last_name columns are equal.*

Sort the result set by vendor_contact_last_name.

6. Write a SELECT statement that returns these three columns:

    account_number   The account_number column from the
                             General_Ledger_Accounts table

    account_description   The account_description column from the
                             General_Ledger_Accounts table

    invoice_id   The invoice_id column from the
                             Invoice_Line_Items table

    Return one row for each account number that has never been used. This
    should return 54 rows. *Hint: Use an outer join and only return rows where the
    invoice_id column contains a null value.*

    Remove the invoice_id column from the SELECT clause.

    Sort the final result set by the account_number column.

7. Use the UNION operator to generate a result set consisting of two columns
    from the Vendors table: vendor_name and vendor_state. If the vendor is in
    California, the vendor_state value should be "CA"; otherwise, the
    vendor_state value should be "Outside CA." Sort the final result set by
    vendor_name.

5

How to code summary queries

In this chapter, you'll learn how to code queries that summarize data. For example, you can use summary queries to report sales totals by vendor or state or to get a count of the number of invoices that were processed each day of the month. But first, you'll learn how to use a special type of function called an aggregate function. Aggregate functions allow you to do jobs like calculate averages, summarize totals, or find the highest value for a given column, and you'll use them in summary queries.

How to work with aggregate functions **152**

How to code aggregate functions 152

Queries that use aggregate functions 154

How to group and summarize data **156**

How to code the GROUP BY and HAVING clauses 156

Queries that use the GROUP BY and HAVING clauses 158

How the HAVING clause compares to the WHERE clause 160

How to code compound search conditions 162

How to use the WITH ROLLUP operator 164

Perspective **166**

How to work with aggregate functions

In chapter 3, you learned how to use *scalar functions*, which operate on a single value and return a single value. In this chapter, you'll learn how to use *aggregate functions*, which operate on a series of values and return a single summary value. Because aggregate functions typically operate on the values in columns, they are sometimes referred to as *column functions*. A query that contains one or more aggregate functions is typically referred to as a *summary query*.

How to code aggregate functions

Figure 5-1 presents the syntax of the most common aggregate functions. Most of these functions operate on an expression. Typically, the expression is just a column name. For example, you could get the average of all values in the invoice_total column like this:

```
AVG(invoice_total)
```

However, an expression can also be more complex. In this figure, for example, the expression that's coded for the SUM function calculates the balance due of an invoice using the invoice_total, payment_total, and credit_total columns. The result is a single value that represents the total amount due for all the selected invoices. In this case, the WHERE clause selects only those invoices with a balance due.

When you use these functions, you can also code the ALL or DISTINCT keyword. The ALL keyword is the default, which means that all values are included in the calculation. The exceptions are null values, which are always excluded from these functions.

If you don't want duplicate values included, you can code the DISTINCT keyword. In most cases, you'll use DISTINCT only with the COUNT function as shown in the next figure. You won't use it with MIN or MAX because it has no effect on those functions. And it doesn't usually make sense to use it with the AVG and SUM functions.

Unlike the other aggregate functions, you can't use the ALL or DISTINCT keywords or an expression with COUNT(*). Instead, you code this function exactly as shown in the syntax. The value returned by this function is the number of rows in the base table that satisfy the search condition of the query, including rows with null values. In this figure, for example, the COUNT(*) function in the query indicates that the Invoices table contains 11 invoices with a balance due.

The syntax of the aggregate functions

Function syntax	Result
`AVG([ALL|DISTINCT] expression)`	The average of the non-null values in the expression.
`SUM([ALL|DISTINCT] expression)`	The total of the non-null values in the expression.
`MIN([ALL|DISTINCT] expression)`	The lowest non-null value in the expression.
`MAX([ALL|DISTINCT] expression)`	The highest non-null value in the expression.
`COUNT([ALL|DISTINCT] expression)`	The number of non-null values in the expression.
`COUNT(*)`	The number of rows selected by the query.

A summary query that counts unpaid invoices and calculates the total due

```
SELECT COUNT(*) AS number_of_invoices,
    SUM(invoice_total - payment_total - credit_total) AS total_due
FROM invoices
WHERE invoice_total - payment_total - credit_total > 0
```

number_of_invoices	total_due
11	32020.42

Description

- *Aggregate functions*, also called *column functions*, perform a calculation on the values in a set of selected rows.

- A *summary query* is a SELECT statement that includes one or more aggregate functions.

- The expression you specify for the AVG and SUM functions must result in a numeric value. The expression for the MIN, MAX, and COUNT functions can result in a numeric, date, or string value.

- By default, all values are included in the calculation regardless of whether they're duplicated. If you want to omit duplicate values, code the DISTINCT keyword. This keyword is typically used with the COUNT function.

- All of the aggregate functions except for COUNT(*) ignore null values.

- If you code an aggregate function in the SELECT clause, that clause can't include non-aggregate columns from the base table unless those columns are named on a GROUP BY clause. See figure 5-3 for more information.

Figure 5-1   How to code aggregate functions

Queries that use aggregate functions

This figure presents four more queries that use aggregate functions. The first two queries use the COUNT(*) function to count the number of rows in the Invoices table that satisfy the search condition. In both cases, only those invoices with invoice dates after 1/1/2011 are included in the count. In addition, the first query uses the AVG function to calculate the average amount of those invoices and the SUM function to calculate the total amount of those invoices. In contrast, the second query uses the MIN and MAX functions to get the minimum and maximum invoice amounts.

Although the MIN, MAX, and COUNT functions are typically used on columns that contain numeric data, they can also be used on columns that contain character or date data. In the third query, for example, they're used on the vendor_name column in the Vendors table. Here, the MIN function returns the name of the vendor that's lowest in the sort sequence, the MAX function returns the name of the vendor that's highest in the sort sequence, and the COUNT function returns the total number of vendors. Note that since the vendor_name column can't contain null values, the COUNT(*) function would have returned the same result.

The fourth query shows how using the DISTINCT keyword can affect the result of a COUNT function. Here, the first COUNT function uses the DISTINCT keyword to count the number of vendors that have invoices dated 1/1/2011 or later in the Invoices table. To do that, it looks for distinct values in the vendor_id column. In contrast, since the second COUNT function doesn't include the DISTINCT keyword, it counts every invoice that's dated 1/1/2011 or later. Although you could use COUNT or the COUNT(*) function instead, this example uses COUNT(vendor_id) to clearly show the difference between coding and not coding the DISTINCT keyword.

With two exceptions, a SELECT clause that contains an aggregate function can contain only aggregate functions. The first exception is if the column specification results in a literal value. This is shown by the first column in the first two queries in figure 5-2. The second exception is if the query includes a GROUP BY clause. Then, the SELECT clause can include any columns specified in the GROUP BY clause as shown in the next two figures.

A summary query that uses the COUNT(*), AVG, and SUM functions

```
SELECT 'After 1/1/2011' AS selection_date,
    COUNT(*) AS number_of_invoices,
    ROUND(AVG(invoice_total), 2) AS avg_invoice_amt,
    SUM(invoice_total) AS total_invoice_amt
FROM invoices
WHERE invoice_date > '2011-01-01'
```

selection_date	number_of_invoices	avg_invoice_amt	total_invoice_amt
After 1/1/2011	114	1879.74	214290.51

A summary query that uses the MIN and MAX functions

```
SELECT 'After 1/1/2011' AS selection_date,
    COUNT(*) AS number_of_invoices,
    MAX(invoice_total) AS highest_invoice_total,
    MIN(invoice_total) AS lowest_invoice_total
FROM invoices
WHERE invoice_date > '2011-01-01'
```

selection_date	number_of_invoices	highest_invoice_total	lowest_invoice_total
After 1/1/2011	114	37966.19	6.00

A summary query that works on non-numeric columns

```
SELECT MIN(vendor_name) AS first_vendor,
    MAX(vendor_name) AS last_vendor,
    COUNT(vendor_name) AS number_of_vendors
FROM vendors
```

first_vendor	last_vendor	number_of_vendors
Abbey Office Furnishings	Zylka Design	122

A summary query that uses the DISTINCT keyword

```
SELECT COUNT(DISTINCT vendor_id) AS number_of_vendors,
    COUNT(vendor_id) AS number_of_invoices,
    ROUND(AVG(invoice_total), 2) AS avg_invoice_amt,
    SUM(invoice_total) AS total_invoice_amt
FROM invoices
WHERE invoice_date > '2011-01-01'
```

number_of_vendors	number_of_invoices	avg_invoice_amt	total_invoice_amt
34	114	1879.74	214290.51

[handwritten note in margin: Distinct is diff between]

Description

- To count all of the selected rows, you typically use the COUNT(*) function. Alternately, you can use the COUNT function with the name of any column that can't contain null values.

- To count only the rows with unique values in a specified column, you can code the COUNT function with the DISTINCT keyword followed by the name of the column.

Figure 5-2   Queries that use aggregate functions

How to group and summarize data

Now that you understand how aggregate functions work, you're ready to learn how to group data and use aggregate functions to summarize the data in each group. To do that, you can use two new clauses of the SELECT statement: GROUP BY and HAVING.

How to code the GROUP BY and HAVING clauses

Figure 5-3 shows the syntax of the SELECT statement with the GROUP BY and HAVING clauses. The GROUP BY clause determines how the selected rows are grouped, and the HAVING clause determines which groups are included in the final results. These clauses are coded after the WHERE clause but before the ORDER BY clause. That makes sense because the WHERE clause is applied before the rows are grouped, and the ORDER BY clause is applied after the rows are grouped.

In the GROUP BY clause, you list one or more columns or expressions separated by commas. Then, the rows in the result set are grouped by those columns or expressions in ascending sequence. That means that a single row is returned for each unique set of values in the GROUP BY columns. In this figure, for instance, the example groups the results by a single column. In the next figure, you can see examples that group by multiple columns.

The example in this figure calculates the average invoice amount for each vendor who has invoices in the Invoices table. To do that, it uses a GROUP BY clause to group the invoices by vendor_id. As a result, the AVG function calculates the average of the invoice_total column for each group rather than for the entire result set.

The example in this figure also includes a HAVING clause. The search condition in this clause specifies that only those vendors with invoices that average over $2,000 should be included. Note that this condition must be applied after the rows are grouped and the average for each group has been calculated.

In addition to the AVG function, the SELECT clause includes the vendor_id column. That's usually what you want since the rows are grouped by this column. However, if you don't want to include the columns used in the GROUP BY clause in the SELECT clause, you don't have to.

The syntax of a SELECT statement with GROUP BY and HAVING clauses

```
SELECT select_list
FROM table_source
[WHERE search_condition]
[GROUP BY group_by_list]
[HAVING search_condition]
[ORDER BY order_by_list]
```

A summary query that calculates the average invoice amount by vendor

```
SELECT vendor_id, ROUND(AVG(invoice_total), 2) AS average_invoice_amount
FROM invoices
GROUP BY vendor_id
HAVING AVG(invoice_total) > 2000
ORDER BY average_invoice_amount DESC
```

vendor_id	average_invoice_amount
110	23978.48
72	10963.66
104	7125.34
99	6940.25
119	4901.26
122	2575.33
86	2433.00
100	2184.50

(8 rows)

Description

- The GROUP BY clause groups the rows of a result set based on one or more columns or expressions. To include two or more columns or expressions, separate them by commas.

- If you include aggregate functions in the SELECT clause, the aggregate is calculated for each group specified by the GROUP BY clause.

- If you include two or more columns or expressions in the GROUP BY clause, they form a hierarchy where each column or expression is subordinate to the previous one.

- The HAVING clause specifies a search condition for a group or an aggregate. MySQL applies this condition after it groups the rows that satisfy the search condition in the WHERE clause.

- When a SELECT statement includes a GROUP BY clause, the SELECT clause can include the columns used for grouping, aggregate functions, and expressions that result in a constant value.

Figure 5-3 How to code the GROUP BY and HAVING clauses

Queries that use the GROUP BY and HAVING clauses

Figure 5-4 presents three more queries that group data. The first query in this figure groups the rows in the Invoices table by vendor_id and returns a count of the number of invoices for each vendor.

The second query shows how you can group by more than one column. Here, a join is used to combine the vendor_state and vendor_city columns from the Vendors table with a count and average of the invoices in the Invoices table. Because the rows are grouped by both state and city, a row is returned for each state and city combination.

The third query is identical to the second query except that it includes a HAVING clause. This clause uses the COUNT function to limit the state and city groups that are included in the result set to those that have two or more invoices. In other words, it excludes groups that have only one invoice.

By default, the GROUP BY clause sorts the columns in ascending order. Usually, that's what you want. However, you can change this sort order by coding the DESC keyword after the column name in the GROUP BY clause. Or, if you don't want to sort the result set at all, you can code an ORDER BY NULL clause at the end of the query. Since this avoids sorting overhead, it can improve the performance of your query.

A summary query that counts the number of invoices by vendor

```
SELECT vendor_id, COUNT(*) AS invoice_qty
FROM invoices
GROUP BY vendor_id
```

vendor_id	invoice_qty
34	2
37	3
48	1
72	2

(34 rows)

A summary query that calculates the number of invoices and the average invoice amount for the vendors in each state and city

```
SELECT vendor_state, vendor_city, COUNT(*) AS invoice_qty,
    ROUND(AVG(invoice_total), 2) AS invoice_avg
FROM invoices JOIN vendors
    ON invoices.vendor_id = vendors.vendor_id
GROUP BY vendor_state, vendor_city
```

vendor_state	vendor_city	invoice_qty	invoice_avg
AZ	Phoenix	1	662.00
CA	Fresno	19	1208.75
CA	Los Angeles	1	503.20
CA	Oxnard	3	188.00

(20 rows)

A summary query that limits the groups to those with two or more invoices

```
SELECT vendor_state, vendor_city, COUNT(*) AS invoice_qty,
    ROUND(AVG(invoice_total), 2) AS invoice_avg
FROM invoices JOIN vendors
    ON invoices.vendor_id = vendors.vendor_id
GROUP BY vendor_state, vendor_city
HAVING COUNT(*) >= 2
```

vendor_state	vendor_city	invoice_qty	invoice_avg
CA	Fresno	19	1208.75
CA	Oxnard	3	188.00
CA	Pasadena	5	196.12
CA	Sacramento	7	253.00

(12 rows)

Description

- By default, the GROUP BY clause sorts the columns in ascending order. To change this sort order, you can code the DESC keyword after the column name in the GROUP BY clause.

- To get your results faster, you can code an ORDER BY NULL clause to prevent MySQL from sorting the rows in the GROUP BY clause.

Figure 5-4   Queries that use the GROUP BY and HAVING clauses

How the HAVING clause compares to the WHERE clause

As you've seen, you can limit the groups included in a result set by coding a search condition in the HAVING clause. In addition, you can apply a search condition to each row before it's included in a group. To do that, you code the search condition in the WHERE clause just as you would for any SELECT statement. To make sure you understand the differences between search conditions coded in the HAVING and WHERE clauses, figure 5-5 presents two examples.

The first example groups the invoices in the Invoices table by vendor name and calculates a count and average invoice amount for each group. Then, the HAVING clause limits the groups in the result set to those that have an average invoice total greater than $500.

In contrast, the second example includes a WHERE clause that limits the invoices included in the groups to those that have an invoice total greater than $500. In other words, the search condition in this example is applied to every row. In the previous example, it was applied to each group of rows. As a result, these examples show that there are eight invoices for Zylka Design in the Invoices table, but only seven of them are over $500.

Beyond this, there are two differences in the expressions that you can include in the WHERE and HAVING clauses. First, the HAVING clause can include aggregate functions as shown in the first example, but the WHERE clause can't. That's because the search condition in a WHERE clause is applied before the rows are grouped. Second, although the WHERE clause can refer to any column in the base tables, the HAVING clause can only refer to columns included in the SELECT clause. That's because it filters the summarized result set that's defined by the SELECT, FROM, WHERE, and GROUP BY clauses. In other words, it doesn't filter the base tables.

A summary query with a search condition in the HAVING clause

```
SELECT vendor_name,
    COUNT(*) AS invoice_qty,
    ROUND(AVG(invoice_total),2) AS invoice_avg
FROM vendors JOIN invoices
    ON vendors.vendor_id = invoices.vendor_id
GROUP BY vendor_name
HAVING AVG(invoice_total) > 500
ORDER BY invoice_qty DESC
```

vendor_name	invoice_qty	invoice_avg
United Parcel Service	9	2575.33
Zylka Design	8	867.53
Malloy Lithographing Inc	5	23978.48
Data Reproductions Corp	2	10963.66

(19 rows)

A summary query with a search condition in the WHERE clause

```
SELECT vendor_name,
    COUNT(*) AS invoice_qty,
    ROUND(AVG(invoice_total),2) AS invoice_avg
FROM vendors JOIN invoices
    ON vendors.vendor_id = invoices.vendor_id
WHERE invoice_total > 500
GROUP BY vendor_name
ORDER BY invoice_qty DESC
```

vendor_name	invoice_qty	invoice_avg
United Parcel Service	9	2575.33
Zylka Design	7	946.67
Malloy Lithographing Inc	5	23978.48
Ingram	2	1077.21

(20 rows)

Description

- When you include a WHERE clause in a SELECT statement that uses grouping and aggregates, MySQL applies the search condition before it groups the rows and calculates the aggregates.

- When you include a HAVING clause in a SELECT statement that uses grouping and aggregates, MySQL applies the search condition after it groups the rows and calculates the aggregates.

- A WHERE clause can refer to any column in the base tables.

- A HAVING clause can only refer to a column included in the SELECT clause.

- A WHERE clause can't contain aggregate functions.

- A HAVING clause can contain aggregate functions.

Figure 5-5   How the HAVING clause compares to the WHERE clause

How to code compound search conditions

You can code compound search conditions in a HAVING clause just as you can in a WHERE clause. The first example in figure 5-6 shows how this works. This query groups invoices by invoice date and calculates a count of the invoices and the sum of the invoice totals for each date. In addition, the HAVING clause specifies three conditions. First, the invoice date must be between 5/1/2011 and 5/31/2011. Second, the invoice count must be greater than 1. And third, the sum of the invoice totals must be greater than $100.

In the HAVING clause of this query, the second and third conditions include aggregate functions. As a result, they must be coded in the HAVING clause. The first condition, however, doesn't include an aggregate function, so it could be coded in either the HAVING or WHERE clause. The second example shows this condition coded in the WHERE clause. Either way, both queries return the same result set.

So, where should you code your search conditions? In general, I think queries are easier to read when they include all the search conditions in the HAVING clause. However, if you prefer to code non-aggregate search conditions in the WHERE clause, that's OK too.

A summary query with a compound condition in the HAVING clause

```
SELECT
    invoice_date,
    COUNT(*) AS invoice_qty,
    SUM(invoice_total) AS invoice_sum
FROM invoices
GROUP BY invoice_date
HAVING invoice_date BETWEEN '2011-05-01' AND '2011-05-31'
    AND COUNT(*) > 1
    AND SUM(invoice_total) > 100
ORDER BY invoice_date DESC
```

The same query coded with a WHERE clause

```
SELECT
    invoice_date,
    COUNT(*) AS invoice_qty,
    SUM(invoice_total) AS invoice_sum
FROM invoices
WHERE invoice_date BETWEEN '2011-05-01' AND '2011-05-31'
GROUP BY invoice_date
HAVING COUNT(*) > 1
    AND SUM(invoice_total) > 100
ORDER BY invoice_date DESC
```

The result set returned by both queries

invoice_date	invoice_qty	invoice_sum
2011-05-31	2	453.75
2011-05-25	3	2201.15
2011-05-23	2	347.75
2011-05-21	2	8078.44

(7 rows)

Description

- You can use the AND and OR operators to code compound search conditions in a HAVING clause just as you can in a WHERE clause.

- If a search condition includes an aggregate function, it must be coded in the HAVING clause. Otherwise, it can be coded in either the HAVING or the WHERE clause.

Figure 5-6   How to code compound search conditions

How to use the WITH ROLLUP operator

So far, this chapter has discussed standard SQL keywords and functions. However, MySQL provides an extension to standard SQL that's useful for summarizing data: the WITH ROLLUP operator.

You can use the WITH ROLLUP operator to add one or more summary rows to a result set that uses grouping and aggregates. The two examples in figure 5-7 show how this works.

The first example shows how the WITH ROLLUP operator works when you group by a single column. This statement groups the invoices by vendor_id and calculates an invoice count and invoice total for each vendor group. In addition, since the GROUP BY clause includes the WITH ROLLUP operator, this query adds a summary row to the end of the result set. This row summarizes all of the aggregate columns in the result set. In this case, it summarizes the invoice_count and invoice_total columns. Since the vendor_id column can't be summarized, it's assigned a null value.

The second query in this figure shows how the WITH ROLLUP operator works when you group by two columns. This query groups vendors by state and city and counts the number of vendors in each group. Then, this query adds summary rows for each state, and it adds a final summary row at the end of the result set.

When you use the WITH ROLLUP operator, you can't use an ORDER BY clause to sort the result set. Instead, you can sort the individual columns by coding the ASC or DESC keyword after the column name in the GROUP BY clause. In the second example, for instance, the ASC keyword is coded after both GROUP BY columns. In this case, the ASC keyword is optional since the columns are sorted in ascending order by default. However, if you wanted to sort in descending order, you would need to include the DESC keyword.

A summary query that includes a final summary row

```
SELECT vendor_id, COUNT(*) AS invoice_count,
    SUM(invoice_total) AS invoice_total
FROM invoices
GROUP BY vendor_id WITH ROLLUP
```

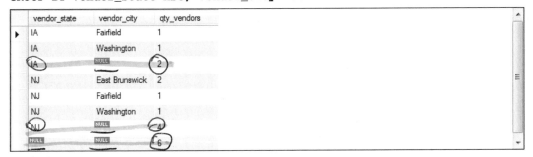

```
(35 rows)
```

A summary query that includes a summary row for each grouping level

```
SELECT vendor_state, vendor_city, COUNT(*) AS qty_vendors
FROM vendors
WHERE vendor_state IN ('IA', 'NJ')
GROUP BY vendor_state ASC, vendor_city ASC WITH ROLLUP
```

vendor_state	vendor_city	qty_vendors
IA	Fairfield	1
IA	Washington	1
IA	NULL	2
NJ	East Brunswick	2
NJ	Fairfield	1
NJ	Washington	1
NJ	NULL	4
NULL	NULL	6

Description

- You can use the WITH ROLLUP operator in the GROUP BY clause to add summary rows to the final result set.

- The WITH ROLLUP operator adds a summary row for each group specified in the GROUP BY clause. It also adds a summary row to the end of the result set that summarizes the entire result set.

- If the GROUP BY clause specifies a single group, the WITH ROLLUP operator only adds the final summary row.

- When you use the WITH ROLLUP operator, you can't use the ORDER BY clause. To sort individual columns, you can code the ASC or DESC keyword after the column in the GROUP BY clause.

- When you use the WITH ROLLUP operator, you can't use the DISTINCT keyword in any of the aggregate functions.

Figure 5-7   How to use the WITH ROLLUP operator

Perspective

In this chapter, you learned how to code queries that group and summarize data. In most cases, you'll be able to use the techniques presented here to get the summary information you need.

Terms

scalar function
aggregate function
column function
summary query

Exercises

1. Write a SELECT statement that returns one row for each vendor in the Invoices table that contains these columns :

    The vendor_id column from the Vendors table

    The sum of the invoice_total columns in the Invoices table for that vendor

    This should return 34 rows.

2. Write a SELECT statement that returns one row for each vendor that contains these columns:

    The vendor_name column from the Vendors table

    The sum of the payment_total columns in the Invoices table for that vendor

    Sort the result set in descending sequence by the payment total sum for each vendor.

3. Write a SELECT statement that returns one row for each vendor that contains three columns:

    The vendor_name column from the Vendors table

    The count of the invoices in the Invoices table for each vendor

    The sum of the invoice_total columns in the Invoices table for each vendor

    Sort the result set so the vendor with the most invoices appears first.

4. Write a SELECT statement that returns one row for each general ledger account number that contains three columns:

    The account_description column from the General_Ledger_Accounts table

    The count of the items in the Invoice_Line_Items table that have the same account_number

    The sum of the line_item_amount columns in the Invoice_Line_Items table that have the same account_number

    Return only those rows where the count of line items is greater than 1. This should return 10 rows.

    Group the result set by account description.

    Sort the result set in descending sequence by the sum of the line item amounts.

5. Modify the solution to exercise 4 so it returns only invoices dated in the second quarter of 2011 (April 1, 2011 to June 30, 2011). This should still return 10 rows but with some different line item counts for each vendor. *Hint: Join to the Invoices table to code a search condition based on invoice_date.*

6. Write a SELECT statement that answers this question: What is the total amount invoiced for each general ledger account number? Return these columns:

    The account number from the Invoice_Line_Items table

    The sum of the line item amounts from the Invoice_Line_Items table

    Use the WITH ROLLUP operator to include a row that gives the grand total. This should return 22 rows.

    Note: Once you add the WITH ROLLUP operator, you may need to use MySQL Workbench's Execute SQL Script button instead of its Execute Current Statement button to execute this statement.

7. Write a SELECT statement that answers this question: Which vendors are being paid from more than one account? Return these columns:

    The vendor name from the Vendors table

    The count of distinct general ledger accounts that apply to that vendor's invoices

    This should return 2 rows.

6

How to code subqueries

Subqueries allow you to build queries that would be difficult or impossible to build otherwise. In this chapter, you'll learn how to use subqueries in SELECT statements. Then, in the next chapter, you'll learn how to use them in INSERT, UPDATE, and DELETE statements.

An introduction to subqueries **170**
Where to code subqueries 170
When to use subqueries 172
How to code subqueries in the WHERE clause **174**
How to use the IN operator 174
How to use the comparison operators 176
How to use the ALL keyword 178
How to use the ANY and SOME keywords 180
How to code correlated subqueries 182
How to use the EXISTS operator 184
How to code subqueries in other clauses **186**
How to code subqueries in the HAVING clause 186
How to code subqueries in the SELECT clause 186
How to code subqueries in the FROM clause 188
How to work with complex queries **190**
A complex query that uses three subqueries 190
A procedure for building complex queries 192
Perspective **194**

An introduction to subqueries

A *subquery* is a SELECT statement that's coded within another SQL statement. Since you already know how to code SELECT statements, you already know how to code subqueries. Now you just need to learn where you can code them and when you should use them.

Where to code subqueries

Figure 6-1 shows that a subquery can be coded, or *introduced*, in the WHERE, HAVING, FROM, or SELECT clause of a SELECT statement. In this figure, for example, the SELECT statement shows how you can use a subquery in a WHERE clause. This statement retrieves all the invoices from the Invoices table that have invoice totals greater than the average of all the invoices. To do that, the subquery calculates the average of all the invoices. Then, the search condition tests each invoice to see if its invoice total is greater than that average.

When a subquery returns a single value as it does in this example, you can use it anywhere you would normally use a single value. However, a subquery can also return a list of values (a result set that has one column). In that case, you can use the subquery in place of a list of values, such as the list for an IN operator. In addition, a subquery can return a table of values (a result set that has multiple columns). In that case, you can use the subquery in the FROM clause in place of a table. In this chapter, you'll learn about all of these different types of subqueries.

Finally, you can code a subquery within another subquery. In that case, the subqueries are said to be nested. Because *nested subqueries* can be difficult to read, you should use them only when necessary.

Four ways to introduce a subquery in a SELECT statement

1. In a WHERE clause as a search condition
2. In a HAVING clause as a search condition
3. In the FROM clause as a table specification
4. In the SELECT clause as a column specification

Use a subquery in the WHERE clause

```
SELECT invoice_number, invoice_date, invoice_total
FROM invoices
WHERE invoice_total >
    (SELECT AVG(invoice_total)
     FROM invoices)
ORDER BY invoice_total
```

The value returned by the subquery

```
1879.741316
```

The result set

invoice_number	invoice_date	invoice_total
989319-487	2011-06-20	1927.54
97/522	2011-06-28	1962.13
989319-417	2011-07-23	2051.59
989319-427	2011-06-16	2115.81
989319-477	2011-06-08	2184.11
587056	2011-06-30	2184.50

```
(21 rows)
```

Description

- A *subquery* is a SELECT statement that's coded within another SQL statement. For this to work, you must enclose the subquery in parentheses.
- A subquery can return a single value, a list of values (a result set that has a single column), or a table of values (a result set that has multiple columns).
- A subquery can be coded, or *introduced*, anywhere a single value, a list of values, or a table is allowed.
- The syntax for a subquery is the same as for a standard SELECT statement. However, a subquery can't include an ORDER BY clause.
- Subqueries can be *nested* within other subqueries.

Figure 6-1   Where to code subqueries

When to use subqueries

In the last figure, you saw an example of a subquery that returns an aggregate value that's used in the search condition of a WHERE clause. This type of subquery provides for processing that can't be done any other way. However, most subqueries can be restated as joins, and most joins can be restated as subqueries as shown by the SELECT statements in figure 6-2.

Both SELECT statements in this figure return a result set that consists of selected rows and columns from the Invoices table. In this case, only the invoices for vendors in California are returned. The first statement uses a join to combine the Vendors and Invoices tables so the vendor_state column can be tested for each invoice. In contrast, the second statement uses a subquery to return a result set that consists of the vendor_id column for each vendor in California. Then, that result set is used with the IN operator in the search condition so only invoices with a vendor_id in that result set are included in the final result set.

So if you have a choice, which technique should you use? In general, we recommend that you use the technique that results in the most readable code. For example, a join tends to be more intuitive than a subquery when it uses an existing relationship between two tables. That's the case with the Vendors and Invoices tables used in this figure. On the other hand, a subquery tends to be more intuitive when it uses an ad hoc relationship.

You should also realize that when you use a subquery in a WHERE clause, its results can't be included in the final result set. For instance, the second example in this figure can't be changed to include the vendor_name column from the Vendors table. That's because the Vendors table isn't named in the FROM clause of the main query. So if you need to include information from both tables in the result set, you need to use a join.

A query that uses an inner join

```
SELECT invoice_number, invoice_date, invoice_total
FROM invoices JOIN vendors
    ON invoices.vendor_id = vendors.vendor_id
WHERE vendor_state = 'CA'
ORDER BY invoice_date
```

The same query restated with a subquery

```
SELECT invoice_number, invoice_date, invoice_total
FROM invoices
WHERE vendor_id IN
    (SELECT vendor_id
     FROM vendors
     WHERE vendor_state = 'CA')
ORDER BY invoice_date
```

The result set returned by both queries

invoice_number	invoice_date	invoice_total
125520-1	2011-04-24	95.00
97/488	2011-04-24	601.95
111-92R-10096	2011-04-30	16.33
25022117	2011-05-01	6.00

(40 rows)

Advantages of joins

- The SELECT clause of a join can include columns from both tables.
- A join tends to be more intuitive when it uses an existing relationship between the two tables, such as a primary key to foreign key relationship.

Advantages of subqueries

- You can use a subquery to pass an aggregate value to the main query.
- A subquery tends to be more intuitive when it uses an ad hoc relationship between the two tables.
- Long, complex queries can sometimes be easier to code using subqueries.

Description

- Like a join, a subquery can be used to code queries that work with two or more tables.
- Most subqueries can be restated as joins and most joins can be restated as subqueries.

Figure 6-2   When to use subqueries

How to code subqueries in the WHERE clause

You can use a variety of techniques to work with a subquery in a WHERE clause. You'll learn about these techniques in the topics that follow.

How to use the IN operator

In chapter 3, you learned how to use the IN operator to test whether an expression is contained in a list of values. One way to provide that list of values is to use a subquery as shown by figure 6-3.

The example in this figure retrieves the vendors from the Vendors table that don't have invoices in the Invoices table. To do that, it uses a subquery to return a list of IDs for each vendor that's in the Invoices table. Then, the main query returns some data about the vendors whose IDs aren't in that list.

When you use the IN operator with a subquery, the subquery must return a single column that provides the list of values. In this figure, the subquery also includes the DISTINCT keyword. That way, if more than one invoice exists for a vendor, the subquery only includes a single ID for the vendor. However, this keyword is optional and has no effect on the final result set.

In the previous figure, you saw that a query that uses a subquery with the IN operator can be restated using an inner join. Similarly, a query that uses a subquery with the NOT IN operator can typically be restated using an outer join. In this figure, for instance, the first query can be restated as shown in the second query. In this case, though, the first query is more readable.

The syntax of a WHERE clause that uses an IN phrase

```
WHERE test_expression [NOT] IN (subquery)
```

Get vendors without invoices

```
SELECT vendor_id, vendor_name, vendor_state
FROM vendors
WHERE vendor_id NOT IN
    (SELECT DISTINCT vendor_id
     FROM invoices)
ORDER BY vendor_id
```

The result of the subquery

vendor_id
34
37
48
72
80
81
82

(34 rows)

The result set

vendor_id	vendor_name	vendor_state
33	Nielson	OH
35	Cal State Termite	CA
36	Graylift	CA
38	Venture Communications Int1	NY
39	Custom Printing Company	MO
40	Nat Assoc of College Stores	OH

(88 rows)

The query restated without a subquery

```
SELECT v.vendor_id, vendor_name, vendor_state
FROM vendors v LEFT JOIN invoices i
    ON v.vendor_id = i.vendor_id
WHERE i.vendor_id IS NULL
ORDER BY v.vendor_id
```

Description

- You can introduce a subquery with the IN operator to provide the list of values that are tested against the test expression.

- When you use the IN operator, the subquery must return a single column of values.

- A query that uses the NOT IN operator with a subquery can typically be restated using an outer join.

Figure 6-3   How to use the IN operator

How to use the comparison operators

Figure 6-4 shows how you can use the comparison operators to compare an expression with the result of a subquery. In this example, the subquery returns the average balance due of the invoices in the Invoices table that have a balance due greater than zero. Then, it uses that value to retrieve all invoices with a balance due that's less than the average.

When you use a comparison operator as shown in this figure, the subquery must return a single value. In most cases, that means that it uses an aggregate function. However, you can also use the comparison operators with subqueries that return a list of values. To do that, you use the SOME, ANY, or ALL keywords as shown in the next two figures.

The syntax of a WHERE clause that uses a comparison operator

```
WHERE expression comparison_operator [SOME|ANY|ALL] (subquery)
```

Get invoices with a balance due less than the average

```
SELECT invoice_number, invoice_date,
    invoice_total - payment_total - credit_total AS balance_due
FROM invoices
WHERE invoice_total - payment_total - credit_total > 0
  AND invoice_total - payment_total - credit_total <
    (
      SELECT AVG(invoice_total - payment_total - credit_total)
      FROM invoices
      WHERE invoice_total - payment_total - credit_total > 0
    )
ORDER BY invoice_total DESC
```

(handwritten annotations: ← AVG, any invoice balance > 0)

The value returned by the subquery

```
2910.947273
```

The result set

invoice_number	invoice_date	balance_due
31361833	2011-07-21	579.42
9982771	2011-07-24	503.20
547480102	2011-08-01	224.00
134116	2011-07-28	90.36
39104	2011-07-10	85.31
263253270	2011-07-22	67.92

```
(9 rows)
```

Description

- You can use a comparison operator in a WHERE clause to compare an expression with the results of a subquery.

- If you code a search condition without the ANY, SOME, and ALL keywords, the subquery must return a single value.

- If you include the ANY, SOME, or ALL keyword, the subquery can return a list of values. See figures 6-5 and 6-6 for more information on using these keywords.

Figure 6-4   How to use the comparison operators

How to use the ALL keyword

Figure 6-5 shows how to use the ALL keyword to modify the comparison operator so the condition must be true for all the values returned by a subquery. The table at the top of this figure shows how this works.

If you use the greater than operator (>), the expression must be greater than the maximum value returned by the subquery. Conversely, if you use the less than operator (<), the expression must be less than the minimum value returned by the subquery. If you use the equal operator (=), the expression must be equal to all of the values returned by the subquery. And if you use the not equal operator (<>), the expression must not equal any of the values returned by the subquery. However, a not equal condition can be restated using the NOT IN operator, which is easier to read. As a result, it's a better practice to use the NOT IN operator for this type of condition.

The query in this figure shows how to use the greater than operator with the ALL keyword. Here, the subquery selects the invoice_total column for all the invoices with a vendor_id value of 34. This results in a list of two values. Then, the main query retrieves the rows from the Invoices table that have invoice totals greater than both of the values returned by the subquery. In other words, this query returns all the invoices that have totals greater than 1083.58, which is the largest invoice for vendor number 34.

When you use the ALL operator, the comparison evaluates to true if the subquery doesn't return any rows. In contrast, the comparison evaluates to false if the subquery returns only null values.

In many cases, you can rewrite a condition with the ALL keyword so it's easier to read. For example, you could rewrite the query in this figure to use the MAX function like this:

```
WHERE invoice_total >
    (SELECT MAX(invoice_total)
     FROM invoices
     WHERE vendor_id = 34)
```

As a result, we recommend replacing the ALL keyword with an equivalent condition whenever it makes the query easier to read.

How the ALL keyword works

Condition	Equivalent expression	Description
`x > ALL (1, 2)`	`x > 2`	Evaluates to true if x is greater than the maximum value returned by the subquery.
`x < ALL (1, 2)`	`x < 1`	Evaluates to true if x is less than the minimum value returned by the subquery.
`x = ALL (1, 2)`	`(x = 1) AND (x = 2)`	Evaluates to true if the subquery returns a single value that's equal to x or if the subquery returns multiple values that are the same and these values are all equal to x.
`x <> ALL (1, 2)`	`x NOT IN (1, 2)`	Evaluates to true if *x* is not one of the values returned by the subquery.

Get invoices larger than the largest invoice for vendor 34

```
SELECT vendor_name, invoice_number, invoice_total
FROM invoices i JOIN vendors v ON i.vendor_id = v.vendor_id
WHERE invoice_total > ALL
    (SELECT invoice_total
    FROM invoices
    WHERE vendor_id = 34)
ORDER BY vendor_name
```

The result of the subquery

invoice_total
116.54
1083.58

The result set

vendor_name	invoice_number	invoice_total
Bertelsmann Industry Svcs. Inc	509786	6940.25
Cahners Publishing Company	587056	2184.50
Computerworld	367447	2433.00
Data Reproductions Corp	40318	21842.00

`(25 rows)`

Description

- You can use the ALL keyword to test that a comparison condition is true for all of the values returned by a subquery.
- If no rows are returned by the subquery, a comparison that uses the ALL keyword is always true.
- If all of the rows returned by the subquery contain a null value, a comparison that uses the ALL keyword is always false.

Figure 6-5   How to use the ALL keyword

How to use the ANY and SOME keywords

Figure 6-6 shows how to use the ANY and SOME keywords to test whether a comparison is true for any of the values returned by a subquery. Since both of these keywords work the same, you can use whichever one you prefer. For the sake of brevity, this figure uses the ANY keyword in its examples. However, you can substitute the SOME keyword for the ANY keyword to get the same results.

The example in this figure shows how you can use the ANY keyword with the less than operator. This statement is similar to the one you saw in the previous figure, except that it retrieves invoices with invoice totals that are less than at least one of the invoice totals for a given vendor. Like the statement in the previous figure, this condition can be rewritten using the MAX function, as follows:

```
WHERE invoice_total <
    (SELECT MAX(invoice_total)
     FROM invoices
     WHERE vendor_id = 115)
```

Since this statement is easier to read, we recommend using statements like this one instead of statements that use the ANY keyword whenever possible.

How the ANY keyword works

Condition	Equivalent expression	Description
`x > ANY (1, 2)`	`x > 1`	Evaluates to true if x is greater than the minimum value returned by the subquery.
`x < ANY (1, 2)`	`x < 2`	Evaluates to true if x is less than the maximum value returned by the subquery.
`x = ANY (1, 2)`	`x IN (1, 2)`	Evaluates to true if x is equal to any of the values returned by the subquery.
`x <> ANY (1, 2)`	`(x <> 1) OR (x <> 2)`	Evaluates to true if *x* is not equal to at least one of the values returned by the subquery.

Get invoices smaller than the largest invoice for vendor 115

```
SELECT vendor_name, invoice_number, invoice_total
FROM vendors JOIN invoices ON vendors.vendor_id = invoices.invoice_id
WHERE invoice_total < ANY
    (SELECT invoice_total
    FROM invoices
    WHERE vendor_id = 115)
```

all have to be less than any of subquery results (25.67)

The result of the subquery

The result set

vendor_name	invoice_number	invoice_total
Newbrige Book Clubs	963253251	15.50
Golden Eagle Insurance Co	111-92R-10096	16.33
Expedata Inc	25022117	6.00
Internal Revenue Service	21-4748363	9.95
Blanchard & Johnson Ass...	4-321-2596	10.00

`(17 rows)`

Description

- You can use the ANY keyword to test that a condition is true for one or more of the values returned by a subquery.
- If the subquery doesn't return any values, or if it only returns null values, a comparison that uses the ANY keyword evaluates to false.
- The SOME keyword works the same as the ANY keyword.

Figure 6-6   How to use the ANY and SOME keywords

How to code correlated subqueries

So far, all of the subqueries in this chapter have been uncorrelated subqueries. An *uncorrelated subquery* is executed only once for the entire query. However, you can also code a *correlated subquery* that's executed once for each row that's processed by the main query. This type of query is similar to using a loop to do repetitive processing in a procedural programming language like PHP or Java.

Figure 6-7 shows how correlated subqueries work. The example retrieves rows from the Invoices table for those invoices that have an invoice total that's greater than the average of all the invoices for the same vendor. To do that, the WHERE clause of the subquery refers to the vendor_id value of the main query. That way, only the invoices for the current vendor are included in the average.

Each time MySQL processes a row in the main query, it substitutes the value in the vendor_id column for the column reference in the subquery. Then, MySQL executes the subquery based on that value. For example, if the vendor_id value is 95, MySQL executes this subquery:

```
SELECT AVG(invoice_total)
FROM invoices
WHERE vendor_id = 95
```

After MySQL executes this subquery, it uses the returned value to determine whether to include the current invoice in the result set. For example, for vendor 95, the subquery returns a value of 28.501667. Then, MySQL compares that value with the invoice total of the current invoice. If the invoice total is greater than that value, MySQL includes the invoice in the result set. Otherwise, it doesn't. MySQL repeats this process until it has processed each of the invoices in the Invoices table.

In this figure, the WHERE clause of the subquery qualifies the vendor_id column from the main query with the alias that's assigned to the Invoices table in that query. This is necessary because this statement uses the same table in the sub and main queries. So, the use of a table alias avoids ambiguity. However, if a subquery uses a different table than the main query, a table alias isn't necessary.

Since correlated subqueries can be difficult to code, you may want to test a subquery separately before using it within another SELECT statement. To do that, however, you'll need to substitute a constant value for the variable that refers to a column in the outer query. That's what we did to get the average invoice total for vendor 95. Once you're sure that the subquery works on its own, you can replace the constant value with a reference to the outer query so you can use it within a SELECT statement.

Get each invoice amount that's higher than the vendor's average invoice amount

```
SELECT vendor_id, invoice_number, invoice_total
FROM invoices i
WHERE invoice_total >
    (SELECT AVG(invoice_total)
     FROM invoices
     WHERE vendor_id = i.vendor_id)
ORDER BY vendor_id, invoice_total
```

The value returned by the subquery for vendor 95

```
28.501667
```

The result set

vendor_id	invoice_number	invoice_total
83	31359783	1575.00
95	111-92R-10095	32.70
95	111-92R-10093	39.77
95	111-92R-10092	46.21
110	P-0259	26881.40

(36 rows)

Description

- A *correlated subquery* is a subquery that is executed once for each row in the main query. In contrast, an *uncorrelated subquery* is executed only once. All of the subqueries in the previous figures are uncorrelated subqueries.

- A correlated subquery refers to a value that's provided by a column in the main query. For each different value that's returned by the main query for that column, the subquery returns a different result.

- To refer to a column in the main query, you can qualify the column with a table name or alias. If a correlated subquery uses the same table as the main query, you can use table aliases to remove ambiguity.

Figure 6-7   How to code correlated subqueries

How to use the EXISTS operator

Figure 6-8 shows how to use the EXISTS operator with a subquery. This operator tests whether the subquery returns a result set. In other words, it tests whether the result set exists. When you use this operator, the subquery doesn't actually return a result set to the outer query. Instead, it returns an indication of whether any rows satisfy the search condition of the subquery. Because of that, queries that use this operator execute quickly.

You typically use the EXISTS operator with a correlated subquery as shown in this figure. This query retrieves all the vendors in the Vendors table that don't have invoices in the Invoices table. Although this query returns the same vendors as the queries shown in figure 6-3, it executes more quickly than either of those queries.

In this example, the correlated subquery selects all invoices that have the same vendor_id value as the current vendor in the outer query. Because the subquery doesn't actually return a result set, it doesn't matter what columns are included in the SELECT clause. As a result, it's customary to just code an asterisk.

After the subquery is executed, the search condition in the WHERE clause of the main query uses the NOT EXISTS operator to test whether any invoices were found for the current vendor. If not, the vendor row is included in the result set.

The syntax of a subquery that uses the EXISTS operator

```
WHERE [NOT] EXISTS (subquery)
```

Get all vendors that don't have invoices

```
SELECT vendor_id, vendor_name, vendor_state
FROM vendors
WHERE NOT EXISTS
    (SELECT *
     FROM invoices
     WHERE vendor_id = vendors.vendor_id)
```

The result set

vendor_id	vendor_name	vendor_state
33	Nielson	OH
35	Cal State Termite	CA
36	Graylift	CA
38	Venture Communications Int1	NY
39	Custom Printing Company	MO
40	Nat Assoc of College Stores	OH

(88 rows)

Description

- You can use the EXISTS operator to test that one or more rows are returned by the subquery.

- You can use the NOT EXISTS operator to test that no rows are returned by the subquery.

- When you use these operators with a subquery, it doesn't matter what columns you specify in the SELECT clause. As a result, you typically just code an asterisk (*).

Figure 6-8   How to use the EXISTS operator

How to code subqueries in other clauses

Now that you know how to code subqueries in the WHERE clause of a SELECT statement, you're ready to learn how to code them in the HAVING, FROM, and SELECT clauses.

How to code subqueries in the HAVING clause

When you code a HAVING clause, you specify a search condition just as you do when you code a WHERE clause. That includes search conditions that contain subqueries. To learn how to code subqueries in a HAVING clause, then, you can refer back to figures 6-3 through 6-8.

How to code subqueries in the SELECT clause

Figure 6-9 shows how to use subqueries in the SELECT clause. To do that, you code the subquery in place of a column specification. As a result, the subquery must return a single value for that column.

In most cases, you code correlated subqueries in the SELECT clause. In this figure, for example, the subquery calculates the maximum invoice date for each vendor in the Vendors table. To do that, the subquery refers to the vendor_id column from the Vendors table in the main query.

Subqueries coded in the SELECT clause are typically difficult to read. As a result, you shouldn't use them if you can find another solution. In most cases, you can replace the subquery with a join. In this figure, for example, the first query can be restated as shown in the second query. This query joins the Vendors and Invoices tables, groups the rows by vendor_name, and uses the MAX function to calculate the maximum invoice date for each vendor. As a result, this query is easier to read.

Get the most recent invoice date for each vendor

```
SELECT vendor_name,
    (SELECT MAX(invoice_date) FROM invoices
      WHERE vendor_id = vendors.vendor_id) AS latest_inv
FROM vendors
ORDER BY latest_inv DESC
```

The result set

vendor_name	latest_inv
Federal Express Corporation	2011-08-02
Blue Cross	2011-08-01
Malloy Lithographing Inc	2011-07-31
Cardinal Business Media, ...	2011-07-28
Zylka Design	2011-07-25
Ford Motor Credit Company	2011-07-24
United Parcel Service	2011-07-24

(122 rows)

The same query restated using a join

```
SELECT vendor_name, MAX(invoice_date) AS latest_inv
FROM vendors v
    LEFT JOIN invoices i ON v.vendor_id = i.vendor_id
GROUP BY vendor_name
ORDER BY latest_inv DESC
```

Description

- When you code a subquery in the SELECT clause, the subquery must return a single value.

- When you code a subquery in the SELECT clause, you typically use a correlated subquery.

- A query that includes a subquery in its SELECT clause can typically be restated using a join instead of the subquery. Because a join is usually faster and easier to read, subqueries are seldom coded in the SELECT clause.

Figure 6-9   How to code subqueries in the SELECT clause

How to code subqueries in the FROM clause

Figure 6-10 shows how to code a subquery in the FROM clause. To do that, you code a subquery in place of a table specification. When you code a subquery in the FROM clause, it can return a result set that contains any number of rows and columns. This result set is sometimes referred to as an *inline view*.

Subqueries are typically used in the FROM clause to create inline views that provide summarized data to another summary query. In this figure, for example, the subquery returns a result set that contains the vendor state, the vendor name, and the sum of invoice totals for each vendor. To do that, it groups the vendors by state and name. Once the subquery returns this result set, the main query groups the result set by vendor state and gets the largest sum of invoice totals for each state. This returns the invoice total for the top vendor in each state.

When you code a subquery in the FROM clause, you must assign a table alias to the subquery. This is required even if you don't use the table alias in the main query. In this figure, for example, the query assigns a table alias of *t* (for temporary table) to the subquery.

In addition, you should assign a column alias to all calculated columns in a subquery. In this figure, for example, the subquery assigns a column alias of sum_of_invoices to the result of the SUM function. That makes it easier to refer to these columns from other clauses in the subquery if you need to do that.

Get the largest invoice total for the top vendor in each state

```
SELECT vendor_state, MAX(sum_of_invoices) AS max_sum_of_invoices
FROM
(
    SELECT vendor_state, vendor_name,
        SUM(invoice_total) AS sum_of_invoices
    FROM vendors v JOIN invoices i
        ON v.vendor_id = i.vendor_id
    GROUP BY vendor_state, vendor_name
) t
GROUP BY vendor_state
```

The result of the subquery (an inline view)

vendor_state	vendor_name	sum_of_invoices
AZ	Wells Fargo Bank	662.00
CA	Abbey Office Furnishings	17.50
CA	Bertelsmann Industry Svcs. Inc	6940.25
CA	Blue Cross	564.00
CA	Coffee Break Service	41.80
CA	Computerworld	2433.00
CA	Digital Dreamworks	7125.34
CA	Dristas Groom & McCormick	220.00

(34 rows)

The result set

vendor_state	max_sum_of_invoices
AZ	662.00
CA	7125.34
DC	600.00

(10 rows)

Description

- A subquery that's coded in the FROM clause returns a result set that can be referred to as an *inline view.*

- When you code a subquery in the FROM clause, you must assign an alias to it. Then, you can use that alias just as you would any other table name or alias.

- When you code a subquery in the FROM clause, you should use an alias for any columns in the subquery that perform calculations. Then, the inline view can use these aliases as the column names of the table.

Figure 6-10   How to code subqueries in the FROM clause

How to work with complex queries

So far, the examples you've seen of queries that use subqueries have been relatively simple. However, these types of queries can get complicated in a hurry, particularly if the subqueries are nested. Because of that, you'll want to be sure that you plan and test these queries carefully. In a moment, you'll learn how to do that. But first, this chapter presents an example of a complex query.

A complex query that uses subqueries

Figure 6-11 presents a complex query that uses multiple subqueries. The first subquery is used in the FROM clause of the outer query to create a result set that contains the state, name, and total invoice amount for each vendor in the Vendors table. The second subquery is also used in the FROM clause of the outer query to create a result set that's joined with the first result set. This subquery uses a nested subquery and is the same query that was described in figure 6-10. As a result, you should already understand how it works.

After this statement creates the two result sets, it joins them based on the columns in each table that contain the state and the total invoice amount. The final result set includes the state, name, and total invoice amount for the vendor in each state with the largest invoice total. This result set is sorted by state.

At this point, you might be wondering if there is an easier solution to this problem. For example, you might think that you could solve the problem by joining the Vendors and Invoices tables, grouping by vendor state, and calculating the sum of invoices for each vendor. However, if you group by vendor state, you can't include the name of the vendor in the result set. And if you group by vendor state and vendor name, the result set includes all vendors, not just the top vendor from each state. As a result, the query presented here is a fairly straightforward way of solving the problem.

When you code a complex subquery, it's often helpful to include comments. You can use *comments* to describe the different parts of the query without changing how the query operates. To code a single-line comment, you start the line with two dashes (--).

In this figure, the query includes three comments. The first comment identifies the first subquery, the second comment identifies the second subquery, and the third comment identifies the third subquery. These comments make it easier to read the main query by making it easier to identify the three subqueries and determine what they do. For example, these comments clearly show that the subqueries that have aliases of t1 and t2 return the same result set.

A complex query that uses subqueries

```
SELECT t1.vendor_state, vendor_name, t1.sum_of_invoices
FROM
    (
        -- invoice totals by vendor
        SELECT vendor_state, vendor_name,
            SUM(invoice_total) AS sum_of_invoices
        FROM vendors v JOIN invoices i
            ON v.vendor_id = i.vendor_id
        GROUP BY vendor_state, vendor_name
    ) t1
    JOIN
        (
            -- top invoice totals by state
            SELECT vendor_state,
                MAX(sum_of_invoices) AS sum_of_invoices
            FROM
                (
                    -- invoice totals by vendor
                    SELECT vendor_state, vendor_name,
                        SUM(invoice_total) AS sum_of_invoices
                    FROM vendors v JOIN invoices i
                        ON v.vendor_id = i.vendor_id
                    GROUP BY vendor_state, vendor_name
                ) t2
            GROUP BY vendor_state
        ) t3
    ON t1.vendor_state = t3.vendor_state AND
        t1.sum_of_invoices = t3.sum_of_invoices
ORDER BY vendor_state
```

The result set

vendor_state	vendor_name	sum_of_invoices
AZ	Wells Fargo Bank	662.00
CA	Digital Dreamworks	7125.34
DC	Reiter's Scientific & Pro Books	600.00
MA	Dean Witter Reynolds	1367.50

```
(10 rows)
```

Description

- This query retrieves the vendor from each state that has the largest invoice total. To do that, it uses three subqueries.

- This query uses comments to clearly identify its subqueries.

- The subqueries named t1 and t2 return the same result set. This result set includes the vendor state, name, and sum of invoices.

- The subquery named t3 returns a result set that includes the vendor state and the largest sum of invoices for any vendor in that state. To do that, this subquery uses a nested subquery named t2.

- The subqueries named t1 and t3 are joined on both the vendor_state and sum_of_invoices columns.

Figure 6-11   A complex query that uses subqueries

A procedure for building complex queries

To build a complex query like the one in the previous figure, you can use a procedure like the one in figure 6-12. To start, you should state the question in English so you're clear about what you want the query to answer. In this case, the question is, "Which vendor in each state has the largest invoice total?"

Once you're clear about the problem, you can outline the query using *pseudocode*. Pseudocode is code that represents the intent of the query, but doesn't necessarily use SQL code. The pseudocode shown in this figure, for example, uses part SQL code and part English. This pseudocode identifies the three columns returned by the main query, two subqueries, and even the join condition for the two subqueries.

The next step in the procedure is to code and test the subqueries to be sure they work the way you want them to. For example, this figure shows the code for the first subquery along with its result set. This returns all of the data that you want, but it also includes extra rows that you don't want. To remove the extra rows from the first query, you can code the second subquery shown in this figure. This subquery uses the first subquery as a nested subquery. Although this removes the extra rows, it also removes the vendor_name column.

Once you're sure that both subqueries work the way you want them to, you can use them in the main query. For example, the pseudocode in this figure shows that you should join the result sets returned by the subqueries on the vendor_state and sum_of_invoices columns. In addition, the code in the previous figure shows how these two subqueries are used in the main query. This allows you to get all of the columns you want in the final result set without any of the extra rows that you don't want.

Writing complex queries is difficult, but following a procedure like the one shown in this figure can make it a little easier. At first, you might not be able to use pseudocode to identify subqueries. In that case, it's OK to skip ahead to step 3 and begin experimenting with possible subqueries. This may give you some ideas for how to solve the problem. Once you get these subqueries working correctly, you can begin coding a main query, and you can cut and paste the subqueries into the main query.

A procedure for building complex queries

1. State the problem to be solved by the query in English.
2. Use pseudocode to outline the query.
3. Code the subqueries and test them to be sure that they return the correct data.
4. Code and test the final query.

The problem to be solved by the query in figure 6-11

Which vendor in each state has the largest invoice total?

Pseudocode for the query

```
SELECT vendor_state, vendor_name, sum_of_invoices
FROM (subquery returning vendor_state, vendor_name, sum_of_invoices)
JOIN (subquery returning vendor_state, largest_sum_of_invoices)
    ON vendor_state AND sum_of_invoices
ORDER BY vendor_state
```

The code for the first subquery

```
SELECT vendor_state, vendor_name, SUM(invoice_total) AS sum_of_invoices
FROM vendors v JOIN invoices i
    ON v.vendor_id = i.vendor_id
GROUP BY vendor_state, vendor_name
```

The result set for the first subquery

vendor_state	vendor_name	sum_of_invoices
AZ	Wells Fargo Bank	662.00
CA	Abbey Office Furnishings	17.50
CA	Bertelsmann Industry Svcs. Inc	6940.25

(34 rows)

The code for the second subquery

```
SELECT vendor_state, MAX(sum_of_invoices) AS sum_of_invoices
FROM
(
    SELECT vendor_state, vendor_name,
        SUM(invoice_total) AS sum_of_invoices
    FROM vendors v JOIN invoices i
        ON v.vendor_id = i.vendor_id
    GROUP BY vendor_state, vendor_name
) t
GROUP BY vendor_state
```

The result set for the second subquery

vendor_state	sum_of_invoices
AZ	662.00
CA	7125.34
DC	600.00

(10 rows)

Figure 6-12   A procedure for building complex queries

Perspective

Subqueries are a powerful tool that you can use to solve difficult problems. Before you use a subquery, however, remember that a subquery can often be restated more clearly by using a join. If so, you'll typically want to use a join instead of a subquery.

If you find yourself coding the same subqueries in multiple places, you should consider creating a view for that subquery as described in chapter 12. This will help you develop queries more quickly since you can use the view instead of coding the subquery again. In addition, since views typically execute more quickly than subqueries, this may improve the performance of your queries.

Terms

subquery
introduce a subquery
nested subquery
correlated subquery
uncorrelated subquery
inline view
comment
pseudocode

Exercises

1. Write a SELECT statement that returns the same result set as this SELECT statement, but don't use a join. Instead, use a subquery in a WHERE clause that uses the IN keyword.

    ```
    SELECT DISTINCT vendor_name
    FROM vendors JOIN invoices
        ON vendors.vendor_id = invoices.vendor_id
    ORDER BY vendor_name
    ```

2. Write a SELECT statement that answers this question: Which invoices have a payment total that's greater than the average payment total for all invoices with a payment total greater than 0?

    Return the invoice_number and invoice_total columns for each invoice. This should return 20 rows.

    Sort the results by the invoice_total column in descending order.

3. Write a SELECT statement that returns two columns from the General_Ledger_Accounts table: account_number and account_description.

    Return one row for each account number that has never been assigned to any line item in the Invoice_Line_Items table. To do that, use a subquery introduced with the NOT EXISTS operator. This should return 54 rows.

    Sort the results by the account_number column.

4. Write a SELECT statement that returns four columns: vendor_name, invoice_id, invoice_sequence, and line_item_amount.

    Return a row for each line item of each invoice that has more than one line item in the Invoice_Line_Items table. This should return 6 rows. *Hint: Use a subquery that tests for invoice_sequence > 1.*

5. Write a SELECT statement that returns two columns: vendor_id and the largest unpaid invoice for each vendor. To do this, you can group the result set by the vendor_id column. This should return 7 rows.

    Write a second SELECT statement that uses the first SELECT statement in its FROM clause. The main query should return a single value that represents the sum of the largest unpaid invoices for each vendor.

6. Write a SELECT statement that returns the name, city, and state of each vendor that's located in a unique city and state. In other words, don't include vendors that have a city and state in common with another vendor. This should return 38 rows.

    Sort the results by the vendor_state and vendor_city columns.

7. Use a correlated subquery to return one row per vendor, representing the vendor's oldest invoice (the one with the earliest date). Each row should include these four columns: vendor_name, invoice_number, invoice_date, and invoice_total. This should return 34 rows.

    Sort the results by the vendor_name column.

8. Rewrite exercise 7 so it gets the same result but uses an inline view instead of a correlated subquery.

7

How to insert, update, and delete data

In the last four chapters, you learned how to code the SELECT statement to retrieve and summarize data. Now, you'll learn how to code the INSERT, UPDATE, and DELETE statements to modify the data in a table. When you're done with this chapter, you'll know how to code the four statements that are used every day by professional application developers.

As you read this chapter, keep in mind that by default, MySQL automatically commits changes to the database immediately after each INSERT, UPDATE, or DELETE statement is executed. Usually, that's what you want. If it isn't, you can refer to chapter 14 to learn how to turn off auto-commit mode.

How to create test tables **198**
How to create the tables for this book 198
How to create a copy of a table 198

How to insert new rows **200**
How to insert a single row 200
How to insert multiple rows 200
How to insert default values and null values 202
How to use a subquery in an INSERT statement 204

How to update existing rows **206**
How to update rows 206
How to use a subquery in an UPDATE statement 208

How to delete existing rows **210**
How to delete rows 210
How to use a subquery in a DELETE statement 210

Perspective **212**

How to create test tables

Before you begin experimenting with INSERT, UPDATE, and DELETE statements, you need to make sure that your experimentation won't affect "live" data that's used by other people at your business or school.

How to create the tables for this book

If you're only working with the tables for this book, you can use the procedure shown in appendix A (PC) or B (Mac) to create the tables for this book. Then, you can experiment all you want without worrying about how much you change these tables. If you ever want to restore these tables to their original state, you can use the procedure shown in the appendix to do that.

How to create a copy of a table

If you're working with tables that are running on a server that's available from your business or school, it's usually a good idea to create a copy of some or all of a table before you do any testing. To do that, you can use the CREATE TABLE AS statement with a SELECT statement as shown in figure 7-1. When you use this technique, the result set that's defined by the SELECT statement is copied into a new table. Then, you can experiment all you want with the test table and delete it when you're done.

When you use this technique to create tables, MySQL only copies the column definitions and data. In other words, MySQL doesn't retain other parts of the column definitions such as primary keys, foreign keys, and indexes. As a result, when you experiment with copied tables, you may get different results than you would get with the original tables. Still, this is usually preferable to experimenting with live data.

The examples in this figure show how to use the CREATE TABLE AS statement. Here, the first example copies all of the columns from all of the rows in the Invoices table into a new table named Invoices_Copy. The second example copies all of the columns in the Invoices table into a new table named Old_Invoices, but only for rows where the balance due is zero. And the third example creates a table that contains summary data from the Invoices table.

When you're done experimenting with test tables, you can use the DROP TABLE statement that's shown in this figure to delete any tables you don't need anymore. In this figure, for instance, the fourth example shows how to drop the Old_Invoices table.

The syntax of the CREATE TABLE AS statement

```
CREATE TABLE table_name AS select_statement
```

Create a complete copy of the Invoices table

```
CREATE TABLE invoices_copy AS
SELECT *
FROM invoices
```

Create a partial copy of the Invoices table

```
CREATE TABLE old_invoices AS
SELECT *
FROM invoices
WHERE invoice_total - payment_total - credit_total = 0
```

Create a table with summary rows from the Invoices table

```
CREATE TABLE vendor_balances AS
SELECT vendor_id, SUM(invoice_total) AS sum_of_invoices
FROM invoices
WHERE (invoice_total - payment_total - credit_total) <> 0
GROUP BY vendor_id
```

Delete a table

```
DROP TABLE old_invoices
```

Description

- You can use the CREATE TABLE AS statement to create a new table based on the result set defined by a SELECT statement.

- Each column name in the SELECT clause must be unique. If you use calculated values in the select list, you must name the column.

- You can code the other clauses of the SELECT statement just as you would for any other SELECT statement, including grouping, aggregates, joins, and subqueries.

- The table you name must not exist. If it does, you must delete the table by using the DROP TABLE statement before you execute the CREATE TABLE AS statement.

- When you use the CREATE TABLE AS statement to create a table, only the column definitions and data are copied. Definitions of primary keys, foreign keys, indexes, and so on are not included in the new table.

Figure 7-1   How to create a table from a SELECT statement

How to insert new rows

To add rows to a table, you use the INSERT statement. In most cases, you use this statement to add a single row to a table. However, you can also use it to add multiple rows to a table.

How to insert a single row

Figure 7-2 starts by showing how to code INSERT statements that insert a single row. Because the examples in this figure insert rows into the Invoices table, this figure reviews the column definitions for this table. This shows the sequence of the columns in the table and which columns have default values or allow null values. It also shows that invoice_id is an auto increment column.

When you code an INSERT statement, you name the table on the INSERT clause, followed by an optional list of columns. Then, you list the values to be inserted on the VALUES clause.

The first two examples in this figure illustrate how this works. The first example doesn't include a column list. Because of that, the VALUES clause must include a value for every column in the table, and those values must be listed in the same sequence that the columns appear in the table. That way, MySQL knows which value to assign to which column. Notice that this statement uses the NULL keyword to assign a null value to the payment_date column. You'll learn more about using this keyword in the next figure.

The second INSERT statement includes a column list. However, this list doesn't include four columns. It doesn't include the invoice_id column since MySQL automatically increments this column if a value isn't specified. It doesn't include the payment_total and credit_total columns since these columns provide a default value of 0. And it doesn't include the payment_date column since this column allows a null value. In addition, the columns aren't listed in the same sequence as the columns in the table. When you include a list of columns, you can code the columns in any sequence you like. Then, you just need to be sure you code the values in the VALUES clause in the same sequence.

When you specify the values for the columns to be inserted, you must be sure that those values are compatible with the data types of the columns. For example, you must enclose literal values for dates and strings within quotes. However, the quotes are optional when you code literal values for numbers. In the next chapter, you'll learn more about working with data types. For now, just realize that if any of the values aren't compatible with the corresponding column data types, MySQL returns an error and the row isn't inserted.

How to insert multiple rows

The third example in figure 7-2 shows how to insert multiple rows. When you do that, you follow the same rules as you do for inserting a single row. Then, you separate each list of values with a comma. This technique is often useful when you need to create a script that inserts data into a database.

The syntax of the INSERT statement

```
INSERT [INTO] table_name [(column_list)]
VALUES (expression_1[, expression_2]...)[,
        (expression_1[, expression_2]...)]...
```

The column definitions for the Invoices table

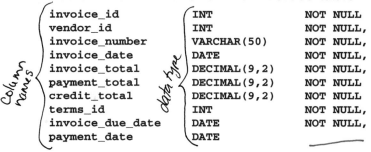

```
invoice_id        INT            NOT NULL    AUTO_INCREMENT,
vendor_id         INT            NOT NULL,
invoice_number    VARCHAR(50)    NOT NULL,
invoice_date      DATE           NOT NULL,
invoice_total     DECIMAL(9,2)   NOT NULL,
payment_total     DECIMAL(9,2)   NOT NULL    DEFAULT 0,
credit_total      DECIMAL(9,2)   NOT NULL    DEFAULT 0,
terms_id          INT            NOT NULL,
invoice_due_date  DATE           NOT NULL,
payment_date      DATE
```

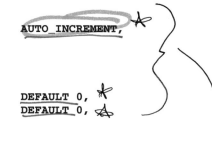

Insert a single row without using a column list

```
INSERT INTO invoices VALUES
(115, 97, '456789', '2011-08-01', 8344.50, 0, 0, 1, '2011-08-31', NULL)
```

(1 row affected)

Insert a single row using a column list

```
INSERT INTO invoices
     (vendor_id, invoice_number, invoice_total, terms_id, invoice_date,
      invoice_due_date)
VALUES
     (97, '456789', 8344.50, 1, '2011-08-01', '2011-08-31')
```

(1 row affected)

Insert multiple rows

```
INSERT INTO invoices VALUES
(116, 97, '456701', '2011-08-02', 270.50, 0, 0, 1, '2011-09-01', NULL),
(117, 97, '456791', '2011-08-03', 4390.00, 0, 0, 1, '2011-09-02', NULL),
(118, 97, '456792', '2011-08-03', 565.60, 0, 0, 1, '2011-09-02', NULL)
```

(3 rows affected)

Description

- You use the INSERT statement to add one or more rows to a table.

- In the INSERT clause, you specify the name of the table that you want to add a row to, along with an optional column list. The INTO keyword is also optional.

- In the VALUES clause, you specify the values to be inserted. If you don't include a column list in the INSERT clause, you must specify the column values in the same order as in the table, and you must code a value for each column. If you include a column list, you must specify the column values in the same order as in the column list, and you can omit columns that have default values, accept null values, or are automatically generated.

- To insert a null value into a column, you can use the NULL keyword. To insert a default value or to have MySQL generate a value for an auto increment column, you can use the DEFAULT keyword. For more information, see figure 7-3.

Figure 7-2   How to insert rows

How to insert default values and null values

If a column allows null values, you can use the INSERT statement to insert a null value into that column. Similarly, if a column is defined with a default value, you can use the INSERT statement to insert that value. Finally, if a column is defined as an auto increment column, you can have MySQL generate a value for the column. The technique you use depends on whether the INSERT statement includes a column list, as shown by the examples in figure 7-3.

All of these INSERT statements use a table named Color_Sample from the EX database. This table contains the three columns shown at the top of this figure. The first column, color_id, is defined so MySQL automatically generates its value whenever necessary. The second column, color_number, is defined with a default value of 0. And the third column, color_name, is defined so it allows null values.

The first two statements show how to assign an automatically incremented value, a default value, or a null value using a column list. To do that, you omit the column from the list. In the first statement, for example, the column list names only the color_number column. As a result, MySQL automatically assigns a value of 1 to the color_id column (assuming the table doesn't contain any rows) and a null value to the color_name column. Similarly, in the second statement, the column list names only the color_name column. As a result, MySQL assigns a value of 2 to the color_id column and a null value to the color_number column.

The next three statements show how to assign an automatically incremented, default, or null value to a column without including a column list. To do that, you can use the DEFAULT and NULL keywords. For example, the third statement specifies a value for the color_name column, but uses the DEFAULT keyword for the color_id and color_number columns. As a result, MySQL assigns an automatically incremented value of 3 to the color_id column and a default value of 0 to the color_number column. The fourth statement uses the NULL keyword to assign a null value to the color_name column. Finally, the fifth statement shows what happens if you use the DEFAULT keyword for the first two columns and the NULL keyword for the third column.

The column definitions for the Color_Sample table

```
color_id        INT              NOT NULL     AUTO_INCREMENT,
color_number    INT              NOT NULL     DEFAULT 0,
color_name      VARCHAR(50)
```

Five INSERT statements for the Color_Sample table

```
INSERT INTO color_sample (color_number)
VALUES (606)

INSERT INTO color_sample (color_name)
VALUES ('Yellow')

INSERT INTO color_sample
VALUES (DEFAULT, DEFAULT, 'Orange')

INSERT INTO color_sample
VALUES (DEFAULT, 808, NULL)

INSERT INTO color_sample
VALUES (DEFAULT, DEFAULT, NULL)
```

The Color_Sample table after the rows have been inserted

color_id	color_number	color_name
1	606	NULL
2	0	Yellow
3	0	Orange
4	808	NULL
5	0	NULL

Description

- If a column is defined so it allows null values, you can use the NULL keyword in the list of values to insert a null value into that column.

- If a column is defined with a default value, you can use the DEFAULT keyword in the list of values to insert the default value for that column.

- If a column is defined as an auto increment column, you can use the DEFAULT keyword in the list of values to have MySQL generate the value for the column.

- If you include a column list, you can omit columns with default values and null values. Then, the default value or null value is assigned automatically. You can also omit an auto increment column. Then, MySQL generates the value for the column.

Figure 7-3   How to insert default values and null values

How to use a subquery in an INSERT statement

Instead of using the VALUES clause of the INSERT statement to specify the values for each row to be inserted, you can use a subquery to select the rows from another table. Figure 7-4 shows you how to do that.

Both examples in this figure retrieve rows from the Invoices table and insert them into a table named Invoice_Archive. This table is defined with the same columns as the Invoices table. However, the invoice_id column isn't defined as an auto increment column, and the payment_total and credit_total columns aren't defined with default values. As a result, you must include values for these columns.

The first example shows how you can use a subquery in an INSERT statement without a column list. In this example, the SELECT clause of the subquery use an asterisk to retrieve all the columns in the Invoices table. Then, after MySQL applies the search condition in the WHERE clause, all the rows in the result set are inserted into the Invoice_Archive table.

The second example shows how you can use a subquery in an INSERT statement with a column list. Just as when you use the VALUES clause, you can list the columns in any sequence. However, the columns must be listed in the same sequence in the SELECT clause of the subquery. In addition, you can omit auto increment columns, columns that are defined with default values, and columns that allow null values.

Note that the subqueries in these statements aren't coded within parentheses as a subquery in a SELECT statement is. That's because they're not coded within a clause of the INSERT statement. Instead, they're coded in place of the VALUES clause.

Before you execute an INSERT statement that uses a subquery, you should make sure that the rows and columns retrieved by the subquery are the ones you want to insert. To do that, you can execute the SELECT statement by itself. Then, when you're sure it retrieves the correct data, you can add the INSERT clause to insert the rows into another table.

The syntax for using a subquery to insert one or more rows

```
INSERT [INTO] table_name [(column_list)] select_statement
```

Insert paid invoices into the Invoice_Archive table

```
INSERT INTO invoice_archive
SELECT *
FROM invoices
WHERE invoice_total - payment_total - credit_total = 0
```

```
(103 rows affected)
```

The same statement with a column list

```
INSERT INTO invoice_archive
    (invoice_id, vendor_id, invoice_number, invoice_total, credit_total,
    payment_total, terms_id, invoice_date, invoice_due_date)
SELECT
    invoice_id, vendor_id, invoice_number, invoice_total, credit_total,
    payment_total, terms_id, invoice_date, invoice_due_date
FROM invoices
WHERE invoice_total - payment_total - credit_total = 0
```

balance = ∅

```
(103 rows affected)
```

Description

- To insert rows selected from one or more tables into another table, you can code a subquery in place of the VALUES clause. Then, MySQL inserts the rows returned by the subquery into the target table. For this to work, the target table must already exist.

- The rules for working with a column list are the same as they are for any INSERT statement.

Figure 7-4   How to use a subquery in an INSERT statement

How to update existing rows

To modify the data in one or more rows of a table, you use the UPDATE statement. Although most of the UPDATE statements you code will perform simple updates, you can also code more complex UPDATE statements that include subqueries if necessary.

How to update rows

Figure 7-5 presents the syntax of the UPDATE statement. Most UPDATE statements include all three of the clauses shown here. The UPDATE clause names the table to be updated. The SET clause names the columns to be updated and the values to be assigned to those columns. And the WHERE clause specifies the condition a row must meet to be updated.

When you use MySQL Workbench, you should realize that it will execute an UPDATE statement only if the condition on the WHERE clause refers to a primary or foreign key. That's because, by default, Workbench runs in "safe update" mode. If that's not what you want, you can turn safe update mode off as described in this figure. For example, because the WHERE clause in the first and third UPDATE statements in this figure refer to the invoice_number column, which isn't a key column, you have to turn safe mode off to execute them.

The first UPDATE statement modifies the values of two columns in the Invoices table: payment_date and payment_total. Since the WHERE clause in this statement identifies a single row, MySQL only updates the columns in that row. In this example, the values for the columns are coded as a literal values. You should realize, though, that you can assign any valid expression to a column as long as it evaluates to a value that's compatible with the data type of the column. You can also use the NULL keyword to assign a null value to a column that allows nulls, and you can use the DEFAULT keyword to assign the default value to a column that's defined with a default value.

The second UPDATE statement modifies a single column in the Invoices table: terms_id. This time, however, the WHERE clause specifies that all the rows for vendor 95 should be updated. Since this vendor has six rows in the Invoices table, MySQL updates all six rows.

The third UPDATE statement shows how you can use an expression to assign a value to a column. In this case, the expression increases the value of the credit_total column by 100. Like the first UPDATE statement, this statement updates a single row.

Before you execute an UPDATE statement, you may want to make sure that you've selected the correct rows. To do that, you can code a SELECT statement with the same search condition. Then, if the SELECT statement returns the correct rows, you can copy its WHERE clause into your UPDATE statement.

The syntax of the UPDATE statement

```
UPDATE table_name
SET column_name_1 = expression_1[, column_name_2 = expression_2]...
[WHERE search_condition]
```

Update two columns for a single row

```
UPDATE invoices
SET payment_date = '2011-09-21',
    payment_total = 19351.18
WHERE invoice_number = '97/522'
```

2 columns

```
(1 row affected)
```

Update one column for multiple rows

```
UPDATE invoices
SET terms_id = 1
WHERE vendor_id = 95
```

literal

```
(6 rows affected)
```

Update one column for one row

```
UPDATE invoices
SET credit_total = credit_total + 100
WHERE invoice_number = '97/522'
```

expression

```
(1 row affected)
```

Description

- You use the UPDATE statement to modify one or more rows in a table.
- In the SET clause, you name each column and its new value. You can specify the value for a column as a literal or an expression.
- In the WHERE clause, you can specify the conditions that must be met for a row to be updated.
- You can use the DEFAULT and NULL keywords to specify default and null values as described in figure 7-3.
- By default, MySQL Workbench runs in safe update mode. That prevents you from updating rows if the WHERE clause is omitted or doesn't refer to a primary key or foreign key column.
- To get around the restrictions of safe update mode, you can turn this mode off. To do that, select the Edit→Preferences command, select the SQL Editor tab, change the "safe update" option, and restart MySQL Workbench.

Warning

- If you turn off safe update mode and omit the WHERE clause, all rows in the table will be updated.

Figure 7-5   How to update rows

How to use a subquery in an UPDATE statement

When you code the search condition on the WHERE clause of an UPDATE statement, you can include a subquery to identify the rows to be updated. Figure 7-6 presents two statements that illustrate how you do that.

In the first statement, a subquery is used in the WHERE clause to identify the invoices to be updated. This subquery returns the vendor_id value for the vendor in the Vendors table with the name "Pacific Bell." Then, all the invoices with that vendor_id value are updated.

The second UPDATE statement also uses a subquery in the WHERE clause. This subquery returns a list of the vendor_id values for all vendors in California, Arizona, and Nevada. Then, the IN operator is used to update all the invoices with vendor_id values in that list. Although this subquery returns 80 vendors, many of these vendors don't have invoices. As a result, the UPDATE statement only affects 40 invoices.

To execute the second UPDATE statement from MySQL Workbench, you have to turn safe update mode off. That's because the WHERE clause in this statement uses the IN operator. This may be a bug in Workbench, or it may be designed to work this way.

Update all invoices for a vendor

```
UPDATE invoices
SET terms_id = 1
WHERE vendor_id =
    (SELECT vendor_id
     FROM vendors
     WHERE vendor_name = 'Pacific Bell')
```

(handwritten: all terms-id =1 For all invoices for 'Pacific Bell')

(6 rows affected)

Update the terms for all invoices for vendors in three states

```
UPDATE invoices
SET terms_id = 1
WHERE vendor_id IN
    (SELECT vendor_id
     FROM vendors
     WHERE vendor_state IN ('CA', 'AZ', 'NV'))
```

(handwritten: all terms-id =1 for all vendors in CA, AZ, NV)

(40 rows affected)

Description

- You can code a subquery in the WHERE clause of an UPDATE statement to provide one or more values used in the search condition.

Figure 7-6   How to use a subquery in an UPDATE statement

How to delete existing rows

To delete one or more rows from a table, you use the DELETE statement. If necessary, you can use subqueries in a DELETE statement to help identify the rows to be deleted.

How to delete rows

Figure 7-7 presents the syntax of the DELETE statement along with four examples that show how it works. To start, the DELETE clause specifies the name of the table and must include the FROM keyword.

The WHERE clause specifies a search condition that identifies the rows to be deleted. Although this clause is optional, you'll almost always include it. If you don't, you could inadvertently delete all of the rows in the table. Fortunately, MySQL Workbench runs in safe update mode by default, which prevents a DELETE statement from executing if it doesn't include a WHERE clause that refers to a primary key or foreign key column.

If you want to make sure that you've selected the correct rows before you delete them, you can code a SELECT statement that retrieves those rows. Then, once you're sure the SELECT statement is retrieving the correct rows, you can convert the SELECT statement to a DELETE statement.

The first DELETE statement in this figure deletes a single row from the General_Ledger_Accounts table. To do that, it specifies the account_number value of the row to be deleted in the WHERE clause. The second DELETE statement deletes a single row from the Invoice_Line_Items table. To do that, it specifies the invoice_id value and the invoice_sequence value of the row to be deleted in the WHERE clause. Finally, the third DELETE statement deletes four rows from the Invoice_Line_Items table. To do that, it specifies 12 as the invoice_id value of the row to be deleted. Since the invoice for this ID has four line items, this deletes all four line items.

If you try to delete a row that has one or more related rows in another table, MySQL typically returns an error message and doesn't delete the row. For example, MySQL returns an error message if you attempt to delete a row from the Vendors table that has related rows in the Invoices table. Usually, that's what you want.

How to use a subquery in a DELETE statement

If you want to delete a row from the Vendors table that has related rows in the Invoices table, you need to start by deleting the rows in the Invoice_Line_Items table for the vendor's invoices. To do that, you can use a subquery as shown in the fourth example in figure 7-7. Here, the subquery selects all the invoice IDs for the vendor from the Invoices table. Then, the DELETE statement deletes all the invoice line items with those IDs.

The syntax of the DELETE statement

```
DELETE FROM table_name
[WHERE search_condition]
```

Delete one row

```
DELETE FROM general_ledger_accounts
WHERE account_number = 306
```

```
(1 row affected)
```

Delete one row using a compound condition

```
DELETE FROM invoice_line_items
WHERE invoice_id = 78 AND invoice_sequence = 2
```

```
(1 row affected)
```

Delete multiple rows

```
DELETE FROM invoice_line_items
WHERE invoice_id = 12
```

```
(4 rows affected)
```

Use a subquery in a DELETE statement

```
DELETE FROM invoice_line_items
WHERE invoice_id IN
    (SELECT invoice_id
     FROM invoices
     WHERE vendor_id = 115)
```

```
(4 rows affected)
```

Description

- You can use the DELETE statement to delete one or more rows from the table you name in the DELETE clause.

- You specify the conditions that must be met for a row to be deleted in the WHERE clause.

- You can use a subquery within the WHERE clause.

- A foreign-key constraint may prevent you from deleting a row. In that case, you can only delete the row if you delete all child rows for that row first.

- By default, MySQL Workbench runs in safe update mode. That prevents you from deleting rows if the WHERE clause is omitted or doesn't refer to a primary key or foreign key column. For information on turning safe update mode off, see figure 7-5.

Warning

- If you turn safe update mode off and omit the WHERE clause from a DELETE statement, all the rows in the table will be deleted.

Figure 7-7   How to delete rows

Perspective

In this chapter, you learned how to use the INSERT, UPDATE, and DELETE statements to modify the data in a database. In chapters 10 and 11, you'll learn more about how table definitions can affect the way these statements work. And in chapter 14, you'll learn more about executing groups of INSERT, UPDATE, and DELETE statements as a single transaction.

Exercises

To test whether a table has been modified correctly as you do these exercises, you can write and run an appropriate SELECT statement. Or, when you're using MySQL Workbench, you can right-click on a table name in the Object Browser window and select the Select Rows - Limit 1000 command to display the data for the table in a Result tab. To refresh the data in this tab after modifying the table data, click the Refresh button in the toolbar at the top of the tab.

1. Write an INSERT statement that adds this row to the Terms table:

   terms_id: 6
   terms_description: Net due 120 days
   terms_due_days: 120

   Use MySQL Workbench to review the column definitions for the Terms table, and include a column list with the required columns in the INSERT statement.

2. Write an UPDATE statement that modifies the row you just added to the Terms table. This statement should change the terms_description column to "Net due 125 days", and it should change the terms_due_days column to 125.

3. Write a DELETE statement that deletes the row you added to the Terms table in exercise 1.

4. Write an INSERT statement that adds this row to the Invoices table:

   invoice_id: The next automatically generated ID
   vendor_id: 32
   invoice_number: AX-014-027
   invoice_date: 8/1/2011
   invoice_total: $434.58
   payment_total: $0.00
   credit_total: $0.00
   terms_id: 2
   invoice_due_date: 8/31/2011
   payment_date: null

   Write this statement without using a column list.

5. Write an INSERT statement that adds these rows to the Invoice_Line_Items table:

invoice_sequence:	1	2
account_number:	160	527
line_item_amount:	$180.23	$254.35
line_item_description:	Hard drive	Exchange Server update

   Set the invoice_id column of these two rows to the invoice ID that was generated by MySQL for the invoice you added in exercise 4.

6. Write an UPDATE statement that modifies the invoice you added in exercise 4. This statement should change the credit_total column so it's 10% of the invoice_total column, and it should change the payment_total column so the sum of the payment_total and credit_total columns are equal to the invoice_total column.

7. Write an UPDATE statement that modifies the Vendors table. Change the default_account_number column to 403 for the vendor with an ID of 44.

8. Write an UPDATE statement that modifies the Invoices table. Change the terms_id column to 2 for each invoice that's for a vendor with a default_terms_id of 2.

9. Write a DELETE statement that deletes the row that you added to the Invoices table in exercise 4. When you execute this statement, it will produce an error since the invoice has related rows in the Invoice_Line_Items table. To fix that, precede the DELETE statement with another DELETE statement that deletes the line items for this invoice. (Remember that to code two or more statements in a script, you must end each statement with a semicolon.)

8

How to work with data types

So far, you have been using SQL statements to work with the three most common types of data: strings, numbers, and dates. Now, this chapter takes a more in-depth look at the data types that are available with MySQL and shows some basic skills for working with them. When you complete this chapter, you'll have a thorough understanding of the data types, and you'll know how to use some functions to convert one data type to another.

The data types **216**
Overview 216
The character types 218
The integer types 220
The fixed-point and floating-point types 222
The date and time types 224
The ENUM and SET types 228
The large object types 230

How to convert data **232**
How implicit data conversion works 232
How to convert data using the CAST and CONVERT functions 234
How to convert data using the FORMAT and CHAR functions 236

Perspective **238**

The data types

A column's *data type* specifies the kind of information the column is intended to store. In addition, a column's data type determines the operations that can be performed on the column.

Overview

The MySQL data types can be divided into the five categories shown in figure 8-1. To start, the *character data types* are intended for storing a string of one or more characters, which can include letters, numbers, symbols, or special characters. The terms *character*, *string*, and *text* are used interchangeably to describe this type of data.

The *numeric data types* are intended for storing numbers that can be used for mathematical calculations. As you'll see in this chapter, MySQL can store numbers in a variety of formats. At a basic level, you can divide numbers into two categories: integers and real numbers. *Integers* are numbers that don't have a decimal point, and *real numbers* are numbers that have a decimal point.

The *date and time data types* are intended for storing dates, times, or both dates and times. These data types are typically referred to as *date/time* or *temporal data types*.

Since the first three categories are the most widely used, this book focuses on these data types. However, MySQL also provides *large object (LOB) data types* that are useful for storing images, sound, video, and large amounts of character data. In addition, MySQL provides *spatial data types* that are useful for storing geometric and geographical values such as *global positioning system* (*GPS*) data.

Data types

Category	Description
Character	Strings of character data
Numeric	Numbers that don't include a decimal point (integers) and numbers that include a decimal point (real numbers)
Date and time	Dates, times, or both
Large Object (LOB)	Large strings of character or binary data
Spatial	Geometric or geographical values

Description

- MySQL provides *data types* for storing many types of data.
- Numbers that don't include a decimal point are known as *integers*.
- Numbers that include a decimal point are known as *real numbers.*
- The *date and time data types* are often referred to as the *date/time* or *temporal data types*.
- The *large object (LOB) data types* are useful for storing images, sound, video, and large amounts of text.
- The *spatial data types* are useful for storing geometric or geographical values such as *global positioning system (GPS)* data.

Figure 8-1   Data type overview

The character types

Figure 8-2 presents the two most common character data types supported by MySQL: CHAR and VARCHAR. These data types store strings of characters. By default, the CHAR and VARCHAR types use the *latin1 character set*. This character set uses one byte to store each character. As a result, it's referred to as a *single-byte character set*. This character set supports all of the characters that are used in English and by most western European languages.

Because a *byte* of computer storage consists of eight *bits* and eight bits can be combined in 256 different ways, each byte can represent one of 256 different characters. These characters are assigned numeric codes from 0 to 255. Most character sets including latin1 use the same codes for the first 128 characters. These are the codes defined by *ASCII* (*American Standard Code for Information Interchange*). The other codes, however, vary depending on the character set.

In chapter 11, you'll learn how to change the default character set to a *multiple-byte character set* such as the *UTF-8 character set*. This character set supports most characters from most of the world's languages. If you use UTF-8, the number of bytes per character increases, usually to 2 bytes per character. This provides for all of the characters specified by the *Unicode standard*. Because of that, you should use the UTF-8 character set if you want to use your database in a multi-language environment. Otherwise, you can use the latin1 character set to keep storage requirements to a minimum.

You use the CHAR type to store *fixed-length strings*. Data stored using this data type always occupies the same number of bytes regardless of the actual length of the string. This data type is typically used to define columns that have a fixed number of characters. For example, the vendor_state column in the Vendors table is defined as CHAR(2) because it always contains two characters. However, if two characters are stored in a CHAR(10) column, MySQL appends eight spaces to the string so it contains 10 characters.

You use the VARCHAR data type to store *variable-length strings*. Data stored using this data type occupies only the number of bytes needed to store the string plus an extra byte to store the length of the string. This data type is typically used to define columns whose lengths vary from one row to the next. For example, the vendor_name column in the Vendors table is defined as VARCHAR(50) because the length of each vendor's name varies. As a result, you can save storage by using the VARCHAR type instead of the CHAR type for this column.

Although you typically store numeric values using numeric types, the character types may be a better choice for some numeric values. For example, you typically store zip codes, telephone numbers, and social security numbers in character columns even if they contain only numbers. That's because their values aren't used in numeric operations. In addition, if you store these numbers in numeric columns, MySQL may strip leading zeroes in some situations, which isn't what you want.

In this figure, the first five examples use single quotes to specify a string literal. However, the sixth example uses double quotes to specify a string literal. This allows the string literal to include a single quote, and it shows that you can

The character types

Type	Bytes	Description
CHAR(M)	M	Fixed-length strings of character data where M is the number of characters, between 0 and 255.
VARCHAR(M)	L+1	Variable-length strings of character data where M is the maximum number of characters, between 0 and 255. The number of bytes used to store the string is equal to length of the string (L) plus one byte to record its length.

How the character types work

Data type	Original value	Value stored	Bytes used
CHAR(2)	'CA'	'CA'	2
CHAR(10)	'CA'	'CA '	10
VARCHAR(10)	'CA'	'CA'	3
VARCHAR(20)	'California'	'California'	11
VARCHAR(20)	'New York'	'New York'	9
VARCHAR(20)	"Murach's MySQL"	"Murach's MySQL"	15

length of string + 1 (handwritten annotation)

Description

- The CHAR type is used for *fixed-length strings*. A column with this type uses the same amount of storage for each value regardless of the actual length of the string.

- The VARCHAR type is used for *variable-length strings*. A column with this type uses a varying amount of storage for each value depending on the length of the string.

- By default, the CHAR and VARCHAR types use the *latin1 character set*, which is a *single-byte character set*. This character set supports all of the characters that are used in English and by most western European languages.

- To learn how to change the default character set to a *multiple-byte character set* such as the *UTF-8 character set*, please see chapter 11. If you do that, the number of bytes per character increases, usually to 2 bytes per character. However, the UTF-8 format provides for all characters in most languages by providing support for all of the characters in the *Unicode standard*.

Figure 8-2   The character types

use single or double quotes for string literals. Although it's common to use single quotes, double quotes are useful if you need to include a single quote in the string.

The integer types

Figure 8-3 shows the *integer types*, which are numbers that don't include a decimal point. The integer data types differ in the amount of storage they use and the range of values they can store. Since the INT type can store a wide range of numbers and only requires 4 bytes of storage, it's the most commonly used of the integer types.

By default, the integer types can store positive and negative numbers. However, you can include the UNSIGNED attribute for an integer type to prevent negative values from being stored in the column. In that case, the range of acceptable positive values for the column is doubled.

If the ZEROFILL attribute for the integer is set, the UNSIGNED attribute is automatically set, and the integer is displayed with zeroes padded from the left, up to the maximum display size. For the INT type, for instance, the maximum display size is 10 digits. If the default display size is too wide, you can specify a smaller display size by coding it in parentheses after the data type. In this figure, for instance, the last example specifies a display size of 4 digits. This only affects how MySQL displays the value, not how it stores the value.

The INTEGER type is a synonym for the INT type. As a result, you can use these types interchangeably. However, it's a common programming practice to use INT as an abbreviation for INTEGER.

The BOOL and BOOLEAN types are synonyms for TINYINT(1). When you work with these types, you can use a value of 0 to store false values and a value of 1 to store true values. To make that more intuitive, you can use the FALSE keyword, which is an alias for 0, and the TRUE keyword, which is an alias for 1.

can use aliases instead

The integer types

Type	Bytes	Value ranges
BIGINT	8	Signed: -9,223,372,036,854,775,808 to 9,223,372,036,854,775,807 Unsigned: 0 to 18,446,744,073,709,551,615
INT	4	Signed: -2,147,483,648 to 2,147,483,647 Unsigned: 0 to 4,294,967,295
MEDIUMINT	3	Signed: -8,388,608 5to 8,388,607 Unsigned: 0 and 16,777,215
SMALLINT	2	Signed: -32,768 and 32,767 Unsigned: 0 and 65,535
TINYINT	1	Signed: -128 and 127 Unsigned: 0 and 255

How the UNSIGNED and ZEROFILL attributes work

Data type	Original value	Value stored	Value displayed
INT	99	99	99
INT	-99	-99	-99
INT UNSIGNED	99	99	99
INT UNSIGNED	-99	ERROR	ERROR
INT ZEROFILL	99	99	0000000099
INT(4) ZEROFILL	99	99	0099

Description

- The *integer types* store numbers without any digits to the right of the decimal point.
- If the UNSIGNED attribute for the integer is set, it changes the range of acceptable values and prevents storing negative values in the column.
- If the ZEROFILL attribute for the integer is set, MySQL displays the integer with zeroes padded from the left, up to the maximum display size.
- If the ZEROFILL attribute is set, MySQL automatically sets the UNSIGNED attribute.
- To specify a display size, you can code it in parentheses after the data type. This only affects how MySQL displays the value, not how it stores the value.
- The INTEGER type is a synonym for the INT type.
- The BOOL and BOOLEAN types are synonyms for TINYINT(1). You can use these types to store TRUE and FALSE values, where 1 represents a true value and 0 represents a false value.

Figure 8-3   The integer types

The fixed-point and floating-point types

Figure 8-4 presents the data types for storing real numbers, which are numbers that have digits to the right of the decimal point. To start, you can use the DECIMAL type to store *fixed-point numbers*, which are numbers that have a fixed number of digits to the right of the decimal point.

The number of digits a value has to the right of the decimal point is called its *scale*, and the total number of digits is called its *precision*. You can customize the precision and scale of the DECIMAL type so they're right for the data to be stored. For instance, if you need to store monetary values, it's common to use two digits to the right of the decimal place as shown in the first three examples.

When you use the DECIMAL type, MySQL uses a varying number of bytes to store the value. In general, it packs 9 digits into 4 bytes. However, it stores the digits to the left and right of the decimal point separately, and it can use less than 4 bytes if there are less than 9 digits. As a result, DECIMAL(9, 2) requires 5 bytes, while DECIMAL(18, 9) requires 8 bytes. For more details about how this works, you can check the MySQL Reference Manual.

In contrast to the DECIMAL type, the **DOUBLE** and **FLOAT** types store *floating-point numbers*. These data types provide for very large and very small numbers, but with a limited number of *significant digits*. The FLOAT type can be used to store a *single-precision number*, which provides for numbers with up to 7 significant digits. And the DOUBLE type can be used to store a *double-precision number*, which provides for numbers with up to 15 significant digits.

To express the value of a floating-point number, you can use *scientific notation*. To use this notation, you type the letter E followed by a power of 10. For instance, 3.65E+9 is equal to 3.65×10^9, or 3,650,000,000. Conversely, 3.65E-9 is equal to 3.65×10^{-9}, or 0.00000000365. If you have a mathematical background, of course, you're already familiar with this notation.

Because the precision of the integer types and the DECIMAL type is exact, these data types are considered *exact numeric types*. In contrast, the DOUBLE and FLOAT types are considered *approximate numeric types* because they may not represent a value exactly. That can happen, for example, when a number is rounded to the appropriate number of significant digits. In this figure, for instance, the last example shows that the FLOAT type rounds the original value and only stores 7 significant digits. For business applications, you typically use the exact numeric types, as there's seldom the need to work with the very large and very small numbers that the floating-point data types are designed for. However, for scientific applications, you may sometimes need to use the DOUBLE and FLOAT types.

The DECIMAL, DOUBLE, and FLOAT types have numerous synonyms. Sometimes these synonyms are helpful because they make it easier to work with data from other databases. However, when working with a MySQL database, most programmers use the DECIMAL, DOUBLE, and FLOAT types.

When you work with real numbers, you can use the UNSIGNED and ZEROFILL attributes. These attributes work similarly to the way they do with integer types.

The fixed-point type

Type	Bytes	Description
DECIMAL(M, D)	Vary	Fixed-precision numbers where M specifies the maximum number of total digits (the precision) and D specifies the number of digits to the right of the decimal (the scale). M can range from 1 to 65. D can range from 0 to 30 but can't be larger than M. The default is 0.

The floating-point types

Type	Bytes	Description
DOUBLE	8	Double-precision floating-point numbers from -1.7976×10^{308} to 1.7976×10^{308}.
FLOAT	4	Single-precision floating-point numbers from -3.4028×10^{38} to 3.4028×10^{38}.

How the fixed-point (exact) and floating-point (approximate) types work

Data type	Original value	Value stored	Bytes used
DECIMAL(9,2)	1.2	1.20	5
DECIMAL(9,2)	1234567.89	1234567.89	5
DECIMAL(9,2)	-1234567.89	-1234567.89	5
DECIMAL(18,9)	1234567.89	1234567.890000000	8
DOUBLE	1234567.89	1234567.89	8
FLOAT	1234567.89	1234570	4

Description

- *Real numbers* can include digits to the right of the decimal point. The *precision* of a real number indicates the total number of digits that can be stored, and the *scale* indicates the number of digits that can be stored to the right of the decimal point.

- The DECIMAL type is considered an *exact numeric type* because its precision is exact.

- The DOUBLE and FLOAT types store *floating-point numbers*, which have a limited number of *significant digits*. These data types are considered *approximate numeric data types* because they may not represent a value exactly.

- If the UNSIGNED attribute for a real number is set, it prevents storing negative values in the column but does not affect the range of acceptable values.

- If the ZEROFILL attribute for a real number is set, the number is displayed with zeroes padded from the left, and the UNSIGNED attribute is automatically set.

- The DEC, NUMERIC, and FIXED types are synonyms for the DECIMAL type.

- The REAL and DOUBLE PRECISION types are synonyms for the DOUBLE type.

Figure 8-4   The fixed-point and floating-point types

The date and time types

Part 1 of figure 8-5 presents the five date and time types supported by MySQL. You can use the DATE type to store a date without a time. You can use the TIME type to store a time without a date. And you can use either the DATETIME or TIMESTAMP types to store both a date and a time.

You typically use the TIMESTAMP type to keep track of when a row was inserted or last updated. For example, you might use this type to keep track of the entries on a blog. MySQL makes that easy by automatically setting the TIMESTAMP column to the current date and time whenever a row is inserted or updated. If that's not what you want, you can use the DATETIME type instead.

The problem with the TIMESTAMP type is that it can only store dates up to the year 2038. This is known as the *year 2038 problem*, the *Y2K38 problem*, and the *Unix Millennium bug*. As a result, if you want your database to be able to store dates that go beyond 2038, you should use the DATETIME type instead of the TIMESTAMP type. Otherwise, you can use the TIMESTAMP type since it only requires 4 bytes to store a TIMESTAMP value, compared to 8 bytes for a DATETIME value.

If you need to store a year without any other temporal data, you can use the YEAR type. By default, the YEAR type stores 4-digit years from 1901 to 2155. Usually, that's what you want. However, if necessary, you can use the YEAR(2) type to store a 2-digit year.

The date and time types

Type	Bytes	Description
DATE	3	Dates from January 1, 1000 through December 31, 9999. The default format for entry and display is "yyyy-mm-dd".
TIME	3	Times in the range -838:59:59 through 838:59:59. The default format for display and entry is "hh:mm:ss".
DATETIME	8	Combination date and time from midnight January 1, 1970 to December 31, 9999. The default format for display and entry is "yyyy-mm-dd hh:mm:ss".
TIMESTAMP	4	Combination date and time from midnight January 1, 1970 to the year 2037. The default format is "yyyy-mm-dd hh:mm:ss".
YEAR[(2|4)]	1	Years in 2-digit or 4-digit format. The default is 4-digit format. In 4-digit format, allowable values are from 1901 to 2155. In 2-digit format, from (19)70 to (20)69.

Description

- A column of TIMESTAMP type is automatically updated to the current date and time when a row is inserted or updated. If a table has multiple TIMESTAMP columns, only the first one is updated automatically.

- The TIMESTAMP type can only store dates up to the year 2038. This is known as the *year 2038 problem*, the *Y2K38 problem*, and the *Unix Millennium bug*. To fix this problem, use the DATETIME type instead of the TIMESTAMP type and update the value manually as needed.

Figure 8-5   The date and time types (part 1 of 2)

When you work with the date and time types, you need to know how to code date and time literals. Part 2 of figure 8-5 shows how to do that. The default date format for MySQL is "yyyy-mm-dd", which is why we've used this format in most of the examples in this book. By default, MySQL doesn't support other common date formats such as "mm/dd/yy". If you attempt to use an unsupported format, MySQL returns an error message.

You also need to be aware of the two-digit year cutoff that's defined on your system. When you code a two-digit year, the two-digit year cutoff determines how MySQL interprets the year. By default, MySQL interprets the years 00 through 69 as 2000 through 2069, and it interprets the years 70 through 99 as 1970 through 1999. Usually, that's what you want. However, the two-digit year cutoff can be modified if necessary. In general, it's considered a good coding practice to use four-digit years. That way, you can be sure that MySQL is interpreting the year correctly.

MySQL interprets any punctuation character in a literal as a delimiter between date parts or time parts. If you don't use any delimiters, you can code the value as a numeric literal. In that case, you don't need to use single quotes.

When storing a date in a DATE column, the values are loosely checked for valid data. For instance, months must be in the range 0-12 and days must be in the range 0-31. For illegal dates, such as February 31, MySQL returns an error. However, MySQL allows you to store unconventional date values, such as "2011-12-00", which represents a month and year without a specific day.

The default time format for MySQL is "hh:mm:ss", using a 24-hour clock. Many of the same rules for coding date literals also apply to time literals. For instance, you can use any punctuation character as a delimiter. Similarly, for valid values, you can omit the delimiters. In that case, you can use a numeric literal (no quotes) instead of a string literal (quotes). Finally, MySQL checks times for validity. For illegal times, such as "19:61:11", MySQL returns an error.

The default date/time format for MySQL is a combination of the date and time formats. Most of the rules for coding date/time literals are a combination of the rules for coding date and time literals. In addition, if you don't specify a time when storing a TIMESTAMP or DATETIME value, the time defaults to 00:00:00, which is midnight.

How MySQL interprets literal date/time values

Literal value	Value stored in DATE column
'2011-08-15'	2011-08-15
'2011-8-15'	2011-08-15
'11-8-15'	2011-08-15
'20110815'	2011-08-15
20110815	2011-08-15
'2011.08.15'	2011-08-15
'11/8/15'	2011-08-15
'8/15/11'	ERROR
'2011-02-31'	ERROR

Literal value	Value stored in TIME column
'7:32'	07:32:00
'19:32:11'	19:32:11
'193211'	19:32:11
193211	19:32:11
'19:61:11'	ERROR

Literal value	Value stored in DATETIME or TIMESTAMP column
'2011-08-15 19:32:11'	2011-08-15 19:32:11
'2011-08-15'	2011-08-15 00:00:00

Description

- You can specify date and time values by coding a literal value. In most cases, you enclose the literal value in single quotes.

- For dates, MySQL uses the "yyyy-mm-dd" format. For times, MySQL uses the "hh:mm:ss" format, using a 24-hour clock.

- By default, MySQL does not support common date formats used by other systems such as "mm/dd/yy" and "mon/dd/yyyy".

 • By default, MySQL interprets 2-digit years from 00 to 69 as 2000 to 2069 and the years from 70 to 99 as 1970 to 1999.

- MySQL interprets any punctuation character as a delimiter between date parts. If you don't use any delimiters, you can code the value as a numeric literal without quotes.

- If you don't specify a time when storing a DATETIME or TIMESTAMP value, MySQL stores a time value of 00:00:00 (12:00 midnight).

- If you don't specify seconds when storing a TIME value, MySQL stores 00 for the seconds.

- When storing date and time values, MySQL loosely checks the values to make sure they are valid. For example, months must be in the range 0-12, days must be in the range 0-31, and so on. If MySQL determines that a date or time isn't valid, it returns an error.

- MySQL 5.5 is stricter than previous versions of MySQL for storing date and time values. If MySQL can't interpret a value, it returns an error or a warning.

Figure 8-5   The date and time types (part 2 of 2)

The ENUM and SET types

The ENUM and SET types can be considered character data types since they allow you to restrict the values for a column to a limited set of strings as shown in figure 8-6. However, MySQL internally stores these values as integers, which reduces the number of bytes needed to store each string.

The main difference between the ENUM and SET types is that an ENUM column can store exactly one value, but a SET column can store zero, one, or up to 64 different values. In other words, an ENUM column can consist of only one member in a set of values, while the SET column may consist of any, or all, members in a set.

You can use the ENUM type to store values that are mutually exclusive, such as Yes, No, or Maybe. In other words, you can use the ENUM type to represent a choice of one value, but not two. For example, delivery or pickup; cash, credit, or debit; small, medium, or large; paper or plastic; soup or salad, although I suppose you might want both soup and salad. For that, you could use a SET column.

You can use a SET column when you want to choose more than one value. For example, the toppings on a pizza, the software on a computer, or the features of a car could be SET values.

The acceptable values for an ENUM or SET column are defined when the table is created. An ENUM column can specify up to 65,535 acceptable values. However, a SET column is limited to 64 values.

To store a value in an ENUM column, you code a single text string. If the string is one of the acceptable values for the column, MySQL stores that value. Otherwise, MySQL assigns an empty string to the column.

When you add a row to a table that contains an ENUM column, MySQL assigns a default value to that column if you don't explicitly specify a value. If the column allows null values, MySQL assigns a null value to the column. If the column doesn't allow null values, MySQL assigns the first value in the set of acceptable values. If you want MySQL to use a specific value as the default value, then, you'll want to code that value as the first value in the set.

To store values in a SET column, you code a single string with one or more values separated by commas. Then, MySQL stores each acceptable value and ignores any other values. Since commas are used to separate values, you can't use commas within a value when you define the SET column.

When storing multiple values in a SET column, the order of the values doesn't matter. That's because MySQL stores the values in the same order as in the column definition. It also doesn't matter if you repeat a value because MySQL doesn't store duplicate values.

The ENUM and SET types

Type	Bytes	Description
ENUM	1-2	Stores one value selected from a list of acceptable values.
SET	1-8	Stores zero or more values selected from a list of acceptable values.

large list of possible values, but only 1 value possible

smaller list, but can include 0, 1, or more, all

How values are stored in ENUM columns

Value	Stored in column ENUM ('Yes', 'No', 'Maybe')
'Yes'	'Yes'
'No'	'No'
'Maybe'	'Maybe'
'Possibly'	''

How values are stored in SET columns

Value	Stored in column SET ('Pepperoni', 'Mushrooms', 'Olives')
'Pepperoni'	'Pepperoni'
'Mushrooms'	'Mushrooms'
'Pepperoni, Bacon'	'Pepperoni'
'Olives, Pepperoni'	'Pepperoni, Olives'

Description

- The ENUM and SET types can be used to restrict the values that you store to a limited set of values. The ENUM column can take on exactly one value, but a SET column can take on zero, one, or up to 64 different values.
- You can define the set of acceptable values for an ENUM or SET column when you create a table. An ENUM column can have up to 65,535 acceptable values, but a SET column is limited to 64 acceptable values.
- To specify a value for an ENUM column, you code a single text string. If the string contains an acceptable value, that value is stored in the column. Otherwise, the column is assigned an empty string.
- If you don't specify a value for an ENUM column when you insert a row, MySQL assigns a default value that depends on whether the column allows null values. If the column allows null values, MySQL assigns a null value to the column. If it doesn't allow null values, MySQL assigns the first value in the set of acceptable values to the column.
- To specify values for a SET column, you code a single string with the values separated by commas. Each acceptable value is stored in the column, and any other values are ignored.
- When you store values in a SET column, MySQL stores the values using the order specified in the column definition, and it does not store duplicate values.

Figure 8-6   The ENUM and SET types

The large object types

Figure 8-7 presents the large object (LOB) types. These data types are designed to store large amounts of binary or character data.

The *BLOB* (*Binary Large Object*) types store strings of binary data. This data type is often used to store images, sounds, and video. However, the BLOB types can be used to store any type of binary data, including the binary data that's normally stored in application files such as PDF files or Word files.

The TEXT types work similarly to the BLOB types, but they store strings of characters. As a result, in other database systems, they are sometimes referred to as *character large object* (*CLOB*) types. These data types can be used to store large amounts of character data including data that's normally stored in text or XML files.

To read and write data from a column defined with a BLOB or TEXT type, you typically use another programming language such as Java or PHP. As a result, we don't cover these types in this book. However, if you want to use these types, you can learn more about how to do that by reading about them in the MySQL Reference Manual.

The large object types

Type	Bytes	Description
LONGBLOB	L+4	Variable-length strings of binary data up to 4GB in length (L).
MEDIUMBLOB	L+3	Variable-length strings of binary data up to 16MB in length (L).
BLOB	L+2	Variable-length strings of binary data up to 65KB in length (L).
TINYBLOB	L+1	Variable-length strings of binary data up to 255 bytes in length (L).
LARGETEXT	L+4	Variable-length strings of characters up to 4GB in length (L).
MEDIUMTEXT	L+3	Variable-length strings of characters up to 16MB in length (L).
TEXT	L+2	Variable-length strings of characters up to 65KB in length (L).
TINYTEXT	L+1	Variable-length strings of characters up to 255 bytes in length (L).

Description

- The BLOB types store strings of binary data and are referred to as *binary large object* (*BLOB*) types.
- The TEXT types store strings of character data and are sometimes referred to as *character large object* (*CLOB*) types.

Figure 8-7   The large object types

How to convert data

As you work with the various data types, you'll find that you frequently need to convert data from one type to another. Although MySQL performs many conversions automatically, it doesn't always perform the conversion the way you want. Because of that, you need to be aware of how data conversion works, and you need to know when and how to specify the type of conversion you want.

How implicit data conversion works

Before MySQL can operate on two values, it must convert those values to the same data type. To understand how this works, consider the three expressions shown in figure 8-8.

In the first example, the second column joins a string literal of "$" to the invoice_total column, which is defined with the DECIMAL type. As a result, MySQL converts the DECIMAL value to its corresponding characters, appends those characters to the $ character, and stores them as a CHAR type.

In the second example, the second column divides the INT literal of 989319 by the VARCHAR type that's stored in the invoice_number column. As a result, MySQL attempts to convert the invoice_number column to an INT type before it performs the division operation. If the invoice_number column contains only numbers, this works as you would expect. However, if the invoice_number column contains letters or special characters, MySQL converts only the numeric characters that precede the letters or special characters. For example, in the first row in the result set, MySQL only converts the numbers before the dash in the invoice_number column.

In the third example, the second column adds an INT literal of 1 to the invoice_date column, which is defined with the DATE type. As a result, MySQL converts the DATE value in the invoice_date column to an INT value before it performs the addition. In the result set, the first column uses the DATE type, which includes dashes between the parts of the date. The second column, on the other hand, uses the INT type, which doesn't include dashes between parts of the date.

When MySQL performs a conversion automatically, it's called an *implicit conversion*. However, if you want to control how a conversion is performed, you can code an *explicit conversion*. To do that, you can use the CAST and CONVERT functions shown in the next figure.

SELECT statements that implicitly convert data from one type to another

Number to string

```
SELECT invoice_total, CONCAT('$', invoice_total)
FROM invoices
```

invoice_total	CONCAT('$', invoice_total)
3813.33	$3813.33
40.20	$40.20

String to number

```
SELECT invoice_number, 989319/invoice_number
FROM invoices
```

invoice_number	989319/invoice_number
989319-457	1
263253241	0.0037580505988908225
963253234	0.0010270601385803393

Date to number

```
SELECT invoice_date, invoice_date + 1
FROM invoices
```

invoice_date	invoice_date + 1
2011-04-08	20110409
2011-04-10	20110411

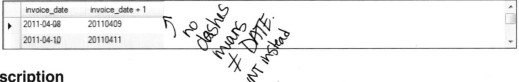

Description

- When MySQL automatically converts one data type to another, it's known as an *implicit conversion*.

- If you code an expression that involves values with different data types, MySQL implicitly converts them when it evaluates the expression.

- If you use a string in a numeric expression, MySQL attempts to convert the string to a number before evaluating the expression. If the string starts with a letter or special character, MySQL returns a value of zero. If it starts with a number, MySQL returns that number and each successive number until it encounters a letter or special character.

- If you add or subtract an integer to or from a DATE value, MySQL implicitly converts the DATE value to an integer value.

Figure 8-8   How implicit data conversion works

How to convert data using the CAST and CONVERT functions

Because MySQL's rules for implicit conversion are more flexible than those for other SQL databases, you generally don't need to explicitly convert data from one type to another. However, whenever necessary, you can use the CAST and CONVERT functions to convert, or *cast*, an expression to the data type you specify as shown in figure 8-9. Since CAST is an ANSI-standard function, it is used more frequently than CONVERT, but both functions work equally well for most tasks.

The first SELECT statement shows how to use the CAST function. Here, the fourth column in the result set casts the DATE values of the invoice_date column to CHAR values. Although the fourth column looks the same as the second column, it stores a CHAR value, not a DATE value. In this case, MySQL converted all of the characters in the DATE value to a CHAR value. If that's not what you want, you can truncate the number of characters in the result by specifying a value less than 10 after the CHAR keyword.

The fifth column in the result set casts the DECIMAL values in the invoice_total column to signed INT values. Before the digits to the right of the decimal point are dropped, the numbers are rounded to the nearest whole number. For brevity, this statement only uses the SIGNED keyword. For clarity, it could also include the optional INTEGER keyword immediately after the SIGNED keyword.

The second SELECT statement in this figure shows how to use the CONVERT function. If you compare this statement to the first SELECT statement, you'll see that it uses a slightly different syntax. However, both SELECT statements accomplish the same task.

The syntax of the CAST function

```
CAST(expression AS cast_type)
```

The syntax of the CONVERT function

```
CONVERT(expression, cast_type)
```

The cast types you can use in the CAST and CONVERT functions

Cast type	Description
CHAR[(N)]	A string of characters where N is the maximum number of characters.
DATE	A DATE value.
DATETIME	A DATETIME value.
TIME	A TIME value.
SIGNED [INTEGER]	A signed INT value. The INTEGER keyword is optional.
UNSIGNED [INTEGER]	An unsigned INT value. The INTEGER keyword is optional.
DECIMAL[(M[,D])]	A DECIMAL value where M specifies the precision and D specifies the scale.

A statement that uses the CAST function

```
SELECT invoice_id, invoice_date, invoice_total,
    CAST(invoice_date AS CHAR(10)) AS char_date,
    CAST(invoice_total AS SIGNED) AS integer_total
FROM invoices
```

invoice_id	invoice_date	invoice_total	char_date	integer_total
1	2011-04-08	3813.33	2011-04-08	3813
2	2011-04-10	40.20	2011-04-10	40
3	2011-04-13	138.75	2011-04-13	139

A statement that uses the CONVERT function

```
SELECT invoice_id, invoice_date, invoice_total,
    CONVERT(invoice_date, CHAR(10)) AS char_date,
    CONVERT(invoice_total, SIGNED) AS integer_total
FROM invoices
```

invoice_id	invoice_date	invoice_total	char_date	integer_total
1	2011-04-08	3813.33	2011-04-08	3813
2	2011-04-10	40.20	2011-04-10	40
3	2011-04-13	138.75	2011-04-13	139

Description

- You can use the CAST or CONVERT function to perform an *explicit conversion*. This allows you to convert, or *cast*, an expression from one data type to another.
- CAST is an ANSI-standard function and is used more frequently than CONVERT.

Figure 8-9   How to convert data using the CAST and CONVERT functions

How to convert data using the FORMAT and CHAR functions

In addition to the CAST and CONVERT functions, MySQL provides some functions that perform other types of data conversion. In particular, it provides the FORMAT and CHAR functions shown in figure 8-10.

You can use the FORMAT function to convert a number to a string of characters. This function uses commas to group the thousands to the left of the decimal point. This makes large numbers easier to read. In addition, the FORMAT function rounds the number to the specified number of decimal places. If you specify 0 decimal places, the function returns a string that doesn't include a decimal point.

The CHAR function returns a binary string for each specified integer. This function is typically used to output ASCII control characters that can't be typed on your keyboard. The three most common control characters are presented in this figure. These characters can be used to format output so it's easy to read. In this figure, for example, the SELECT statement uses the CHAR(13) and CHAR(10) control characters to start new lines after the vendor name and vendor address in the output.

The FORMAT and CHAR functions

Function	Description
`FORMAT(number,decimal)`	Converts the specified number to a character string with grouped digits separated by commas, rounded to the specified number of decimal digits. If *decimal* is zero, then the decimal point is omitted.
`CHAR(value1[,value2]...)`	Converts one or more numbers to a binary string. Each number is interpreted as an integer between 0 and 255.

The FORMAT function

Function	Result
`FORMAT(1234567.8901,2)`	`1,234,567.89`
`FORMAT(1234.56,4)`	`1,234.5600`
`FORMAT(1234.56,0)`	`1,235`

The CHAR function for common control characters

Function	Control character
`CHAR(9)`	Tab
`CHAR(10)`	Line feed
`CHAR(13)`	Carriage return

A statement that uses the CHAR function to format output

```
SELECT CONCAT(vendor_name, CHAR(13,10), vendor_address1, CHAR(13,10),
       vendor_city, ', ', vendor_state, ' ', vendor_zip_code)
FROM vendors
WHERE vendor_id = 1;
```

```
US Postal Service
Attn:  Supt. Window Services
Madison, WI 53707
```

Description

- The CHAR function is typically used to insert control characters into a character string.

Figure 8-10   How to convert data using the FORMAT and CHAR functions

Perspective

In this chapter, you learned about the different MySQL data types. In addition, you learned how to use some functions to convert data from one type to another. In the next chapter, you'll learn some of the additional functions for working with data.

Terms

data type
character data types
string data
text data
numeric data types
integer
real number
date and time data types
date/time data types
temporal data types
large object (LOB) data types
spatial data types
global positioning system (GPS)
single-byte character set
latin1 character set
byte
bit
ASCII (American Standard Code
    for Information Interchange)
multiple-byte character set
UTF-8 character set
Unicode standard

fixed-length string
variable-length string
integer types
fixed-point number
scale
precision
floating-point number
significant digits
single-precision number
double-precision number
scientific notation
exact numeric types
approximate numeric types
year 2038 problem
Y2K38 problem
Unix Millennium bug
BLOB (Binary Large Object)
character large object (CLOB)
implicit conversion
explicit conversion
cast

Exercises

1. Write a SELECT statement that returns these columns from the Invoices table:

    The invoice_total column

    A column that uses the FORMAT function to return the invoice_total column with 1 digit to the right of the decimal point

    A column that uses the CONVERT function to return the invoice_total column as an integer

    A column that uses the CAST function to return the invoice_total column as an integer

2. Write a SELECT statement that returns these columns from the Invoices table:

    The invoice_date column

    A column that uses the CAST function to return the invoice_date column with its full date and time

    A column that uses the CAST function to return the invoice_date column with just the day and the month

9

How to use functions

In chapter 3, you were introduced to some of the scalar functions that you can use in a SELECT statement. Now, this chapter expands on that coverage by presenting many more of the scalar functions. When you complete this chapter, you'll have a thorough understanding of the functions that you can use with MySQL.

How to work with string data **242**
A summary of the string functions 242
Examples that use string functions 244
How to sort by a string column that contains numbers 246
How to parse a string 248

How to work with numeric data **250**
How to use the numeric functions 250
How to search for floating-point numbers 252

How to work with date/time data **254**
How to get the current date and time 254
How to parse dates and times with date/time functions 256
How to parse dates and times with the EXTRACT function 258
How to format dates and times 260
How to perform calculations on dates and times 262
How to search for a date 264
How to search for a time 266

Other functions you should know about **268**
How to use the CASE function 268
How to use the IF, IFNULL, and COALESCE functions 270

Perspective **272**

How to work with string data

This topic shows how to use the most useful functions that MySQL provides for working with string data. In addition, it shows how to solve two common problems that can occur when you work with string data.

A summary of the string functions

Figure 9-1 summarizes the most useful string functions that are available with MySQL. To start, it summarizes the CONCAT function that you learned about in chapter 3. Then, it summarizes a related function, the CONCAT_WS function, that you can use to specify a separator string that goes between the other strings that you are concatenating. (WS stands for *with separator*.)

The next three functions allow you to remove, or *trim*, characters from the beginning or end of the string. To remove spaces from the left or right side of a string, you can use the LTRIM or RTRIM functions. To remove spaces from both sides of a string, you can use the TRIM function. You can also use the TRIM function to remove characters other than the space character from the left or right side of a string.

To find the number of characters in a string, you can use the LENGTH function. However, this function counts spaces at the beginning of the string (leading spaces), but not spaces at the end of the string (trailing spaces). As a result, you need to take this into account if the string ends with spaces.

To locate the first occurrence of a substring within another string, you can use the LOCATE function. This function returns an integer value that indicates the position of the substring. Note that you can start the search at a position other than the beginning of the string by including the optional start argument. This function is often used within other functions such as the SUBSTRING function.

The next four functions return a substring of the specified string. To start, you can use the LEFT and RIGHT functions to get the specified number of characters from the left or right side of a string. You can also use the SUBSTRING_INDEX function to get characters from the left or right side of a string. This function returns the characters before or after a delimiter string occurs the specified number of times. Or, you can use the SUBSTRING function to get the specified number of characters from anywhere in a string.

You can use the next two functions to modify the specified string. First, you can use the REPLACE function to replace a substring within the string with another substring. Second, you can use the INSERT function to insert another string into the string.

Finally, you can use the last seven functions to transform the string in other ways. To start, you can use the REVERSE function to reverse the order of the characters in a string. You can use the LOWER and UPPER functions to convert the characters in a string to lower or uppercase. You can use the LPAD and RPAD functions to pad a string on the left or right until it's a specified length. You can use the SPACE function to return a string that repeats the space character the specified number of times. And you can use the REPEAT function to repeat any string the specified number of times.

Some of the string functions

Function	Description
`CONCAT(str1[,str2]...)`	Concatenates the specified strings. If one of the strings is null, then the result is null.
`CONCAT_WS(sep,str1[,str2]...)`	Concatenates the strings with the specified *separator* string added in between. If one of the strings is null or empty, it's ignored. If the separator is null, then the result is null.
`LTRIM(str)`	Returns the string with any leading spaces removed.
`RTRIM(str)`	Returns the string with any trailing spaces removed.
`TRIM([[BOTH|LEADING|TRAILING]` `[remove] FROM] str)`	Returns the string without leading or trailing occurrences of the specified *remove* string. If remove string is omitted, spaces are removed.
`LENGTH(str)`	Returns the number of characters in the string.
`LOCATE(find,search[,start])`	Returns the position of the first occurrence of the *find* string in the *search* string, starting at the specified *start* position. If the *start* position is omitted, the search starts at the beginning of the string. If the string isn't found, the function returns zero.
`LEFT(str,length)`	Returns the specified number of characters from the beginning of the string.
`RIGHT(str,length)`	Returns the specified number of characters from the end of the string.
`SUBSTRING_INDEX(str,delimiter,` `count)`	Returns the substring before the specified number of occurrences of the specified *delimiter* string. If *count* is positive, it returns from the beginning of the string. If *count* is negative, it returns from the end of the string.
`SUBSTRING(str,start[,length])`	Returns the specified number of characters from the string starting at the specified *start* position. If *length* is omitted, it returns from the start position to the end of the string.
`REPLACE(search,find,replace)`	Returns the *search* string with all occurrences of the *find* string replaced with the *replace* string.
`INSERT(str,start,length,insert)`	Returns the string with the specified *insert* string inserted into it starting at the specified *start* position and replacing the specified *length*.
`REVERSE(str)`	Returns the string with the characters in reverse order.
`LOWER(str)`	Returns the string converted to lowercase letters.
`UPPER(str)`	Returns the string converted to uppercase letters.
`LPAD(str,length,pad)`	Returns the string padded on the left with the specified *pad* string until it's the specified *length*. If the string is longer than the length, it's truncated.
`RPAD(str,length,pad)`	Returns the string padded on the right with the specified *pad* string until it's the specified *length*. If the string is longer than the length, it's truncated.
`SPACE(count)`	Returns the space character repeated *count* times.
`REPEAT(str,count)`	Returns the specified string repeated *count* times.

Figure 9-1   A summary of the string functions

Examples that use string functions

Figure 9-2 presents examples of most of the string functions. If you study these examples, you shouldn't have any trouble figuring out how they work. If you're confused by any of them, though, you can refer back to the previous figure to check the syntax and results.

The SELECT statement shown at the bottom of this figure shows how you can use the CONCAT_WS and RIGHT functions to format columns in a result set. In this case, the second column uses the CONCAT_WS function to retrieve two columns from the Vendors table and separate them with a comma and a space.

The third column in the result set lists the vendor's phone number without an area code. To accomplish that, this column uses the RIGHT function to extract the eight rightmost characters of the vendor_phone column. This assumes that the area code is enclosed in parentheses and that all of the phone numbers are stored in the same format. Since the vendor_phone column is defined with the VARCHAR(50) data type, this isn't necessarily the case.

This SELECT statement also shows how you can use a function in a WHERE clause. This WHERE clause uses the LEFT function to select only those rows that begin with an area code of "(559". Again, this assumes that the area code is enclosed in parentheses and that the phone numbers are all in the same format.

String function examples

Function	Result
CONCAT('Last', 'First')	'LastFirst'
CONCAT_WS(', ', 'Last', 'First')	'Last, First'
LTRIM(' MySQL ')	'MySQL '
RTRIM(' MySQL ')	' MySQL'
TRIM(' MySQL ')	'MySQL'
TRIM(BOTH '*' FROM '****MySQL****')	'MySQL'
LOWER('MySQL')	'mysql'
UPPER('ca')	'CA'
LEFT('MySQL', 3)	'MyS'
RIGHT('MySQL', 3)	'SQL'
SUBSTRING('(559) 555-1212', 7, 8)	'555-1212'
SUBSTRING_INDEX('http://www.murach.com', '.', -2)	'murach.com'
LENGTH('MySQL')	5
LENGTH(' MySQL ')	9
LOCATE('SQL', ' MySQL')	5
LOCATE('-', '(559) 555-1212')	10
REPLACE(RIGHT('(559) 555-1212', 13),') ', '-')	'559-555-1212'
INSERT("MySQL", 1, 0, "Murach's ")	"Murach's MySQL"
INSERT('MySQL', 1, 0, 'Murach''s ')	"Murach's MySQL"

A SELECT statement that uses three functions

```
SELECT vendor_name,
       CONCAT_WS(', ', vendor_contact_last_name,
                 vendor_contact_first_name) AS contact_name,
       RIGHT(vendor_phone, 8) AS phone
FROM vendors
WHERE LEFT(vendor_phone, 4) = '(559'
ORDER BY contact_name
```

vendor_name	contact_name	phone
Dristas Groom & McCormick	Aaronsen, Thom	555-8484
Yale Industrial Trucks-Fresno	Alexis, Alexandro	555-2993
Lou Gentile's Flower Basket	Anum, Trisha	555-6643
Pollstar	Aranovitch, Robert	555-2631

Figure 9-2   Examples that use string functions

How to sort by a string column that contains numbers

Figure 9-3 presents solutions to a common problem that can occur when you attempt to sort string data that's stored in a numeric column. To illustrate the problem, look at the first example in this figure. Here, the emp_id column in the String_Sample table, which contains numeric IDs, is defined with a character type. Because of that, when you sort by this column, the rows aren't in numeric sequence. That's because MySQL interprets the values as characters, not as numbers.

One way to solve this problem is to convert the values in the emp_id column to integers for sorting purposes. This is illustrated in the second SELECT statement in this figure, which uses the CAST function. As you can see, the rows are now sorted in numeric sequence. The third example is similar, but it implicitly casts the character values to integers by adding 0 to the values.

Another way to solve this problem is to pad the numbers with leading zeros or spaces, as shown in the last example. Here, the LPAD function is used to pad the emp_id column with zeros so the result always contains two columns. Then, the columns that start with a zero are sorted before the other columns, so the rows are returned in numeric sequence.

Of course, if you know that a column will always contain numbers, you'll typically define it with a numeric type. If that isn't possible, though, you can solve the sorting problem by using one of the techniques shown in this figure.

How to sort by a string column that contains numbers

Sorted by the emp_id column

```
SELECT *
FROM string_sample
ORDER BY emp_id
```

emp_id	emp_name
1	Lizbeth Darien
17	Lance Pinos-Potter
2	Darnell O'Sullivan
20	Jean Paul Renard
3	Alisha von Strump

Sorted by the emp_id column explicitly cast as an integer

```
SELECT *
FROM string_sample
ORDER BY CAST(emp_id AS SIGNED)
```

emp_id	emp_name
1	Lizbeth Darien
2	Darnell O'Sullivan
3	Alisha von Strump
17	Lance Pinos-Potter
20	Jean Paul Renard

Sorted by the emp_id column implicitly cast as an integer

```
SELECT *
FROM string_sample
ORDER BY emp_id + 0
```

emp_id	emp_name
1	Lizbeth Darien
2	Darnell O'Sullivan
3	Alisha von Strump
17	Lance Pinos-Potter
20	Jean Paul Renard

Sorted by the emp_id column after it has been padded with leading zeros

```
SELECT LPAD(emp_id, 2, '0') AS emp_id, emp_name
FROM string_sample
ORDER BY emp_id
```

emp_id	emp_name
01	Lizbeth Darien
02	Darnell O'Sullivan
03	Alisha von Strump
17	Lance Pinos-Potter
20	Jean Paul Renard

Description

- The emp_id column in the String_Sample table used in the examples above is defined with the type VARCHAR(3). However, this column contains numeric values.

Figure 9-3   How to sort by a string column that contains numbers

How to parse a string

Another problem you may encounter when working with string data occurs when two or more values are stored in the same string. For example, the emp_name column in the String_Sample table contains both a first and a last name. If you want to work with the first and last names independently, you have to parse the string using the string functions. Figure 9-4 shows how this works.

The first example uses the SUBSTRING_INDEX function to parse the first and last names. To start, the second column uses the SUBSTRING_INDEX function to return all characters from the start of the string in the emp_name column up to the first space in that column. Then, the third column uses the SUBSTRING_INDEX function to return all characters from the end of the string in the emp_name column up to the last space in that column. To do that, a negative value is coded for the count parameter.

Unfortunately, this example doesn't work correctly for all rows. In particular, the last name for the fifth row should probably be "von Strump" not "Strump". To solve this problem, you can sometimes use the SUBSTRING function as shown in the third example.

But first, it's helpful to understand how the LOCATE function works as illustrated by the second example. Here, the second column returns an integer value for the location of the first space. Then, the third column returns the location of the second space. To get the location of the second space, this LOCATE function uses a nested LOCATE function as its third parameter. This starts the search at the character after the first space.

The third example uses the SUBSTRING function to parse a string. To start, the second column uses the SUBSTRING and LOCATE functions to return all characters from the beginning of the string to the first space. Then, the third column uses the SUBSTRING and LOCATE functions to return all characters after the first space to the end of the string.

Unfortunately, this example also doesn't work correctly for all rows. In particular, the last name for the fourth row should probably be "Renard" not "Paul Renard". However, this example does return "von Strump" not "Strump" for the last row, which is probably correct.

As you review these examples, you can focus on how the string functions are used. As I've indicated, though, this code doesn't work correctly for all names. This illustrates the importance of designing a database so this type of problem doesn't occur. You'll learn more about that in the next chapter. For now, just realize that if a database is designed correctly, you won't have to worry about this type of problem. Instead, this problem should occur only if you're importing data from another file or database system.

How to use the SUBSTRING_INDEX function to parse a string

```
SELECT emp_name,
    SUBSTRING_INDEX(emp_name, ' ', 1) AS first_name,
    SUBSTRING_INDEX(emp_name, ' ', -1) AS last_name
FROM string_sample
```

emp_name	first_name	last_name
Lizbeth Darien	Lizbeth	Darien
Darnell O'Sullivan	Darnell	O'Sullivan
Lance Pinos-Potter	Lance	Pinos-Potter
Jean Paul Renard	Jean	Renard
Alisha von Strump	Alisha	Strump

How to use the LOCATE function to find a character in a string

```
SELECT emp_name,
    LOCATE(' ', emp_name) AS first_space,
    LOCATE(' ', emp_name, LOCATE(' ', emp_name) + 1) AS second_space
FROM string_sample
```

emp_name	first_space	second_space
Lizbeth Darien	8	0
Darnell O'Sullivan	8	0
Lance Pinos-Potter	6	0
Jean Paul Renard	5	10
Alisha von Strump	7	11

How to use the SUBSTRING function to parse a string

```
SELECT emp_name,
    SUBSTRING(emp_name, 1, LOCATE(' ', emp_name) - 1) AS first_name,
    SUBSTRING(emp_name, LOCATE(' ', emp_name) + 1) AS last_name
FROM string_sample
```

emp_name	first_name	last_name
Lizbeth Darien	Lizbeth	Darien
Darnell O'Sullivan	Darnell	O'Sullivan
Lance Pinos-Potter	Lance	Pinos-Potter
Jean Paul Renard	Jean	Paul Renard
Alisha von Strump	Alisha	von Strump

Description

- If a string consists of two or more components, you can parse it into its individual components. To do that, you can use the SUBSTRING_INDEX, SUBSTRING, and LOCATE functions.

Figure 9-4   How to parse a string

How to work with numeric data

In addition to the string functions, MySQL provides several functions for working with numeric data. Although you'll probably use only a couple of these functions regularly, you should be aware of them in case you ever need them.

How to use the numeric functions

Figure 9-5 summarizes some of the numeric functions that MySQL provides. The function you'll probably use most often is the ROUND function that you saw back in chapter 3. This function rounds a number to the precision specified by the length argument. Note that you can round the digits to the left of the decimal point by coding a negative value for this argument. However, you're more likely to code a positive number to round the digits to the right of the decimal point.

Another function that you might use regularly is the TRUNCATE function. This function works like the ROUND function, but it truncates the number instead of rounding to the nearest number. In other words, this function chops off the end of the number without doing any rounding. For example, if you round 19.99 to the nearest integer, you get a value of 20. However, if you truncate 19.99, you get a value of 19.

You can use the next two functions, CEILING and FLOOR, to get the smallest integer greater than or equal to a number and the largest integer less than or equal to a number. You can use the ABS function to get the absolute value of a number. And you can use the SIGN function to return a value that indicates if a number is positive, negative, or zero. If you study the examples, you shouldn't have any trouble figuring out how these functions work.

You can use the next two functions, SQRT and POWER, to calculate the square root of a number or raise a number to a specified power. And you can use the last function, RAND, to generate a floating-point number with a random value between 0 and 1.

In addition to the functions shown in this figure, MySQL provides many other functions for performing mathematical calculations, including trigonometric calculations. Since you're not likely to use these functions, they aren't presented in this book. However, if you need a function that isn't shown here, you can search for the function in the MySQL Reference Manual.

Some of the numeric functions

Function	Description
ROUND(number[,length])	Returns the number rounded to the precision specified by *length*. If *length* is 0, the decimal digits are omitted. This is the default. If *length* is negative, the digits to the left of the decimal point are rounded.
TRUNCATE(number,length)	Returns the number truncated to the precision specified by *length*. If *length* is 0, the decimal digits are omitted.
CEILING(number)	Returns the smallest integer that is greater than or equal to the number.
FLOOR(number)	Returns the largest integer that is less than or equal to the number.
ABS(number)	Returns the absolute value of the number.
SIGN(number)	Returns the sign of the number as -1 for a negative number, 1 for a positive number, and 0 if the number is zero.
SQRT(number)	Returns the square root of the number.
POWER(number,power)	Returns the number raised to the specified *power*.
RAND([integer])	Returns a random floating-point number between 0 and 1. If *integer* is omitted, the function returns the same number each time it's invoked within the same query. Otherwise, *integer* provides a seed value for the random number generator.

Examples that use the numeric functions

Function	Result
ROUND(12.49,0)	12
ROUND(12.50,0)	13
ROUND(12.49,1)	12.5
TRUNCATE(12.51,0)	12
TRUNCATE(12.49,1)	12.4
CEILING(12.5)	13
CEILING(-12.5)	-12
FLOOR(-12.5)	-13
FLOOR(12.5)	12
ABS(-1.25)	1.25
ABS(1.25)	1.25
SIGN(-1.25)	-1
SIGN(1.25)	1
SQRT(125.43)	11.199553562530964
POWER(9,2)	81
RAND()	0.2444132019248

Note

- If an error occurs, each of the numeric functions returns a null value.

Figure 9-5   How to use the numeric functions

How to search for floating-point numbers

In chapter 8, you learned that floating-point types such as the DOUBLE and FLOAT types store approximate values, not exact values. The details of why that is are beyond the scope of this book. From a practical point of view, though, that means that you don't want to search for exact values when you're working with floating-point numbers. If you do, you'll miss values that are approximately equal to the value you're looking for.

To illustrate, consider the table shown in figure 9-6. This table includes a column named float_value that's defined with the DOUBLE type. Now, consider what would happen if you selected all the rows where the value of float_value is equal to 1 as shown in the first SELECT statement. In that case, the result set includes only the second row, even though the table contains two other rows that have values approximately equal to 1.

This figure shows two ways to search for approximate values. First, you can search for a range of values. In this figure, for example, the second SELECT statement searches for values between .99 and 1.01. Second, you can search for values that round to an exact value. This is illustrated by the third SELECT statement. Both of these statements return the three rows from the Float_Sample table that are approximately equal to 1. In addition, both of these statements only check whether the numbers are equal down to two decimal places. However, if you want, you can modify these statements to check for more decimal places.

The Float_Sample table

	float_id	float_value
▶	1	0.999999999999999
	2	1
	3	1.000000000000001
	4	1234.56789012345
	5	999.04440209348
	6	24.04849

A search for an exact value that doesn't include two approximate values

```
SELECT *
FROM float_sample
WHERE float_value = 1
```

	float_id	float_value
▶	2	1

How to search for approximate values

Search for a range of values

```
SELECT *
FROM float_sample
WHERE float_value BETWEEN 0.99 AND 1.01
```

	float_id	float_value
▶	1	0.999999999999999
	2	1
	3	1.000000000000001

Search for rounded values

```
SELECT *
FROM float_sample
WHERE ROUND(float_value, 2) = 1.00
```

	float_id	float_value
▶	1	0.999999999999999
	2	1
	3	1.000000000000001

Description

- Because floating-point values are approximate, you'll want to search for approximate values when working with floating-point data types such as the DOUBLE and FLOAT types.

Figure 9-6   How to search for floating-point numbers

How to work with date/time data

In the topics that follow, you'll learn how to use some of the functions that MySQL provides for working with dates and times. As you'll see, these include functions for extracting different parts of a date/time value and for performing operations on dates and times. In addition, you'll learn how to perform different types of searches on date/time values.

How to get the current date and time

Figure 9-7 presents some of the date/time functions and shows how they work. The NOW, CURDATE, and CURTIME functions return the local dates and/or times based on your system's clock. However, if a session time zone has been set, the value returned by the CURDATE and CURTIME functions is adjusted to accommodate that time zone.

The UTC_DATE and UTC_TIME functions work similarly, but they return the *Universal Time Coordinate* (*UTC*) date, also known as *Greenwich Mean Time* (*GMT*). Although you probably won't use the UTC functions often, they're useful if your system operates in different time zones. That way, the date/time values always reflect Greenwich Mean Time, regardless of the time zone in which they're entered. For example, a date/time value entered at 11:00 a.m. Los Angeles time is given the same value as a date/time value entered at 2:00 p.m. New York time. That makes it easy to compare and operate on these values.

When you use functions to get the current date and time, you should be aware that the CURRENT_TIMESTAMP, CURRENT_DATE, and CURRENT_TIME functions are synonymous with the NOW, CURDATE, and CURTIME functions. In practice, the NOW, CURDATE, and CURTIME functions are typically used by MySQL programmers because they've been around the longest and because they're shorter, which makes them easier to type. However, the CURRENT_TIMESTAMP, CURRENT_DATE, and CURRENT_TIME functions are the ANSI standard, so they're more likely to work with other databases. As a result, if portability is a priority for you, you might want to use these functions.

When you use the NOW, SYSDATE, CURDATE, and CURTIME functions, you must enter an empty set of parentheses after the name of the function as shown in this figure. However, when you use the other functions shown in this figure, the parentheses are optional. For example, you can code the CURRENT_DATE function like this:

```
CURRENT_DATE
```

The advantage of coding the empty set of parentheses is that it clearly indicates that the code is calling a function. The disadvantage is that it requires a little more typing.

Functions that get the current date and time

Function	Description
NOW() SYSDATE() CURRENT_TIMESTAMP()	Returns the current local date and time based on the system's clock.
CURDATE() CURRENT_DATE()	Returns the current local date.
CURTIME() CURRENT_TIME()	Returns the current local time.
UTC_DATE()	Returns the current date in Greenwich Mean Time (GMT).
UTC_TIME()	Returns the current time in Greenwich Mean Time (GMT).

Examples

Function	Result
NOW()	2011-09-29 14:12:04
SYSDATE()	2011-09-29 14:12:04
CURDATE()	2011-09-29
CURTIME()	14:12:04
UTC_DATE()	2011-09-29
UTC_TIME()	21:12:04
CURRENT_TIMESTAMP()	2011-09-29 14:12:04
CURRENT_DATE()	2011-09-29
CURRENT_TIME()	14:12:04

Description

- Parentheses are required after the NOW, SYSDATE, CURDATE, and CURTIME functions.
- Parentheses are optional after the UTC_DATE, UTC_TIME, CURRENT_TIMESTAMP, CURRENT_DATE, and CURRENT_TIME functions.

Figure 9-7   How to get the current date and time

How to parse dates and times
with date/time functions

Figure 9-8 shows you how to use some of MySQL's functions to parse dates and times. When you use these functions, you can retrieve any of the date parts listed in this figure.

If you need to get an integer value for part of a date/time value, you can use the first group of functions as shown in the first group of examples in this figure. For example, you can use the DAYOFWEEK function to return a number that represents the day of the week. You can use the MONTH function to return a number that represents the month. And you can use the HOUR function to return a number that represents the hour. However, if you need to get the name of a day or month as a string, you can use the DAYNAME or MONTHNAME functions as shown in the second group of examples in this figure.

Some of the date/time parsing functions

Function	Description
DAYOFMONTH(date)	Returns the day of the month as an integer.
MONTH(date)	Returns the month as an integer.
YEAR(date)	Returns the 4-digit year as an integer.
HOUR(time)	Returns the hours as an integer.
MINUTE(time)	Returns the minutes as an integer.
SECOND(time)	Returns the seconds as an integer.
DAYOFWEEK(date)	Returns the day of the week as an integer where 1=Sunday, 2=Monday, etc.
QUARTER(date)	Returns the quarter of the year as an integer between 1 and 4.
DAYOFYEAR(date)	Returns the day of the year as an integer.
WEEK(date[,first])	Returns the week of the year as an integer. If the *first* parameter is 1, the week starts on Monday. Otherwise, the week starts on Sunday.
LAST_DAY(date)	Returns the last day of the month as an integer.
DAYNAME(date)	Returns the name of the day of the week as a string.
MONTHNAME(date)	Returns the name of the month as a string.

Examples

Function	Result
DAYOFMONTH('2011-09-03')	3
MONTH('2011-09-03')	9
YEAR('2011-09-03')	2011
HOUR('11:35:00')	11
MINUTE('11:35:00')	35
SECOND('11:35:00')	0
DAYOFWEEK('2011-09-03')	7
QUARTER('2011-09-03')	3
DAYOFYEAR('2011-09-03')	246
WEEK('2011-09-03')	35
LAST_DAY('2011-09-03')	30
DAYNAME('2011-09-03')	Saturday
MONTHNAME('2011-09-03')	September

Description

- The argument for the date functions can be either a DATE value or a DATETIME value.
- The argument for the time functions can be either a TIME value or a DATETIME value.

Figure 9-8   How to parse dates and times with date/time functions

How to parse dates and times with the EXTRACT function

In the previous figure, you learned about some common date/time functions for parsing dates and times. In addition to these functions, you can use the EXTRACT function to parse dates and times as shown in figure 9-9. Because this function is part of the ANSI standard, you may want to use it to make your code more portable. Or, you may just prefer how this function works.

When you use the EXTRACT function, you can code any of the date/time units shown in this figure, followed by the FROM keyword and a date/time value. Then, MySQL extracts the specified unit from the date/time value and returns an integer value that corresponds with that unit. For example, you can use the MONTH unit to get an integer for the month. You can also use some units to get multiple parts of the date. For example, you can use the HOUR_SECOND unit to get an integer that represents the hours, minutes, and seconds parts of a date/time value. In that case, the returned integer contains one or two digits for the hour (a leading zero is dropped), two digits for the minute, and two digits for the second.

Of course, the EXTRACT function won't work correctly if you don't specify a date/time value that makes sense for the specified unit. For example, if you specify the SECOND unit for a DATE value, the EXTRACT function won't work correctly. Conversely, if you specify the MONTH unit for a TIME value, the EXTRACT function won't work correctly. However, if you specify a DATETIME value as shown in this figure, the EXTRACT function should always work correctly.

The EXTRACT function

Function	Description
`EXTRACT(unit FROM date)`	Returns an integer that corresponds with the specified *unit* for the specified date/time.

Date/time units

Unit	Description
`SECOND`	Seconds
`MINUTE`	Minutes
`HOUR`	Hours
`DAY`	Day
`MONTH`	Month
`YEAR`	Year
`MINUTE_SECOND`	Minutes and seconds
`HOUR_MINUTE`	Hour and minutes
`DAY_HOUR`	Day and hours
`YEAR_MONTH`	Year and month
`HOUR_SECOND`	Hours, minutes, and seconds
`DAY_MINUTE`	Day, hours, and minutes
`DAY_SECOND`	Day, hours, minutes, and seconds

Examples that use the EXTRACT function

Function	Result
`EXTRACT(SECOND FROM '2011-09-03 11:35:00')`	0
`EXTRACT(MINUTE FROM '2011-09-03 11:35:00')`	35
`EXTRACT(HOUR FROM '2011-09-03 11:35:00')`	11
`EXTRACT(DAY FROM '2011-09-03 11:35:00')`	3
`EXTRACT(MONTH FROM '2011-09-03 11:35:00')`	9
`EXTRACT(YEAR FROM '2011-09-03 11:35:00')`	2011
`EXTRACT(MINUTE_SECOND FROM '2011-09-03 11:35:00')`	3500
`EXTRACT(HOUR_MINUTE FROM '2011-09-03 11:35:00')`	1135
`EXTRACT(DAY_HOUR FROM '2011-09-03 11:35:00')`	311
`EXTRACT(YEAR_MONTH FROM '2011-09-03 11:35:00')`	201109
`EXTRACT(HOUR_SECOND FROM '2011-09-03 11:35:00')`	113500
`EXTRACT(DAY_MINUTE FROM '2011-09-03 11:35:00')`	31135
`EXTRACT(DAY_SECOND FROM '2011-09-03 11:35:00')`	3113500

Figure 9-9   How to parse dates and times with the EXTRACT function

How to format dates and times

Figure 9-10 shows how to use the DATE_FORMAT function to format dates and times. This function accepts two parameters. The first parameter specifies the DATE or DATETIME value that you want to format. Then, the second parameter specifies a *format string* that includes special codes for formatting the various parts of the date or time. To use one of these codes within the format string, you code the percent sign (%) followed by a single case-sensitive letter.

In this figure, for instance, the first example uses the %m code to get the numeric month, the %d code to get the numeric day, and the %y code to get the two-digit year. This example also uses front slashes (/) to separate the month, day, and year.

The next three examples use other formatting codes, but they work similarly to the first example. Namely, the format string contains some date/time formatting codes to display the different parts of the date. In addition, it contains other characters such as spaces, commas, or dashes to separate the different parts of the date.

This figure also shows how to use the TIME_FORMAT function to format TIME values. This function is illustrated by the last two examples. Although you can also use the TIME_FORMAT function to format the time part of a DATETIME value, it's more common to use the DATE_FORMAT function to do that as shown in the fourth example.

Two functions for formatting dates and times

Function	Description
`DATE_FORMAT(date,format)`	Returns a string for the specified DATE or DATETIME value with the formatting specified by the *format* string.
`TIME_FORMAT(time,format)`	Works like the DATE_FORMAT function but accepts TIME or DATETIME values, and the *format* string can only specify times, not dates.

Common codes for date/time format strings

Code	Description
`%m`	Month, numeric (01…12)
`%c`	Month, numeric (1…12)
`%M`	Month name (January…December)
`%b`	Abbreviated month name (Jan…Dec)
`%d`	Day of the month, numeric (00…31)
`%e`	Day of the month, numeric (0…31)
`%D`	Day of the month with suffix (1st, 2nd, 3rd, etc.)
`%y`	Year, numeric, 2 digits
`%Y`	Year, numeric, 4 digits
`%W`	Weekday name (Sunday…Saturday)
`%a`	Abbreviated weekday name (Sun…Sat)
`%H`	Hour (00…23)
`%k`	Hour (0…23)
`%h`	Hour (01…12)
`%l`	Hour (1…12)
`%i`	Minutes (00…59)
`%r`	Time, 12-hour (hh:mm:ss AM or PM)
`%T`	Time, 24-hour (hh:mm:ss)
`%S`	Seconds (00…59)
`%p`	AM or PM

Examples

Function	Result
`DATE_FORMAT('2011-09-03', '%m/%d/%y')`	`09/03/11`
`DATE_FORMAT('2011-09-03', '%W, %M %D, %Y')`	`Saturday, September 3rd, 2011`
`DATE_FORMAT('2011-09-03', '%e-%b-%y')`	`3-Sep-11`
`DATE_FORMAT('2011-09-03 16:45', '%r')`	`04:45:00 PM`
`TIME_FORMAT('16:45', '%r')`	`04:45:00 PM`
`TIME_FORMAT('16:45', '%l:%i %p')`	`4:45 PM`

Figure 9-10   How to format dates and times

How to perform calculations on dates and times

Figure 9-11 shows you how to use the DATE_ADD, DATE_SUB and DATEDIFF functions to perform calculations on dates and times. You can use the DATE_ADD function to add a specified number of date parts to a date. In this figure, for instance, the first three examples show how you can add days, months, or seconds to a date/time value.

You can also use the DATE_ADD function to subtract date parts from a date/time value. To do that, you code the expression argument as a negative value as shown by the fourth example. This performs the same calculation as the DATE_SUB function shown in the fifth example.

When you use these date functions, MySQL checks for dates that include leap years and returns a NULL value if a date doesn't exist. For example, 2008 was a leap year, so it has a day for February 29. However, 2009 wasn't a leap year, so it doesn't have a day for February 29. As a result, when the sixth example adds one year to February 29, 2008, MySQL returns February 28, 2009. On the other hand, the seventh example tries to add one year to an invalid date (February 29, 2009). As a result, MySQL returns a NULL value.

The eighth example shows how to use the DATE_ADD function with the DAY_HOUR unit to add the specified number of days and hours to a date/time value. Here, the example adds 2 days and 12 hours to the specified date.

If you need to find the number of days between two date/time values, you can use the DATEDIFF function as shown by the second group of examples. Note that this function only returns days, not hours, minutes, or seconds. This is true even if the arguments are DATETIME values that include time values, as shown in the second DATEDIFF example. When you use the DATEDIFF function, you typically specify the later date as the first argument and the earlier date as the second argument. That way, the result of the function is a positive value. If you code the earlier date as the first argument, the result is a negative value as shown in the third DATEDIFF example.

The last group of examples shows how to use the TO_DAYS and TIME_TO_SEC functions to perform calculations on dates and times. To start, the TO_DAYS example shows how you can use this function to calculate the number of days between two dates. This performs the same calculation as the first two DATEDIFF examples. Since the DATEDIFF function is easier to write and read, you'll typically use it instead of the TO_DAYS function for this type of calculation.

The last example shows how to use the TIME_TO_SEC function to calculate the number of seconds between two times. This type of calculation can be useful when you're working with time values.

Some of the functions for calculating dates and times

Function	Description
`DATE_ADD(date,INTERVAL expression unit)`	Returns a DATE or DATETIME value equal to the specified *date* plus the specified interval.
`DATE_SUB(date,INTERVAL expression unit)`	Returns a DATE or DATETIME value equal to the *date* minus the specified interval.
`DATEDIFF(date1, date2)`	Returns the number of days from one date to the other. For DATETIME values, this function ignores the time parts of the value.
`TO_DAYS(date)`	Returns the number of days since the year 0. This function does not return reliable results for dates before 1582.
`TIME_TO_SEC(time)`	Returns the number of seconds elapsed since midnight, which is useful for calculating elapsed time.

Examples

Function	Result
`DATE_ADD('2011-12-31', INTERVAL 1 DAY)`	`2012-01-01`
`DATE_ADD('2011-12-31', INTERVAL 3 MONTH)`	`2012-03-31`
`DATE_ADD('2011-12-31 23:59:59', INTERVAL 1 SECOND)`	`2012-01-01 00:00:00`
`DATE_ADD('2012-01-01', INTERVAL -1 DAY)`	`2011-12-31`
`DATE_SUB('2012-01-01', INTERVAL 1 DAY)`	`2011-12-31`
`DATE_ADD('2008-02-29', INTERVAL 1 YEAR)`	`2009-02-28`
`DATE_ADD('2009-02-29', INTERVAL 1 YEAR)`	`NULL`
`DATE_ADD('2011-12-31 12:00', INTERVAL '2 12' DAY_HOUR)`	`2012-01-03 00:00:00`
`DATEDIFF('2011-09-30', '2011-09-03')`	`27`
`DATEDIFF('2011-09-30 23:59:59', '2011-09-03')`	`27`
`DATEDIFF('2011-09-03', '2011-09-30')`	`-27`
`TO_DAYS('2011-09-30') - TO_DAYS('2011-09-03')`	`27`
`TIME_TO_SEC('10:00') - TIME_TO_SEC('09:59')`	`60`

Description

- If the expression you specify in the DATE_ADD function is a negative integer, the interval is subtracted from the date.
- If the expression you specify in the DATE_SUB function is a negative integer, the interval is added to the date.

Figure 9-11   How to perform calculations on dates and times

How to search for a date

Figure 9-12 illustrates a problem you can encounter when searching for dates in a column that's defined with the DATETIME data type. The examples in this figure use a table named Date_Sample. This table includes a date_id column that's defined with the INT type and a start_date column that's defined with the DATETIME type. The time components in the first three rows in this table have a zero value. In contrast, the time components in the next three rows have non-zero time components.

The problem occurs when you try to search for a date value. In this figure, for instance, the first SELECT statement searches for rows in the Date_Sample table with a date of '2011-02-28'. Because this code doesn't specify a time component, MySQL adds a zero time component ('00:00:00') when it converts the date string to a DATETIME value. However, because the row with this date has a non-zero time value, MySQL doesn't return any rows for this statement.

To solve this problem, you can use one of the three techniques shown in this figure. First, you can search for a range of dates that includes only the date you're looking for as shown by the second SELECT statement in this figure. The WHERE clause in this statement searches for dates that are greater than or equal to the date you're looking for and less than the date that follows the date you're looking for. Because a time component of zero is implicitly added to both of the dates in the search condition, this statement returns the one row with the date you want.

Because this SELECT statement doesn't use any functions in the WHERE clause, it provides the most efficient technique for searching for dates. That's particularly true if the start_date column is indexed. In contrast, the second technique uses the MONTH, DAYOFMONTH, and YEAR functions in the WHERE clause to search for just for those components. And the third technique uses the DATE_FORMAT function in the WHERE clause to return a formatted string that only contains the month, day, and year.

If you want, you can use other date functions to search for a date. For example, you can use the EXTRACT function shown earlier in this chapter. Whenever possible, though, you should avoid using functions so the search is as efficient as possible.

The contents of the Date_Sample table

date_id	start_date
1	1979-03-01 00:00:00
2	1999-02-28 00:00:00
3	2003-10-31 00:00:00
4	2011-02-28 10:00:00
5	2012-02-28 13:58:32
6	2012-03-01 09:02:25

A SELECT statement that fails to return a row

```
SELECT *
FROM date_sample
WHERE start_date = '2011-02-28'
```

date_id	start_date

Three techniques for ignoring time values

Search for a range of dates

```
SELECT *
FROM date_sample
WHERE start_date >= '2011-02-28' AND start_date < '2011-03-01'
```

date_id	start_date
4	2011-02-28 10:00:00

Search for month, day, and year integers

```
SELECT *
FROM date_sample
WHERE MONTH(start_date) = 2 AND
      DAYOFMONTH(start_date) = 28 AND
      YEAR(start_date) = 2011
```

date_id	start_date
4	2011-02-28 10:00:00

Search for a formatted date

```
SELECT *
FROM date_sample
WHERE DATE_FORMAT(start_date, '%m-%d-%Y') = '02-28-2011'
```

date_id	start_date
4	2011-02-28 10:00:00

Description

- You can search for a date in a DATETIME column by searching for a range of dates, by using functions to specify the month, day, and year of the date, or by searching for a formatted date. Of these techniques, searching for a range of dates is the most efficient.

Figure 9-12   How to search for a date

How to search for a time

When you search for a time value in a DATETIME column without specifying a date component, MySQL automatically uses the default date of January 1, 1900. That's why the first SELECT statement in figure 9-13 doesn't return a row even though one row matches the specified time.

The second SELECT statement shows one way to solve this problem. Here, the WHERE clause uses the DATE_FORMAT function to return a string for the start_date column in the hh:mm:ss format. Then, the WHERE clause compares this string to a literal string of 10:00:00.

The third SELECT statement in this figure shows another way to solve this problem. This statement works similarly to the second statement, but it uses the EXTRACT function to extract an integer that represents the hours, minutes, and seconds in the start_date column. Then, the WHERE clause compares this integer to an integer value of 100000. Although this approach might run slightly faster, it's also more difficult to read. As a result, I recommend using the first approach unless performance is critical.

The fourth and fifth SELECT statements show that you can use a similar technique to search for a range of times. Here, the fourth statement uses the HOUR function to search for a particular hour of the day, and the fifth statement uses the EXTRACT function to search for times between two times. Of course, you could also use the DATE_FORMAT function to get the same results.

Before I go on, you should realize that many of the problems that can occur when searching for dates and times can be avoided by designing the database properly. For example, if you know that only the date portion of a date/time value is significant, you can store the date in a column with the DATE type. Conversely, if you know that only the time portion of a date/time value is significant, you can store the time in a column with the TIME type. That way, you won't need to use functions in your searches, and you can create an index for the search column to significantly speed searches.

However, if both the date and time are significant, you can store them in a column with the DATETIME type. Then, you can use the techniques shown in this figure and the previous figure to search for dates and times. Remember, though, that if you need to use functions in your searches, MySQL can't use the column's index and the search will run significantly slower.

The contents of the Date_Sample table

date_id	start_date
1	1979-03-01 00:00:00
2	1999-02-28 00:00:00
3	2003-10-31 00:00:00
4	2011-02-28 10:00:00
5	2012-02-28 13:58:32
6	2012-03-01 09:02:25

A SELECT statement that fails to return a row

```
SELECT * FROM date_sample
WHERE start_date = '10:00:00'
```

date_id	start_date

Examples that ignore date values

Search for a time that has been formatted

```
SELECT * FROM date_sample
WHERE DATE_FORMAT(start_date, '%T') = '10:00:00'
```

date_id	start_date
4	2011-02-28 10:00:00

Search for a time that hasn't been formatted

```
SELECT * FROM date_sample
WHERE EXTRACT(HOUR_SECOND FROM start_date) = 100000
```

date_id	start_date
4	2011-02-28 10:00:00

Search for an hour of the day

```
SELECT * FROM date_sample
WHERE HOUR(start_date) = 9
```

date_id	start_date
6	2012-03-01 09:02:25

Search for a range of times

```
SELECT * FROM date_sample
WHERE EXTRACT(HOUR_MINUTE FROM start_date) BETWEEN 900 AND 1200
```

date_id	start_date
4	2011-02-28 10:00:00
6	2012-03-01 09:02:25

Description

- You can search for a time in a DATETIME column without specifying a date by using date/time functions to get the time part of the DATETIME value. Then, you can use the time parts in your WHERE clause.

Figure 9-13   How to search for a time

Other functions you should know about

This topic describes four other functions that you should know about: CASE, IF, IFNULL, and COALESCE.

How to use the CASE function

Figure 9-14 presents the two versions of the CASE function. This function returns a value that's determined by the conditions you specify. The easiest way to describe how this function works is to look at the two examples shown in this figure.

The first example uses a simple CASE function. When you use this function, MySQL compares the input expression you code in the CASE clause with the expressions you code in the WHEN clauses. In this example, the input expression is a value in the terms_id column of the Invoices table, and the when expressions are the valid values for this column. When MySQL finds an expression in a WHEN clause that's equal to the input expression, it returns the expression specified in the matching THEN clause. For example, if the value of the terms_id column is 3, this function returns a value of "Net due 30 days." Although it's not shown in this example, you can also code an ELSE clause at the end of the CASE function. Then, if none of the expressions in the WHEN clause are equal to the input expression, the function returns the value specified in the ELSE clause.

The second example uses a search CASE function to determine the status of the invoices in the Invoices table. To do that, the CASE function uses the DATEDIFF and NOW functions to get the number of days between the current date and the invoice due date. If the difference is greater than 30, the CASE function returns the value "Over 30 days past due." Otherwise, if the difference is greater than 0, the function returns the value "1 to 30 days past due." Note that if the condition in the first WHEN clause is true, the condition in the second WHEN clause is also true. In that case, the function returns the expression associated with the first condition since this condition is evaluated first. In other words, the sequence of the conditions is critical to getting the correct results. If neither of the conditions is true, the function returns the value "Current."

The simple CASE function is typically used with columns that can contain a limited number of values, such as the terms_id column used in the first example. In contrast, the searched CASE function can be used for a wide variety of purposes. For example, this function can be used to test for conditions other than equal, such as greater than or less than. This is shown in the second example, which couldn't be coded using the simple syntax. In addition, each condition in a searched CASE function can be based on a different column or expression. Of course, CASE functions can be more complicated than the ones that are shown here, but this should give you an idea of what you can do with this function.

The syntax of the simple CASE function

```
CASE input_expression
    WHEN when_expression_1 THEN result_expression_1
    [WHEN when_expression_2 THEN result_expression_2]...
    [ELSE else_result_expression]
END
```

A SELECT statement that uses a simple CASE function

```
SELECT invoice_number, terms_id,
    CASE terms_id
        WHEN 1 THEN 'Net due 10 days'
        WHEN 2 THEN 'Net due 20 days'
        WHEN 3 THEN 'Net due 30 days'
        WHEN 4 THEN 'Net due 60 days'
        WHEN 5 THEN 'Net due 90 days'
    END AS terms
FROM invoices
```

invoice_number	terms_id	terms
111-92R-10096	2	Net due 20 days
25022117	4	Net due 60 days
P02-88D77S7	3	Net due 30 days

The syntax of the searched CASE function

```
CASE
    WHEN conditional_expression_1 THEN result_expression_1
    [WHEN conditional_expression_2 THEN result_expression_2]...
    [ELSE else_result_expression]
END
```

A SELECT statement that uses a searched CASE function

```
SELECT invoice_number, invoice_total, invoice_date, invoice_due_date,
    CASE
        WHEN DATEDIFF(NOW(), invoice_due_date) > 30
            THEN 'Over 30 days past due'
        WHEN DATEDIFF(NOW(), invoice_due_date) > 0
            THEN '1 to 30 days past due'
        ELSE 'Current'
    END AS invoice_status
FROM invoices
WHERE invoice_total - payment_total - credit_total > 0
```

invoice_number	invoice_total	invoice_date	invoice_due_date	invoice_status
39104	85.31	2011-07-10	2011-08-09	Over 30 days past due
963253264	52.25	2011-07-18	2011-08-17	Over 30 days past due
31361833	579.42	2011-07-21	2011-08-10	Over 30 days past due

Description

- The simple CASE function tests the expression in the CASE clause against the expressions in the WHEN clauses. Then, the function returns the result expression for the first test that's true.

- The searched CASE function tests the expression in each WHEN clause and returns the result expression for the first test that's true.

Figure 9-14   How to use the CASE function

How to use the IF, IFNULL, and COALESCE functions

Figure 9-15 presents three functions: IF, IFNULL, and COALESCE. To start, you can use the IF function to test a condition and return one value if the condition is true or another value if the condition is false. For instance, the first example uses the IF function to return a string value of "Yes" if the vendor_city column is equal to a value of "Fresno". Otherwise, the IF function returns a value of "No".

Both the IFNULL and COALESCE functions let you substitute non-null values for null values. Although these functions are similar, the COALESCE function is more flexible because it lets you specify a list of values. Then, it returns the first non-null value in the list. In contrast, the IFNULL function only lets you specify two expressions. If the first expression is not null, it returns the first expression. Otherwise, it returns the second expression.

The second example uses the IFNULL function to return the value of the payment_date column if that column doesn't contain a null value. Otherwise, it returns a string that says "No Payment". The third example performs the same operation using the COALESCE function.

The syntax of the IF function

```
IF(test_expression, if_true_expression, else_expression)
```

A SELECT statement that uses the IF function

```
SELECT vendor_name,
       IF(vendor_city = 'Fresno', 'Yes', 'No') AS is_city_fresno
FROM vendors
```

vendor_name	is_city_fresno
Towne Advertiser's Mailing...	No
BFI Industries	Yes
Pacific Gas & Electric	No
Robbins Mobile Lock And ...	Yes
Bill Marvin Electric Inc	Yes

The syntax of the IFNULL function

```
IFNULL(test_expression, replacement_value)
```

A SELECT statement that uses the IFNULL function

```
SELECT payment_date,
       IFNULL(payment_date, 'No Payment') AS new_date
FROM invoices
```

payment_date	new_date
2011-08-11	2011-08-11
NULL	No Payment
2011-08-11	2011-08-11

The syntax of the COALESCE function

```
COALESCE(expression_1[, expression_2]...)
```

A SELECT statement that uses the COALESCE function

```
SELECT payment_date,
       COALESCE(payment_date, 'No Payment') AS new_date
FROM invoices
```

payment_date	new_date
2011-08-11	2011-08-11
NULL	No Payment
2011-08-11	2011-08-11

Description

- The IF function lets you test an expression and return one value if the expression is true and another value if the expression is false.
- The IFNULL and COALESCE functions let you substitute non-null values for null values.
- The IFNULL function returns the first expression if it isn't null. Otherwise, it returns the replacement value you specify.
- The COALESCE function returns the first expression in the list that isn't null. If all of the expressions are null, this function returns a null value.

Figure 9-15   How to use the IF, IFNULL, and COALESCE functions

Perspective

In this chapter, you learned about the different functions that you can use to operate on MySQL data. At this point, you have all of the skills you need to develop SQL code at a professional level.

However, there's a lot more to learn about MySQL. In the next section of this book, then, you'll learn the basic skills for designing a database. Even if you never need to design your own database, understanding this material will help you work more efficiently with databases that have been designed by others.

Exercises

1. Write a SELECT statement that returns these columns from the Invoices table:

    The invoice_total column

    A column that uses the ROUND function to return the invoice_total column with 1 decimal digit

    A column that uses the ROUND function to return the invoice_total column with no decimal digits

2. Write a SELECT statement that returns these columns from the Date_Sample table in the EX database:

    The start_date column

    A column that uses the DATE_FORMAT function to return the start_date column with its month name abbreviated and its month, day, and two-digit year separated by slashes

    A column that uses the DATE_FORMAT function to return the start_date column with its month and day returned as integers with no leading zeros, a two-digit year, and all date parts separated by slashes

    A column that uses the DATE_FORMAT function to return the start_date column with only the hours and minutes on a 12-hour clock with an am/pm indicator

    A column that uses the DATE_FORMAT function to return the start_date column with its month returned as an integer with no leading zeros, its month, day, and two-digit year separated by slashes, and its hours and minutes on a 12-hour clock with an am/pm indicator

3. Write a SELECT statement that returns these columns from the Vendors table:

   The vendor_name column

   The vendor_name column in all capital letters

   The vendor_phone column

   A column that displays the last four digits of each phone number

   When you get that working right, add the columns that follow to the result set. This is more difficult because these columns require the use of functions within functions.

   The vendor_phone column with the parts of the number separated by dots, as in 555.555.5555

   A column that displays the second word in each vendor name if there is one and blanks if there isn't

4. Write a SELECT statement that returns these columns from the Invoices table:

   The invoice_number column

   The invoice_date column

   The invoice_date column plus 30 days

   The payment_date column

   A column named days_to_pay that shows the number of days between the invoice date and the payment date

   The number of the invoice date's month

   The four-digit year of the invoice date

   When you have this working, add a WHERE clause that retrieves just the invoices for the month of May based on the invoice date, not the number of the invoice month.

Section 3

Database design and implementation

For large applications, a developer who specializes in database design may be responsible for designing and creating the databases that are used by production applications. This developer may also be responsible for designing and creating the databases that are used for testing those applications. Then, a database administrator (DBA) may be responsible for maintaining these databases. For smaller applications, programmers are often asked to fill one or both of these roles. In other words, programmers often need to design, create, and maintain the databases that are used for testing and production.

So, whether you're a database designer, a database administrator, or a SQL programmer, you need the skills and knowledge presented in this section. That's true even if you aren't ever called upon to design, create, or maintain a database. By understanding what's going on behind the scenes, you'll be able to use SQL more effectively.

In chapter 10, you'll learn how to design a database. In chapter 11, you'll learn how to use the Data Definition Language (DDL) statements to create and maintain databases, tables, and indexes. Finally, in chapter 12, you'll learn how to create and maintain views, which are database objects that provide another way to look at tables.

10

How to design a database

In this chapter, you'll learn how to design a new database. This is useful information whether or not you ever design a database on your own. To illustrate this process, I'll use the accounts payable (AP) database that you've seen throughout this book.

How to design a data structure **278**
The basic steps for designing a data structure 278
How to identify the data elements 280
How to subdivide the data elements 282
How to identify the tables and assign columns 284
How to identify the primary and foreign keys 286
How to enforce the relationships between tables 288
How normalization works 290
How to identify the columns to be indexed 292

How to normalize a data structure **294**
The seven normal forms 294
How to apply the first normal form 296
How to apply the second normal form 298
How to apply the third normal form 300
When and how to denormalize a data structure 302

How to use MySQL Workbench for database design **304**
How to open an existing EER model 304
How to create a new EER model 304
How to work with an EER model 306
How to work with an EER diagram 308

Perspective **310**

How to design a data structure

Databases are often designed by database administrators (DBAs) or design specialists. This is especially true for large, multiuser databases. How well this is done can directly affect your job as a MySQL programmer. In general, a well-designed database is easy to understand and query, while a poorly designed database is difficult to work with. In fact, when you work with a poorly designed database, you will often need to figure out how it is designed before you can code your queries appropriately.

The topics that follow present a basic approach for designing a *data structure*. We use that term to refer to a model of the database rather than the database itself. Once you design the data structure, you can use the techniques presented in the next two chapters to create a database with that design. By understanding the right way to design a database, you'll work more effectively as a MySQL programmer.

The basic steps for designing a data structure

In many cases, you can design a data structure based on an existing real-world system. The illustration at the top of figure 10-1 presents a conceptual view of how this works. Here, you can see that all of the information about the people, documents, and facilities within a real-world system is mapped to the tables, columns, and rows of a database system.

As you design a data structure, each table represents one object, or *entity*, in the real-world system. Then, within each table, each column stores one item of information, or *attribute*, for the entity, and each row stores one occurrence, or *instance*, of the entity.

This figure also presents the six steps you can follow to design a data structure. You'll learn more about each of these steps in the topics that follow. In general, though, step 1 is to identify all the data elements that need to be stored in the database. Step 2 is to break complex elements down into smaller components whenever that makes sense. Step 3 is to identify the tables that will make up the system and to determine which data elements are assigned as columns in each table. Step 4 is to define the relationships between the tables by identifying the primary and foreign keys. Step 5 is to normalize the database to reduce data redundancy. And step 6 is to identify the indexes that are needed for each table.

To model a database system after a real-world system, you can use a technique called *entity-relationship (ER) modeling*. Because this is a complex subject of its own, I won't present it in this book. However, I have applied some of the basic elements of this technique to the design diagrams presented in this chapter. In effect, then, you'll be learning some of the basics of this modeling technique.

A database system is modeled after a real-world system

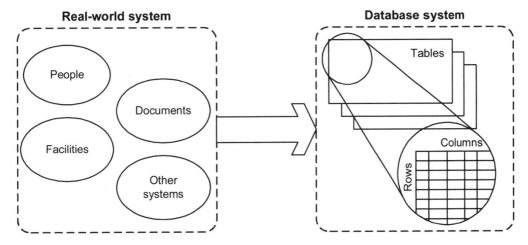

The six basic steps for designing a data structure

Step 1:   Identify the data elements

Step 2:   Subdivide each element into its smallest useful components

Step 3:   Identify the tables and assign columns

Step 4:   Identify the primary and foreign keys

Step 5:   Review whether the data structure is normalized

Step 6:   Identify the indexes

Description

- A relational database system should model the real-world environment where it's used. The job of the designer is to analyze the real-world system and then map it onto a relational database system.

- A table in a relational database typically represents an object, or *entity*, in the real world. Each column of a table is used to store an *attribute* associated with the entity, and each row represents one *instance* of the entity.

- To model a database and the relationships between its tables after a real-world system, you can use a technique called *entity-relationship (ER) modeling*. Some of the diagrams you'll see in this chapter apply the basic elements of ER modeling.

Figure 10-1   The basic steps for designing a data structure

How to identify the data elements

The first step for designing a data structure is to identify the data elements required by the system. You can use several techniques to do that, including analyzing the existing system if there is one, evaluating comparable systems, and interviewing anyone who will be using the system. One particularly good source of information is the documents used by an existing system.

In figure 10-2, for example, you can see an invoice that's used by an accounts payable system. We'll use this document as the main source of information for the database design presented in this chapter. Keep in mind, though, that you'll want to use all available resources when you design your own database.

If you study this document, you'll notice that it contains information about three different entities: vendors, invoices, and line items. First, the form itself has preprinted information about the vendor who issued the invoice, such as the vendor's name and address. If this vendor were to issue another invoice, this information wouldn't change.

This document also contains specific information about the invoice. Some of this information, such as the invoice number, invoice date, and invoice total, is general in nature. Although the actual information will vary from one invoice to the next, each invoice will include this information. In addition to this general information, each invoice includes information about the items that were purchased. Although each line item contains similar information, each invoice can contain a different number of line items.

One of the things you need to consider as you review a document like this is how much information your system needs to track. For an accounts payable system, for example, you may not need to store detailed data such as the information about each line item. Instead, you may just need to store summary data like the invoice total. As you think about what data elements to include in the database, then, you should have an idea of what information you'll need to get back out of the system.

An invoice that can be used to identify data elements

Acme Fabrication, Inc.

Custom Contraptions, Contrivances and Confabulations

1234 West Industrial Way   East Los Angeles   California 90022

800.555.1212   fax 562.555.1213   www.acmefabrication.com

Invoice Number:	I01-1088
Invoice Date:	10/05/11
Terms:	Net 30

Part No.	Qty.	Description	Unit Price	Extension
CUST345	12	Design service, hr	100.00	1200.00
457332	7	Baling wire, 25x3ft roll	79.90	559.30
50173	4375	Duct tape, black, yd	1.09	4768.75
328771	2	Rubber tubing, 100ft roll	4.79	9.58
CUST281	7	Assembly, hr	75.00	525.00
CUST917	2	Testing, hr	125.00	250.00
		Sales Tax		245.20

Your salesperson:	Ruben Goldberg, ext 4512
Accounts receivable:	Inigo Jones, ext 4901

$7,557.83

PLEASE PAY THIS AMOUNT

Thanks for your business!

The data elements identified on the invoice document

Vendor name	Invoice date	Item extension
Vendor address	Invoice terms	Vendor sales contact name
Vendor phone number	Item part number	Vendor sales contact extension
Vendor fax number	Item quantity	Vendor AR contact name
Vendor web address	Item description	Vendor AR contact extension
Invoice number	Item unit price	Invoice total

Description

- Depending on the nature of the system, you can identify data elements in a variety of ways, including interviewing users, analyzing existing systems, and evaluating comparable systems.

- The documents used by a real-world system, such as the invoice shown above, can often help you identify the data elements of the system.

- As you identify the data elements of a system, you should begin thinking about the entities that those elements are associated with. That will help you identify the tables of the database later on.

Figure 10-2   How to identify the data elements

How to subdivide the data elements

Some of the data elements you identify in step 1 of the design procedure will consist of multiple components. The next step, then, is to divide these elements into their smallest useful values. Figure 10-3 shows how you can do that.

The first example in this figure shows how you can divide the name of the sales contact for a vendor. Here, the name is divided into two elements: a first name and a last name. When you divide a name like this, you can easily perform operations like sorting by last name and using the first name in a salutation, such as "Dear Ruben." In contrast, if the full name is stored in a single column, you have to use the string functions to extract the component you need. But as you learned in the last chapter, that can lead to inefficient and complicated code. In general, then, you should separate a name like this whenever you'll need to use the name components separately. Later, when you need to use the full name, you can concatenate the first and last names.

The second example shows how you typically divide an address. Notice in this example that the street number and street name are stored in a single column. Although you could store these components in separate columns, that usually doesn't make sense since these values are typically used together. That's what I mean when I say that the data elements should be divided into their smallest *useful* values.

With that guideline in mind, you might even need to divide a single string into two or more components. A bulk mail system, for example, might require a separate column for the first three digits of the zip code. And a telephone number could require as many as four columns: one for the area code, one for the three-digit prefix, one for the four-digit number, and one for the extension.

As in the previous step, knowledge of the real-world system and of the information that will be extracted from the database is critical. In some circumstances, it may be okay to store data elements with multiple components in a single column. That can simplify your design and reduce the overall number of columns. In general, though, most designers divide data elements as much as possible. That way, it's easy to accommodate almost any query, and you don't have to change the database design later on when you realize that you need to use just part of a column value.

A name that's divided into first and last names

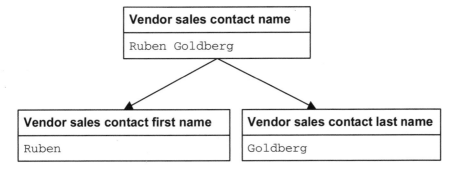

An address that's divided into street address, city, state, and zip code

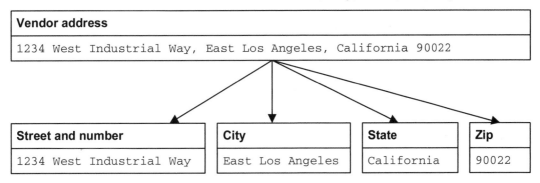

Description

- If a data element contains two or more components, you should consider subdividing the element into those components. That way, you won't need to parse the element each time you use it.

- The extent to which you subdivide a data element depends on how it will be used. Because it's difficult to predict all future uses for the data, most designers subdivide data elements as much as possible.

- When you subdivide a data element, you can easily rebuild it when necessary by concatenating the individual components.

Figure 10-3   How to subdivide the data elements

How to identify the tables and assign columns

Figure 10-4 presents the three main entities for the accounts payable system and lists the possible data elements that can be associated with each one. In most cases, you'll recognize the main entities that need to be included in a data structure as you identify the data elements. As I reviewed the data elements represented on the invoice document in figure 10-2, for example, I identified the three entities shown in this figure: vendors, invoices, and invoice line items. Although you may identify additional entities later on in the design process, it's sufficient to identity the main entities at this point. These entities will become the tables of the database.

After you identify the main entities, you need to determine which data elements are associated with each entity. These elements will become the columns of the tables. In many cases, the associations are obvious. For example, it's easy to determine that the vendor name and address are associated with the vendors entity and the invoice date and invoice total are associated with the invoices entity. Some associations, however, aren't so obvious. In that case, you may need to list a data element under two or more entities. In this figure, for example, you can see that the invoice number is included in both the invoices and invoice line items entities and the account number is included in all three entities. Later, when you normalize the data structure, you may be able to remove these repeated elements. For now, though, it's okay to include them.

Before I go on, I want to point out the notation I used in this figure. To start, any data elements I included that weren't identified in previous steps are shown in italics. Although you should be able to identify most of the data elements in the first two steps of the design process, you'll occasionally think of additional elements during the third step. In this case, since the initial list of data elements was based on a single document, I added several data elements to this list.

Similarly, you may decide during this step that you don't need some of the data elements you've identified. For example, I decided that I didn't need the fax number or web address of each vendor. So I used the strikethrough feature of my word processor to indicate that these data elements should not be included.

Finally, I identified the data elements that are included in two or more tables by coding an asterisk after them. Although you can use any notation you like for this step of the design process, you'll want to be sure that you document your design decisions. For a complicated design, you will probably want to use a *CASE (computer-aided software engineering)* tool.

By the way, a couple of the new data elements I added may not be clear to you if you haven't worked with a corporate accounts payable system before. "Terms" refers to the payment terms that the vendor offers. For example, the terms might be net 30 (the invoice must be paid in 30 days) or might include a discount for early payment. "Account number" refers to the general ledger accounts that a company uses to track its expenses. For example, one account number might be assigned for advertising expenses, while another might be for office supplies. Each invoice that's paid is assigned to an account, and in some cases, different line items on an invoice are assigned to different accounts.

Possible tables and columns for an accounts payable system

Vendors	Invoices	Invoice line items
Vendor name	Invoice number*	Invoice number*
Vendor address	Invoice date	~~Item part number~~
Vendor city	Terms*	Item quantity
Vendor state	Invoice total	Item description
Vendor zip code	*Payment date*	Item unit price
Vendor phone number	*Payment total*	Item extension
~~Vendor fax number~~	*Invoice due date*	*Account number**
~~Vendor web address~~	*Credit total*	*Sequence number*
Vendor contact first name	*Account number**	
Vendor contact last name		
~~Vendor contact phone~~		
~~Vendor AR first name~~		
~~Vendor AR last name~~		
~~Vendor AR phone~~		
*Terms**		
*Account number**		

Description

- After you identify and subdivide all of the data elements for a database, you should group them by the entities with which they're associated. These entities will later become the tables of the database, and the elements will become the columns.

- If a data element relates to more than one entity, you can include it under all of the entities it relates to. Then, when you normalize the database, you may be able to remove the duplicate elements.

- As you assign the elements to entities, you should omit elements that aren't needed, and you should add any additional elements that are needed.

The notation used in this figure

- Data elements that were previously identified but aren't needed are crossed out.

- Data elements that were added are displayed in italics.

- Data elements that are related to two or more entities are followed by an asterisk.

- You can use a similar notation or develop one of your own. You can also use a *CASE (computer-aided software engineering)* tool if one is available to you.

Figure 10-4 How to identify the tables and assign columns

How to identify the primary and foreign keys

Once you identify the entities and data elements of a system, the next step is to identify the relationships between the tables. To do that, you need to identify the primary and foreign keys as shown in figure 10-5.

As you know, a primary key is used to uniquely identify each row in a table. In some cases, you can use an existing column as the primary key. For example, you might consider using the vendor_name column as the primary key of the Vendors table. Because the values for this column can be long, however, and because it would be easy to enter a value like that incorrectly, that's not a good candidate for a primary key. Instead, you should use an ID column like vendor_id that's incremented by one for each new row.

Similarly, you might consider using the invoice_number column as the primary key of the Invoices table. However, it's possible for different vendors to use the same invoice number, so this value isn't necessarily unique. Because of that, another ID column like invoice_id can be used as the primary key.

To uniquely identify the rows in the Invoice_Line_Items table, this design uses a composite key. This composite key uses two columns to identify each row. The first column is the invoice_id column from the Invoices table, and the second column is the invoice_sequence column. This is necessary because this table may contain more than one row (line item) for each invoice. And that means that the invoice_id value by itself may not be unique.

After you identify the primary key of each table, you need to identify the relationships between the tables and add foreign key columns as necessary. In most cases, two tables will have a one-to-many relationship with each other. For example, each vendor can have many invoices, and each invoice can have many line items. To identify the vendor that each invoice is associated with, a vendor_id column is included in the Invoices table. Because the Invoice_Line_Items table already contains an invoice_id column, it's not necessary to add another column to this table.

The diagram at the top of this figure illustrates the relationships I identified between the tables in the accounts payable system. As you can see, the primary keys are displayed in bold. Then, the lines between the tables indicate how the primary key in one table is related to the foreign key in another table. Here, a small, round connector indicates the "one" side of the relationship, and the connector with three lines indicates the "many" side of the relationship.

In addition to the one-to-many relationships shown in this diagram, you can also use many-to-many relationships and one-to-one relationships. The second diagram in this figure, for example, shows a many-to-many relationship between an Employees table and a Committees table. As you can see, this type of relationship can be implemented by creating a *linking table*, also called a *connecting table* or an *associate table*. This table contains the primary key columns from the two tables. Then, each table has a one-to-many relationship with the linking table. Notice that the linking table doesn't have its own primary key. Because this table doesn't correspond to an entity and because it's used only in conjunction with the Employees and Committees tables, a primary key isn't needed.

The relationships between the tables in the accounts payable system

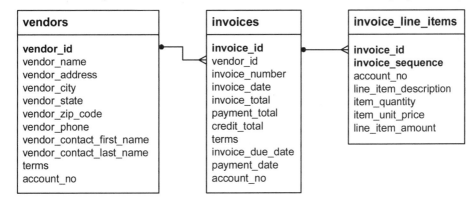

Two tables with a many-to-many relationship

Linking table

Two tables with a one-to-one relationship

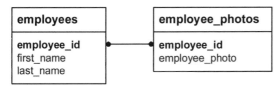

Description

- Each table should have a primary key that uniquely identifies each row. If possible, you should use an existing column for the primary key.

- The values of the primary keys should seldom, if ever, change. The values should also be short and easy to enter correctly.

- If a suitable column doesn't exist for a primary key, you can create an ID column that is incremented by one for each new row as the primary key.

- If two tables have a one-to-many relationship, you may need to add a foreign key column to the table on the "many" side. The foreign key column must have the same data type as the primary key column it's related to.

- If two tables have a many-to-many relationship, you'll need to define a *linking table* to relate them. Then, each of the tables in the many-to-many relationship will have a one-to-many relationship with the linking table. The linking table doesn't usually have a primary key.

- If two tables have a one-to-one relationship, they should be related by their primary keys. This type of relationship is typically used to improve performance. Then, columns with large amounts of data can be stored in a separate table.

Figure 10-5   How to identify the primary and foreign keys

The third example illustrates two tables that have a one-to-one relationship. With this type of relationship, both tables have the same primary key, which means that the information could be stored in a single table. This type of relationship is often used when a table contains one or more columns with large amounts of data. In this case, the Employee_Photos table contains a large binary column with a photo of each employee. Because this column is used infrequently, storing it in a separate table will make operations on the Employees table more efficient. Then, when this column is needed, it can be combined with the columns in the Employees table using a join.

How to enforce the relationships between tables

Although the primary keys and foreign keys indicate how the tables in a database are related, the database management system doesn't always enforce those relationships automatically. In that case, any of the operations shown in the table at the top of figure 10-6 would violate the *referential integrity* of the tables. If you deleted a row from a primary key table, for example, and the foreign key table included rows related to that primary key, the referential integrity of the two tables would be destroyed. In that case, the rows in the foreign key table that no longer have a related row in the primary key table would be *orphaned*. Similar problems can occur when you insert a row into the foreign key table or update a primary key or foreign key value.

To enforce those relationships and maintain the referential integrity of the tables, MySQL provides for *declarative referential integrity*. To use it, you define *foreign key constraints* that indicate how the referential integrity between the tables is enforced. You'll learn more about defining foreign key constraints in the next chapter. For now, just realize that these constraints can prevent all of the operations listed in this figure that violate referential integrity.

Operations that can violate referential integrity

This operation...	Violates referential integrity if...
Delete a row from the primary key table	The foreign key table contains one or more rows related to the deleted row
Insert a row in the foreign key table	The foreign key value doesn't have a matching primary key value in the related table
Update the value of a foreign key	The new foreign key value doesn't have a matching primary key value in the related table
Update the value of a primary key	The foreign key table contains one or more rows related to the row that's changed

Description

- *Referential integrity* means that the relationships between tables are maintained correctly. That means that a table with a foreign key doesn't have rows with foreign key values that don't have matching primary key values in the related table.

- In MySQL, you can enforce referential integrity by using declarative referential integrity.

- To use *declarative referential integrity (DRI)*, you define *foreign key constraints*. You'll learn how to do that in the next chapter.

- When you define foreign key constraints, you can specify how referential integrity is enforced when a row is deleted from the primary key table. The options are to return an error, to delete the related rows in the foreign key table, or to set the foreign key values in the related rows to null.

- If referential integrity isn't enforced and a row is deleted from the primary key table that has related rows in the foreign key table, the rows in the foreign key table are said to be *orphaned*.

Figure 10-6   How to enforce the relationships between tables

How normalization works

The next step in the design process is to review whether the data structure is *normalized*. To do that, you look at how the data is separated into related tables. If you follow the first four steps for designing a database that are presented in this chapter, your database will already be partially normalized when you get to this step. However, almost every design can be normalized further.

Figure 10-7 illustrates how *normalization* works. The first two tables in this figure show some of the problems caused by an *unnormalized data structure*. In the first table, you can see that each row represents an invoice. Because an invoice can have one or more line items, however, the item_description column must be repeated to provide for the maximum number of line items. But since most invoices have fewer line items than the maximum, this can waste storage space.

In the second table, each line item is stored in a separate row. That eliminates the problem caused by repeating the item_description column, but it introduces a new problem: the invoice number must be repeated in each row. This, too, can cause storage problems, particularly if the repeated column is large. In addition, it can cause maintenance problems if the column contains a value that's likely to change. Then, when the value changes, each row that contains the value must be updated. And if a repeated value must be reentered for each new row, it would be easy for the value to vary from one row to another.

To eliminate the problems caused by *data redundancy*, you can normalize the data structure. To do that, you apply the *normal forms* you'll learn about later in this chapter. As you'll see, there are a total of seven normal forms. However, it's common to apply only the first three. The diagram in this figure, for example, shows the accounts payable system in third normal form. Although it may not be obvious at this point how this reduces data redundancy, that will become clearer as you learn about the different normal forms.

A table that contains repeating columns

vendor_name	invoice_number	item_description_1	item_description_2	item_description_3
Cahners Publishing	112897	VB ad	SQL ad	Library directory
Zylka Design	97/552	Catalogs	SQL flyer	NULL
Zylka Design	97/553B	Card revision	NULL	NULL

A table that contains redundant data

vendor_name	invoice_number	item_description
Cahners Publishing	112897	VB ad
Cahners Publishing	112897	SQL ad
Cahners Publishing	112897	Library directory
Zylka Design	97/522	Catalogs
Zylka Design	97/522	SQL flyer
Zylka Design	97/553B	Card revision

The accounts payable system in third normal form

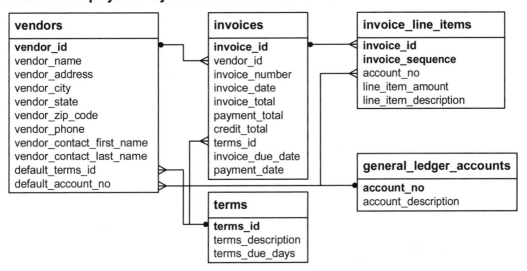

Description

- *Normalization* is a formal process you can use to separate the data in a data structure into related tables. Normalization reduces *data redundancy*, which can cause storage and maintenance problems.

- In an *unnormalized data structure*, a table can contain information about two or more entities. It can also contain repeating columns, columns that contain repeating values, and data that's repeated in two or more rows.

- In a *normalized data structure*, each table contains information about a single entity, and each piece of information is stored in exactly one place.

- To normalize a data structure, you apply the *normal forms* in sequence. Although there are a total of seven normal forms, a data structure is typically considered normalized if the first three normal forms are applied.

Figure 10-7   How normalization works

How to identify the columns to be indexed

The last step in the design process is to identify the columns that should be indexed. An *index* is a structure that provides for locating one or more rows directly. Without an index, a database management system has to perform a *table scan*, which involves searching through the entire table.

Just as the index of a book has page numbers that direct you to a specific subject, a database index has pointers that direct the system to a specific row. This can speed performance not only when you're searching for rows based on a search condition, but also when you're joining data from tables. If a join is done based on a primary key to foreign key relationship, for example, and an index is defined for the foreign key column, the database management system can use that index to locate the rows for each primary key value.

When you use MySQL, an index is automatically created for the primary and foreign keys in each table that you create. But you should consider creating indexes for other columns in some of the tables based on the guidelines at the top of figure 10-8.

To start, you should index a column if it will be used frequently in search conditions or joins. The column should also contain mostly distinct values, and the values in the column should be updated infrequently. If these conditions aren't met, the overhead of maintaining the index will probably outweigh the advantages of using it.

When you create indexes, you should be aware that MySQL must update the indexes whenever you add, update, or delete rows. Because that can affect performance, you don't want to define more indexes than you need.

As you identify the indexes for a table, keep in mind that, like a key, an index can consist of two or more columns. This type of index is called a *composite index*.

When to create an index

- When the column is used frequently in search conditions or joins
- When the column contains a large number of distinct values
- When the column is updated infrequently

Description

- MySQL automatically creates an index for primary keys and foreign keys.
- An *index* provides a way for a database management system to locate information more quickly. When it uses an index, the database management system can go directly to a specific row rather than having to search through all the rows until it finds it.
- Indexes speed performance when searching and joining tables.
- You can create *composite indexes* that include two or more columns. You should use this type of index when the columns in the index are updated infrequently or when the index covers almost every search condition on the table.
- Because indexes must be updated each time you add, update, or delete a row, you shouldn't create more indexes than you need.

Figure 10-8   How to identify the columns to be indexed

How to normalize a data structure

The topics that follow describe the seven normal forms and teach you how to apply the first three. As I said earlier, you apply these three forms to some extent in the first four database design steps, but these topics will give you more insight into the process. Then, the last topic explains when and how to denormalize a data structure. When you finish these topics, you'll have the basic skills for designing databases that are efficient and easy to use.

The seven normal forms

Figure 10-9 summarizes the seven normal forms. Each normal form assumes that the previous forms have already been applied. Before you can apply the third normal form, for example, the design must already be in the second normal form.

Strictly speaking, a data structure isn't normalized until it's in the fifth or sixth normal form. However, the normal forms past the third normal form are applied infrequently. Because of that, I won't present those forms in detail here. Instead, I'll just describe them briefly so you'll have an idea of how to apply them if you need to.

The *Boyce-Codd normal form* can be used to eliminate *transitive dependencies*. With this type of dependency, one column depends on another column, which depends on a third column. To illustrate, consider the city, state, and zip code columns in the Vendors table. Here, a zip code identifies a city and state, which means that the city and state are dependent on the zip code. The zip code, in turn, is dependent on the vendor_id column. To eliminate this dependency, you could store the city and state values in a separate table that uses zip code as its primary key.

The fourth normal form can be used to eliminate multiple *multivalued dependencies* from a table. A multivalued dependency is one where a primary key column has a one-to-many relationship with a non-key column. To illustrate, consider the vendor contact phone number in the Vendors table. If you wanted to accommodate alternate phone numbers, such as a cellular or home phone, you could add extra columns for each type of number. However, this creates a multivalued dependency between the phone numbers and the vendor_id. To be in fourth normal form, therefore, you'd need to store phone numbers in a separate table that uses vendor_id as a foreign key.

To apply the fifth normal form, you continue to divide the tables of the data structure into smaller tables until all redundancy has been removed. When further splitting would result in tables that couldn't be used to reconstruct the original table, the data structure is in fifth normal form. In this form, most tables consist of little more than key columns with one or two data elements.

The *domain-key normal form*, sometimes called the sixth normal form, is only of academic interest since no database system has implemented a way to apply it. For this reason, even normalization purists might consider a database to be normalized in fifth normal form.

The seven normal forms

Normal form	Description
First (1NF)	The value stored at the intersection of each row and column must be a scalar value, and a table must not contain any repeating columns.
Second (2NF)	Every non-key column must depend on the entire primary key.
Third (3NF)	Every non-key column must depend only on the primary key.
Boyce-Codd (BCNF)	A non-key column can't be dependent on another non-key column. This prevents *transitive dependencies*, where column A depends on column C and column B depends on column C. Since both A and B depend on C, A and B should be moved into another table with C as the key.
Fourth (4NF)	A table must not have more than one *multivalued dependency*, where the primary key has a one-to-many relationship to non-key columns. This form gets rid of misleading many-to-many relationships.
Fifth (5NF)	The data structure is split into smaller and smaller tables until all redundancy has been eliminated. If further splitting would result in tables that couldn't be joined to recreate the original table, the structure is in fifth normal form.
Domain-key (DKNF) or Sixth (6NF)	Every constraint on the relationship is dependent only on key constraints and domain constraints, where a *domain* is the set of allowable values for a column. This form prevents the insertion of any unacceptable data by enforcing constraints at the level of a relationship, rather than at the table or column level. DKNF is less a design model than an abstract "ultimate" normal form.

The benefits of normalization

- Since a normalized database has more tables than an unnormalized database, and since each table has an index on its primary key, the database has more indexes. That makes data retrieval more efficient.

- Since each table contains information about a single entity, each index has fewer columns (usually one) and fewer rows. That makes data retrieval and insert, update, and delete operations more efficient.

- Each table has fewer indexes, which makes insert, update, and delete operations more efficient.

- Data redundancy is minimized, which simplifies maintenance and reduces storage.

Description

- Each normal form assumes that the design is already in the previous normal form.

- A database is typically considered to be normalized if it is in third normal form. The other four forms are not commonly used and are not covered in detail in this book.

Figure 10-9   The seven normal forms

Figure 10-9 also lists the benefits of normalizing a data structure. To summarize, normalization produces smaller, more efficient tables. In addition, it reduces data redundancy, which makes the data easier to maintain and reduces the amount of storage needed for the database. Because of these benefits, you should always consider normalizing your data structures.

You should also be aware that the subject of normalization is a contentious one in the database community. In the academic study of computer science, normalization is considered a form of design perfection that should always be strived for. In practice, though, database designers and DBAs tend to use normalization as a flexible design guideline.

How to apply the first normal form

Figure 10-10 illustrates how you apply the first normal form to an unnormalized invoice data structure consisting of the data elements that are shown in figure 10-2. The first two tables in this figure illustrate structures that aren't in first normal form. Both of these tables contain a single row for each invoice. Because each invoice can contain one or more line items, though, the first table allows for repeating values in the item_description column. The second table is similar, except it includes a separate column for each line item description. Neither of these structures is acceptable in first normal form.

The third table in this figure has eliminated the repeating values and columns. To do that, it includes one row for each line item. Notice, however, that this has increased the data redundancy. Specifically, the vendor name and invoice number are now repeated for each line item. This problem can be solved by applying the second normal form.

Before I describe the second normal form, I want you to realize that I intentionally omitted many of the columns in the invoice data structure from the examples in this figure and the next figure. In addition to the columns shown here, for example, each of these tables would also contain the vendor address, invoice date, invoice total, etc. By eliminating these columns, it will be easier for you to focus on the columns that are affected by applying the normal forms.

The invoice data with a column that contains repeating values

vendor_name	invoice_number	item_description
Cahners Publishing	112897	VB ad, SQL ad, Library directory
Zylka Design	97/522	Catalogs, SQL Flyer
Zylka Design	97/533B	Card revision

The invoice data with repeating columns

vendor_name	invoice_number	item_description_1	item_description_2	item_description_3
Cahners Publishing	112897	VB ad	SQL ad	Library directory
Zylka Design	97/552	Catalogs	SQL flyer	NULL
Zylka Design	97/553B	Card revision	NULL	NULL

The invoice data in first normal form

vendor_name	invoice_number	item_description
Cahners Publishing	112897	VB ad
Cahners Publishing	112897	SQL ad
Cahners Publishing	112897	Library directory
Zylka Design	97/522	Catalogs
Zylka Design	97/522	SQL flyer
Zylka Design	97/553B	Card revision

Description

- For a table to be in first normal form, its columns must not contain repeating values. Instead, each column must contain a single, scalar value. In addition, the table must not contain repeating columns that represent a set of values.

- A table in first normal form often has repeating values in its rows. This can be resolved by applying the second normal form.

Figure 10-10   How to apply the first normal form

How to apply the second normal form

Figure 10-11 shows how to apply the second normal form. To be in second normal form, every column in a table that isn't a key column must be dependent on the entire primary key. This form only applies to tables that have composite primary keys, which is often the case when you start with data that is completely unnormalized. The table at the top of this figure, for example, shows the invoice data in first normal form after key columns have been added. In this case, the primary key consists of the invoice_id and invoice_sequence columns. The invoice_sequence column is needed to uniquely identify each line item for an invoice.

Now, consider the three non-key columns shown in this table. Of these three, only one, item_description, depends on the entire primary key. The other two, vendor_name and invoice_number, depend only on the invoice_id column. Because of that, these columns should be moved to another table. The result is a data structure like the second one shown in this figure. Here, all of the information related to an invoice is stored in the Invoices table, and all of the information related to an individual line item is stored in the Invoice_Line_Items table.

Notice that the relationship between these tables is based on the invoice_id column. This column is the primary key of the Invoices table, and it's the foreign key in the Invoice_Line_Items table that relates the rows in that table to the rows in the Invoices table. This column is also part of the primary key of the Invoice_Line_Items table.

When you apply second normal form to a data structure, it eliminates some of the redundant row data in the tables. In this figure, for example, you can see that the invoice number and vendor name are now included only once for each invoice. In first normal form, this information was included for each line item.

The invoice data in first normal form with keys added

invoice_id	vendor_name	invoice_number	invoice_sequence	item_description
1	Cahners Publishing	112897	1	VB ad
1	Cahners Publishing	112897	2	SQL ad
1	Cahners Publishing	112897	3	Library directory
2	Zylka Design	97/522	1	Catalogs
2	Zylka Design	97/522	2	SQL flyer
3	Zylka Design	97/533B	1	Card revision

The invoice data in second normal form

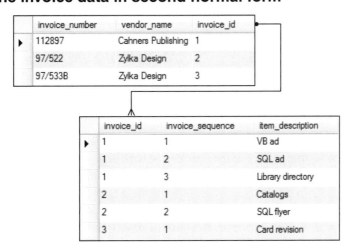

invoice_number	vendor_name	invoice_id
112897	Cahners Publishing	1
97/522	Zylka Design	2
97/533B	Zylka Design	3

invoice_id	invoice_sequence	item_description
1	1	VB ad
1	2	SQL ad
1	3	Library directory
2	1	Catalogs
2	2	SQL flyer
3	1	Card revision

Description

- For a table to be in second normal form, every non-key column must depend on the entire primary key. If a column doesn't depend on the entire key, it indicates that the table contains information for more than one entity. This can happen if the table contains a composite primary key.
- To apply second normal form, you move columns that don't depend on the entire primary key to another table and then establish a relationship between the two tables.
- Second normal form helps remove redundant row data, which can save storage space, make maintenance easier, and reduce the chance of storing inconsistent data.

Figure 10-11   How to apply the second normal form

How to apply the third normal form

To apply the third normal form, you make sure that every non-key column depends *only* on the primary key. Figure 10-12 illustrates how you can apply this form to the data structure for the accounts payable system. At the top of this figure, you can see all of the columns in the Invoices and Invoice_Line_Items tables in second normal form. Then, you can see a list of questions that you might ask about some of the columns in these tables when you apply third normal form.

First, does the vendor information depend only on the invoice_id column? Another way to phrase this question is, "Will the information for the same vendor change from one invoice to another?" If the answer is no, the vendor information should be stored in a separate table. That way, can you be sure that the vendor information for each invoice for a vendor will be the same. In addition, you will reduce the redundancy of the data in the Invoices table. This is illustrated by the diagram in this figure that shows the accounts payable system in third normal form. Here, a Vendors table has been added to store the information for each vendor. This table is related to the Invoices table by the vendor_id column, which has been added as a foreign key to the Invoices table.

Second, does the terms column depend only on the invoice_id column? The answer to that question depends on how this column is used. In this case, I'll assume that this column is used not only to specify the terms for each invoice, but also to specify the default terms for a vendor. Because of that, the terms information could be stored in both the Vendors and the Invoices tables. To avoid redundancy, however, the information related to different terms can be stored in a separate table, as illustrated by the Terms table in this figure. As you can see, the primary key of this table is an auto increment column named terms_id. Then, a foreign key column named default_terms_id has been added to the Vendors table, and a foreign key column named terms_id has been added to the Invoices table.

Third, does the account_no column depend only on the invoice_id column? Again, that depends on how this column is used. In this case, it's used to specify the general ledger account number for each line item, so it depends on the invoice_id and the invoice_sequence columns. In other words, this column should be stored in the Invoice_Line_Items table. In addition, each vendor has a default account number, which should be stored in the Vendors table. Because of that, another table named General_Ledger_Accounts has been added to store the account numbers and account descriptions. Then, foreign key columns have been added to the Vendors and Invoice_Line_Items tables to relate them to this table.

Fourth, can the invoice_due_date column in the Invoices table and the line_item_amount column in the Invoice_Line_Items table be derived from other data in the database? If so, they depend on the columns that contain that data rather than on the primary key columns. In this case, the value of the line_item_amount column can always be calculated from the item_quantity and item_unit_price columns. Because of that, this column could be omitted. Alternatively, you could omit the item_quantity and item_unit_price columns and keep just the line_item_amount column. That's what I did in the data

The accounts payable system in second normal form

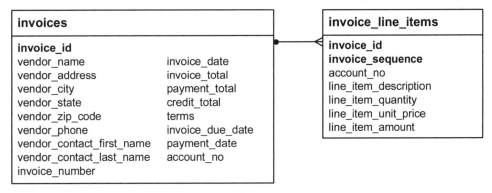

Questions about the structure

1. Does the vendor information (vendor_name, vendor_address, etc.) depend only on the invoice_id column?

2. Does the terms column depend only on the invoice_id column?

3. Does the account_no column depend only on the invoice_id column?

4. Can the invoice_due_date and line_item_amount columns be derived from other data?

The accounts payable system in third normal form

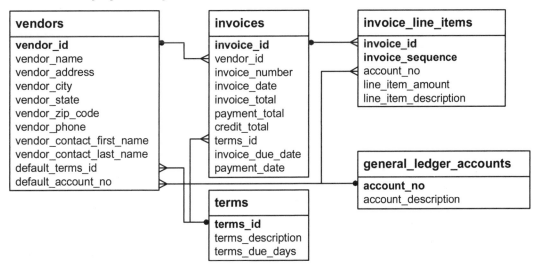

Description

- For a table to be in third normal form, every non-key column must depend *only* on the primary key.

- If a column doesn't depend only on the primary key, it implies that the column is assigned to the wrong table or that it can be computed from other columns in the table. A column that can be computed from other columns contains *derived data*.

Figure 10-12   How to apply the third normal form

structure shown in this figure. The solution you choose, however, depends on how the data will be used.

In contrast, although the invoice_due_date column could be calculated from the invoice_date column in the Invoices table and the terms_due_days column in the related row of the Terms table, the system also allows this date to be overridden. Because of that, the invoice_due_date column should not be omitted. If the system didn't allow this value to be overridden, however, this column could be safely omitted.

When and how to denormalize a data structure

Denormalization is the deliberate deviation from the normal forms. Most denormalization occurs beyond the third normal form. In contrast, the first three normal forms are almost universally applied.

To illustrate when and how to *denormalize* a data structure, figure 10-13 presents the design of the accounts payable system in fifth normal form. Here, the vendor zip codes are stored in a separate table that contains the city and state for each zip code. In addition, the area codes are stored in a separate table. Because of that, a query that retrieves vendor addresses and phone numbers would require two joins. In contrast, if you left the city, state, and area code information in the Vendors table, no joins would be required, but the Vendors table would be larger.

In general, you should denormalize based on the way the data will be used. In this case, we'll seldom need to query phone numbers without the area code. Likewise, we'll seldom need to query city and state without the zip code. For these reasons, I've denormalized my design by eliminating the Zip_Codes and Area_Codes tables.

You might also consider denormalizing a table if the data it contains is updated infrequently. In that case, redundant data isn't as likely to cause problems.

Finally, you should consider including derived data in a table if that data is used frequently in search conditions. For example, if you frequently query the Invoices table based on invoice balances, you might consider including a column that contains the balance due. That way, you won't have to calculate this value each time it's queried. Keep in mind, though, that if you store derived data, it's possible for it to deviate from the derived value. For this reason, you may need to protect the derived column so it can't be updated directly. Alternatively, you could update the table periodically to reset the value of the derived column.

Because normalization eliminates the possibility of data redundancy errors and optimizes the use of storage, you should carefully consider when and how to denormalize a data structure. In general, you should denormalize only when the increased efficiency outweighs the potential for redundancy errors and storage problems. Of course, your decision to denormalize should also be based on your knowledge of the real-world environment in which the system will be used. If you've carefully analyzed the real-world environment as outlined in this chapter, you'll have a good basis for making that decision.

The accounts payable system in fifth normal form

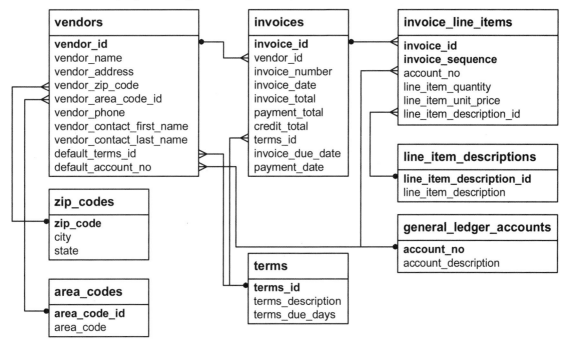

When to denormalize

- When a column from a joined table is used repeatedly in search criteria, you should consider moving that column to the primary key table if it will eliminate the need for a join.

- If a table is updated infrequently, you should consider denormalizing it to improve efficiency. Because the data remains relatively constant, you don't have to worry about data redundancy errors once the initial data is entered and verified.

- Include columns with derived values when those values are used frequently in search conditions. If you do that, you need to be sure that the column value is always synchronized with the value of the columns it's derived from.

Description

- Data structures that are normalized to the fourth normal form and beyond typically require more joins than tables normalized to the third normal form and can therefore be less efficient.

- MySQL statements that work with tables that are normalized to the fourth normal form and beyond are typically more difficult to code and debug.

- Most designers *denormalize* data structures to some extent, usually to the third normal form.

- *Denormalization* can result in larger tables, redundant data, and reduced performance.

- Only denormalize when necessary. It is better to adhere to the normal forms unless it is clear that performance will be improved by denormalizing.

Figure 10-13   When and how to denormalize a data structure

How to use MySQL Workbench for database design

When you're ready to create a database diagram, it usually makes sense to use a design tool that's specifically designed for that purpose. Fortunately, dozens of tools for designing databases are available. This topic introduces you to one of them: MySQL Workbench.

MySQL Workbench makes it easy to create one or more database diagrams from an *enhanced entity-relationship model (EER model)*. This model extends the original *entity-relationship model (ER model)*. In addition, you can create a visual representation of an EER model by creating one or more *EER diagrams* from that model.

When working with MySQL Workbench, you can generate an EER model from an existing MySQL database or SQL creation script. Conversely, you can generate a SQL creation script from an EER model. This makes it easy to implement your design when you're done with it.

How to open an existing EER model

When you start MySQL Workbench, it displays the Home page that's shown in figure 10-14. Then, you can open an existing EER model that was created with MySQL Workbench. If you opened the model recently, it should be displayed in the list of recently opened models in the Data Modeling section of the Home page. In this figure, for example, two models are shown in this list. One is named AP, and the other is named OM. Then, you can open the model by double-clicking on it. If the model you want to open isn't displayed in this list, you can click the "Open Existing EER Model" link and use the resulting dialog box to select the file for the model.

How to create a new EER model

If you're designing a new database from scratch, you can click the "Create New EER Model" link to create a model that doesn't contain any tables. Then, you can add tables to the model as shown in the next figure.

Alternatively, if you're redesigning an existing database, you can start by creating a model from that database. To do that, you can click the "Create EER Model From Existing Database" link. Then, you can use the resulting dialog boxes to connect to the server and select a database. When you do, MySQL Workbench creates a model and a diagram that includes all of the tables and columns of the selected database.

If you don't have access to the database but you have access to the script that creates it, you can create a model from that script. To do that, you can click the "Create EER Model From SQL Script" link. Then, you can use the resulting dialog box to select the script file.

The Home page of MySQL Workbench

Description

- MySQL Workbench allows you to create an *enhanced entity-relationship model* (*EER model*). This type of model extends the original *entity-relationship model* (*ER model*).

- Once you have created or opened an EER model, you can work with one or more *EER diagrams* that are associated with that model.

- To open an existing EER model, double-click on a recently used model in the list of models in the Data Modeling section. Or, click the "Open Existing EER Model" link and use the resulting dialog box to select the file for the model.

- To create a new EER model that's blank, click the "Create New EER Model" link.

- To create an EER model from an existing database, click the "Create EER Model From Existing Database" link and use the resulting dialog boxes to connect to the server and select a database.

- To create an EER model from a SQL creation script, click the "Create EER Model From SQL Script" link and use the resulting dialog box to select the script file.

- To remove an existing model from the list of recently used models, right-click on the model and select the "Remove Model From List" command.

Figure 10-14   How to create and open an EER model

How to work with an EER model

Figure 10-15 shows how to work with an EER model. In particular, it shows the Model tab for the AP database. From this tab, you can work with the tables of the database.

To edit one of these tables, you can double-click on it. When you do, MySQL Workbench displays a tab for the table at the bottom of the window. Within this tab are additional tabs that you can use to modify the columns, indexes, and foreign keys for the table. For example, this figure shows the Columns tab for the Vendors table. From this tab, you can modify the names, data types, and other attributes of the columns. You can also add a new column by entering the information for the column at the bottom of the table. And, you can modify the name of the table.

If you want to add a table to the model, you can double-click on the Add Table icon. Then, you can edit the table to set its name, columns, indexes, and foreign keys. You'll learn more about how to do that in the next chapter. Or, if you want to remove a table from the model, you can right-click on the table and select the Delete command.

Since you typically begin designing a database by creating the tables of the database, this figure focuses on how to work with tables. However, you can use similar skills to work with other database objects that are stored in the model, such as views and stored programs.

Since it's usually easier to work with a visual representation of the model, you can open a diagram that corresponds with the model. As you'll see in the next figure, this can make it easier to see the relationships between tables. When you work with a diagram, some changes that you make affect the corresponding model. As a result, you can think of working with a diagram as a more visual way of working with the model.

To open an existing diagram for a model, you can double-click on the name of the diagram. In this figure, for example, the model for the AP database contains a diagram named EER Diagram. For small databases, you may only need a single diagram like this. However, for larger databases, you may need to create multiple diagrams that provide ways to view different parts of the database. To create a new diagram for the model, you can double-click the Add Diagram icon. Then, the diagram is given a name such as EER Diagram 1, EER Diagram 2, and so on.

When you're done creating your model, you can create a MySQL database creation script from the diagram. To do that, you can select the File→Forward Engineer MySQL Create Script command. Then, you can implement your design by using MySQL Workbench to run the script. This creates the database that corresponds with the model.

The EER model for the AP database

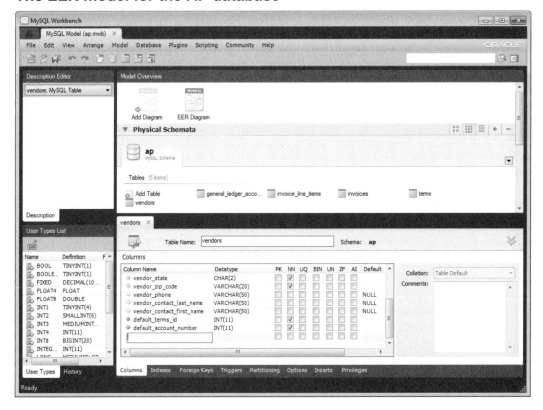

Description

- An EER model is a representation of the entities, or objects, of the database including the tables, views, and stored programs.

- To edit a table, double-click on it. Then, use the tabs that appear across the bottom of the window to modify the table's columns, indexes, and foreign keys.

- To add a new table, double-click on the Add Table icon. Then, use the tab that appears to define the table.

- To delete a table, right-click on it and select the Delete command.

- The skills for working with tables also apply to other database objects such as views and stored programs.

- The EER model typically includes at least one diagram named EER Diagram.

- To open a diagram, double-click on the name of the diagram.

- To create a new diagram, double-click on the Add Diagram icon or select the Model→Add Diagram command.

- To export a database creation script from the model, select the File→Export→ Forward Engineer SQL Create Script command.

Figure 10-15   How to work with an EER model

How to work with an EER diagram

When you open a model, MySQL Workbench often opens the diagrams associated with the model. If not, you can open a diagram as described in the previous figure. You can also create a new diagram for the model as described in the previous figure. When you do, a tab is opened for the diagram as shown in figure 10-16.

In this figure, you can see the diagram that's associated with the model for the AP database. This diagram shows the definitions of the columns in the tables as well as the relationships between the tables. For example, it shows that there's a one-to-many relationship between the Vendors and Invoices tables.

To edit a table, you can double-click on it. This displays a tab for the table that works the same as the one you saw in the last figure. As you learned in that figure, you can use this tab to make changes to the columns, indexes, and foreign keys.

To add a table that exists in the model to the diagram, you can drag the table from the Catalog Tree pane onto the diagram. Or, if you want to create a new table, you can click the Place a New Table button in the vertical toolbar to the left of the diagram and then click on the diagram. This adds a new table to the diagram and to the model.

Since a diagram provides a visual representation of the relationships between tables, you often use it to define those relationships. To do that, you can use the six relationship buttons at the bottom of the toolbar. The first five buttons generate foreign keys for the table, so you can use these buttons when the column for a foreign key doesn't exist yet. You can use the last relationship button if the foreign key column already exists in your diagram. For example, to create a relationship between the Vendors and Invoices tables, I clicked on the last button (the Place a Relationship Using Existing Columns button). Then, I clicked on the vendor_id column in the Invoices table to identify the foreign key, and I clicked on the vendor_id column in the Vendors table to identify the primary key.

In the next chapter, you'll learn more about the SQL statements that are generated by a tool like this. This will help you understand how to use MySQL Workbench, and it will allow you to edit the SQL statements that are generated by your database design tools.

The EER diagram for the AP database

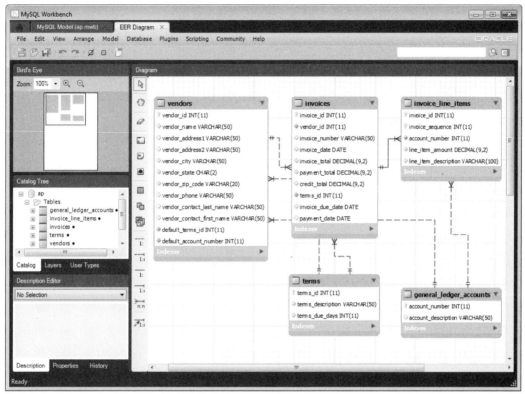

Description

- An EER diagram is a visual representation of an EER model. As a result, when you modify the tables in the diagram, you also modify the model.

- To add a table that already exists in the model to the diagram, drag the table from the Catalog Tree window onto the diagram.

- To add a new table to the diagram, click the Place a New Table button in the vertical toolbar at the left edge of the diagram. Then, click on the diagram where you want to add the table.

- To display the model for a table, double-click on the table. Then, a tab is displayed for the table, and you can use the techniques you learned in the previous figure to edit the table.

- To define the relationship between two tables, click one of the relationship buttons in the vertical toolbar. Then, click on the column in each table that defines the relationship.

- To edit or delete a relationship, right-click on the relationship icon and select the appropriate command.

- To remove a table from the diagram, right-click on the table and select the Delete command. Then, you can choose whether to also remove the table from the model or to only remove it from the diagram.

Figure 10-16   How to work with an EER diagram

Perspective

Database design is a complicated subject. Because of that, it's impossible to teach you everything you need to know in a single chapter. With the skills you've learned in this chapter, though, you should now be able to design simple databases of your own. More important, you should be able to evaluate the design of any database that you work with. That way, you can be sure that the queries you code will be as efficient and as effective as possible.

In the next chapter, you'll learn how to implement the database designs you develop using DDL statements. As you read that chapter, though, keep in mind that you can also implement a database design by generating a SQL creation script from an EER model and then executing that script. Even so, you'll want to be sure you understand the DDL statements the generated script contains.

Terms

data structure	unnormalized data structure
entity	normalized data structure
attribute	normal forms
instance	index
entity-relationship (ER) modeling	table scan
CASE (computer-aided software engineering)	composite index
	derived data
linking table	Boyce-Codd normal form
connecting table	transitive dependency
associate table	multivalued dependency
referential integrity	domain-key normal form
declarative referential integrity (DRI)	denormalization
foreign key constraint	entity-relationship (ER) model
orphaned row	enhanced entity-relationship (EER) model
normalization	
data redundancy	EER diagram

Exercises

1. Use MySQL Workbench to create an EER diagram for a database that stores information about products.

   Each product must have a product name, description, and price.

   Each product must belong to one category.

   Each category must have a category name and description.

   Each category can include multiple products.

2. Use MySQL Workbench to create an EER diagram for a database that stores information about customers.

   Each customer must have an email address, first name, and last name.

   Each customer can have two or more addresses.

   Each customer can have a default billing address and a default shipping address.

   Each address must have a street address, city, state, postal code, and country.

   Each country name should be stored in one place only. In other words, you shouldn't store the name of the country, which may be many characters, in the address.

3. Use MySQL Workbench to create an EER diagram for a database that tracks the memberships for an association and for the groups within the association.

   Each member must have an email address, first name, and last name.

   Each member can belong to any number of groups.

   Each group must have a name.

   Each group can have any number of members.

11

How to create databases, tables, and indexes

Now that you've learned how to design a database, you're ready to learn how to implement your design. To do that, you use the set of SQL statements that are known as the data definition language (DDL). In this chapter, you'll learn how to use DDL statements or MySQL Workbench to work with databases, tables, and indexes. In addition, you'll learn how to change the character set, collation, and storage engine if you need to do that.

How to work with databases	**314**
How to create and drop a database	314
How to select a database	314
How to work with tables	**316**
How to create a table	316
How to code a primary key constraint	318
How to code a foreign key constraint	320
How to alter the columns of a table	322
How to alter the constraints of a table	324
How to rename, truncate, and drop a table	326
How to work with indexes	**328**
How to create an index	328
How to drop an index	328
A script that creates a database	**330**
How to use MySQL Workbench	**334**
How to work with the columns of a table	334
How to work with the indexes of a table	336
How to work with the foreign keys of a table	338
How to work with character sets and collations	**340**
An introduction to character sets and collations	340
How to view character sets and collations	342
How to specify a character set and a collation	344
How to work with storage engines	**346**
An introduction to storage engines	346
How to view storage engines	346
How to specify a storage engine	348
Perspective	**350**

How to work with databases

Before you can begin creating the tables of a database, you must create the database. Then, since multiple databases may be running on a single MySQL server, you usually select the database before you begin working with it. Of course, if you decide that you no longer need a database, you can drop it, which causes the database and all of its tables and data to be deleted.

If you're working on a large database project, you probably won't need to code DDL statements like these because that will be handled by a database design specialist or a database administrator (DBA). For small projects, though, the SQL programmer may often have to serve as the DBA too. And even when working with large projects, the SQL programmer often needs to use DDL to create smaller tables that are needed for testing.

How to create and drop a database

Figure 11-1 starts by presenting the CREATE DATABASE statement. The first example in this figure uses the CREATE DATABASE statement to create a database named AP. If a database already exists with that name, this statement generates an error and doesn't execute. To prevent this, you can add the IF NOT EXISTS keywords to the CREATE DATABASE statement as shown in the second example. Then, the statement only executes if the database doesn't already exist.

The syntax of the DROP DATABASE statement is also shown in this figure. The third example uses this statement to delete the database named AP that was created in the first two examples. This permanently deletes everything in the entire database, so use it with caution! If the specified database doesn't exist, this statement generates an error. To prevent this, you can add the IF EXISTS keywords to the statement as shown in the fourth example. Then, the statement only drops the database if it exists.

How to select a database

Figure 11-1 also shows how to select a database using the USE statement. The example shown here uses this statement to select the database that was created by the CREATE DATABASE statement in the first example. Although the USE statement isn't a standard SQL statement, it's a MySQL extension that's commonly used when working with MySQL databases.

How to use the CREATE DATABASE statement

Syntax

```
CREATE DATABASE [IF NOT EXISTS] db_name
```

Attempt to create a database named AP

```
CREATE DATABASE ap
```

Create a database named AP only if it doesn't exist

```
CREATE DATABASE IF NOT EXISTS ap
```

How to use the DROP DATABASE statement

Syntax

```
DROP DATABASE [IF EXISTS] db_name
```

Attempt to drop a database named AP

```
DROP DATABASE ap
```

Drop a database named AP only if it exists

```
DROP DATABASE IF EXISTS ap
```

How to use the USE statement

Syntax

```
USE db_name
```

Select a database named AP

```
USE ap
```

Description

- The CREATE DATABASE statement creates a database with the specified name on the server.
- The DROP DATABASE statement deletes the database with the specified name from the server. This deletes all of the tables and data that are stored in the database.
- The USE statement selects the specified database and makes it the current database.

Figure 11-1   How to create, drop, and select a database

How to work with tables

This topic shows how to code the DDL statements that work with the tables of a database. Because the syntax for these statements is complex, this chapter doesn't present complete syntax diagrams for these statements. Instead, the diagrams present only the commonly used clauses. If you're interested in the complete syntax of any statement, though, you can refer to the MySQL Reference Manual.

How to create a table

Figure 11-2 presents a simplified syntax for the CREATE TABLE statement. By default, this statement creates a new table in the current database. If that's not what you want, you can qualify the table name with the database name. For example, you can qualify the Vendors table with the EX database like this:

```
CREATE TABLE ex.vendors
```

Before I continue, you should realize that if you run the statements shown in this figure against the AP database, the statements will fail. That's because the AP database already contains tables named Vendors and Invoices. As a result, if you want to test these statements, you can run them against the EX database. Then, the Vendors and Invoices tables will be created in that database.

In its simplest form, the CREATE TABLE statement consists of the name of the new table followed by the names and data types of its columns. This is illustrated by the first example in this figure. However, in most cases, you'll code one or more *attributes* for each column as illustrated by the second example. For instance, to indicate that a column doesn't accept null values, you can code the NOT NULL attribute. If you omit this attribute, the column allows null values.

To indicate that each row in a column must contain a unique value, you can code the UNIQUE attribute. Since two null values aren't considered to be the same, a unique column can contain null values. However, it's common to use the NOT NULL and UNIQUE attributes to define a column that can't contain null values and where each value in the column must be unique.

To generate unique numbers in sequence, you use the AUTO_INCREMENT attribute. This attribute can only be specified for one column in a table, and that column must be defined as either the primary key or a unique key. When you define a column with the AUTO_INCREMENT attribute, MySQL automatically generates the next number in sequence for the column if you don't specify a value. By default, MySQL starts numbering with 1, but you can start with a value other than 1 by coding the AUTO_INCREMENT attribute like this:

```
AUTO_INCREMENT = 3
```

Finally, to specify a default value for a column, you can use the DEFAULT attribute. This value is used if another value isn't specified when a row is added to the database. The default value you specify must correspond to the data type for the column. For example, the default value for the payment_total column is set to a value of zero.

The syntax of the CREATE TABLE statement

```
CREATE TABLE [db_name.]table_name
(
  column_name_1 data_type [column_attributes]
  [, column_name_2 data_type [column_attributes]]...
  [, table_level_constraints]
)
```

Common column attributes

Attribute	Description
NOT NULL	Indicates that the column doesn't accept null values. If omitted, the column can accept null values.
UNIQUE	Specifies that each value stored in the column must be unique.
DEFAULT default_value	Specifies a default value for the column.
AUTO_INCREMENT	Identifies a column whose value is automatically incremented by MySQL when a new row is added. An auto increment column must be defined as an integer or a floating-point number.

A statement that creates a table without column attributes

```
CREATE TABLE vendors
(
  vendor_id      INT,
  vendor_name    VARCHAR(50)
)
```

A statement that creates a table with column attributes

```
CREATE TABLE vendors
(
  vendor_id      INT           NOT NULL    UNIQUE AUTO_INCREMENT,
  vendor_name    VARCHAR(50)   NOT NULL    UNIQUE
)
```

Another statement that creates a table with column attributes

```
CREATE TABLE invoices
(
  invoice_id       INT            NOT NULL    UNIQUE,
  vendor_id        INT            NOT NULL,
  invoice_number   VARCHAR(50)    NOT NULL,
  invoice_date     DATE,
  invoice_total    DECIMAL(9,2)   NOT NULL,
  payment_total    DECIMAL(9,2)               DEFAULT 0
)
```

Description

- To test the code in this figure and in the figures that follow, you can select the EX database.

- The CREATE TABLE statement creates a table based on the column names, data types, and *attributes* that you specify. In addition, it allows you to specify some attributes and constraints at the table level as described later in this chapter.

Figure 11-2   How to create a table

How to code a primary key constraint

Whether you realize it or not, the NOT NULL and UNIQUE keywords are examples of *constraints*. A constraint restricts the type of data that can be stored in a column. For example, the NOT NULL keyword prevents null values from being stored in a column, and the UNIQUE keyword only allows unique values.

Figure 11-3 shows how to code another type of constraint that's known as a *primary key constraint*. The easiest way to define a primary key is to code the PRIMARY KEY keywords after the data type for the column as shown in the first example. When you identify a column as the primary key, two of the column's attributes are changed automatically. First, the column is forced to be NOT NULL. Second, the column is forced to contain a unique value for each row. In addition, an index is automatically created based on the column.

When you define a constraint in a column definition as shown in the first example, it's called a *column-level constraint*. You can also define a constraint at the table level using the CONSTRAINT keyword. When you code a *table-level constraint*, you can provide a name for the constraint. In the second example in this figure, for instance, the first constraint provides a name of vendors_pk for the primary key of the Vendors table. Note how the constraint names used in this example begin with a table name or a column name. In addition, they use a two-letter suffix to identify the type of constraint.

Although you can't name them at the column level, the vendors_pk and vendor_name_uq constraints work the same regardless of whether they are coded at the column level or the table level. As a result, where you code these constraints is largely a matter of personal preference. I prefer to code the primary key and unique key constraints at the column level as shown in the first example. However, when MySQL Workbench generates code from an EER model, it usually codes these constraints at the table level as shown in the second example.

In addition to allowing you to name a primary key, a table-level constraint provides another capability that isn't available from column-level constraints: it can refer to multiple columns in the table. As a result, if you need to refer to multiple columns, you must use a table-level constraint. For example, to create the primary key for the Invoice_Line_Items table, I coded the constraint at the table level as shown in the third example. Unlike the constraint name for the primary key in the second example, I used an abbreviated form of the table name for the constraint name in this example. That keeps the constraint name shorter, but the name still clearly identifies the table that it applies to.

When you code a constraint at the table level, you must code a comma at the end of the preceding column definition. If you don't, you will get an error when you try to run the statement.

The syntax of a column-level primary key constraint

```
column_name data_type PRIMARY KEY column_attributes
```

The syntax of a table-level primary key constraint

```
[CONSTRAINT [constraint_name]]
PRIMARY KEY (column_name_1[, column_name_2]...)
```

A table with column-level constraints

```
CREATE TABLE vendors
(
  vendor_id      INT          PRIMARY KEY   AUTO_INCREMENT,
  vendor_name    VARCHAR(50)  NOT NULL      UNIQUE
)
```

A table with table-level constraints

```
CREATE TABLE vendors
(
  vendor_id      INT          AUTO_INCREMENT,
  vendor_name    VARCHAR(50)  NOT NULL,
  CONSTRAINT vendors_pk PRIMARY KEY (vendor_id),
  CONSTRAINT vendor_name_uq UNIQUE (vendor_name)
)
```

A table with a two-column primary key constraint

```
CREATE TABLE invoice_line_items
(
  invoice_id             INT            NOT NULL,
  invoice_sequence       INT            NOT NULL,
  line_item_description   VARCHAR(100)   NOT NULL,
  CONSTRAINT line_items_pk PRIMARY KEY (invoice_id, invoice_sequence)
)
```

Description

- *Constraints* are used to enforce the integrity of the data in a table by defining rules about the values that can be stored in the columns of the table.

- You code a *column-level constraint* as part of the definition of the column it constrains. You code a *table-level constraint* as if it is a separate column definition, and you name the columns it constrains within that definition.

- A *not null constraint* prevents null values from being stored in the column. A *unique constraint* requires that each row has a unique value in the column but allows null values to be stored in the column.

- A *primary key constraint* requires that each row has a unique value for the column or columns for the primary key, and it does not allow null values.

Figure 11-3   How to code a primary key constraint

How to code a foreign key constraint

Figure 11-4 shows how to code a *foreign key constraint*, which is also known as a *reference constraint*. This type of constraint is used to define the relationships between tables and to enforce referential integrity.

Before I describe foreign key constraints, you should know that MySQL only enforces these constraints if you are using the InnoDB storage engine for your tables. If you are using another storage engine such as MyISAM, you can still code foreign key constraints to show the relationships between the tables, but MySQL doesn't enforce these relationships. You'll learn more about working with the storage engines that are available from MySQL later in this chapter.

To create a foreign key constraint at the column level, you code the REFER-ENCES keyword followed by the name of the related table and the name of the related column in parentheses. In this figure, for instance, the first example creates a table with a vendor_id column that includes a REFERENCES clause that identifies the vendor_id column in the Vendors table as the related column.

The second example shows how to code the same foreign key constraint shown in the first example at the table level. When you use this syntax, you can include the CONSTRAINT keyword followed by a name, followed by the FOREIGN KEY keywords. Although this requires a little more code, it allows you to provide a name for the foreign key, which is a good programming practice. It also lets you reference a foreign key that consists of multiple columns.

The third example in this figure shows what happens when you try to insert a row into the Invoices table with a vendor_id value that isn't matched by the vendor_id column in the Vendors table. Because of the foreign key constraint, the system enforces referential integrity by refusing to do the operation. It also displays an error message that indicates the constraint that was violated.

Similarly, if you try to delete a row from the Vendors table that has related rows in the Invoices table, the delete operation will fail and the system will display an error message. Since this prevents rows in the Invoices table from being orphaned, this is usually what you want.

In some cases, though, you may want to automatically delete the related rows in the Invoices table when a row in the Vendors table is deleted. To do that, you can code the ON DELETE clause on the foreign key constraint as illus-trated by the fourth example. Here, this clause is coded with the CASCADE option. Then, when you delete a row from the primary key table, the delete is *cascaded* to the related rows in the foreign key table. If, for example, you delete a row from the Vendors table, all related rows in the Invoices table will also be deleted. Because a *cascading delete* makes it easier to delete data that you didn't intend to delete, you should use it with caution.

You can also code the SET NULL option on the ON DELETE clause. Then, when you delete a row from the primary key table, the values in the foreign key column of the foreign key table are set to null. Since this creates rows in the foreign key table that aren't related to the primary key table, you'll rarely want to use this option.

The syntax of a column-level foreign key constraint

```
[CONSTRAINT] REFERENCES table_name (column_name)
  [ON DELETE {CASCADE|SET NULL}]
```

The syntax of a table-level foreign key constraint

```
[CONSTRAINT constraint_name]
  FOREIGN KEY (column_name_1[, column_name_2]...)
  REFERENCES table_name (column_name_1[, column_name_2]...)
  [ON DELETE {CASCADE|SET NULL}]
```

A table with a column-level foreign key constraint

```
CREATE TABLE invoices
(
  invoice_id       INT           PRIMARY KEY,
  vendor_id        INT           REFERENCES vendors (vendor_id),
  invoice_number   VARCHAR(50)   NOT NULL       UNIQUE
)
```

A table with a table-level foreign key constraint

```
CREATE TABLE invoices
(
  invoice_id       INT           PRIMARY KEY,
  vendor_id        INT           NOT NULL,
  invoice_number   VARCHAR(50)   NOT NULL       UNIQUE,
  CONSTRAINT invoices_fk_vendors
    FOREIGN KEY (vendor_id) REFERENCES vendors (vendor_id)
)
```

An INSERT statement that fails because a related row doesn't exist

```
INSERT INTO invoices
VALUES (1, 1, '1')
```

The response from the system

```
Error Code: 1452. Cannot add or update a child row: a foreign key constraint
fails ('ex'.'invoices', CONSTRAINT 'invoices_fk_vendors' FOREIGN KEY
('vendor_id') REFERENCES 'vendors' ('vendor_id'))
```

A constraint that uses the ON DELETE clause

```
CONSTRAINT invoices_fk_vendors
  FOREIGN KEY (vendor_id) REFERENCES vendors (vendor_id)
  ON DELETE CASCADE
```

Description

- A *foreign key constraint* requires values in one table to match values in another table. This defines the relationship between two tables and enforces referential integrity.

- To define a relationship that consists of two or more columns, you must define the constraint at the table level.

Figure 11-4   How to code a foreign key constraint

How to alter the columns of a table

After you create tables, you may need to change the columns of a table. For example, you may need to add, modify, or drop a column. To do that, you can use the ALTER TABLE statement shown in figure 11-5.

The first example in this figure shows how to add a new column to a table. To do that, you code the column definition the same way you do when you create a new table. To start, you specify the column name. Then, you code the data type and column attributes.

The second example shows how to drop an existing column. Note that MySQL prevents you from dropping some columns. For example, you can't drop a column if it's the primary key column.

The third example shows how to modify the length of the data type for an existing column. In this case, a column that was defined as VARCHAR(50) is changed to VARCHAR(100). Since the new data type is bigger than the old data type, you can be sure that the existing data will still fit.

The fourth example shows how to change the data type to a different data type. In this case, a column that was defined as VARCHAR(100) is changed to CHAR(100). Since these data types both store the same type of characters, you know that no data will be lost.

The fifth example shows how to change the default value for a column. In this case, a default value of "New Vendor" is assigned to the vendor_name column.

In the first five statements, MySQL can alter the table without losing any data. As a result, these statements execute successfully and alter the table. However, if the change will result in a loss of data, it's not allowed. For example, the sixth statement attempts to change the length of the vendor_name column to a length that's too small for existing data that's stored in this column. As a result, MySQL doesn't modify the column, and the system returns an error message like the one shown in this figure.

The syntax for modifying the columns of a table

```
ALTER TABLE [db_name.]table_name
{
ADD          column_name data_type [column_attributes] |
DROP COLUMN column_name |
MODIFY       column_name data_type [column_attributes]
}
```

A statement that adds a new column

```
ALTER TABLE vendors
ADD last_transaction_date DATE
```

A statement that drops a column

```
ALTER TABLE vendors
DROP COLUMN last_transaction_date
```

A statement that changes the length of a column

```
ALTER TABLE vendors
MODIFY vendor_name VARCHAR(100) NOT NULL UNIQUE
```

A statement that changes the data type of a column

```
ALTER TABLE vendors
MODIFY vendor_name CHAR(100) NOT NULL UNIQUE
```

A statement that changes the default value of a column

```
ALTER TABLE vendors
MODIFY vendor_name VARCHAR(100) NOT NULL DEFAULT 'New Vendor'
```

A statement that fails because it would cause data to be lost

```
ALTER TABLE vendors
MODIFY vendor_name VARCHAR(10) NOT NULL UNIQUE
```

The response from the system

```
Error Code: 1265. Data truncated for column 'vendor_name' at row 1
```

Description

- You can use the ALTER TABLE statement to add, drop, or modify the columns of an existing table.
- MySQL won't allow you to change a column if that change would cause data to be lost.

Warning

- You should never alter a table or other database object in a production database without first consulting the DBA.

Figure 11-5 How to alter the columns of a table

How to alter the constraints of a table

You may also need to change the constraints of a table after you create it. For example, you may need to add or drop a constraint. To do that, you can use the ALTER TABLE statement as shown in figure 11-6.

The first example shows how to add a primary key to a table. To do that, you code the ADD PRIMARY KEY keywords followed by the names of the key columns in parentheses.

The second example shows how to add a foreign key to a table. This example uses the FOREIGN KEY keywords to identify the vendor_id column as the foreign key, and it uses the REFERENCES clause to identify the vendor_id column in the Vendors table as the related column. In addition, this example includes the optional CONSTRAINT keyword to provide a name for the foreign key, which is a good programming practice.

The third example uses the DROP PRIMARY KEY keywords to delete the primary key for the Vendors table. Depending on how this table and the other tables in the database are defined, MySQL may not allow you to drop the primary key for a table. That's true if the primary key is an auto increment column or if it's referred to by foreign keys. Since most primary keys are referred to by at least one foreign key, you can't typically delete a primary key.

The last example uses the DROP FOREIGN KEY keywords to drop the invoices_fk_vendors foreign key from the Invoices table. Because a table can contain more than one foreign key, you must know the name of the key you want to drop. If you don't know its name, you can use MySQL Workbench to look it up as shown later in this chapter.

The syntax for modifying the constraints of a table

```
ALTER TABLE [db_name.]table_name
{
ADD      PRIMARY KEY constraint_definition |
ADD      [CONSTRAINT  constraint_name] FOREIGN KEY constraint_definition |
DROP     PRIMARY KEY |
DROP     FOREIGN KEY constraint_name
}
```

A statement that adds a primary key constraint

```
ALTER TABLE vendors
ADD PRIMARY KEY (vendor_id)
```

A statement that adds a foreign key constraint

```
ALTER TABLE invoices
ADD CONSTRAINT invoices_fk_vendors
FOREIGN KEY (vendor_id) REFERENCES vendors (vendor_id)
```

A statement that drops a primary key constraint

```
ALTER TABLE vendors
DROP PRIMARY KEY
```

A statement that drops a foreign key constraint

```
ALTER TABLE invoices
DROP FOREIGN KEY invoices_fk_vendors
```

Description

- You can use the ALTER TABLE statement to add or drop the constraints of an existing table.
- To drop a foreign key constraint, you must know its name. If you don't know its name, you can use MySQL Workbench to look up the name as shown later in this chapter.

Figure 11-6   How to alter the constraints of a table

How to rename, truncate, and drop a table

Figure 11-7 shows how to use the RENAME TABLE, TRUNCATE TABLE, and DROP TABLE statements. When you use these statements, use them cautiously, especially when you're working on a production database.

To start, you can use the RENAME TABLE statement to rename an existing table. This is useful if you want to change the name of a table without modifying its column definitions or the data that's stored in the table. In this figure, for instance, the first example changes the name of the Vendors table to Vendor. If you rename a table, you should probably update the names of any constraints that use the name of the table. To do that, you have to drop the constraint and then add it back.

You can use the TRUNCATE TABLE statement to delete all of the data from a table without deleting the column definitions for the table. In this figure, for instance, the second example deletes all rows from the newly renamed Vendor table.

You can use the DROP TABLE statement to delete all of the data from a table and also delete the definition of the table, including the constraints for the table. In this figure, for instance, the third and fourth examples drop the Vendor table. However, the fourth example explicitly specifies that it is dropping the Vendor table that's stored in the EX database, not the Vendor table in another database such as the AP database.

When you issue a DROP TABLE statement, MySQL checks to see if other tables depend on the table you're trying to delete. If they do, MySQL won't allow the deletion. For instance, you can't delete the Vendors table from the AP database because a foreign key constraint in the Invoices table refers to the Vendors table. If you try to delete the Vendors table, the system will return an error message like the one shown in the fifth example. In that case, you must drop the Invoices table before you can drop the Vendors table.

When you drop a table, any indexes or triggers that have been defined for the table are also dropped. You'll learn how to create indexes for a table in just a moment. You'll learn how to create triggers for a table in chapter 16.

A statement that renames a table

```
RENAME TABLE vendors TO vendor
```

A statement that deletes all data from a table

```
TRUNCATE TABLE vendor
```

A statement that deletes a table from the current database

```
DROP TABLE vendor
```

A statement that qualifies the table to be deleted

```
DROP TABLE ex.vendor
```

A statement that returns an error due to a foreign key reference

```
DROP TABLE vendors
```

The response from the system

```
Error Code: 1217. Cannot delete or update a parent row: a foreign key
constraint fails
```

Description

- You can use the RENAME TABLE statement to change the name of an existing table.
- You can use the TRUNCATE TABLE statement to delete all data from a table without deleting the definition for the table.
- You can use the DROP TABLE statement to delete a table from the current database.
- To rename, truncate, or drop a table from another database, you must qualify the table name with the database name.
- You can't truncate or drop a table if a foreign key constraint in another table refers to that table.
- When you drop a table, all of its data, constraints, and indexes are deleted.

Warnings

- You shouldn't use these statements on a production database without first consulting the DBA.

Figure 11-7   How to rename, truncate, and drop a table

How to work with indexes

An *index* speeds up joins and searches by providing a way for a database management system to go directly to a row rather than having to search through all the rows until it finds the one you want. By default, MySQL creates indexes for the primary keys, foreign keys, and unique keys of a table. Usually, that's what you want. In addition, you may want to create indexes for other columns that are used frequently in search conditions or joins. However, you'll want to avoid creating indexes on columns that are updated frequently since this slows down insert, update, and delete operations.

How to create an index

Figure 11-8 presents the basic syntax of the CREATE INDEX statement, which creates an index based on one or more columns of a table. To create an index, you name the table and columns that the index will be based on in the ON clause. For each column, you can specify the ASC or DESC keyword to indicate whether you want the index sorted in ascending or descending sequence. If you don't specify a sort order, ASC is the default. In addition, you can use the UNIQUE keyword to specify that an index contains only unique values.

In the examples in this figure, the names follow a standard naming convention. To start, the index name specifies the name of the table, followed by the name of the column or columns, followed by a suffix of IX. This naming convention makes it easy to see which columns of which tables have been indexed. However, if the table or column names are lengthy, you can abbreviate their names in the name of the index.

How to drop an index

The last example in figure 11-8 shows how to use the DROP INDEX statement to drop an index. You may want to drop an index if you suspect that it isn't speeding up your joins and searches and that it may be slowing down your insert, update, and delete operations.

The syntax of the CREATE INDEX statement

```
CREATE [UNIQUE] INDEX index_name
  ON [db_name.]table_name (column_name_1 [ASC|DESC][,
                           column_name_2 [ASC|DESC]]...)
```

A statement that creates an index based on a single column

```
CREATE INDEX invoices_invoice_date_ix
  ON invoices (invoice_date)
```

A statement that creates an index based on two columns

```
CREATE INDEX invoices_vendor_id_invoice_number_ix
  ON invoices (vendor_id, invoice_number)
```

A statement that creates a unique index

```
CREATE UNIQUE INDEX vendors_vendor_phone_ix
  ON vendors (vendor_phone)
```

A statement that creates an index that's sorted in descending order

```
CREATE INDEX invoices_invoice_total_ix
  ON invoices (invoice_total DESC)
```

A statement that drops an index

```
DROP INDEX vendors_vendor_phone_ix ON vendors
```

Description

- MySQL automatically creates an *index* for primary key, foreign key, and unique constraints.

- You can use the CREATE INDEX statement to create other indexes for a table. An index can improve performance when MySQL searches for rows in the table.

- You can use the DROP INDEX statement to drop an index from a table.

Figure 11-8   How to create and drop an index

A script that creates a database

Figure 11-9 presents the DDL statements that are used to create the AP database that's used throughout this book. In this figure, these statements are coded as part of a script.

As you learned in earlier chapters, a *script* is a file that contains one or more SQL statements. Scripts are often used to create the objects for a database as shown in this figure. When you code a script, you code a semicolon at the end of each SQL statement.

The DROP DATABASE IF EXISTS statement that begins this script drops the entire database if it already exists, including all of its tables. This suppresses any error messages that would be displayed if you attempted to drop a database that didn't exist. Then, the CREATE DATABASE statement creates the AP database.

The USE statement selects the AP database. As a result, the rest of the statements in the script are executed against the AP database.

The CREATE TABLE statements create the five main tables of the AP database. For each statement, I coded the primary key column (or columns) first. Although this isn't required, it's a good programming practice. After the primary key, I coded the remaining columns in a logical order. That way, if you use a SELECT * statement to retrieve all of the columns, they're returned in a logical order.

When you create tables, you must create the tables that don't have foreign keys first. That way, the other tables can define foreign keys that refer to them. In this figure, for example, I created the General_Ledger_Accounts and Terms tables first since they don't have foreign keys. Then, I coded the Vendors table, which has foreign keys that refer to these tables. And so on. Conversely, when you drop tables, you must drop the last table that was created first. Then, you can work back to the first table that was created. Otherwise, the foreign keys might not allow you to delete the tables.

The SQL script that creates the AP database   **Page 1**

```
-- create the database
DROP DATABASE IF EXISTS ap;
CREATE DATABASE ap;

-- select the database
USE ap;

-- create the tables
CREATE TABLE general_ledger_accounts
(
  account_number       INT            PRIMARY KEY,
  account_description  VARCHAR(50)    UNIQUE
);

CREATE TABLE terms
(
  terms_id             INT            PRIMARY KEY,
  terms_description    VARCHAR(50)    NOT NULL,
  terms_due_days       INT            NOT NULL
);

CREATE TABLE vendors
(
  vendor_id                   INT            PRIMARY KEY    AUTO_INCREMENT,
  vendor_name                 VARCHAR(50)    NOT NULL       UNIQUE,
  vendor_address1             VARCHAR(50),
  vendor_address2             VARCHAR(50),
  vendor_city                 VARCHAR(50)    NOT NULL,
  vendor_state                CHAR(2)        NOT NULL,
  vendor_zip_code             VARCHAR(20)    NOT NULL,
  vendor_phone                VARCHAR(50),
  vendor_contact_last_name    VARCHAR(50),
  vendor_contact_first_name   VARCHAR(50),
  default_terms_id            INT            NOT NULL,
  default_account_number      INT            NOT NULL,
  CONSTRAINT vendors_fk_terms
    FOREIGN KEY (default_terms_id)
    REFERENCES terms (terms_id),
  CONSTRAINT vendors_fk_accounts
    FOREIGN KEY (default_account_number)
    REFERENCES general_ledger_accounts (account_number)
);
```

Figure 11-9   The script used to create the AP database (part 1 of 2)

For most of the columns in these tables, I coded a NOT NULL constraint or a DEFAULT attribute. In general, I only allow a column to accept null values when I want to allow for unknown values. If, for example, a vendor doesn't supply an address, the address is unknown. In that case, you can store a null value in the vendor_address1 and vendor_address2 columns.

Another option is to store an empty string for these columns. To do that, I could have defined the vendor address columns like this:

```
vendor_address1     VARCHAR(50)     DEFAULT '',
vendor_address2     VARCHAR(50)     DEFAULT '',
```

In this case, empty strings will be stored for these columns unless other values are assigned to them.

In practice, a null value is a more intuitive representation of an unknown value than a default value is. Conversely, it makes sense to use a default value like an empty string to indicate that a value is known but the column is empty. For example, an empty string might indicate that a vendor hasn't provided its street address. Although how you use nulls and empty strings is largely a matter of personal preference, it does of course affect the way you query a table.

When a primary key consisted of a single column, I coded the PRIMARY KEY constraint at the column level. Similarly, I coded the UNIQUE constraint at the column level. As a result, I didn't provide names for these constraints. However, whenever I coded a primary key or foreign key constraint at the table level, I followed a convention that begins with the name of the table or an abbreviated name for the table.

As you know, when MySQL creates a table, it automatically creates indexes for the primary key, foreign keys, and unique keys. MySQL uses the name "PRIMARY" for the name of the index for a table's primary key. It uses the name of the column for the name of the index for a unique key. And it uses the name of the foreign key for the name of the index for a foreign key column. For the Invoices table, for example, MySQL automatically creates an index named "PRIMARY" for the invoice_id column, it creates an index named invoices_fk_vendors for the vendor_id column, and it creates an index named invoices_fk_terms for the terms_id column.

In addition to the indexes that are created automatically, I used a CREATE INDEX statement to create an index for the invoice_date column in the Invoices table. Since this column is frequently used to search for rows in this table, this index should improve performance of the database. To name this index, I followed the naming conventions presented earlier in this chapter. As a result, when you view the name of an index, you can easily identify the table and column that's being indexed.

The SQL script that creates the AP database   **Page 2**

```sql
CREATE TABLE invoices
(
  invoice_id              INT               PRIMARY KEY    AUTO_INCREMENT,
  vendor_id               INT               NOT NULL,
  invoice_number          VARCHAR(50)       NOT NULL,
  invoice_date            DATE              NOT NULL,
  invoice_total           DECIMAL(9,2)      NOT NULL,
  payment_total           DECIMAL(9,2)      NOT NULL       DEFAULT 0,
  credit_total            DECIMAL(9,2)      NOT NULL       DEFAULT 0,
  terms_id                INT               NOT NULL,
  invoice_due_date        DATE              NOT NULL,
  payment_date            DATE,
  CONSTRAINT invoices_fk_vendors
    FOREIGN KEY (vendor_id)
    REFERENCES vendors (vendor_id),
  CONSTRAINT invoices_fk_terms
    FOREIGN KEY (terms_id)
    REFERENCES terms (terms_id)
);

CREATE TABLE invoice_line_items
(
  invoice_id              INT               NOT NULL,
  invoice_sequence        INT               NOT NULL,
  account_number          INT               NOT NULL,
  line_item_amount        DECIMAL(9,2)      NOT NULL,
  line_item_description   VARCHAR(100)      NOT NULL,
  CONSTRAINT line_items_pk
    PRIMARY KEY (invoice_id, invoice_sequence),
  CONSTRAINT line_items_fk_invoices
    FOREIGN KEY (invoice_id)
    REFERENCES invoices (invoice_id),
  CONSTRAINT line_items_fk_acounts
    FOREIGN KEY (account_number)
    REFERENCES general_ledger_accounts (account_number)
);

-- create an index
CREATE INDEX invoices_invoice_date_ix
  ON invoices (invoice_date DESC);
```

Figure 11-9   The script used to create the AP database (part 2 of 2)

How to use MySQL Workbench

Since you often use a script to create tables and other database objects, it's important to understand the DDL skills presented in this chapter. Once you understand these skills, it's easy to learn how to use a graphical user interface such as MySQL Workbench to work with database objects such as tables and indexes. For example, it's often useful to view these database objects before writing the SELECT, INSERT, UPDATE, or DELETE statements that use them.

How to work with the columns of a table

Figure 11-10 shows how to work with the column definitions of a table. To start, you can view the column definitions for a table by right-clicking on the table in the Object Browser window and selecting Alter Table to display the table in the main window. Then, click on the Columns tab at the bottom of the window.

For example, this figure shows the columns for the Invoices table. Here, you can see the name, data type, and other attributes of each column. For instance, you can see that the invoice_id column is the primary key column and an auto increment column. The payment_total and credit_total columns specify a default value of 0.00. And the payment_date column allows null values and its default value is NULL.

If you need to add a new column, you can double-click below the last name in the Column Name column. Then, you can type in a name for the new column, and you can specify its attributes to the right of the column name.

You can also work with a new or existing column using the controls below the list of columns. In this figure, for example, I've selected the invoice_id column, so the information for that column is displayed below the column list. This is useful if you aren't familiar with the abbreviations that are used for the check boxes in the column list, since these attributes are clearly identified by the check boxes below the list. You can also use the Collation drop-down list to change the character set and collation for some columns. You'll learn more about that later in this chapter.

The column definitions for the Invoices table

Description

- To view the columns for a table, right-click on the table in the Object Browser window, select the Alter Table command, and click on the Columns tab.

- To rename a column, double-click on the column name and enter the new name.

- To change the data type for a column, click on the data type in the Datatype column. Then, select a data type from the drop-down list that's displayed.

- To change the default value for a column, enter a new default value in the Default column.

- To change other attributes of the column, check or uncheck the attribute check boxes to the right of the column.

- To drop a column, right-click on the column name and select the Delete Selected Columns command.

- To move a column up or down, right-click on the column name and select the Move Up or Move Down command. You can also use the Up and Down keys on the keyboard.

- To add a new column, double-click in the Column Name column below the last column and type in a new name. Then, specify the attributes for the new column.

- To apply the changes to the table, click the Apply button. To reverse the changes, click the Revert button.

Figure 11-10   How to work with the columns of a table

How to work with the indexes of a table

Although MySQL Workbench provides several ways to work with indexes, one of the easiest is to right-click on the table in the Object Browser window and select the Alter Table command to display the table definition. Then, you can click on the Indexes tab to display the indexes of the table. For example, figure 11-11 shows the indexes for the Invoices table.

In most cases, you'll use this tab to add indexes to a table. To do that, you start by double-clicking below the last index name and then entering the name of the new index. Then, you can select the type of index you want to create, the column or columns you want to index, and the order for each column. To change or drop an index, you can use the skills presented in this figure.

The indexes for the Invoices table

Description

- To view the indexes for a table, right-click on the table in the Object Browser window, select the Alter Table command, and click on the Indexes tab.

- To rename an index, double-click on the name and enter the new name.

- To change the type of an index, click on the Type column. Then, select a type from the drop-down list that appears.

- To change the column that's indexed, select the index and then select its column in the list of columns that appears. You can also change the sort order of the index by clicking in the Order column and then selecting ASC or DESC from the drop-down list that appears.

- To drop an index, right-click on the index name and select the Delete Selected Indices command.

- To add a new index, double-click below the last index name and type in a new name. Then, specify the type, column, and order for the index.

- To apply the changes to the table, click the Apply button. To reverse the changes, click the Revert button.

Figure 11-11   How to work with the indexes of a table

How to work with the foreign keys of a table

To work with the foreign keys of a table, you use the Foreign Keys tab. For example, figure 11-12 shows the foreign keys for the Invoices table, and the foreign key named invoices_fk_terms is selected. Here, MySQL Workbench shows the table that's referenced by the foreign key, the foreign key column, and the column that's referenced by the foreign key. If you need to, you can change any of the information that defines the foreign key as described in this figure. You can also add new foreign keys, and you can drop existing keys.

The foreign keys for the Invoices table

Description

- To view the foreign keys for a table, right-click on the table in the Object Browser window, select the Alter Table command, and click on the Foreign Keys tab.

- To rename a foreign key, double-click on the name and enter the new name.

- To change the referenced table, click on the table name in the Referenced Table column and select a table from the drop-down list that appears.

- To change the column or referenced column for a foreign key, select the foreign key and then select the column or referenced column in the list that appears.

- To drop a foreign key, right-click on its name and select the Delete Selected FKs command.

- To add a new foreign key, double-click below the last foreign key name and type in a new name. Then, specify the referenced table, foreign key column, and referenced column.

- To apply the changes to the table, click the Apply button. To reverse the changes, click the Revert button.

Figure 11-12   How to work with the foreign keys of a table

How to work with character sets and collations

So far, this book has assumed that you're working with the default character set and collation for your MySQL server. In this topic, you'll learn more about characters sets and collations and why you might want to use a character set or collation that's different from the default. Then, you'll learn how to specify the character set and collation for a database, a table, or even a column.

An introduction to character sets and collations

When a column is defined with a string type such as CHAR or VARCHAR, MySQL stores a numeric value for each character. Then, it uses a *character set* to map the numeric values to the characters of the string.

Figure 11-13 begins by presenting two character sets that are commonly used by MySQL. To start, it presents the default character set for MySQL: the latin1 character set. This character set uses one byte per character to provide for most characters in Western European languages. If these are the only types of characters you need to store, the latin1 character set is an excellent choice. However, if you need to store other characters, you can use the utf8 character set.

The advantage of the utf8 character set is that it provides for all characters specified by the Unicode character set. This includes most characters from most languages worldwide. As a result, it's appropriate when you're going to be working with a global application that needs to be able to store characters from multiple languages. The disadvantage of the utf8 character set is that it can use up to three bytes per character.

Every character set has a corresponding *collation* that determines how the characters within the set are sorted. For example, the latin1 character set uses the collation named latin1_swedish_ci by default. Here, the beginning of the name shows that it corresponds with the latin1 character set. In addition, the *ci* at the end shows that it is *case-insensitive*. This means that MySQL sorts uppercase letters such as *A* and lowercase letters such as *a* at the same level, which is usually what you want.

If MySQL isn't sorting characters the way you want, you can use another collation. For example, if you want a case-sensitive sort, you can use a collation with a name that ends with *cs*. Or, you can use a collation with a name that ends with *bin*, which stands for *binary*. This sorts characters by their numeric values instead of by their character values.

Two commonly used character sets

Name	Description
latin1	The latin1 character set uses one byte per character to provide for most characters in Western European languages.
utf8	The utf8 character set uses one to three bytes per character to provide for all characters specified by the Unicode character set. This character set provides for most characters in most of the world's languages.

Four collations for the latin1 character set

Name	Description
latin1_swedish_ci	The default collation for the latin1 character set.
latin1_general_ci	A case-insensitive collation for the latin1 character set.
latin1_general_cs	A case-sensitive collation for the latin1 character set.
latin1_bin	The binary collation for the latin1 character set.

Three collations for the utf8 character set

Name	Description
utf8_general_ci	The default collation for the utf8 character set.
utf8_spanish_ci	A case-insensitive collation for the utf8 character set.
utf8_bin	The binary collation for the utf8 character set.

Description

- The *character set* that's used by a database, table, or column determines which characters can be stored and how many bytes are used to store the characters.
- Every character set has a corresponding *collation* that determines how the characters within the set are sorted.
- If the name of a collation ends with *ci*, the collation is *case-insensitive*.
- If the name of a collation ends with *cs*, the collation is *case-sensitive*.
- If the name of a collation ends with *bin*, the collation is *binary*, which means that the characters are sorted according to the binary numbers that correspond with each character.

Figure 11-13   An introduction to character sets and collations

How to view character sets and collations

Figure 11-14 starts by showing how to view all character sets that are available on your MySQL server. To do that, you use the SHOW CHARSET statement as shown in the first example. As the results of this statement show, the SHOW CHARSET statement displays information about each character set in addition to its name.

You can also use the SHOW CHARSET statement to view information about a single character set. To do that, you can use a LIKE clause to identify the character set as shown in the second example.

This figure also shows how to use the SHOW COLLATION statement to view information about collations. For instance, the third example in this figure shows how to view information about all the collations that are available on the current server. In the result set that's returned by this statement, you can see the collations for the latin1 character set as well as some of the collations for the latin2 character set.

If you only want to view the collations for a specific character set, you can use a LIKE clause with the % wildcard character. In this figure, for example, the second SHOW COLLATION statement shows the collations for the latin1 character set.

The next four examples in this figure show how to use the SHOW VARI-ABLES statement to view the default character set and collation for your current server or database. In these examples, the LIKE clause is used to specify the name of a variable. For example, to view the default character set for a server, you use the character_set_server variable.

You can also view the character set and collation for all the tables in a database. To do that, you can query the table named Tables in the database named Information_Schema as shown in the last example. Here, the SELECT statement returns the table name and table collation for each table in the AP database. Since the collation identifies the character set, this indicates the character set for each table.

How to view all available character sets for a server

```
SHOW CHARSET
```

Charset	Description	Default collation	Maxlen
latin1	cp1252 West European	latin1_swedish_ci	1
latin2	ISO 8859-2 Central European	latin2_general_ci	1
swe7	7bit Swedish	swe7_swedish_ci	1
ascii	US ASCII	ascii_general_ci	1
ujis	EUC-JP Japanese	ujis_japanese_ci	3

How to view a specific character set

```
SHOW CHARSET LIKE 'latin1'
```

How to view all available collations for a server

```
SHOW COLLATION
```

Collation	Charset	Id	Default	Compiled	Sortlen
latin1_swedish_ci	latin1	8	Yes	Yes	1
latin1_danish_ci	latin1	15		Yes	1
latin1_german2_ci	latin1	31		Yes	2
latin1_bin	latin1	47		Yes	1
latin1_general_ci	latin1	48		Yes	1
latin1_general_cs	latin1	49		Yes	1
latin1_spanish_ci	latin1	94		Yes	1
latin2_czech_cs	latin2	2		Yes	4
latin2_general_ci	latin2	9	Yes	Yes	1

How to view all available collations for a specific character set

```
SHOW COLLATION LIKE 'latin1%'
```

How to view the default character set for a server

```
SHOW VARIABLES LIKE 'character_set_server'
```

How to view the default collation for a server

```
SHOW VARIABLES LIKE 'collation_server'
```

How to view the default character set for a database

```
SHOW VARIABLES LIKE 'character_set_database'
```

How to view the default collation for a database

```
SHOW VARIABLES LIKE 'collation_database'
```

How to view the character set and collation for all the tables in a database

```
SELECT table_name, table_collation
FROM information_schema.tables
WHERE table_schema = 'ap'
```

table_name	table_collation
invoice_line_items	latin1_swedish_ci
invoices	latin1_swedish_ci
terms	latin1_swedish_ci

Figure 11-14 How to view character sets and collations

How to specify a character set and a collation

Figure 11-15 shows how to specify a character set and a collation at three levels: database, table, and column. In most cases, you want to specify the character set and collation at the database level as shown in the first group of examples. Then, all the columns in all of the tables that store string data are defined with that character set and collation. If necessary, though, you can also set the character set and collation at the table or column level as shown by the second and third groups of examples.

To specify a character set or collation, you can use the CHARSET or COLLATE clauses. For a new database or table, you can add these clauses to the CREATE statement for the database or table. For an existing database or table, you can add these clauses to the ALTER statement for the database or table.

Most of the examples in this figure use both the CHARSET and COLLATE clauses. This clearly shows the character set and collation that are being specified. In most cases, though, you only need to use one clause or the other. That's because every character set has a default collation, and every collation has a corresponding character set. As a result, if you omit the COLLATE clause, MySQL uses the default collation for the specified character set. And, if you omit the CHARSET clause, MySQL uses the character set that corresponds with the specified collation. If you want to use a collation other than the default for a character set, then, you can do that by coding the COLLATE clause without the CHARSET clause.

You can also use MySQL Workbench to change the character set and collation for a table or column. To do that, you use the Columns tab that you saw in figure 11-10. To change the character set and collation for a table, you use the Collation drop-down list at the top of this tab. To change the character set and collation for a column, you select the column and then use the Collation drop-down list below the list of columns.

The clauses used to specify a character set and collation

```
[CHARSET character_set] [COLLATE collation]
```

How to specify a character set and collation at the database level

For a new database

```
CREATE DATABASE ar CHARSET latin1 COLLATE latin1_swedish_ci
```

For an existing database

```
ALTER DATABASE ar CHARSET utf8 COLLATE utf8_general_ci
```

For an existing database using the CHARSET clause only

```
ALTER DATABASE ar CHARSET utf8
```

For an existing database using the COLLATE clause only

```
ALTER DATABASE ar COLLATE utf8_general_ci
```

How to specify a character set and collation at the table level

For a new table

```
CREATE TABLE employees
(
  emp_id      INT             PRIMARY KEY,
  emp_name    VARCHAR(25)
)
CHARSET latin1 COLLATE latin1_swedish_ci
```

For an existing table

```
ALTER TABLE employees
CHARSET utf8 COLLATE utf8_general_ci
```

How to specify a character set and collation at the column level

For a column in a new table

```
CREATE TABLE employees
(
  emp_id      INT          PRIMARY KEY,
  emp_name    VARCHAR(25)   CHARSET latin1 COLLATE latin1_swedish_ci
)
```

For a column in an existing table

```
ALTER TABLE employees
MODIFY emp_name VARCHAR(25) CHARSET utf8 COLLATE utf8_general_ci
```

Description

- You can use the CHARSET and COLLATE clauses to set the character set and collation at the database, table, or column level.
- If you omit the CHARSET clause, MySQL uses the character set that corresponds with the specified collation.
- If you omit the COLLATE clause, MySQL uses the default collation for the specified character set.
- The CHARACTER SET keywords are a synonym for the CHARSET keyword.

Figure 11-15   How to specify a character set and a collation

How to work with storage engines

A *storage engine* determines how MySQL stores data and which database features are available to you. Unlike many other databases, MySQL provides several different storage engines that you can use, and each of these engines provides slightly different features.

An introduction to storage engines

Figure 11-16 begins by presenting the two most commonly used storage engines: InnoDB and MyISAM. The InnoDB engine is the default engine for MySQL 5.5 and later. As a result, if you installed the software as described in appendix A or B of this book, you have been using the InnoDB engine so far. This engine supports foreign keys as described earlier in this chapter. In addition, it supports transactions, which are described in chapter 14.

Prior to MySQL 5.5, the MyISAM engine was the default storage engine. As a result, if you ever work on an older MySQL database, there's a good chance its tables use the MyISAM engine. This engine supports some features that aren't supported by InnoDB tables, including full-text searches and spatial data types. However, the MyISAM engine doesn't support foreign keys, an important feature for maintaining referential integrity.

Although this chapter doesn't cover the full-text search feature that's provided by the MyISAM engine, you should know that this feature makes it easier and faster to search string data using natural language search strings. To use this feature, you create a special type of index called a FULLTEXT index. Then, you can use full-text search features in your SELECT statements. For more information about how this works, you can search the Internet.

How to view storage engines

Figure 11-16 also shows how to view information about storage engines. To start, it shows how to use the SHOW ENGINES statement to view all available storage engines for the current server. In this figure, for example, the result set shows that the InnoDB storage engine is the default storage engine for the server. In addition, it shows that several other storage engines are available to the server. Of these, the MyISAM storage engine is the most significant since it was the default storage engine in earlier versions of MySQL.

If you want to quickly view the default storage engine for the server, you can use the SHOW VARIABLES statement shown in this figure. This statement returns a single row that includes the name of the default storage engine.

If you want to view the storage engine that's used for all the tables in a database, you can use a SELECT statement to query the tables in the Information_Schema database as shown in the last example. Here, the SELECT statement displays the table name and storage engine for the tables in the AP database. You can also display this information for all tables on the server by removing the WHERE clause from this SELECT statement.

Two commonly used storage engines

Name	Description
InnoDB	The default storage engine for MySQL 5.5 and later. This engine supports foreign keys and transactions.
MyISAM	The default storage engine prior to MySQL 5.5. This engine supports full-text searching and the spatial data types.

How to view all storage engines for a server

```
SHOW ENGINES
```

Engine	Support	Comment	Transactions	XA	Savepoints
▶ FEDERATED	NO	Federated MySQL storage engine	NULL	NULL	NULL
MRG_MYISAM	YES	Collection of identical MyISAM tables	NO	NO	NO
MyISAM	YES	MyISAM storage engine	NO	NO	NO
BLACKHOLE	YES	/dev/null storage engine (anything you write to it disappears)	NO	NO	NO
CSV	YES	CSV storage engine	NO	NO	NO
MEMORY	YES	Hash based, stored in memory, useful for temporary tables	NO	NO	NO
ARCHIVE	YES	Archive storage engine	NO	NO	NO
InnoDB	DEFAULT	Supports transactions, row-level locking, and foreign keys	YES	YES	YES
PERFORMANCE_SCHEMA	YES	Performance Schema	NO	NO	NO

How to view the default storage engine for a server

```
SHOW VARIABLES LIKE 'storage_engine'
```

How to view the storage engine for all the tables in a database

```
SELECT table_name, engine
FROM information_schema.tables
WHERE table_schema = 'ap'
```

table_name	engine
invoice_line_items	InnoDB
invoices	InnoDB
terms	InnoDB

Description

- The *storage engine* determines how MySQL stores data and which database features are available to you.

- You can use multiple storage engines on the same server and within the same database.

Figure 11-16   How to view storage engines

How to specify a storage engine

If you don't specify a storage engine when you create your tables, MySQL uses the default storage engine for the server. However, if the default storage engine doesn't provide the features that you want, you can use the ENGINE clause to change the storage engine for the tables that you create. For example, suppose you want to create a table that can take advantage of the full-text searching features available from the MyISAM storage engine. To do that, you can code a CREATE TABLE statement that uses the ENGINE clause as shown in the first example of figure 11-17.

You can also use the ENGINE clause on the ALTER TABLE statement to change the storage engine that an existing table uses, as shown in the second example. You might want to do that for older tables that use the MyISAM storage engine so you can take advantage of the foreign key features provided by the InnoDB storage engine. When you change the storage engine for an existing table, you should know that it can take MySQL a significant amount of time to rebuild the table. In addition, the table can't be accessed while this is happening. As a result, you shouldn't attempt to change the storage engine on a production database unless you are ready to stop all applications from accessing the database while MySQL rebuilds the table.

You can also change the storage engine for a table from MySQL Workbench. To do that, you use the Columns tab shown in figure 11-10. Then, you use the Engine drop-down list to choose a storage engine.

If you find that you are often using a storage engine that's different than the default engine for your server, you can change the default storage engine for the current session. To do that, you can code a SET SESSION statement to set the storage_engine variable for the current session. Since that only changes the storage engine for the current session, you may want to change the storage engine permanently. To do that, though, you need to modify the configuration file for the server as shown in chapter 17.

The clause used to specify a storage engine

```
ENGINE = engine_name
```

How to specify a storage engine for a table

For a new table

```
CREATE TABLE product_descriptions
(
  product_id            INT                 PRIMARY KEY,
  product_description   VARCHAR(200)
)
ENGINE = MyISAM
```

For an existing table

```
ALTER TABLE product_descriptions ENGINE = InnoDB
```

How to set the default storage engine for the current session

```
SET SESSION storage_engine = InnoDB
```

Description

- To specify a storage engine for a table, you can use the ENGINE clause.
- To change the default storage engine for the current session, you can use the SET SESSION statement to set the storage_engine variable for the current session.
- To permanently change the default storage engine for a server, you can modify the configuration file for the server. For more information about how to do this, see chapter 17.

Figure 11-17   How to specify a storage engine

Perspective

Now that you've completed this chapter, you should be able to create and modify the tables of a database by coding DDL statements. In addition, you should be able to use a graphical tool like MySQL Workbench to work with the tables of a database.

Before you move on, though, take a moment to consider the advantages and disadvantages of using MySQL Workbench to work with database objects. The advantage, of course, is that MySQL Workbench provides a graphical user interface that makes it easy to view and work with database objects. The disadvantage is that no record is kept of any changes that you make to the database. For example, if you add a column to a table, that change isn't stored anywhere for future use.

In contrast, if you use a script to add a column to a table, that change is stored for future use. This makes it easy to recreate the database if you ever need to do that. And that's why it's common to use scripts to make any changes to the structure of a database. On the other hand, MySQL Workbench is an excellent tool for quickly viewing the objects of a database or for quickly creating temporary tables or other objects that won't need to be recreated later.

Terms

attribute
constraint
column-level constraint
table-level constraint
not null constraint
unique constraint
primary key constraint
foreign key constraint
reference constraint
cascading delete
index
script
character set
collation
storage engine

Exercises

1. Write a script that adds an index to the AP database for the zip code field in the Vendors table.

2. Write a script that contains the CREATE TABLE statements needed to implement the following design in the EX database:

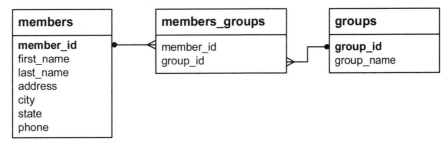

These tables provide for members of an association, and each member can be registered in one or more groups within the association.

The member_id and group_id columns are the primary keys of the Members and Groups tables, and these columns are foreign keys in the Members_Groups table.

Include any constraints or default values that you think are necessary.

Include statements to drop the tables if they already exist.

3. Write INSERT statements that add rows to the tables that are created in exercise 2.

Add two rows to the Members table for the first two member IDs.

Add two rows to the Groups table for the first two group IDs.

Add three rows to the Group_Membership table: one row for member 1 and group 2; one for member 2 and group 1; and one for member 2 and group 2.

Write a SELECT statement that joins the three tables and retrieves the group name, member last name, and member first name. Sort the results by the group name, member last name, and member first name.

4. Write an ALTER TABLE statement that adds two new columns to the Members table created in exercise 2.

Add one column for annual dues that provides for three digits to the left of the decimal point and two to the right. This column should have a default value of 52.50.

Add one column for the payment date.

5. Write an ALTER TABLE statement that modifies the Groups table created in exercise 2 so the group name in each row has to be unique. Then, use an INSERT statement to attempt to insert a duplicate name. This statement should fail due to the unique constraint.

12

How to create views

As you've seen throughout this book, SELECT queries can be complicated, particularly if they use multiple joins, subqueries, or complex functions. Because of that, you may want to save the queries you use regularly. One way to do that is to store the statement in a script. Another way is to create a view.

Unlike scripts, which are stored in files, views are stored as part of the database. As a result, they can be used by SQL programmers and by custom applications that have access to the database. This provides some advantages over using tables directly.

An introduction to views **354**
How views work 354
Benefits of using views 356
How to work with views **358**
How to create a view 358
How to create an updatable view 362
How to use the WITH CHECK OPTION clause 364
How to insert or delete rows through a view 366
How to alter or drop a view 368
Perspective **370**

An introduction to views

Before you learn the details for working with views, it's helpful to get a general idea of how views work. In addition, it's helpful to consider some of the benefits of views so you can determine whether you want to use them.

How views work

A *view* is a SELECT statement that's stored in the database as a database object. To create a view, you use a CREATE VIEW statement like the one shown in figure 12-1. This statement creates a view named Vendors_Min that retrieves the vendor_name, vendor_state, and vendor_phone columns from the Vendors table.

You can think of a view as a virtual table that consists only of the rows and columns specified in its CREATE VIEW statement. The table or tables that are listed in the FROM clause are called the *base tables* for the view. Since the view refers back to the base tables, it doesn't store any data itself, and it always reflects the most current data in the base tables.

To use a view, you refer to it from another SQL statement. In this figure, for example, the SELECT statement uses the Vendors_Min view in the FROM clause instead of a table. As a result, this SELECT statement extracts its result set from the virtual table that the view represents. In this case, all the rows for vendors in California are retrieved from the view.

When you create a view like the one in this figure, the view is updatable. As a result, it's possible to use the view in an INSERT, UPDATE, or DELETE statement. In this figure, for example, the UPDATE statement uses the Vendors_Min view to update the vendor_phone column in the Vendors table for the specified vendor.

To drop a view, you can use the DROP VIEW statement as shown in this figure. This works similarly to the DROP statements for tables and indexes that you learned about in the previous chapter.

Because a view is stored as an object in a database, it can be used by anyone who has appropriate privileges. That may include users who have access to the database through applications that provide for ad hoc queries and report generation. In addition, that may include custom applications that are written specifically to work with the data in the database. In fact, views are often designed to be used with these types of applications.

A CREATE VIEW statement for a view named Vendors_Min

```
CREATE VIEW vendors_min AS
    SELECT vendor_name, vendor_state, vendor_phone
    FROM vendors
```

The virtual table that's represented by the view

vendor_name	vendor_state	vendor_phone
US Postal Service	WI	(800) 555-1205
National Information Data Ctr	DC	(301) 555-8950
Register of Copyrights	DC	NULL
Jobtrak	CA	(800) 555-8725
Newbrige Book Clubs	NJ	(800) 555-9980

`(122 rows)`

A SELECT statement that uses the Vendors_Min view

```
SELECT * FROM vendors_min
WHERE vendor_state = 'CA'
ORDER BY vendor_name
```

The result set that's returned by the SELECT statement

vendor_name	vendor_state	vendor_phone
Abbey Office Furnishings	CA	(559) 555-8300
American Express	CA	(800) 555-3344
ASC Signs	CA	NULL
Aztek Label	CA	(714) 555-9000
Bertelsmann Industry Svcs. Inc	CA	(805) 555-0584
BFI Industries	CA	(559) 555-1551

`(75 rows)`

An UPDATE statement that uses a view to update the base table

```
UPDATE vendors_min
SET vendor_phone = '(800) 555-3941'
WHERE vendor_name = 'Register of Copyrights'
```

A statement that drops a view

```
DROP VIEW vendors_min
```

Description

- A *view* consists of a SELECT statement that's stored as an object in the database. The tables referenced in the SELECT statement are called the *base tables* for the view.

- When you create a view, you can refer to the view anywhere you would normally use a table in a SELECT, INSERT, UPDATE, or DELETE statement.

- Although a view behaves like a virtual table, it doesn't store any data. Instead, a view always refers back to its base tables.

- A view can also be referred to as a *viewed table* because it provides a view to the underlying base tables.

Figure 12-1   How views work

Benefits of using views

Figure 12-2 describes some of the advantages of using views. To start, you can use views to limit the exposure of the tables in your database to external users and applications. To illustrate, suppose a view refers to a table that you've decided to divide into two tables. To accommodate this change, you simply modify the view. In other words, you don't have to modify any statements that refer to the view. That means that users who query the database using the view don't have to be aware of the change in the database structure, and application programs that use the view don't have to be modified.

You can also use views to restrict access to a database. To do that, you include just the columns and rows you want a user or an application to have access to in the views. Then, you let the user or application access the data only through the views. For example, let's assume you have an Employees table that has a salary column that contains information about each employee's salary. In this case, you can create a view that doesn't include the salary column for the users who need to view and maintain this table, but who shouldn't be able to view salaries. Then, you can create another view that includes the salary column for the users who need to view and maintain salary information.

In addition, you can use views to hide the complexity of a SELECT statement. For example, if you have a long and unwieldy SELECT statement that joins multiple tables, you can create a view for that statement. This makes it easier for you and other database users to work with this data.

Finally, when you create a view, you can allow data in the base table to be updated through the view. To do that, you use INSERT, UPDATE, or DELETE statements to work with the view.

Some of the benefits provided by views

Benefit	Description
Design independence	Views can limit the exposure of tables to external users and applications. As a result, if the design of the tables changes, you can modify the view as necessary so users who query the view don't need to be aware of the change, and applications that use the view don't need to be modified.
Data security	Views can restrict access to the data in a table by using the SELECT clause to include only selected columns of a table or by using the WHERE clause to include only selected rows in a table.
Simplified queries	Views can be used to hide the complexity of retrieval operations. Then, the data can be retrieved using simple SELECT statements that specify a view in the FROM clause.
Updatability	With certain restrictions, views can be used to update, insert, and delete data from a base table.

Description

- You can create a view based on almost any SELECT statement. That means that you can code views that join tables, summarize data, and use subqueries and functions.

Figure 12-2   Benefits of using views

How to work with views

Now that you have a general understanding of how views work and of the benefits that they provide, you're ready to learn the details for working with them.

How to create a view

Figure 12-3 presents the CREATE VIEW statement that you use to create a view. In its simplest form, you code the CREATE VIEW keywords, followed by the name of the view, followed by the AS keyword and the SELECT statement that defines the view. In this figure, for instance, the first statement creates a view named Vendors_Phone_List. This view includes four columns from the Vendors table for all vendors with invoices.

If you execute the first CREATE VIEW statement and a view with that name doesn't already exist in the current database, MySQL adds the view and displays a message to indicate that the statement was successful. However, if a view with this name already exists, MySQL doesn't add the view and displays a message that indicates that the name is already in use. In that case, you need to specify a new name for the view, or you need to drop the view that's already using that name.

When you code a CREATE VIEW statement, you can specify that you want to automatically drop a view that has the same name as the view that you're creating. To do that, you can specify the OR REPLACE keywords after the CREATE keyword as shown in all of the examples in this figure except for the first.

The SELECT statement for a view can use most of the features of a normal SELECT statement. In this figure, for instance, the second example creates a view that joins data from two tables. Similarly, the third statement creates a view that uses a LIMIT clause.

By default, the columns in a view are given the same names as the columns in the base tables. If a view contains a calculated column, however, you'll want to name that column just as you do in other SELECT statements. In addition, you'll need to rename columns from different tables that have the same name. To do that, you can code the column names in the CREATE VIEW clause as shown in the fourth example. Or, you can use the AS clause in the SELECT statement as shown in the fifth example.

Note that if you use the technique shown in the fourth example, you have to assign names to all of the columns. In contrast, if you use the technique shown in the fifth example, you only have to assign names to the columns you need to rename. As a result, you'll typically want to use the technique presented in the fifth example.

The syntax of the CREATE VIEW statement

```
CREATE [OR REPLACE] VIEW view_name
  [(column_alias_1[, column_alias_2]...)]
AS
  select_statement
  [WITH [CHECK OPTION] [CONSTRAINT constraint_name]]
```

A view of vendors that have invoices

```
CREATE VIEW vendors_phone_list AS
  SELECT vendor_name, vendor_contact_last_name,
         vendor_contact_first_name, vendor_phone
  FROM vendors
  WHERE vendor_id IN (SELECT DISTINCT vendor_id FROM invoices)
```

A view that uses a join

```
CREATE OR REPLACE VIEW vendor_invoices AS
  SELECT vendor_name, invoice_number, invoice_date, invoice_total
  FROM vendors
    JOIN invoices ON vendors.vendor_id = invoices.vendor_id
```

A view that uses a LIMIT clause

```
CREATE OR REPLACE VIEW top5_invoice_totals AS
  SELECT vendor_id, invoice_total
  FROM invoices
  ORDER BY invoice_total DESC
  LIMIT 5
```

A view that names all of its columns in the CREATE VIEW clause

```
CREATE OR REPLACE VIEW invoices_outstanding
  (invoice_number, invoice_date, invoice_total, balance_due)
AS
  SELECT invoice_number, invoice_date, invoice_total,
         invoice_total - payment_total - credit_total
  FROM invoices
  WHERE invoice_total - payment_total - credit_total > 0
```

A view that names just the calculated column in its SELECT clause

```
CREATE OR REPLACE VIEW invoices_outstanding AS
  SELECT invoice_number, invoice_date, invoice_total,
         invoice_total - payment_total - credit_total AS balance_due
  FROM invoices
  WHERE invoice_total - payment_total - credit_total > 0
```

Figure 12-3   How to create a view (part 1 of 2)

The example in part 2 of figure 12-3 creates a view that summarizes the rows in the Invoices table by vendor. This shows that a view can use aggregate functions and the GROUP BY clause to summarize data. In this case, the rows are grouped by vendor name, and a count of the invoices and the invoice total are calculated for each vendor.

When you create a view, the SELECT statement you code within the definition of the view can refer to another view instead of a base table. In other words, views can be *nested*. In theory, *nested views* can make it easier to present data to your users. In practice, using nested views can make the dependencies between tables and views confusing, which can make your code difficult to maintain. As a result, if you use nested views, you should use them carefully.

A view that summarizes invoices by vendor

```
CREATE OR REPLACE VIEW invoice_summary AS
  SELECT vendor_name,
    COUNT(*) AS invoice_count,
    SUM(invoice_total) AS invoice_total_sum
  FROM vendors
    JOIN invoices ON vendors.vendor_id = invoices.vendor_id
  GROUP BY vendor_name
```

Description

- You use the CREATE VIEW statement to create a view.

- If you include the OR REPLACE keywords, the CREATE VIEW statement will replace any existing view that has the same name. Otherwise, you must specify a new name for the view.

- If you name the columns of a view in the CREATE VIEW clause, you have to name all of the columns. In contrast, if you name the columns in the SELECT clause, you can name just the columns you need to rename.

- You can create a view that's based on another view rather than on a table. This is known as a *nested view*.

Figure 12-3   How to create a view (part 2 of 2)

How to create an updatable view

Once you create a view, you can refer to it in a SELECT statement. In addition, you can refer to it in INSERT, UPDATE, and DELETE statements to modify the data that's stored in an underlying table. To do that, the view must be updatable. Figure 12-4 lists the requirements for creating *updatable views*.

The first two requirements have to do with what you can code in the select list of the SELECT statement that defines the view. In particular, the select list can't include the DISTINCT keyword or aggregate functions. In addition, the SELECT statement can't include a GROUP BY or HAVING clause, and two SELECT statements can't be joined by a union operation.

The CREATE VIEW statement in this figure creates a view that's updatable. As a result, you can refer to it in an INSERT, UPDATE, or DELETE statement. For example, you can use the first UPDATE statement shown in this figure to update the credit_total column in the Invoices base table.

However, you can't update any calculated columns that are used by the view. For example, you can't use the second UPDATE statement shown in this figure to update the balance_due column that's calculated from the other columns in the view.

In addition, when you update data through a view, you can only update the data in a single base table at a time, even if the view refers to two or more tables. In this figure, for instance, the view includes data from two base tables: Vendors and Invoices. Because of that, you can code an UPDATE statement that updates the data in the Vendors table or the data in the Invoices table, but not in both tables. For example, the first UPDATE statement only refers to columns in the Invoices table, so it's able to update data in that table.

Requirements for creating updatable views

- The select list can't include a DISTINCT clause.
- The select list can't include aggregate functions.
- The SELECT statement can't include a GROUP BY or HAVING clause.
- The view can't include the UNION operator.

A CREATE VIEW statement that creates an updatable view

```
CREATE OR REPLACE VIEW balance_due_view AS
    SELECT vendor_name, invoice_number,
           invoice_total, payment_total, credit_total,
           invoice_total - payment_total - credit_total AS balance_due
    FROM vendors JOIN invoices ON vendors.vendor_id = invoices.vendor_id
    WHERE invoice_total - payment_total - credit_total > 0
```

non-updatable

An UPDATE statement that uses the view to update data

```
UPDATE balance_due_view
SET credit_total = 300
WHERE invoice_number = '9982771'
```

The response from the system

```
(1 row affected)
```

An UPDATE statement that attempts to use the view to update a calculated column

```
UPDATE balance_due_view
SET balance_due = 0
WHERE invoice_number = '9982771'
```

The response from the system

```
Error Code: 1348. Column 'balance_due' is not updatable
```

Description

- An *updatable view* is a view that can be used in an INSERT, UPDATE, or DELETE statement to update the data in the base table. If a view isn't updatable, it's called a *read-only view*.
- The requirements for coding updatable views are more restrictive than for coding read-only views. That's because MySQL must be able to unambiguously determine which base tables and columns are affected.

Figure 12-4   How to create an updatable view

How to use the WITH CHECK OPTION clause

Figure 12-5 shows an example of an updatable view that uses the WITH CHECK OPTION clause to prevent an update if it causes the row to be excluded from the view. To start, the CREATE VIEW statement creates an updatable view named Vendor_Payment that joins data from the Vendors and Invoices tables and retrieves all invoices that have a balance due that's greater than or equal to zero.

Then, the first UPDATE statement uses this view to modify the payment_date and payment_total columns for a specific invoice. This works because this UPDATE statement doesn't exclude the row from the view.

However, the second UPDATE statement causes the balance due to become less than zero. As a result, this statement fails due to the WITH CHECK OPTION clause, and an error is displayed. Since this can prevent users from storing invalid data in a database, this clause can be useful in some situations.

An updatable view that has a WITH CHECK OPTION clause

```
CREATE OR REPLACE VIEW vendor_payment AS
    SELECT vendor_name, invoice_number, invoice_date, payment_date,
           invoice_total, credit_total, payment_total
    FROM vendors JOIN invoices ON vendors.vendor_id = invoices.vendor_id
    WHERE invoice_total - payment_total - credit_total >= 0
WITH CHECK OPTION
```

A SELECT statement that displays a row from the view

```
SELECT * FROM vendor_payment
WHERE invoice_number = 'P-0608'
```

The result set

	vendor_name	invoice_number	invoice_date	payment_date	invoice_total	credit_total	payment_td
▶	Malloy Lithographing Inc	P-0608	2011-07-23	NULL	20551.18	1200.00	0.00

An UPDATE statement that updates the view

```
UPDATE vendor_payment
SET payment_total = 400.00,
    payment_date = '2011-08-01'
WHERE invoice_number = 'P-0608'
```

The response from the system

```
(1 row affected)
```

The same row data after the update

	vendor_name	invoice_number	invoice_date	payment_date	invoice_total	credit_total	payment_td
▶	Malloy Lithographing Inc	P-0608	2011-07-23	2011-08-01	20551.18	1200.00	400.00

An UPDATE statement that attempts to update the view

```
UPDATE vendor_payment
SET payment_total = 30000.00,
    payment_date = '2011-08-01'
WHERE invoice_number = 'P-0608';
```

The response from the system

```
Error Code: 1369. CHECK OPTION failed 'ap.vendor_payment'
```

Description

- If you don't include a WITH CHECK OPTION clause when you create a view, a change you make through the view can cause the modified rows to no longer be included in the view.

- If you specify a WITH CHECK OPTION clause when you create a view, an error will occur if you try to modify a row in such a way that it would no longer be included in the view.

Figure 12-5   How to use the WITH CHECK OPTION clause

How to insert or delete rows through a view

In the previous figures, you learned how to use a view to update data in the underlying tables. Now, figure 12-6 shows how to use a view to insert or delete data in an underlying table. In general, this works the same as it does when you work directly with a table. However, due to table constraints, using a view to insert or delete rows often results in errors like the ones shown in this figure. As a result, it's generally more common to work directly with base tables when inserting or deleting rows.

At the top of this figure, you can see a CREATE VIEW statement for a view named ibm_invoices. This view retrieves columns and rows from the Invoices table for the vendor named IBM, which has a vendor_id of 34. Then, the INSERT statement that follows attempts to insert a row into the Invoices table through this view.

This insert operation fails, though, because the view and the INSERT statement don't include all of the required columns for the Invoices table. In this case, a value is required for other columns in the Invoices table including the vendor_id and invoice_due_date columns. As a result, to use a view to insert rows, you must design a view that includes all required columns for the underlying table.

In addition, an INSERT statement that uses a view can insert rows into only one table. That's true even if the view is based on two or more tables and all of the required columns for those tables are included in the view. In that case, you could use a separate INSERT statement to insert rows into each table through the view.

This figure also shows how to delete rows through a view. To do that, you use a DELETE statement like the ones shown here. To start, the first DELETE statement attempts to delete an invoice from the Invoices table through the ibm_invoices view. However, this DELETE statement fails because the Invoice_Line_Items table contains rows related to the invoice. This causes an error message like the one in this figure to be displayed. To get this DELETE statement to work, you must first delete the related line items for the invoice. This is illustrated by the last two DELETE statements in this figure.

A statement that creates an updatable view

```
CREATE OR REPLACE VIEW ibm_invoices AS
  SELECT invoice_number, invoice_date, invoice_total
  FROM invoices
  WHERE vendor_id = 34
```

The contents of the view

invoice_number	invoice_date	invoice_total
QP58872	2011-05-07	116.54
Q545443	2011-06-09	1083.58

An INSERT statement that fails due to columns that don't have values

```
INSERT INTO ibm_invoices
  (invoice_number, invoice_date, invoice_total)
VALUES
  ('RA23988', '2011-07-31', 417.34)
```

[handwritten: Wont work bc needs other column name values in ibm-invoices]

The response from the system

```
Error Code: 1423. Field of view 'ap.ibm_invoices' underlying table doesn't
have a default value
```

A DELETE statement that fails due to a foreign key constraint

```
DELETE FROM ibm_invoices
WHERE invoice_number = 'Q545443'
```

The response from the system

```
Error Code: 1451. Cannot delete or update a parent row: a foreign key
constraint fails ('ap'.'invoice_line_items', CONSTRAINT
'line_items_fk_invoices' FOREIGN KEY ('invoice_id') REFERENCES 'invoices'
('invoice_id'))
```

Two DELETE statements that succeed

```
DELETE FROM invoice_line_items
WHERE invoice_id = (SELECT invoice_id FROM invoices
                    WHERE invoice_number = 'Q545443');

DELETE FROM ibm_invoices
WHERE invoice_number = 'Q545443';
```

The response from the system

```
(1 row affected)
```

Description

- You can use the INSERT statement to insert rows into a base table through a view. To do that, you name the view in the INSERT clause. Both the view and the INSERT statement must include all of the columns from the base table that require a value.

- If the view names more than one base table, an INSERT statement can insert data into only one of those tables.

- You can use the DELETE statement to delete rows from a base table through a view. To do that, you name the view in the DELETE clause. For this to work, the view must be based on a single table.

Figure 12-6   How to insert or delete rows through a view

How to alter or drop a view

Although MySQL supports an ALTER VIEW statement, it's usually easier to alter a view by using the CREATE OR REPLACE VIEW statement to replace the existing view with a new one. In figure 12-7, for instance, the first example uses a CREATE VIEW statement to create a view named vendors_sw that retrieves rows from the Vendors table for vendors located in four states. Then, the second example uses the CREATE OR REPLACE VIEW statement to modify this view so it includes vendors in two additional states.

To drop a view, you use the DROP VIEW statement to name the view you want to drop. In this figure, for instance, the third example drops the view named vendors_sw. Like the other statements for dropping database objects, this statement permanently deletes the view. As a result, you should be careful when you use it.

A statement that creates a view

```
CREATE VIEW vendors_sw AS
SELECT *
FROM vendors
WHERE vendor_state IN ('CA','AZ','NV','NM')
```

A statement that replaces the view with a new view

```
CREATE OR REPLACE VIEW vendors_sw AS
SELECT *
FROM vendors
WHERE vendor_state IN ('CA','AZ','NV','NM','UT','CO')
```

A statement that drops the view

```
DROP VIEW vendors_sw
```

Description

- To alter a view, use the CREATE OR REPLACE VIEW statement to replace the existing view with a new one.
- To delete a view from the database, use the DROP VIEW statement.

Figure 12-7   How to alter or drop a view

Perspective

In this chapter, you learned how to create and use views. As you've seen, views provide a powerful and flexible way to predefine the data that can be retrieved from a database. By using them, you can restrict the access to a database while providing a consistent and simplified way for end users and application programs to access that data.

Terms

view	nested view
base table	updatable view
viewed table	read-only view

Exercises

1. Create a view named open_items that shows the invoices that haven't been paid.

    This view should return four columns from the Vendors and Invoices tables: vendor_name, invoice_number, invoice_total, and balance_due (invoice_total – payment_total – credit_total).

    A row should only be returned when the balance due is greater than zero, and the rows should be in sequence by vendor_name.

2. Write a SELECT statement that returns all of the columns in the open_items view that you created in exercise 1, with one row for each invoice that has a balance due of $1000 or more.

3. Create a view named open_items_summary that returns one summary row for each vendor that has invoices that haven't been paid.

    Each row should include vendor_name, open_item_count (the number of invoices with a balance due), and open_item_total (the total of the balance due amounts)

    The rows should be sorted by the open item totals in descending sequence.

4. Write a SELECT statement that returns just the first 5 rows from the open_items_summary view that you created in exercise 3.

5. Create an updatable view named vendor_address that returns the vendor_id column and all of the address columns for each vendor.

6. Write an UPDATE statement that changes the address for the row with a vendor ID of 4 so the suite number (Ste 260) is stored in the vendor_address2 column instead of the vendor_address1 column.

Section 4

Stored program development

This section presents the essential skills for using MySQL to create stored programs. These are the skills that will take your SQL capabilities to the next level. In chapter 13, you'll learn the language basics for writing procedural code within stored programs. In chapter 14, you'll learn how manage transactions and locking from within stored programs. In chapter 15, you'll learn how create two types of stored programs: stored procedures and functions. And in chapter 16, you'll learn how to create two more types of stored programs: triggers and events.

13

Language skills
for writing stored programs

This chapter presents the basic language skills that you need to write stored programs. With the skills presented in this chapter, you'll be able to code stored programs that provide functionality similar to procedural programming languages like PHP, Java, C++, C#, and Visual Basic.

If you have experience with another procedural language, you shouldn't have any trouble with the skills presented in this chapter. However, you should know that the programming power of MySQL is limited when compared to other languages. That's because MySQL is designed specifically to work with MySQL databases rather than as a general-purpose programming language. For its intended use, however, MySQL is both powerful and flexible.

An introduction to stored programs **374**
Four types of stored programs 374
A script that creates and calls a stored procedure 374
A summary of statements for coding stored programs 376
How to write procedural code **378**
How to display data 378
How to declare and set variables 380
How to code IF statements 382
How to code CASE statements 384
How to code loops 386
How to use a cursor 388
How to declare a condition handler 390
How to use a condition handler 392
How to use multiple condition handlers 396
Perspective **398**

An introduction to stored programs

MySQL 5.0 and 5.1 introduced extensions to standard SQL that allow you to write *stored programs*. Stored programs can include procedural code that controls the flow of execution.

Four types of stored programs

Figure 13-1 presents the four types of stored programs that you can create in MySQL. A *stored procedure* can be called from an application that has access to the database. For example, a PHP application can call a stored procedure and pass parameters to it. A *stored function* can be called from a SQL statement, just like the functions provided by MySQL that you learned about in chapter 9. However, you can customize stored functions so they perform tasks that are specific to your database. Stored procedures and stored functions are similar in many ways and are also known as *stored routines*.

Triggers and events don't need to be called. Instead, they execute automatically when something happens. A *trigger* executes when an INSERT, UPDATE, or DELETE statement is run against a specific table. And an *event* executes at a scheduled time.

A script that creates and calls a stored procedure

The script shown in figure 13-1 creates a stored procedure named test that doesn't accept any parameters. Then, it calls this procedure to execute the statements that are stored within it. This provides a way for you to experiment with the procedural language features that are available from MySQL. That's why this script is used throughout this chapter.

This script begins with the USE statement, which selects the AP database. Then, the DROP PROCEDURE IF EXISTS command drops the procedure named test if it already exists. This suppresses any error messages that would be displayed if you attempted to drop a procedure that didn't exist.

The DELIMITER statement changes the delimiter from the default delimiter of the semicolon (;) to two slashes (//). This is necessary because the semicolon is used within the CREATE PROCEDURE statement, and it allows you to use two front slashes (//) to identify the end of the CREATE PROCEDURE statement. Although we use two front slashes as the delimiter in this book, it's also common to see two dollar signs ($$) or two semicolons (;;) used as the delimiter.

The CREATE PROCEDURE statement creates the procedure. To indicate that this procedure doesn't accept any parameters, this code includes an empty set of parentheses after the procedure's name.

The code within the CREATE PROCEDURE statement is defined by a *block of code* that begins with the BEGIN keyword and ends with the END keyword. Within this block of code, the DECLARE statement defines a variable named sum_balance_due_var of the DECIMAL type. This data type corresponds with the data types that are used for the invoice_total, payment_total, and credit_total columns of the Invoices table. Then, a SELECT statement sets

Four types of stored programs

Type	Description
Stored procedure	Can be called from an application that has access to the database.
Stored function	Can be called from a SQL statement. A stored function works much like the functions provided by MySQL that are described in chapter 9.
Trigger	Is executed in response to an INSERT, UPDATE, or DELETE statement on a specified table.
Event	Is executed at a scheduled time.

A script that creates and calls a stored procedure named test

```
USE ap;

DROP PROCEDURE IF EXISTS test;

-- Change statement delimiter from semicolon to double front slash
DELIMITER //

CREATE PROCEDURE test()
BEGIN
  DECLARE sum_balance_due_var DECIMAL(9, 2);

  SELECT SUM(invoice_total - payment_total - credit_total)
  INTO sum_balance_due_var
  FROM invoices
  WHERE vendor_id = 95;

  IF sum_balance_due_var > 0 THEN
    SELECT CONCAT('Balance due: $', sum_balance_due_var) AS message;
  ELSE
    SELECT 'Balance paid in full' AS message;
  END IF;
END//

-- Change statement delimiter from double front slash to semicolon
DELIMITER ;

CALL test();
```

block of code

The response from the system

message
▸ Balance paid in full

Description

- A *stored program* consists of one or more SQL statements stored in the database for later use.

- Within a stored program, you can write procedural code that controls the flow of execution. That includes if/else constructs, loops, and error-handling code.

Figure 13-1   An introduction to stored programs

the value that's stored in this variable. To do that, the SELECT statement returns a single value and includes an INTO clause that specifies the name of the variable. As a result, the SELECT statement selects the value into the variable.

After the first SELECT statement, the script uses an IF statement to test the value of the variable. If the variable is greater than zero, the statement in the THEN clause uses a SELECT statement to return a result set that indicates the balance that is due. Otherwise, the statement in the ELSE clause uses a SELECT statement to return a result set that indicates that the balance is paid in full.

After the stored procedure has been created, this script uses the DELIMTER statement to change the delimiter back to the default delimiter of a semicolon (;). Then, it uses a CALL statement to call the stored procedure. This executes the code stored within the procedure. You'll learn more about how the CALL statement works in chapter 15.

For now, don't worry if you don't understand the coding details for this script. Instead, focus on the general ideas. Later in this chapter, you'll learn the details that you need to use the procedural language that's provided by MySQL. Then, in chapter 15, you'll learn more about the details of creating stored procedures.

A summary of statements for coding stored programs

Figure 13-2 begins by summarizing the SQL statements for controlling the flow of execution within stored programs. These statements can be used to add functionality that's similar to the functionality provided by procedural languages.

After the SQL statements for writing procedural code, this figure presents one SQL statement that you're already familiar with that's commonly used within stored programs: the SELECT statement. When working with stored programs, you can use the SELECT statement to return a result set to the calling program. This is often used to display messages that can help the programmer develop and debug a stored program.

In addition, you can use the SELECT statement with an INTO clause to retrieve data from the database and store it in one or more variables. You saw an example of this in the previous figure, and you'll learn more about how this works as you progress through this chapter.

SQL statements for controlling the flow of execution

Keywords	Description
IF...ELSEIF...ELSE	Controls the flow of execution based on a condition.
CASE...WHEN...ELSE	Controls the flow of execution based on a condition.
WHILE...DO...LOOP	Repeats statements while a condition is true.
REPEAT...UNTIL...END REPEAT	Repeats statements while a condition is true.
DECLARE CURSOR FOR	Defines a result set that can be processed by a loop.
DECLARE...HANDLER	Defines a handler that's executed when a stored program encounters an error.

A SQL statement used within stored programs

Statement	Description
SELECT	Returns a result set to the calling program. Or, retrieves data from the database and stores it so it can be processed by the stored program.

Description

- MySQL provides statements that can be used within scripts to add functionality similar to that provided by procedural programming languages.

Figure 13-2   A summary of statements for working with stored programs

How to write procedural code

Now that you have a general idea of how stored programs work, you're ready to learn the details for writing procedural code that's used within stored programs.

How to display data

As you develop stored programs, you often need to display messages as shown in figure 13-3. This can help you to make sure that the stored program is executing correctly, and it can help you debug your programs. To display a message, you can use a SELECT statement. In this figure, for example, the stored procedure uses a SELECT statement to return a result set that contains a single row with a column named message that contains a string that says, "This is a test."

To display more complex messages, you can code more complex SELECT statements. In the next figure, for example, you'll see a stored procedure that uses a SELECT statement that returns a result set with multiple values. Then, the SELECT statement stores those values in variables so the variables can be formatted and displayed.

This figure only shows the DELIMTER statement and the CREATE PRO-CEDURE statement that are necessary to create the stored procedure. Before you execute these statements, you may need to select the appropriate database and drop any procedures with the same name as shown in the figure 13-1. Similarly, after you execute these statements, the stored procedure isn't executed until you call it as shown in figure 13-1.

A stored procedure that displays a message

```
DELIMITER //

CREATE PROCEDURE test()
BEGIN
  SELECT 'This is a test.' AS message;
END//
```

The response from the system when the procedure is called

message
This is a test.

Description

- To display a message from a stored program, you can use the SELECT statement to return a result set.

Figure 13-3   How to display data

How to declare and set variables

A *variable* stores a value that can change as the procedure executes. Figure 13-4 shows how to declare and set variables.

To declare a variable, you code the DECLARE keyword followed by the variable name and data type. In this figure, for example, the stored procedure begins by declaring five variables. The data type for each variable corresponds to the data type that's used for a column that's related to the variable. For example, the first two variables are declared with the DECIMAL type. This is the same data type that's used by the invoice_total column of the Invoices table. The third variable also uses this data type, but with 4 decimal places instead of 2. The last two variables use the INT type, which matches the data type for the invoice_id and vendor_id columns. When specifying the data type for a variable, you can use any of the data types that you can use when you specify the data type for a column.

Once you declare a variable, you can assign a value to it using the SET statement. To assign a literal value or the result of an expression, you can code the assignment operator (=) followed by the literal value or the expression. In the script in this figure, for example, the first SET statement uses the assignment operator to assign a value of 95 to the variable named vendor_id_var. The second SET statement uses the assignment operator to assign the result of a calculation to the variable named percent_difference.

You can also use the DEFAULT keyword to assign a default value to a variable when you declare it. Then, the default value is used if another value isn't assigned to the variable. For this to work, the default value must be a literal value, not an expression. To declare and assign a value to the vendor_id_var variable, for example, you could code a statement like this:

```
DECLARE vendor_id_var INT DEFAULT 95;
```

If you want to assign a value that's returned by a SELECT statement to a variable, you can add an INTO clause to a SELECT statement. In the script in this figure, for example, the first SELECT statement uses the INTO clause to assign the three values that are returned by the SELECT statement to the three corresponding variables that are specified by the INTO clause. For this to work, the SELECT statement must return one value for each of the variables that are specified in the INTO clause. In addition, the data types for the columns must be compatible with the data types for the variables.

To review, the script in this figure uses five variables to calculate the percent difference between the minimum and maximum invoices for a particular vendor. To do that, this script uses the assignment operator to assign a value to two of the variables. In addition, it uses the INTO clause of a SELECT statement to assign values to the other three variables. Finally, a SELECT statement displays the values of four of the variables.

In this figure, the script uses the equals sign (=) as the assignment operator. However, MySQL also allows you to use a colon plus the equals sign (:=) as the assignment operator. So, if you are reviewing another programmer's code, you might see this operator.

The syntax for declaring a variable

```
DECLARE variable_name data_type [DEFAULT literal_value];
```

The syntax for setting a variable to a literal value or an expression

```
SET variable_name = literal_value_or_expression;
```

The syntax for setting a variable to a selected value

```
SELECT column_1[, column_2]...
INTO variable_name_1[, variable_name_2]...
```

A stored procedure that uses variables

```
DELIMITER //

CREATE PROCEDURE test()
BEGIN
    DECLARE max_invoice_total   DECIMAL(9,2);
    DECLARE min_invoice_total   DECIMAL(9,2);
    DECLARE percent_difference  DECIMAL(9,4);
    DECLARE count_invoice_id    INT;
    DECLARE vendor_id_var       INT;

    SET vendor_id_var = 95;        lit value

    SELECT MAX(invoice_total), MIN(invoice_total), COUNT(invoice_id)
    INTO max_invoice_total, min_invoice_total, count_invoice_id
    FROM invoices WHERE vendor_id = vendor_id_var;

    SET percent_difference = (max_invoice_total - min_invoice_total) /
                              min_invoice_total * 100;

    SELECT CONCAT('$', max_invoice_total) AS 'Maximum invoice',
           CONCAT('$', min_invoice_total) AS 'Minimum invoice',
           CONCAT('%', ROUND(percent_difference, 2)) AS 'Percent difference',
           count_invoice_id AS 'Number of invoices';
END//
```

Calculate

The response from the system when the procedure is called

Maximum invoice	Minimum invoice	Percent difference	Number of invoices
$46.21	$16.33	%182.98	6

Description

- A *variable* stores a value that can change as a stored program executes.
- A variable must have a name that's different from the names of any columns used in any SELECT statement within the stored program. To distinguish a variable from a column, you can add a suffix like "_var" to the variable name.

Figure 13-4   How to declare and set variables

How to code IF statements

Figure 13-5 shows how to use an IF statement to execute one or more statements based on a value that's returned by a *Boolean expression*. A Boolean expression is an expression that returns a true value or a false value.

The script in this figure uses an IF statement to test the value of a variable. This variable contains the oldest invoice due date in the Invoices table. If this due date is less than the current date, the Boolean expression evaluates to true, and the statement in the IF clause shows that outstanding invoices are overdue. If the value is equal to the current date, the statement in the ELSEIF clause indicates that outstanding invoices are due today. If neither of these conditions is true, the oldest due date must be greater than the current date. As a result, the script indicates that no invoices are overdue.

In this figure, the IF statement only contains one ELSEIF clause. However, you can add as many ELSEIF clauses as you need. As a result, you can code dozens of these clauses if you need them. But if you don't need an ELSEIF clause, you don't have to code one. For example, it's common to code an IF statement without an ELSEIF clause like this:

```
IF first_invoice_due_date < NOW() THEN
  SELECT 'Outstanding invoices overdue!';
ELSE
  SELECT 'No invoices are overdue.';
END IF;
```

Similarly, the ELSE clause is optional. As a result, it's common to code an IF statement like this:

```
IF first_invoice_due_date < NOW() THEN
  SELECT 'Outstanding invoices overdue!';
END IF;
```

You can also *nest* one IF statement within another like this:

```
IF first_invoice_due_date <= NOW() THEN
  SELECT 'Outstanding invoices are overdue!';
  IF first_invoice_due_date = NOW() THEN
    SELECT 'TODAY!';
  END IF;
END IF;
```

In this case, the outer IF statement is executed when the oldest invoice due date is less than or equal to the current date. However, the nested IF statement is only executed when the oldest invoice due date is equal to the current date. In other words, if the current date equals the oldest invoice due date, this code returns two result sets instead of one. As you'll see later in this chapter, you can also nest an IF statement within other types of statements such as loops.

The syntax of the IF statement

```
IF boolean_expression THEN
  statement_1;
  [statement_2;]...
[ELSEIF boolean_expression THEN
  statement_1;
  [statement_2;]...]...
[ELSE
  statement_1;
  [statement_2;]...]
END IF;
```

A stored procedure that uses an IF statement

```
DELIMITER //

CREATE PROCEDURE test()
BEGIN
  DECLARE first_invoice_due_date DATE;

  SELECT MIN(invoice_due_date)
  INTO first_invoice_due_date
  FROM invoices
  WHERE invoice_total - payment_total - credit_total > 0;

  IF first_invoice_due_date < NOW() THEN
    SELECT 'Outstanding invoices overdue!';
  ELSEIF first_invoice_due_date = NOW() THEN
    SELECT 'Outstanding invoices are due today!';
  ELSE
    SELECT 'No invoices are overdue.';
  END IF;
END//
```

The response from the system when the procedure is called

Outstanding invoices overdue!
▶ Outstanding invoices overdue!

Description

- You can use an *IF statement* to execute one or more statements depending on one or more Boolean expressions. A *Boolean expression* is an expression that evaluates to true or false.

- You can *nest* an IF statement within another IF statement or within other SQL statements such as the statements for coding loops.

- You can also code parentheses around the Boolean expressions in an IF statement like this:

```
IF (first_invoice_due_date < NOW()) THEN ...
```

You may see other programmers use this technique.

Figure 13-5　How to code IF statements

How to code CASE statements

In chapter 9, you learned how to code a CASE expression within a SELECT statement. A CASE expression like that usually runs faster than a CASE statement that's coded within a stored program. As a result, if you can use a CASE expression to solve the task at hand, you should. However, you may sometimes need to use a CASE statement as shown in figure 13-6.

The script in this figure shows how to use a *simple CASE statement* to execute one or more statements depending on a value that's returned by an expression. To do that, you begin by coding the CASE keyword followed by an expression that returns a value. In this script, the variable that's coded after the CASE statement returns an integer value that indicates the payment terms for an invoice.

After the CASE clause, you can code one or more WHEN clauses that contain the statement or statements that are executed for each of the values that may be returned. In this example, the CASE statement includes three WHEN clauses for the values of 1, 2, and 3. Each of these clauses displays an appropriate message.

After the WHEN clauses, you can code an optional ELSE clause that's executed if the value that's returned doesn't match the values coded in any of the WHEN clauses. This works much like the ELSE clause that's available from the IF statement.

Although this figure doesn't show an example of it, you can also use a *searched CASE statement* to execute one or more statements depending on one or more Boolean expressions. This works similarly to an IF statement. For example, you can use a searched CASE statement to replace the IF statement in the previous figure like this:

```
CASE
  WHEN first_invoice_due_date < NOW() THEN
    SELECT ('Outstanding invoices overdue!');
  WHEN first_invoice_due_date = NOW() THEN
    SELECT ('Outstanding invoices are due today!');
  ELSE
    SELECT ('No invoices are overdue.');
END CASE;
```

Conversely, you can easily rewrite the simple CASE statement shown in this figure as an IF statement.

So, when should you use an IF statement and when should you use a CASE statement? Although this is largely a matter of personal preference, you usually should try to use the statement that yields the code that's easiest to read and understand.

The syntax of the simple CASE statement

```
CASE expression
  WHEN expression_value_1 THEN
    statement_1;
    [statement_2;]...
  [WHEN expression_value_2 THEN
    statement_1;
    [statement_2;]...]...
  [ELSE
    statement_1;
    [statement_2;]...]
END CASE;
```

A stored procedure that uses a simple CASE statement

```
DELIMITER //

CREATE PROCEDURE test()
BEGIN
  DECLARE terms_id_var INT;

  SELECT terms_id INTO terms_id_var
  FROM invoices WHERE invoice_id = 4;

  CASE terms_id_var
    WHEN 1 THEN
      SELECT 'Net due 10 days' AS Terms;
    WHEN 2 THEN
      SELECT 'Net due 20 days' AS Terms;
    WHEN 3 THEN
      SELECT 'Net due 30 days' AS Terms;
    ELSE
      SELECT 'Net due more than 30 days' AS Terms;
  END CASE;
END//
```

The response from the system when the procedure is called

Terms
Net due 30 days

The syntax of a searched CASE statement

```
CASE
  WHEN boolean_expression THEN
    statement_1;
    [statement_2;]...
  [WHEN boolean_expression THEN
    statement_1;
    [statement_2;]...]...
  [ELSE
    statement_1;
    [statement_2;]...]
END CASE;
```

Description

- You can use a *simple CASE statement* or a *searched CASE statement* to execute one or more statements depending on a value that's returned by an expression.

Figure 13-6   How to code CASE statements

How to code loops

Figure 13-7 shows how to use a *loop* to repeat a statement or several statements while a condition is true. This figure starts by showing how to use a *WHILE loop* to continue executing while a *counter* is within the specified range. In the example, the stored procedure begins by declaring a counter variable named i that has a default value of 1. Then, it declares a string variable named s that can store up to 400 characters and has a default value of an empty string.

The WHILE statement begins by declaring that the loop should continue while the counter variable is less than four. Since the second SET statement increases the value of the counter variable by 1 each time through the loop, the loop is executed three times (when the counter is equal to 1, 2, and 3). As a result, the first SET statement is executed three times. This statement appends some string literals and the value of the counter variable to the string variable.

After the loop finishes executing, the SELECT statement displays the string variable. This variable provides a string representation of the three values of the counter variable. Although this doesn't accomplish anything useful, it clearly shows how a WHILE loop works and can be useful for debugging.

The next two examples show how to use different types of loops to get the same result as the first example. Although the syntax for these loops isn't presented in this figure, you shouldn't have any trouble understanding how they work if you understand how the WHILE loop works.

Both of these examples focus on the code for the loop. In other words, they don't show the DELIMITER and CREATE PROCEDURE statements that were shown in the first example. In addition, they don't show the code that declares the counter and string variables or the code that displays the string variable. However, for these examples to run, they would need to include this code.

The second example shows how to use a *REPEAT loop*. In this example, the REPEAT loop continues to execute until a counter variable named i equals 4. This works similarly to the WHILE loop, except that the Boolean expression is coded at the end of the loop. As a result, a REPEAT loop always executes at least once. Because of that, you should use a REPEAT loop if you want to execute the code at least once, and you should use a WHILE loop if you don't want the code to execute at all in some cases.

The third example shows how to use a *simple LOOP*. Ironically, a simple LOOP is the most complex to code. To start, you must code a name that identifies the start and end of the loop. In this example, the loop is named testLoop. Then, you can use an IF statement to determine when the loop should end. Within this IF statement, you can use the LEAVE statement to jump to the end of the loop. On this statement, you name the loop you want to leave. Although this can be useful if you nest one loop within another loop, it's a lot of unnecessary code for a loop that isn't nested. As a result, you'll typically want to use a WHILE loop or a REPEAT loop.

In the rare case that you need to jump to the beginning of a loop, you can use an ITERATE statement. This statement works like the LEAVE statement, except that it jumps to the beginning of a loop instead of to the end of a loop.

The syntax of the WHILE loop

```
WHILE boolean_expression DO
  statement_1;
  [statement_2;]...
END WHILE;
```

A stored procedure that uses a WHILE loop

```
DELIMITER //

CREATE PROCEDURE test()
BEGIN
  DECLARE i INT DEFAULT 1;
  DECLARE s VARCHAR(400) DEFAULT '';

  WHILE i < 4 DO
    SET s = CONCAT(s, 'i=', i, ' | ');
    SET i = i + 1;
  END WHILE;

  SELECT s AS message;

END//
```

empty?

The output for this code

message
i=1	i=2	i=3	

A REPEAT loop

```
REPEAT
  SET s = CONCAT(s, 'i=', i, ' | ');
  SET i = i + 1;
UNTIL i = 4
END REPEAT;
```

A simple loop

```
testLoop : LOOP
  SET s = CONCAT(s, 'i=', i, ' | ');
  SET i = i + 1;

  IF i = 4 THEN
    LEAVE testLoop;
  END IF;
END LOOP testLoop;
```

Description

- To execute a SQL statement repeatedly, you can use a *loop*. MySQL provides for three types of loops: a *WHILE loop*, a *REPEAT loop*, and a *simple loop*.
- You can use the LEAVE statement to go to the end of a loop.
- You can use the ITERATE statement to go to the beginning of a loop.

Figure 13-7   How to code loops

How to use a cursor

By default, SQL statements work with an entire result set rather than individual rows. However, you may sometimes need to work with the data in a result set one row at a time. To do that, you can use a *cursor* as described in figure 13-8.

In this figure, the stored procedure begins by declaring four variables. Note that the third variable is assigned a default value of FALSE even though it's declared with the TINYINT type. As you learned in chapter 8, this works because the FALSE keyword is an alias for 0. Although many programmers use 0 to represent a false value and 1 to represent a true value, this chapter uses the FALSE and TRUE keywords instead because they make the code easier to read.

Next, this code declares a variable of the CURSOR type named invoices_cursor. Within this declaration, this code uses a SELECT statement to define the result set for this cursor. This result set contains two columns from the invoices table and all of the rows that have a balance due.

After declaring the cursor, this code declares an error handler that's executed when no more rows are found in the result set for the cursor. This error handler sets the variable named row_not_found to a value of TRUE. Because the WHILE loop that follows executes only while the row_not_found variable is equal to FALSE, this causes the WHILE loop to stop executing.

After declaring the error handler, this code uses the OPEN statement to open the cursor. Then, it uses a WHILE loop to loop through each row in the cursor. This WHILE loop continues until the row_not_found variable is set to TRUE by the error handler.

Within the WHILE loop, the FETCH statement gets the column values from the next row and stores them in the variables that were declared earlier. Then, an IF statement checks whether the value of the invoice_total column for the current row is greater than 1000. If it is, an UPDATE statement adds 10% of the invoice_total column to the credit_total column for the row, and a SET statement increments the count of the number of rows that have been updated.

After the WHILE loop, this code closes the cursor. Finally, it uses a SELECT statement to display a count of the number of rows that have been updated.

Before you use a cursor to work with individual rows in a result set, you should consider other solutions. That's because standard database access is faster and uses fewer server resources than cursor-based access. For example, you can accomplish the same update as the stored procedure in this figure with this UPDATE statement:

```
UPDATE invoices
SET credit_total = credit_total + (invoice_total * .1)
WHERE invoice_total - payment_total - credit_total > 0
AND invoice_total > 1000
```

However, if you encounter a situation where it makes sense to use a cursor, the skills presented in this figure should help you do that.

The syntax

Declare a cursor

```
DECLARE cursor_name CURSOR FOR select_statement;
```

Declare an error handler for when no rows are found in the cursor

```
DECLARE CONTINUE HANDLER FOR NOT FOUND handler_statement;
```

Open the cursor

```
OPEN cursor_name;
```

Get column values from the row and store them in a series of variables

```
FETCH cursor_name INTO variable1[, variable2][, variable3]...;
```

Close the cursor

```
CLOSE cursor_name;
```

A stored procedure that uses a cursor

```
DELIMITER //

CREATE PROCEDURE test()
BEGIN
  DECLARE invoice_id_var     INT;
  DECLARE invoice_total_var  DECIMAL(9,2);
  DECLARE row_not_found      TINYINT DEFAULT FALSE;
  DECLARE update_count       INT DEFAULT 0;

  DECLARE invoices_cursor CURSOR FOR
    SELECT invoice_id, invoice_total  FROM invoices
    WHERE invoice_total - payment_total - credit_total > 0;

  DECLARE CONTINUE HANDLER FOR NOT FOUND
    SET row_not_found = TRUE;

  OPEN invoices_cursor;

  WHILE row_not_found = FALSE DO
    FETCH invoices_cursor INTO invoice_id_var, invoice_total_var;

    IF invoice_total_var > 1000 THEN
      UPDATE invoices
      SET credit_total = credit_total + (invoice_total * .1)
      WHERE invoice_id = invoice_id_var;
      SET update_count = update_count + 1;
    END IF;
  END WHILE;

  CLOSE invoices_cursor;

  SELECT CONCAT(update_count, ' row(s) updated.');
END//
```

(handwritten annotations: "=alias ∅" pointing to `FALSE`)

The response from the system when the procedure is called

CONCAT(update_count, ' row(s) updated.')
2 row(s) updated.

Figure 13-8   How to use a cursor

How to declare a condition handler

Before you declare a condition handler, you need to be familiar with the MySQL error codes and named conditions that are defined by MySQL. Figure 13-9 begins by listing five of the more than 700 MySQL error codes. These error codes should give you an idea of the types of errors MySQL provides for.

Each of these error codes corresponds with a SQLSTATE code that's part of the ANSI standard. However, the MySQL codes are typically more useful since they're more specific. For example, the last four MySQL error codes all correspond with a SQLSTATE code of 23000.

In general, you only need to handle these errors when you encounter them during testing. However, if you're interested in viewing a list of all the error codes, you'll find them in the MySQL Reference Manual.

The second table in this figure lists the three built-in named conditions MySQL provides. To start, it provides the NOT FOUND condition that was used in the stored procedure in figure 13-8. This condition corresponds with MySQL error code 1329 and SQLSTATE code 02000. In addition, MySQL provides the SQLEXCEPTION and SQLWARNING conditions.

The SQLEXCEPTION condition provides a way for you to handle all errors, even ones that you did not encounter during testing. When this condition occurs, you typically execute the SHOW ERRORS statement. This statement returns a result set that contains information about the errors that resulted from the last statement in the current session.

The SQLWARNING condition works like the SQLEXCEPTION condition, but it allows you to catch warnings and errors instead of just errors. If you handle this condition, you may want to use the SHOW WARNINGS statement. This statement works similarly to the SHOW ERRORS statement, but it returns information about all errors and warnings.

This figure also shows how to use the DECLARE...HANDLER statement to handle the errors that may occur in your stored programs. In MySQL, this is referred to as a *condition handler*. In other languages, this is referred to an *error handler* or *exception handler*.

The three examples in this figure show how to declare condition handlers for a MySQL error code, a SQLSTATE code, and a named condition. All three of these condition handlers use the CONTINUE keyword, which causes the stored program to continue executing at the statement after the statement that caused the error to occur. If that's not what you want, you can use the EXIT keyword to continue execution after the current block of code. You'll see an example of that in the next figure.

In most cases, you can use the MySQL error codes and the built-in named conditions to handle the exceptions that you encounter. In some cases, though, you may want to create your own named conditions. Although this doesn't provide any new capabilities, it can sometimes improve the readability of your code. For more information about creating your own named conditions, you can search the MySQL Reference Manual for information about the DECLARE...CONDITION statement.

Commonly used MySQL error codes

Error code	SQLSTATE code	Description
1329	02000	Occurs when a program attempts to fetch data from a row that doesn't exist.
1062	23000	Occurs when a program attempts to store duplicate values in a column that has a unique constraint.
1048	23000	Occurs when a program attempts to insert a NULL value into a column that doesn't accept NULL values.
1216	23000	Occurs when a program attempts to add or update a child row but can't because of a foreign key constraint.
1217	23000	Occurs when a program attempts to delete or update a parent row but can't because of a foreign key constraint.

Built-in named conditions

Named condition	Description
NOT FOUND	Occurs when a program attempts to use a FETCH statement or a SELECT statement to retrieve data and no data is found.
SQLEXCEPTION	Occurs when any error condition other than the NOT FOUND condition occurs.
SQLWARNING	Occurs when any error condition other than the NOT FOUND condition occurs or when any warning messages occur.

The syntax for declaring a condition handler

```
DECLARE {CONTINUE|EXIT} HANDLER
  FOR {mysql_error_code|SQLSTATE sqlstate_code|named_condition}
  handler_actions;
```

How to declare a condition handler for a MySQL error code

```
DECLARE CONTINUE HANDLER FOR 1329
  SET row_not_found = TRUE;
```

How to declare a condition handler for a SQLSTATE code

```
DECLARE CONTINUE HANDLER FOR SQLSTATE '02000'
  SET row_not_found = TRUE;
```

How to declare a condition handler for a named condition

```
DECLARE CONTINUE HANDLER FOR NOT FOUND
  SET row_not_found = TRUE;
```

Description

- You can use the DECLARE...HANDLER statement to declare a handler for errors that may occur. In MySQL, this is referred to as a *condition handler*.
- To continue execution when an error occurs, use the CONTINUE keyword. To exit the current block of code when an error occurs, use the EXIT keyword.
- For a complete list of the MySQL error codes and their corresponding SQLSTATE codes, you can search the MySQL Reference Manual for "Server error codes".

Figure 13-9   How to declare a condition handler

How to use a condition handler

Now that you know how to declare a condition handler, figure 13-10 shows how to use a condition handler. To help you understand the difference between a stored program that handles errors and one that doesn't, the first stored procedure shows what happens when an error occurs and the procedure doesn't handle errors. Here, the INSERT statement attempts to insert a duplicate value ("Cash") into a column (account_description) that has been defined with a unique constraint. Because the error condition this causes isn't handled, MySQL displays an error message like the one that's shown. This message identifies the error code (1062), and it displays a description of the error that helps you identify the cause of the error.

Although an error message like this can be helpful as you develop a stored procedure, it isn't helpful to the end user of an application. As a result, you often want to handle exceptions before you put your stored programs into production. Since the most specific way to handle an error is to use a MySQL error code, you usually want to declare a condition handler for the error code that's occurring. Then, you can handle this error by executing the appropriate code. Often, that just means displaying a more user-friendly message. However, you can also perform other error-handling tasks such as writing information about the error to a log table or rolling back a transaction.

The second stored procedure in this figure handles the error that occurs when the first procedure is run. To do that, it begins by declaring a variable named duplicate_entry_for_key of the TINYINT type and setting its default value to FALSE. Then, it declares a handler for error code 1062. This handler uses the CONTINUE keyword to allow the procedure to continue executing when the error is encountered. However, it also uses a SET statement to set the value of the duplicate_entry_for_key variable to TRUE. As a result, the IF statement can test the value of this variable and handle the error when it occurs. In this figure, this code just handles the error by displaying a message that indicates that the row was not inserted.

To test this procedure, you can change the values in the INSERT statement. If you run the statement as shown in this figure, for example, the error with code 1062 occurs and the stored procedure returns the result set shown in this figure. However, if you enter valid values, this procedure returns a result set that indicates that one row was inserted.

A stored procedure that doesn't handle errors

```
DELIMITER //

CREATE PROCEDURE test()
BEGIN
  INSERT INTO general_ledger_accounts VALUES (130, 'Cash');

  SELECT '1 row was inserted.';
END//
```

The response from the system

```
Error Code: 1062. Duplicate entry 'Cash' for key 'account_description'
```

A stored procedure that uses a CONTINUE handler to handle an error

```
DELIMITER //

CREATE PROCEDURE test()
BEGIN
  DECLARE duplicate_entry_for_key TINYINT DEFAULT FALSE;

  DECLARE CONTINUE HANDLER FOR 1062
    SET duplicate_entry_for_key = TRUE;

  INSERT INTO general_ledger_accounts VALUES (130, 'Cash');

  IF duplicate_entry_for_key = TRUE THEN
    SELECT 'Row was not inserted - duplicate key encountered.' AS message;
  ELSE
    SELECT '1 row was inserted.' AS message;
  END IF;
END//
```

The response from the system

message
Row was not inserted - duplicate key encountered.

Figure 13-10   How to use a condition handler (part 1 of 2)

The first stored procedure in part 2 of figure 13-10 shows how to exit the current block of code as soon as an error occurs. To start, this stored procedure begins by declaring a variable named duplicate_entry_for_key just like the stored procedure in part 1. Then, it uses the BEGIN and END keywords to nest a block of code within the block of code for the procedure. Within the nested block of code, the first statement declares a condition handler for the MySQL error with a code of 1062. This handler uses the EXIT keyword to indicate that it should exit the block of code when this error occurs. Then, the second statement executes the INSERT statement that may cause the error. If no error occurs, the third statement in the block displays a message that indicates that the row was inserted.

If an error occurs, however, the duplicate_entry_for_key variable is set to TRUE. In addition, code execution exits the block of code and jumps to the IF statement that's coded after the block. This statement displays a message that indicates that the row was not inserted.

So, when should you use a CONTINUE handler and when should you use an EXIT handler? In general, it's a matter of personal preference. However, if you want to allow MySQL to attempt to execute statements in a block of code even after it encounters an error, you should use a CONTINUE handler. On the other hand, if allowing MySQL to continue to execute statements in the block causes problems, you should use an EXIT handler.

The last stored procedure in this figure shows how to use a named condition to handle the error that occurs when a row can't be inserted. In this case, the stored procedure uses the SQLEXCEPTION condition. When this condition occurs, the stored procedure uses the SHOW ERRORS statement to display information about the error. This information includes the MySQL error code and a description for each error.

When handling the SQLEXCEPTION condition, many programmers make the mistake of displaying a generic message like this: "An unexpected error occurred." Although this message is user-friendly, it doesn't provide any information that can help a programmer find and fix the error. As a result, it's often better not to handle this exception at all. In that case, the stored procedure displays an error as shown in the first example in part 1 of this figure.

A stored procedure that uses an EXIT handler to handle an error

```
DELIMITER //

CREATE PROCEDURE test()
BEGIN
  DECLARE duplicate_entry_for_key TINYINT DEFAULT FALSE;
  BEGIN
    DECLARE EXIT HANDLER FOR 1062
      SET duplicate_entry_for_key = TRUE;

    INSERT INTO general_ledger_accounts VALUES (130, 'Cash');

    SELECT '1 row was inserted.' AS message;
  END;

  IF duplicate_entry_for_key = TRUE THEN
    SELECT 'Row was not inserted - duplicate key encountered.' AS message;
  END IF;
END//
```

The response from the system

message
▸ Row was not inserted - duplicate key encountered.

A stored procedure that uses a named condition to handle all errors

```
DELIMITER //

CREATE PROCEDURE test()
BEGIN
  DECLARE sql_error TINYINT DEFAULT FALSE;
  BEGIN
    DECLARE EXIT HANDLER FOR SQLEXCEPTION
      SET sql_error = TRUE;

    INSERT INTO general_ledger_accounts VALUES (130, 'Cash');

    SELECT '1 row was inserted.' AS message;
  END;

  IF sql_error = TRUE THEN
    SHOW ERRORS;
  END IF;
END//
```

The response from the system

Level	Code	Message
▸ Error	1062	Duplicate entry 'Cash' for key 'account_description'

Description

- If you want MySQL to exit the current block of code as soon as it encounters an error, use an EXIT handler.
- You can use the SHOW ERRORS statement to return a result set that contains information about the errors that resulted from the last statement in the current session.

Figure 13-10   How to use a condition handler (part 2 of 2)

How to use multiple condition handlers

When coding a stored program, it's common to declare multiple condition handlers as shown in figure 13-11. If you do that, the most specific error handlers are executed first, and the least specific error handlers are executed last.

The stored procedure in this figure begins by declaring three variables that are used to indicate whether an error condition has occurred. Here, all three variables are set to a default value of FALSE.

After declaring these three variables, this stored procedure defines a block of code. Within this block, the first three statements declare three condition handlers that correspond with the three variables. These handlers all exit the block of code if the specified error occurs. Of these handlers, the first two are specific to MySQL error codes 1062 and 1048, but the third is a general handler that catches any other errors that may occur.

After the block of code, an IF statement examines the variables that are set by the condition handlers. Then, it executes the appropriate code. For the first two variables, this code displays a user-friendly message that's appropriate for the corresponding MySQL error code. For the third variable, though, this code uses the SHOW ERRORS statement to display information about the unanticipated error that occurred. In other words, if MySQL error code 1062 or 1048 occurs, this code displays a user-friendly error. Otherwise, it displays an error that's less user-friendly but still provides useful information about the error.

If you run the stored procedure shown in this figure, it returns a result set like the one that's shown. In this case, the row wasn't inserted because the first column contained an illegal NULL value. To test for other errors, you can change the values in the INSERT statement. For example, if you enter 'xx' as the value for the first column, the stored procedure executes the condition handler for the SQLEXCEPTION condition. Then, it executes the SHOW ERRORS statement.

A stored procedure that uses multiple condition handlers

```
DELIMITER //

CREATE PROCEDURE test()
BEGIN
  DECLARE duplicate_entry_for_key TINYINT DEFAULT FALSE;
  DECLARE column_cannot_be_null   TINYINT DEFAULT FALSE;
  DECLARE sql_exception           TINYINT DEFAULT FALSE;

  BEGIN
    DECLARE EXIT HANDLER FOR 1062
      SET duplicate_entry_for_key = TRUE;
    DECLARE EXIT HANDLER FOR 1048
      SET column_cannot_be_null = TRUE;
    DECLARE EXIT HANDLER FOR SQLEXCEPTION
      SET sql_exception = TRUE;

    INSERT INTO general_ledger_accounts VALUES (NULL, 'Test');

    SELECT '1 row was inserted.' AS message;
  END;

  IF duplicate_entry_for_key = TRUE THEN
    SELECT 'Row was not inserted - duplicate key encountered.' AS message;
  ELSEIF column_cannot_be_null = TRUE THEN
    SELECT 'Row was not inserted - column cannot be null.' AS message;
  ELSEIF sql_exception = TRUE THEN
    SHOW ERRORS;
  END IF;
END//
```

The response from the system

message
▶ Row was not inserted - column cannot be null.

Description

- You can declare multiple condition handlers for a single stored program. If you do that, the most specific error handlers are executed first and the least specific error handlers are executed last.
- The MySQL error codes and the NOT FOUND condition identify specific errors. The SQLSTATE codes identify less specific ANSI-standard errors. And the SQLEXCEPTION and SQLWARNING conditions identify general errors.

Figure 13-11   How to use multiple condition handlers

Perspective

In this chapter, you were introduced to stored programs, and you learned how to use MySQL to write procedural code. In the next three chapters, you'll learn more about writing stored programs. In chapter 14, you'll learn how to manage transactions and locking. In chapter 15, you'll learn how to code stored procedures and functions. And in chapter 16, you'll learn how to code triggers and events.

Terms

stored program	searched CASE statement
stored procedure	loop
stored function	WHILE loop
stored routine	REPEAT loop
trigger	simple LOOP
event	counter
block of code	cursor
variable	condition handler
Boolean expression	error handler
nested statement	exception handler
simple CASE statement	named condition

Exercises

Each of the scripts that you create in the following exercises should use the same general structure as the script presented in figure 13-1.

1. Write a script that creates and calls a stored procedure named test. This stored procedure should declare a variable and set it to the count of all rows in the Invoices table that have a balance due that's greater than or equal to $5,000. Then, the stored procedure should display a result set that displays the variable in a message like this:

    `3 invoices exceed $5,000.`

2. Write a script that creates and calls a stored procedure named test. This stored procedure should use two variables to store (1) the count of all of the invoices in the Invoices table that have a balance due and (2) the sum of the balances due for all of those invoices. If that total balance due is greater than or equal to $30,000, the stored procedure should display a result set that displays the values of both variables. Otherwise, the procedure should display a result set that displays a message like this:

    `Total balance due is less than $30,000.`

3. Write a script that creates and calls a stored procedure named test. This procedure should calculate the factorial for the number 10. (To calculate a factorial, you multiply an integer by every positive integer less than itself.) Then, it should display a string that includes the factorial like this:

    `The factorial of 10 is: 3,628,800.`

4. Write a script that creates and calls a stored procedure named test. This stored procedure should create a cursor for a result set that consists of the vendor_name, invoice_number, and balance_due columns for each invoice with a balance due that's greater than or equal to $5,000. The rows in this result set should be sorted in descending sequence by balance due. Then, the procedure should display a string variable that includes the balance due, invoice number, and vendor name for each invoice so it looks something like this:

    `11130.70|P-0608|Malloy Lithographing Inc//6585.62|0-2436|Malloy Lithographing Inc//`

    Here, each column is separated by a pipe character (|) and each row is separated by two front slashes (//).

5. Write a script that creates and calls a stored procedure named test. This procedure should attempt to update the invoice_due_date column so it's equal to NULL for the invoice with an invoice ID of 1. If the update is successful, the procedure should display this message:

    `1 row was updated.`

    If the update is unsuccessful, the procedure should display this message:

    `Row was not updated - column cannot be null.`

6. Write a script that creates and calls a stored procedure named test. This procedure should identify all of the prime numbers less than 100. (A prime number is an integer that can't be divided by another integer other than 1 and itself.) Then, it should display a string variable that includes the prime numbers like this:

    `2 | 3 | 5 | 7 | 11 | 13 | 17 | 19 | 23 | 29 | 31 |...`

    Hint: To get this to work, you will need to nest one loop within another loop. In addition, you will need to code an IF statement within the inner loop.

7. Enhance your script for exercise 4 so it shows the invoice data in three groups based on the balance due amount with these headings:

    `$20,000 or More`
    `$10,000 to $20,000`
    `$5,000 to $10,000`

    When you're done, the string variable that's returned should be in this format:

    `$20,000 or More: $10,000 to $20,000: 11130.70|P-0608|Malloy Lithographing Inc//$5,000 to $10,000: 6585.62|0-2436|Malloy Lithographing Inc//`

    To accomplish this, you can loop through the cursor three times by opening and closing the cursor for each loop. *Hint: For each group of invoices, you can code a separate block of code that contains an EXIT handler for the NOT FOUND condition.*

14

How to use transactions and locking

If you've been working with MySQL on your own computer, you've been the only user of your database. In the real world, though, a database may be used by thousands of users at the same time. Then, what happens when two users try to update the same data at the same time? In this chapter, you'll learn how MySQL handles this situation. But first, you'll learn how to combine multiple SQL statements into a single logical unit of work known as a transaction.

How to work with transactions **402**
How to commit and rollback transactions 402
How to work with save points 404
How to work with concurrency and locking **406**
How concurrency and locking are related 406
The four concurrency problems that locks can prevent 408
How to set the transaction isolation level 410
How to prevent deadlocks 412
Perspective **414**

How to work with transactions

A *transaction* is a group of SQL statements that you combine into a single logical unit of work. By combining SQL statements like this, you can prevent certain kinds of database errors.

Before you begin using MySQL to work with transactions, you should realize that some storage engines don't support transactions. In particular, the MyISAM storage engine doesn't support transactions. As a result, the skills presented in this topic only apply to storage engines such as InnoDB that support transactions.

How to commit and rollback transactions

By default, a MySQL session uses autocommit mode, which automatically commits INSERT, UPDATE, and DELETE statements immediately after you execute them. So far in this book, we have assumed that you have been using autocommit mode. If that's not what you want, though, you can use transactions to control when changes are committed.

Since transactions are often coded within stored procedures, figure 14-1 presents a stored procedure named test that contains three INSERT statements that are coded as a transaction. To start, this stored procedure declares a variable named sql_error and sets it to FALSE to indicate that no SQL error has occurred. Then, the second DECLARE statement creates a condition handler that sets the sql_error variable to TRUE if a SQL error occurs.

The START TRANSACTION statement identifies the start of the transaction, which temporarily turns off autocommit mode. Then, the first INSERT statement adds a new invoice to the Invoices table. Next, two more INSERT statements add the line items for the invoice to the Invoice_Line_Items table.

After the INSERT statements, an IF statement uses the sql_error variable to check whether an error occurred when executing any of the INSERT statements. If a SQL error did not occur, this code uses the COMMIT statement to *commit* the changes to the database, which makes the changes permanent. Otherwise, the ROLLBACK statement *rolls back* the changes, which cancels them.

To understand why this is necessary, suppose that each of these INSERT statements is committed to the database immediately after it's executed. Then, what will happen if the third INSERT statement fails? In that case, the Invoices and Invoice_Line_Items tables won't match. Specifically, the sum of the line_item_amount columns in the Invoice_Line_Items table won't be equal to the invoice_total column in the Invoices table. In other words, the integrity of the data won't be maintained.

Similarly, consider the example of a transfer between a checking and a savings account in a banking system. In that case, one update reduces the balance in the checking account and another update increases the balance in the savings account. Then, if one of these updates fails, the customer either gains or loses the amount of the transaction. But here again, treating the two updates as a single transaction solves this problem. Usually, that's what you want.

A stored procedure that runs three INSERT statements as a transaction

```
DELIMITER //

CREATE PROCEDURE test()
BEGIN
  DECLARE sql_error TINYINT DEFAULT FALSE;

  DECLARE CONTINUE HANDLER FOR SQLEXCEPTION
    SET sql_error = TRUE;

  START TRANSACTION;

  INSERT INTO invoices
  VALUES (115, 34, 'ZXA-080', '2012-01-18',
          14092.59, 0, 0, 3, '2012-04-18', NULL);

  INSERT INTO invoice_line_items
  VALUES (115, 1, 160, 4447.23, 'HW upgrade');

  INSERT INTO invoice_line_items
  VALUES (115, 2, 167, 9645.36, 'OS upgrade');

  IF sql_error = FALSE THEN
    COMMIT;
    SELECT 'The transaction was committed.';
  ELSE
    ROLLBACK;
    SELECT 'The transaction was rolled back.';
  END IF;
END//
```

When to use transactions

- When you code two or more INSERT, UPDATE, or DELETE statements that affect related data.
- When you move rows from one table to another table by using INSERT and DELETE statements.
- Whenever the failure of an INSERT, UPDATE, or DELETE statement would violate data integrity.

Description

- A *transaction* is one or more SQL statements that perform a logical unit of work. By default, MySQL runs in autocommit mode, which automatically commits changes to the database immediately after each INSERT, UPDATE, or DELETE statement is executed.
- To start a transaction, code the START TRANSACTION statement. This turns off autocommit mode until the statements in the transaction are committed or rolled back. To *commit* the changes, code a COMMIT statement. To *roll back* the changes, use a ROLLBACK statement.
- MySQL automatically commits changes after a DDL statement such as a CREATE TABLE statement. As a result, you shouldn't code a DDL statement within a transaction unless you want to commit the changes and end the transaction.

Figure 14-1   How to commit and roll back transactions

How to work with save points

The script in figure 14-2 shows how to use the SAVEPOINT statement to identify one or more *save points* within a transaction. Here, a SAVEPOINT statement is used to identify a save point before each of the three INSERT statements that are included in the script. As a result, the script includes three save points.

This script also shows how to use the ROLLBACK TO SAVEPOINT statement to roll back all or part of a transaction. Here, the three ROLLBACK TO SAVEPOINT statements rollback the transaction to each of the three save points. The first statement rolls back to the point before the second line item was inserted. The second statement rolls back to the point before the first line item was inserted. And the third statement rolls back to the point before the invoice was inserted.

At this point, the script calls the COMMIT statement to commit any changes that have been made. However, the three ROLLBACK TO SAVEPOINT statements have rolled back all three INSERT statements, so this doesn't commit any changes to the database. To verify this, you can use a SELECT statement to view the rows in the Invoices and Invoice_Line_Items tables that have an invoice_id of 115.

In general, save points are used when a transaction contains so many statements that rolling back the entire transaction would be inefficient. In that case, an application can roll back to the last save point before an error occurred. Then, the appropriate processing can be done from there. For most applications, though, you won't need to use save points.

In most cases, a transaction and its save points are coded within a stored procedure as shown in figure 14-1. In this figure, though, the transaction and its statements are coded in a script. Although this isn't a realistic example, it does show how save points work, so you should be able to use them if you ever need to. In addition, this example shows that you can use the statements for working with transactions within a script, which is sometimes helpful when working with database creation scripts like the ones described in chapter 11.

A script that uses save points

```
USE ap;

START TRANSACTION;

SAVEPOINT before_invoice;

INSERT INTO invoices
VALUES (115, 34, 'ZXA-080', '2012-01-18',
        14092.59, 0, 0, 3, '2012-04-18', NULL);

SAVEPOINT before_line_item1;

INSERT INTO invoice_line_items
VALUES (115, 1, 160, 4447.23, 'HW upgrade');

SAVEPOINT before_line_item2;

INSERT INTO invoice_line_items
VALUES (115, 2, 167, 9645.36,'OS upgrade');

ROLLBACK TO SAVEPOINT before_line_item2;

ROLLBACK TO SAVEPOINT before_line_item1;

ROLLBACK TO SAVEPOINT before_invoice;

COMMIT;
```

Description

- When you use *save points*, you can roll back a transaction to the beginning of the transaction or to a particular save point.
- You can use the SAVEPOINT statement to create a save point with the specified name.
- You can use the ROLLBACK TO SAVEPOINT statement to roll back a transaction to the specified save point.
- Save points are useful when a single transaction contains so many SQL statements that rolling back the entire transaction would be inefficient.

Figure 14-2   How to work with save points

How to work with concurrency and locking

When two or more users have access to the same database, it's possible for them to be working with the same data at the same time. This is called *concurrency*. Although concurrency isn't a problem when two users retrieve the same data at the same time, it can become a problem when one user updates data that other users are also viewing or updating. In the topics that follow, you'll learn how to prevent concurrency problems.

How concurrency and locking are related

Figure 14-3 presents two transactions that show how MySQL handles concurrency by default. To start, transaction A submits an UPDATE statement that adds a value of 100 to the value that's stored in the credit_total column of the invoice that has an invoice_id value of 6. Because transaction A hasn't yet committed this change to the database, it retains a *lock* on this row. This is known as *locking*.

At this point, if you run the SELECT statement in transaction B, the result set doesn't include the updated value in the credit_total column. In other words, the SELECT statement only reads changes that have been committed.

In addition, the UPDATE statement in transaction B won't be able to update the row due to the lock that transaction A has on the row. As a result, it will have to wait for transaction A to finish before it updates the row.

Once transaction A commits the change made by the UPDATE statement, the SELECT statement in transaction B will show the updated value in the credit_total column if you run it again. In addition, when transaction A commits the update, it releases its lock on the row. Then, the UPDATE statement in transaction B finishes executing if it has been waiting. Or, if you execute the UPDATE statement in transaction B again, it will execute immediately.

To experiment with concurrency, you need to simulate multiple users by opening multiple connections and using them to execute SQL statements. For example, when you're using MySQL Workbench, you can use the Home tab to open two connections. (You can even open both connections for the same user.) Then, you can use the first connection to execute transaction A and the second connection to execute transaction B. To do that, you can run one statement at a time by placing the cursor in each statement and using the Execute Current Statement button (Ctrl+Enter). This allows you to slow down the execution of each script. Otherwise, if you use the Execute SQL Script button (Ctrl+Shift+Enter), the script runs so quickly that you won't be able to get both scripts to access the same row at the same time.

This example shows that MySQL's default locking behavior prevents most concurrency problems. However, if you find that the default locking behavior is insufficient, you may need to override it. You'll learn how to do that in a moment. But first, you need to understand the four concurrency problems that locks can prevent.

Two transactions that retrieve and then modify the data in the same row

Transaction A
```
-- Execute each statement one at a time.
-- Alternate with Transaction B as described.

START TRANSACTION;

UPDATE invoices SET credit_total = credit_total + 100 WHERE invoice_id = 6;

-- the SELECT statement in Transaction B won't show the updated data
-- the UPDATE statement in Transaction B will wait for transaction A to finish

COMMIT;

-- the SELECT statement in Transaction B will display the updated data
-- the UPDATE statement in Transaction B will execute immdediately
```

Transaction B
```
-- Use a second connection to execute these statements!
-- Otherwise, they won't work as described.

START TRANSACTION;

SELECT invoice_id, credit_total FROM invoices WHERE invoice_id = 6;

UPDATE invoices SET credit_total = credit_total + 200 WHERE invoice_id = 6;

COMMIT;
```

Description

- *Concurrency* is the ability of a system to support two or more transactions working with the same data at the same time.

- MySQL can automatically prevent some concurrency problems by using *locks*. A lock stops the execution of another transaction if it conflicts with a transaction that is already running.

- Concurrency is a problem only when the data is being modified. When two or more SELECT statements read the same data, the SELECT statements don't affect each other.

Figure 14-3   How concurrency and locking are related

The four concurrency problems
that locks can prevent

Figure 14-4 describes the four most common concurrency problems. To start, a *lost update* is the problem that you've already learned about. It occurs when two transactions select the same row and then update the row based on the values originally selected. Since each transaction is unaware of the other, the later update overwrites the earlier update. For many applications, though, this type of problem rarely occurs, and it isn't serious when it does occur.

Like lost updates, the other three problems may not adversely affect a database. In fact, for many applications, these problems occur infrequently. Then, when they do occur, they can be corrected by resubmitting the SQL statement that experienced the problem. On some database systems, however, these problems can compromise data integrity so they need to be dealt with.

Although locks can prevent the problems listed in this figure, MySQL's default locking behavior doesn't prevent *phantom reads*. If this level of locking isn't acceptable, you can change the default locking behavior by setting the transaction isolation level as shown in the next figure.

The four types of concurrency problems

Problem	Description
Lost updates	Occur when two transactions select the same row and then update the row based on the values originally selected. Since each transaction is unaware of the other, the later update overwrites the earlier update.
Dirty reads	Occur when a transaction selects data that hasn't been committed by another transaction. For example, transaction A changes a row. Transaction B then selects the changed row before transaction A commits the change. If transaction A then rolls back the change, transaction B has selected data that doesn't exist in the database.
Nonrepeatable reads	Occur when two SELECT statements that try to get the same data get different values because another transaction has updated the data in the time between the two statements. For example, transaction A selects a row. Transaction B then updates the row. When transaction A selects the same row again, the data is different.
Phantom reads	Occur when you perform an update or delete on a set of rows at the same time that another transaction is performing an insert or delete that affects one or more rows in that same set of rows. For example, transaction A updates the payment total for each invoice that has a balance due, but transaction B inserts a new, unpaid, invoice while transaction A is still running. After transaction A finishes, there is still an invoice with a balance due.

Description

- In a large system with many users, you should expect for these kinds of problems to occur. In general, you don't need to take any action except to anticipate the problem. In many cases, if the SQL statement is resubmitted, the problem goes away.

- On some systems, if two transactions overwrite each other, the validity of the database is compromised and resubmitting one of the transactions won't eliminate the problem. If you're working on such a system, you must anticipate these concurrency problems and account for them in your code.

- If one of these problems could affect the data integrity of your system, you can change the default locking behavior by setting the transaction isolation level as shown in the next figure.

Figure 14-4   The four concurrency problems that locks can prevent

How to set the transaction isolation level

The simplest way to prevent concurrency problems is to change the default locking behavior. To do that, you use the SET TRANSACTION ISOLATION LEVEL statement shown in figure 14-5 to set the *transaction isolation level*. By default, this statement sets the isolation level for the next new transaction in the current session. If you want to set the isolation level for all the transactions in a session, though, you can include the SESSION keyword. And if you want to set the isolation level for all sessions, you can include the GLOBAL keyword. The examples in this figure illustrate how this works.

This figure also lists the four transaction isolation levels that MySQL provides and shows which concurrency problems they prevent or allow. For example, if you use the SERIALIZABLE option, all four concurrency problems will be prevented.

When you set the isolation level to SERIALIZABLE, each transaction is completely isolated from every other transaction and concurrency is severely restricted. The server does this by locking each resource, preventing other transactions from accessing it. Since each transaction must wait for the previous transaction to commit, the transactions are executed serially, one after another.

Since the SERIALIZABLE level eliminates all concurrency problems, you may think that this is always the best option. However, this option requires more overhead to manage all of the locks, so the access time for each transaction is increased. For some systems, this may cause significant performance problems. As a result, you typically want to use the SERIALIZABLE isolation level only for situations in which phantom reads aren't acceptable.

The lowest isolation level is READ UNCOMMITTED, which allows all four of the concurrency problems to occur. It does this by performing SELECT queries without setting any locks and without honoring any existing locks. Since this means that your SELECT statements will always execute immediately, this setting provides the best performance. Since other transactions can retrieve and modify the same data, however, this setting can't prevent concurrency problems.

The READ COMMITTED isolation level prevents transactions from seeing data that has been changed by other transactions but not committed. This prevents dirty reads, but allows for other types of concurrency problems.

The default isolation level for MySQL is REPEATABLE READ. With this level, rows read by a transaction will be read consistently within the same transaction. To accomplish that, the server places locks on all the data used by the transaction that prevent other users from updating the data.

The REPEATABLE READ level allows more concurrency than the SERIALIZABLE level but less than the READ COMMITTED level. As you might expect, then, it results in faster performance than SERIALIZABLE and permits fewer concurrency problems than READ COMMITTED. In most situations, then, the default isolation level of REPEATABLE READ is acceptable.

The concurrency problems prevented by each transaction isolation level

Isolation level	Dirty reads	Lost updates	Nonrepeatable reads	Phantom reads
READ UNCOMMITTED	Allows	Allows	Allows	Allows
READ COMMITTED	Prevents	Allows	Allows	Allows
REPEATABLE READ	Prevents	Prevents	Prevents	Allows
SERIALIZABLE	Prevents	Prevents	Prevents	Prevents

The syntax of the SET TRANSACTION ISOLATION LEVEL statement

```
SET {GLOBAL|SESSION} TRANSACTION ISOLATION LEVEL
    {READ UNCOMMITTED|READ COMMITTED|REPEATABLE READ|SERIALIZABLE};
```

Set the transaction isolation level to SERIALIZABLE for the next transaction

```
SET TRANSACTION ISOLATION LEVEL SERIALIZABLE;
```

Set the transaction isolation level to READ UNCOMMITTED for the current session

```
SET SESSION TRANSACTION ISOLATION LEVEL READ UNCOMMITTED;
```

Set the transaction isolation level to READ COMMITTED for all sessions

```
SET GLOBAL TRANSACTION ISOLATION LEVEL READ COMMITTED;
```

Description

- The *transaction isolation level* controls the degree to which transactions are isolated from one another. At the more restrictive isolation levels, concurrency problems are reduced or eliminated. However, at the least restrictive levels, performance is enhanced.

- To change the transaction isolation level, you use the SET TRANSACTION ISOLATION LEVEL statement.

- If you include the GLOBAL keyword, the isolation level is set globally for all new transactions in all sessions. If you include the SESSION keyword, the isolation level is set for all new transactions in the current session. If you omit both GLOBAL and SESSION, the isolation level is set for the next new transaction in the current session.

- The default transaction isolation level is REPEATABLE READ. This level places locks on all data that's used in a transaction, preventing other users from updating that data. However, this isolation level still allows inserts, so phantom reads can occur.

- The READ UNCOMMITTED isolation level doesn't set any locks and ignores locks that are already held. This level results in the highest possible performance for your query, but at the risk of every kind of concurrency problem. For this reason, you should only use this level for data that is rarely updated.

- The READ COMMITTED isolation level locks data that has been changed but not committed. This prevents dirty reads but allows all other types of concurrency problems.

- The SERIALIZABLE isolation level places a lock on all data that's used in a transaction. Since each transaction must wait for the previous transaction to commit, the transactions are handled in sequence. This is the most restrictive isolation level.

Figure 14-5   How to set the transaction isolation level

How to prevent deadlocks

A *deadlock* occurs when neither of two transactions can be committed because each has a lock on a resource needed by the other transaction. This is illustrated by the banking transactions in figure 14-6. Here, transaction A updates the savings account first and then the checking account, while transaction B updates the checking account first and then the savings account.

Now, suppose that the first statement in transaction A locks the savings account, and the first statement in transaction B locks the checking account. At that point, a deadlock occurs because transaction A needs the savings account and transaction B needs the checking account, but both are locked. Eventually, one of the transactions has to be rolled back so the other can proceed, and the loser is known as a *deadlock victim*.

To prevent deadlocks, you can use the four techniques that are presented in this figure. First, you shouldn't leave transactions open any longer than is necessary. That's because the longer a transaction remains open and uncommitted, the more likely it is that another transaction will need to work with that same resource.

So, when you're coding transactions, make sure to include the appropriate COMMIT and ROLLBACK statements. In addition, don't code statements that take a long time to execute between the START TRANSACTION statement that starts the transaction and the COMMIT or ROLLBACK statement that finishes the transaction.

Second, you shouldn't use a higher isolation level than you need. That's because the higher you set the isolation level, the more likely it is that two transactions will be unable to work with the same resource at the same time.

Third, you should schedule transactions that modify a large number of rows to run when no other transactions, or only a small number of other transactions, will be running. That way, it's less likely that the transactions will try to change the same rows at the same time.

Finally, you should consider how the SQL statements you write could cause a deadlock. To prevent the situation that's illustrated in this figure, for example, you should always update related accounts in the same sequence.

Don't allow transactions to remain open for very long

- Keep transactions short.
- Keep SELECT statements outside of the transaction except when absolutely necessary.
- Never code requests for user input during a transaction.

Don't use a transaction isolation level higher than necessary

- The default level of REPEATABLE READ is usually acceptable, but you should consider changing to READ COMMITTED if deadlocks become a problem.
- Reserve the use of the SERIALIZABLE level for short transactions that make changes to data where integrity is vital.

Make large changes when you can be assured of nearly exclusive access

- If you need to change millions of rows in an active table, don't do so during hours of peak usage.
- If possible, give yourself exclusive access to the database before making large changes.

Take locking behavior into considering when coding your transactions

- If you need to code two or more transactions that update the same resources, code the updates in the same order in each transaction.

UPDATE statements that illustrate deadlocking

Transaction A

```
START TRANSACTION;
UPDATE savings SET balance = balance - transfer_amount;
UPDATE checking SET balance = balance + transfer_amount;
COMMIT;
```

Transaction B (possible deadlock)

```
START TRANSACTION;
UPDATE checking SET balance = balance - transfer_amount;
UPDATE savings SET balance = balance + transfer_amount;
COMMIT;
```

Transaction B (prevents deadlocks)

```
START TRANSACTION;
UPDATE savings SET balance = balance + transfer_amount;
UPDATE checking SET balance = balance - transfer_amount;
COMMIT;
```

Description

- A *deadlock* occurs when neither of two transactions can be committed because each transaction has a lock on a resource needed by the other transaction.

Figure 14-6   How to prevent deadlocks

Perspective

In this chapter, you learned the ways that MySQL protects your data from the problems that can occur on a real-world system. Since the failure of one or more related SQL statements can violate data integrity, you learned how to prevent these problems by grouping the statements into transactions. Since multiple transactions can simultaneously modify the same data, you learned how to prevent concurrency problems by setting the transaction isolation level to change the default locking behavior. And since changing the isolation level can increase the chances of deadlocks, you learned defensive programming techniques to prevent deadlocks.

Terms

transaction
commit a transaction
roll back a transaction
save point
concurrency
locking
lost update
dirty read
nonrepeatable read
phantom read
transaction isolation level
deadlock
deadlock victim

Exercises

1. Write a script that creates and calls a stored procedure named test. This procedure should include a set of three SQL statements coded as a transaction to reflect the following change: United Parcel Service has been purchased by Federal Express Corporation and the new company is named FedUP. Rename one of the vendors and delete the other after updating the vendor_id column in the Invoices table.

   If these statements execute successfully, commit the changes. Otherwise, roll back the changes.

2. Write a script that creates and calls a stored procedure named test. This procedure should include a set of two SQL statements coded as a transaction to delete the row with an invoice ID of 114 from the Invoices table. To do this, you must first delete all line items for that invoice from the Invoice_Line_Items table.

   If these statements execute successfully, commit the changes. Otherwise, roll back the changes.

15

How to create stored procedures and functions

In chapter 13, you learned how to create a stored procedure that didn't accept any parameters. Now, you'll learn how to create stored procedures that accept parameters. In addition, you'll learn how to code stored functions.

Collectively, stored procedures and stored functions are sometimes referred to as stored routines. As you'll see, stored routines allow you to store procedural logic such as data validation in a central location. In addition, they provide a powerful way to control how users are allowed to access the database.

Stored procedures and functions were introduced with MySQL 5.0. As a result, they aren't available in earlier versions of MySQL.

How to code stored procedures **416**
How to create and call a stored procedure 416
How to code input and output parameters 418
How to set a default value for a parameter 420
How to validate parameters and raise errors 422
A stored procedure that inserts a row 424
How to work with user variables 428
How to work with dynamic SQL 430
How to drop a stored procedure 432

How to code stored functions **434**
How to create and call a function 434
A function that calculates balance due 436
How to drop a function 438

How to use MySQL Workbench with stored routines **440**
How to view stored routines 440
How to create stored routines 440
How to drop stored routines 440

Perspective **442**

How to code stored procedures

A *stored procedure*, which can also be referred to as a *sproc* or just a *procedure*, is a database object that contains a block of procedural SQL code. You can use stored procedures to modify the data that's stored within a database. For example, you can use a stored procedure to execute an INSERT, UPDATE, or DELETE statement.

How to create and call a stored procedure

Figure 15-1 shows how to use the CREATE PROCEDURE statement to create a stored procedure. To start, you code the CREATE PROCEDURE keywords followed by the name of the procedure. In this figure, for example, the statement creates a procedure named update_invoices_credit_total. This name clearly indicates that the procedure updates the credit_total column of the invoices table.

After the name of the procedure, you code a set of parentheses. Within the parentheses, you can code one or more *parameters* for the procedure. A parameter is typically used to pass a value to the stored procedure from a calling program.

If a procedure accepts more than one parameter, you must use commas to separate the parameters. When you declare a parameter, you code the name of the parameter followed by its data type. In this figure, for example, the procedure accepts two parameters. The first parameter is named invoice_id_param with a data type of INT, and the second parameter is named credit_total_param with a data type of DECIMAL.

After the parentheses, you code a block of statements. This block is identified by the BEGIN and END keywords. Within the block, you can code most SQL statements including the ones for writing procedural code presented in chapter 13 and the ones for working with transactions presented in chapter 14.

When you run the CREATE PROCEDURE statement, MySQL *compiles* the code for the procedure and stores the compiled code in the database. As part of this process, MySQL's compiler checks the syntax of the code within the procedure. If you've made a coding error, the system responds with an appropriate message and the procedure isn't created.

You can execute, or *call*, a stored procedure by using the CALL statement. In this figure, for example, the CALL statement calls the procedure that was created in the first example. This statement passes one value for each of the parameters that are defined by the procedure. Here, the first parameter is a literal value that specifies the invoice ID, and the second parameter is a literal value that identifies the new amount for the credit total.

When you use the CALL statement, you must pass parameters *by position*. In other words, you must code the parameters in the same order as they are coded in the CREATE PROCEDURE statement.

In chapter 18, you will learn how to grant INSERT, UPDATE, and DELETE privileges to specific users. However, if you want to have more fine-grained control over the privileges that you grant to users, you can create stored

The syntax of the CREATE PROCEDURE statement

```
CREATE PROCEDURE procedure_name
(
    [parameter_name_1 data_type]
    [, parameter_name_2 data_type]...
)
sql_block
```

A script that creates a stored procedure that updates a table

```
DELIMITER //

CREATE PROCEDURE update_invoices_credit_total
(
    invoice_id_param        INT,
    credit_total_param      DECIMAL(9,2)
)
BEGIN
    DECLARE sql_error TINYINT DEFAULT FALSE;

    DECLARE CONTINUE HANDLER FOR SQLEXCEPTION
        SET sql_error = TRUE;

    START TRANSACTION;

    UPDATE invoices
    SET credit_total = credit_total_param
    WHERE invoice_id = invoice_id_param;

    IF sql_error = FALSE THEN
        COMMIT;
    ELSE
        ROLLBACK;
    END IF;
END//
```

A statement that calls the stored procedure

```
CALL update_invoices_credit_total(56, 300);
```

Description

- You use the CREATE PROCEDURE statement to create a stored procedure. A *stored procedure* is an executable database object that contains a block of procedural SQL code. A stored procedure can also be called a *sproc* or a *procedure*.

- You can use *parameters* to pass one or more values from the calling program to the stored procedure or from the procedure to the calling program. For more information on working with parameters, see figures 15-2 and 15-3.

- To declare a parameter within a stored procedure, you code the name of the parameter followed by its data type. If you declare two or more parameters, you separate the parameters with commas.

- You can use the CALL statement to *call a procedure*. When a procedure accepts parameters, you pass them to the procedure by coding them within the parentheses that follow the procedure name, and by separating the parameters with commas.

Figure 15-1   How to create and call a stored procedure

procedures that perform all of the types of data manipulation that you want to allow within your database. Then, you can grant privileges to execute these stored procedures. For systems where security is critical, this can be an excellent way to prevent both accidental errors and malicious damage to your data.

How to code input and output parameters

Figure 15-2 shows how to code input and output parameters for a stored procedure. An *input parameter* is passed to the stored procedure from the calling program. You can explicitly identify an input parameter by coding the IN keyword before the name of the parameter. In this figure, for example, the first two parameters are identified as input parameters. However, if you omit this keyword, the parameter is assumed to be an input parameter. In figure 15-1, for example, both parameters are input parameters.

Within a procedure, you can use input parameters like variables. However, you can't change the value of the parameter. In this figure, for example, the procedure uses the first parameter within an UPDATE statement to specify the invoice ID for the invoice row to be updated.

An *output parameter* is returned to the calling program from the stored procedure. To code an output parameter, you must explicitly identify the parameter by coding the OUT keyword before the name of the parameter. In this figure, for example, the third parameter is an output parameter. If the UPDATE statement executes successfully, a SET statement stores a value of 1 in the output parameter. Otherwise, a SET statement stores a value of 0 in the output parameter. Either way, the value of the output parameter is returned to the calling program when the procedure finishes.

To show how a calling program works, this figure includes a script that calls the procedure. Here, initial values are supplied for the two input parameters. Then, a variable named @row_count is supplied for the output parameter. This variable is a special type of variable known as a *user variable*. A user variable is a global variable that's available to the user for the rest of the current session. You'll learn more about user variables later in this chapter.

After the procedure executes, the value of the output parameter is stored in the @row_count variable. Then, the calling program can access this variable. In this figure, for example, the script uses a SELECT statement to display the value of the variable. However, it could also use an IF statement to check the value of the variable and perform an appropriate action.

In addition to input and output parameters, MySQL provides for a parameter that can be used for both input and output. An *input/output parameter* stores an initial value that's passed in from the calling program like an input parameter. However, the procedure can change this value and return it to a calling program like an output parameter. To identify an input/output parameter, you must code the INOUT keywords before the name of the parameter. Although this can be useful in some situations, it can also be confusing. As a result, it often makes sense to avoid the use of input/output parameters.

The syntax for declaring input and output parameters

```
[IN|OUT|INOUT] parameter_name data_type
```

A stored procedure that uses input and output parameters

```
DELIMITER //

CREATE PROCEDURE update_invoices_credit_total
(
  IN  invoice_id_param    INT,
  IN  credit_total_param  DECIMAL(9,2),
  OUT update_count        INT
)
BEGIN
  DECLARE sql_error TINYINT DEFAULT FALSE;

  DECLARE CONTINUE HANDLER FOR SQLEXCEPTION
    SET sql_error = TRUE;

  START TRANSACTION;

  UPDATE invoices
  SET credit_total = credit_total_param
  WHERE invoice_id = invoice_id_param;

  IF sql_error = FALSE THEN
    SET update_count = 1;
    COMMIT;
  ELSE
    SET update_count = 0;
    ROLLBACK;
  END IF;
END//
```

A script that calls the stored procedure and uses the output parameter

```
CALL update_invoices_credit_total(56, 200, @row_count);
SELECT CONCAT('row_count: ', @row_count) AS update_count;
```

Description

- *Input parameters* accept values that are passed from the calling program. These values cannot be changed by the body of the stored procedure. By default, parameters are defined as input parameters. As a result, the IN keyword is optional for identifying input parameters.

- *Output parameters* store values that are passed back to the calling program. These values must be set by the body of the stored procedure. To identify an output parameter, you must code the OUT keyword.

- *Input/output parameters* can store an initial value that's passed from the calling program. However, the body of the stored procedure can change this parameter. To identify an input/output parameter, you must code the INOUT keyword.

- When you work with output parameters or input/output parameters, the calling program typically passes a *user variable* to the parameter list. For more information about user variables, see figure 15-6.

Figure 15-2   How to code input and output parameters

How to set a default value for a parameter

Figure 15-3 shows how to set a default value for a parameter. This is useful if a null value is passed for the parameter. Then, the default value can be used instead of the null value.

In this figure, the stored procedure sets a default value for the second parameter, which contains the credit total to be assigned to the credit_total column for an invoice. To do that, it uses an IF statement to check if the parameter contains a null value. If it does, the value of the parameter is set to 100.

The two CALL statements in this figure show two ways that you can provide values to the stored procedure. Here, the first CALL statement supplies a value for each parameter. As a result, the credit total for the invoice is set to 200. In contrast, the second CALL statement supplies a value of NULL for the second parameter. In that case, the credit total for the invoice is set to the default value of 100.

When you set default values for one or more parameters, it usually makes sense to code these parameters at the end of the parameter list. That way, when you call the stored procedure, you can code all the non-null values first.

A CREATE PROCEDURE statement that provides a default value

```
DELIMITER //

CREATE PROCEDURE update_invoices_credit_total
(
  invoice_id_param      INT,
  credit_total_param    DECIMAL(9,2)
)
BEGIN
  DECLARE sql_error TINYINT DEFAULT FALSE;

  DECLARE CONTINUE HANDLER FOR SQLEXCEPTION
    SET sql_error = TRUE;

  -- Set default values for NULL values
  IF credit_total_param IS NULL THEN
    SET credit_total_param = 100;
  END IF;

  START TRANSACTION;

  UPDATE invoices
  SET credit_total = credit_total_param
  WHERE invoice_id = invoice_id_param;

  IF sql_error = FALSE THEN
    COMMIT;
  ELSE
    ROLLBACK;
  END IF;
END//
```

A statement that calls the stored procedure

```
CALL update_invoices_credit_total(56, 200);
```

Another statement that calls the stored procedure

```
CALL update_invoices_credit_total(56, NULL);
```

Description

- You can provide a default value for a parameter so that if the calling program passes a null value for the parameter, the default value is used instead.

- To set a default value for a parameter, you can use an IF statement to check if the parameter contains a null value. If it does, you can assign a default value to the parameter.

- It's a good programming practice to code your CREATE PROCEDURE statements so they list parameters that require values first, followed by parameters that allow null values.

Figure 15-3   How to set a default value for a parameter

How to validate parameters and raise errors

Within a stored procedure, it's generally considered a good practice to prevent errors by checking the parameters before they're used to make sure they're valid. This is often referred to as *data validation*. Then, if the data isn't valid, you can execute code that makes it valid, or you can *raise an error*, which returns the error to the calling program.

Figure 15-4 shows how to raise an error using one of the predefined errors that are available from MySQL. To do that, you code the SIGNAL statement followed by the SQLSTATE keyword, followed by a SQLSTATE code. Then, you can optionally include a SET statement that sets a message and MySQL error code for the error.

In this figure, for example, the IF statement checks whether the value of the second parameter is less than zero. If so, the SIGNAL statement raises an error with a SQLSTATE code of 22003, a MySQL code of 1264, and a message that indicates that the credit total column must be greater than or equal to 0. These SQLSTATE and MySQL codes are commonly used to validate parameters since they are used to indicate that the value is out of range for the column.

If the calling program doesn't catch this error, the system displays an error message. In this figure, for example, the CALL statement passes a negative value to the second parameter, which causes the error to be raised. As a result, the system displays an error message that contains the MySQL error code and message specified by the SIGNAL statement. Since this error code and message accurately describe the error, the programmer or user of the calling program should be able to identify and fix the problem.

On the other hand, if the calling program catches this error, it can include code that handles the error. For example, the calling program can handle the error by printing a user-friendly message to the user and asking the user to input data again.

Before you go on, you should know that the SIGNAL statement was introduced in MySQL 5.5, and earlier versions of MySQL didn't provide a good way to raise an error. As a workaround, you can raise an error by coding a bad UPDATE statement that specifies an error message instead of a table name like this:

```
UPDATE `Credit_total column must be greater than or equal to 0.`
SET x = 'This UPDATE statement raises an error';
```

Note that for this to work, you must use back ticks (`) instead of single quotes (') to enclose the error message. Although this statement raises an error, the code isn't easy to read or maintain, and the error message that's raised isn't user-friendly. Still, it provides a useful way to raise an error if you can't use the SIGNAL statement.

The syntax of the SIGNAL statement

```
SIGNAL SQLSTATE [VALUE] sqlstate_value
[SET MESSAGE_TEXT = message[, MYSQL_ERRNO = mysql_error_number]];
```

A stored procedure that raises a predefined exception

```
DELIMITER //

CREATE PROCEDURE update_invoices_credit_total
(
  invoice_id_param      INT,
  credit_total_param    DECIMAL(9,2)
)
BEGIN
  -- Validate paramater values
  IF credit_total_param < 0 THEN
    SIGNAL SQLSTATE '22003'
      SET MESSAGE_TEXT =
        'The credit_total column must be greater than or equal to 0.',
      MYSQL_ERRNO = 1264;
  ELSEIF credit_total_param >= 1000 THEN
    SIGNAL SQLSTATE '22003'
      SET MESSAGE_TEXT =
        'The credit_total column must be less than 1000.',
      MYSQL_ERRNO = 1264;
  END IF;

  -- Set default values for parameters
  IF credit_total_param IS NULL THEN
    SET credit_total_param = 100;
  END IF;

  UPDATE invoices
  SET credit_total = credit_total_param
  WHERE invoice_id = invoice_id_param;
END//
```

A statement that calls the procedure

```
CALL update_invoices_credit_total(56, -100);
```

The response from the system

```
Error Code: 1264.
The credit_total column must be greater than or equal to 0.
```

Description

- It's generally considered a good practice to validate the data within a stored procedure before using the data. This is referred to as *data validation*.

- The SIGNAL statement *raises an error*. When you raise an error, you must specify a SQLSTATE code as specified in chapter 13. In addition, you can optionally specify an error message or MySQL error number.

- When you raise an error, MySQL returns the error to the caller in the same way that it returns errors that are raised by the database engine. Then, the calling program can handle the error.

Figure 15-4   How to validate parameters and raise errors

A stored procedure that inserts a row

Figure 15-5 presents a stored procedure that inserts new rows into the invoices table. This should give you a better idea of how you can use stored procedures.

This procedure uses six parameters that correspond to six of the columns in the Invoices table. All of these parameters are input parameters, and each parameter is assigned the same data type as the matching column in the Invoices table. As a result, if the calling program passes a value that can't be converted to the proper data type, an error will be raised when the procedure is called.

None of these parameters corresponds with the invoice_id column since that column is an auto increment column. Similarly, the stored procedure sets a default value for the last two parameters. As a result, if the calling program provides a null value for these parameters, the procedure automatically sets a default value for them.

The body of the procedure begins by declaring three variables. Of these variables, the first two have data types that correspond with columns in the invoices table. However, the third one uses the INT data type to store the number of days before the invoice is due.

All three of these variables have a suffix of "_var" while all of the parameters defined earlier have a suffix of "_param". This makes it easy to tell the difference between the parameters that are passed to the procedure from the calling program and the variables that are used within the procedure.

After the variables are declared, the procedure begins by using an IF statement to check the value of the parameter for the invoice_total column to see if it is less than zero. If so, the procedure uses the SIGNAL statement to raise an error with an appropriate error code and message. This statement exits the stored procedure and returns the error to the calling program. Similarly, the ELSEIF clause checks whether this parameter is greater than one million. If so, it raises an appropriate error. Although this figure only uses this IF statement to check for two conditions, it's common to code a series of IF statements like this one to provide more extensive data validation.

Next, another IF statement is used to check the terms_id parameter for a null value. If the parameter is null, a SELECT statement gets the value of the default_terms_id column for the vendor and stores it in the terms_id variable. If this parameter isn't null, the value of the terms_id parameter is assigned to the terms_id variable.

The next IF statement is similar. It checks the value of the parameter for the invoice_due_date column for a null value. If the parameter is null, a SELECT statement uses the value of the terms_id variable to get the number of days until the invoice is due from the terms table, and it stores this value in the terms_due_days variable. Then, it calculates a due date for the invoice by using the DATE_ADD function to add the number of days to the invoice date. If the invoice_due_date parameter isn't null, though, this code sets the invoice_due_date variable to the value that's stored in the parameter.

A stored procedure that validates the data in a new invoice

```
DELIMITER //

CREATE PROCEDURE insert_invoice
(
  vendor_id_param         INT,
  invoice_number_param    VARCHAR(50),
  invoice_date_param      DATE,
  invoice_total_param     DECIMAL(9,2),
  terms_id_param          INT,
  invoice_due_date_param  DATE
)
BEGIN
  DECLARE terms_id_var           INT;
  DECLARE invoice_due_date_var   DATE;
  DECLARE terms_due_days_var     INT;

  -- Validate paramater values
  IF invoice_total_param < 0 THEN
    SIGNAL SQLSTATE '22003'
      SET MESSAGE_TEXT =
        'The invoice_total column must be a positive number.',
      MYSQL_ERRNO = 1264;
  ELSEIF invoice_total_param >= 1000000 THEN
    SIGNAL SQLSTATE '22003'
      SET MESSAGE_TEXT =
        'The invoice_total column must be less than 1,000,000.',
      MYSQL_ERRNO = 1264;
  END IF;

  -- Set default values for parameters
  IF terms_id_param IS NULL THEN
    SELECT default_terms_id INTO terms_id_var
    FROM vendors WHERE vendor_id = vendor_id_param;
  ELSE
    SET terms_id_var = terms_id_param;
  END IF;
  IF invoice_due_date_param IS NULL THEN
    SELECT terms_due_days INTO terms_due_days_var
      FROM terms WHERE terms_id = terms_id_var;
    SELECT DATE_ADD(invoice_date_param, INTERVAL terms_due_days_var DAY)
      INTO invoice_due_date_var;
  ELSE
    SET invoice_due_date_var = invoice_due_date_param;
  END IF;

  INSERT INTO invoices
          (vendor_id, invoice_number, invoice_date,
           invoice_total, terms_id, invoice_due_date)
  VALUES (vendor_id_param, invoice_number_param, invoice_date_param,
          invoice_total_param, terms_id_var, invoice_due_date_var);
END//
```

Figure 15-5   A stored procedure that inserts a row (part 1 of 2)

After the values have been set for the variables for the terms_id and invoice_due_date columns, this procedure executes an INSERT statement. If this statement executes successfully, the row is inserted into the database.

In most cases, a stored procedure like this is called from an application program. However, to test a procedure before it's used by an application program, you can use CALL statements like the ones in this figure.

The first two CALL statements provide valid values that successfully insert a new row. Of these statements, the first supplies non-null values for all of the parameters for the procedure. The second supplies non-null values for the first four parameters, but not for the last two. This shows that the first four parameters are the only parameters that require non-null values.

The third CALL statement provides a negative number for the invoice total parameter. As a result, this CALL statement causes the stored procedure to raise an error. Since the CALL statement doesn't handle this error, an error message like the one shown in this figure is displayed. However, if you call the stored procedure from another stored procedure or from an application, you can include code that handles the error.

Two statements that call the stored procedure

```
CALL insert_invoice(34, 'ZXA-080', '2012-01-18', 14092.59,
                    3, '2012-03-18');

CALL insert_invoice(34, 'ZXA-082', '2012-01-18', 14092.59,
                    NULL, NULL);
```

The message from the system for a successful insert

```
1 row(s) affected
```

A statement that raises an error

```
CALL insert_invoice(34, 'ZXA-080', '30-AUG-08', -14092.59);
```

The message from the system when a validation error occurs

```
Error Code: 1264. The invoice_total column must be a positive number.
```

Description

- If the data for each of the columns of the row is valid, the procedure executes an INSERT statement to insert the row. Otherwise, the procedure or database engine raises an error and exits the procedure.

- If an application program calls this procedure, it can handle any errors that are raised by the procedure or by the database engine.

Figure 15-5   A stored procedure that inserts a row (part 2 of 2)

How to work with user variables

In figure 15-3, you learned how to store the value of an output parameter in a user variable. Now, you'll learn more about working with user variables.

A *user variable* is a special type of MySQL variable that's globally available to the current user. However, a user variable is only available as long as the user remains connected to the server and is reset when the user disconnects. In addition, a user variable is only available to the current user and cannot be seen or accessed by other users.

Since a user variable is globally available to the current user, multiple stored programs can share the variable. In figure 15-6, for instance, the stored program named set_global_count sets the user variable named @count to a specified INT value. Then, the stored procedure named increment_global_count increments the @count variable by a value of 1. To set the value of this user variable, both of these stored procedures use the SET statement.

Note that these procedures don't need to include a DECLARE statement for the user variable to declare its data type. That's because a user variable can store various data types including string, numeric, and date/time types. As a result, you can declare or access a user variable anywhere just by coding an at sign (@) followed by the name of the variable.

Although user variables are often used within stored programs, you can also access user variables outside of stored programs. Then, you can use standard SQL statements such as the SELECT statement to work with them. In this figure, for instance, the SELECT statement displays the value of the @count variable after it has been set and incremented by the two CALL statements. You can also use the SET statement outside of a stored program to set the value of a user variable.

The syntax for setting a user variable

```
SET @variable_name = expression;
```

Two stored procedures that work with the same user variable

```
DELIMITER //

CREATE PROCEDURE set_global_count
(
  count_var INT
)
BEGIN
  SET @count = count_var;
END//

CREATE PROCEDURE increment_global_count()
BEGIN
  SET @count = @count + 1;
END//
```

Two statements that call these stored procedures

```
CALL set_global_count(100);
CALL increment_global_count();
```

A SELECT statement that directly accesses the user variable

```
SELECT @count AS count_var
```

count_var
101

Description

- A *user variable* is a special type of MySQL variable that's globally available to the current user.

- A user variable is only available to the current user and cannot be seen or accessed by other users.

- A user variable is available as long as the user remains connected to the server, but it is reset when the user disconnects.

- A user variable can store various data types including string, numeric, and date/time types. However, you don't have to declare a data type for a user variable.

- A user variable is available from statements coded both inside and outside of stored programs.

Figure 15-6   How to work with user variables

How to work with dynamic SQL

Figure 15-7 shows how to work with *dynamic SQL*. Dynamic SQL allows you to use procedural code to build and execute a SQL statement that depends on parameters that aren't known until runtime. To do that, you can build a string that contains the SQL statement. Then, you can use the PREPARE, EXECUTE, and DEALLOCATE statements to execute the statement contained in the string.

Dynamic SQL is often used to build complex WHERE clauses that depend on multiple search conditions that may or may not be specified by the user. In this figure, for instance, the code creates a stored procedure named select_invoices that allows the user to specify two parameters: (1) the minimum invoice date and (2) the minimum invoice total. However, if the user specifies a null value for a parameter, the stored procedure doesn't include that parameter in the search condition.

To start, the stored procedure declares two string variables that can hold up to 200 characters. Then, it sets the variable named select_clause to a SELECT clause that selects four columns from the Invoices table, and it sets the variable named where_clause to a WHERE clause that doesn't include any search conditions.

After setting the variables, a series of IF statements creates the WHERE clause depending on the values of the parameters. The first IF statement checks whether the first parameter contains a non-null value. If it does, the IF statement adds a search condition to the WHERE clause like this:

```
WHERE invoice_date > 'min_invoice_date_param'
```

Note that the parameter is enclosed in single quotes since it contains a date value.

The second IF statement checks whether the second parameter contains a non-null value. If it does, a nested IF statement checks whether the string for the WHERE clause has already had a search condition appended to it. In that case, it appends the AND keyword to the WHERE clause to create a compound condition. Then, a SET statement adds a search condition to the WHERE clause. At this point, the WHERE clause may contain a compound search condition, a single search condition, or no search condition at all.

The third IF statement checks if a search condition has been added to the WHERE clause. If it hasn't, the SELECT statement appends only the SELECT clause to the user variable named @dynamic_sql. Otherwise, it appends both the SELECT clause and the WHERE clause to the user variable. At this point, the @dynamic_sql variable contains the dynamically generated SELECT statement.

The PREPARE statement prepares a statement from the string that's stored in the @dynamic_sql variable. For this to work, the string that contains the statement must be stored in a user variable. That way, MySQL can access it outside of the stored program and prepare it to be executed.

After MySQL prepares the statement, the EXECUTE statement executes the prepared statement. This returns a result set for the dynamically generated SELECT statement to the user. Finally, the DEALLOCATE PREPARE statement releases the prepared statement. Once a prepared statement is released, it can no longer be executed.

A stored procedure that uses dynamic SQL

```
DELIMITER //

CREATE PROCEDURE select_invoices
(
  min_invoice_date_param    DATE,
  min_invoice_total_param   DECIMAL(9,2)
)
BEGIN
  DECLARE select_clause VARCHAR(200);
  DECLARE where_clause  VARCHAR(200);

  SET select_clause = "SELECT invoice_id, invoice_number,
                        invoice_date, invoice_total
                        FROM invoices ";
  SET where_clause =  "WHERE ";

  IF min_invoice_date_param IS NOT NULL THEN
    SET where_clause = CONCAT(where_clause,
        " invoice_date > '", min_invoice_date_param, "'");
  END IF;

  IF min_invoice_total_param IS NOT NULL THEN
    IF where_clause != "WHERE " THEN
      SET where_clause = CONCAT(where_clause, "AND ");
    END IF;
    SET where_clause = CONCAT(where_clause,
        "invoice_total > ", min_invoice_total_param);
  END IF;

  IF where_clause = "WHERE " THEN
    SET @dynamic_sql = select_clause;
  ELSE
    SET @dynamic_sql = CONCAT(select_clause, where_clause);
  END IF;

  PREPARE select_invoices_statement
  FROM @dynamic_sql;

  EXECUTE select_invoices_statement;

  DEALLOCATE PREPARE select_invoices_statement;
END//
```

A @dynamic_sql variable at runtime with parameters inserted

```
SELECT invoice_id, invoice_number, invoice_date, invoice_total
FROM invoices
WHERE invoice_date > '2011-08-29' AND invoice_total > 100
```

Description

- You can use a stored routine to build a string variable that contains a SQL statement. Then, you can use the PREPARE, EXECUTE, and DEALLOCATE statements to execute the statement contained in the string. This is known as *dynamic SQL*.

Figure 15-7   How to work with dynamic SQL

How to drop a stored procedure

Figure 15-8 shows how to drop a stored procedure. To do that, you can code the DROP PROCEDURE keywords followed by the name of the procedure. In this figure, the first example uses the CREATE PROCEDURE statement to create a procedure named clear_invoices_credit_total. Then, the second example uses the DROP PROCEDURE statement to drop that procedure.

If you attempt to drop a stored procedure that doesn't exist, MySQL returns an error. To prevent this error, you can add the optional IF EXISTS keywords to the DROP PROCEDURE statement as shown by the third example. Then, MySQL only attempts to drop the stored procedure if it exists.

If you drop a table or view used by a procedure, you should be sure to drop the procedure as well. If you don't, the procedure can still be called by any user or program that has been granted the appropriate privileges. Then, an error will occur because the table or view that the procedure depends on no longer exists.

The syntax of the DROP PROCEDURE statement

```
DROP PROCEDURE [IF EXISTS] procedure_name
```

A statement that creates a stored procedure

```
DELIMITER //

CREATE PROCEDURE clear_invoices_credit_total
(
  invoice_id_param  INT
)
BEGIN
  UPDATE invoices
  SET credit_total = 0
  WHERE invoice_id = invoice_id_param;
END//
```

A statement that drops the stored procedure

```
DROP PROCEDURE clear_invoices_credit_total
```

A statement that drops the stored procedure only if it exists

```
DROP PROCEDURE IF EXISTS clear_invoices_credit_total
```

Description

- To drop a stored procedure from the database, use the DROP PROCEDURE statement.

Figure 15-8   How to drop a stored procedure

How to code stored functions

In chapter 9, you learned about some of MySQL's built-in functions. Now, you'll learn how to create your own functions. These functions are referred to as *stored functions*, *user-defined functions (UDFs)*, or just *functions*.

If you've worked with databases other than MySQL, you may be familiar with functions that return a result set. With MySQL, though, a function can only return a single value. This type of function is called a *scalar function*.

In many ways, the code for creating a function works similarly to the code for creating a stored procedure. However, there are two primary differences between stored procedures and functions. First, a MySQL function always returns a single value. Second, a function can't make changes to the database such as executing an INSERT, UPDATE, or DELETE statement.

How to create and call a function

To create a function, you use the CREATE FUNCTION statement shown in figure 15-9. To start, you code the CREATE FUNCTION keywords, followed by the name of the function. In this figure, the first example shows how to create a function named get_vendor_id.

After the name of the function, you code a set of parentheses. Within the parentheses, you code the parameters for the function. In this figure, for example, the function contains a single parameter of the VARCHAR type that's named vendor_name_param. Since this is similar to the way you declare parameters for a stored procedure, you shouldn't have much trouble understanding how this works. The main difference is that it rarely makes sense to use output parameters for a function. As a result, functions almost always use input parameters as shown by the examples in this chapter.

After the parentheses, you code the RETURNS keyword, followed by the data type that's returned by the function. In this figure, the example returns a value of the INT type.

After the declaration of the return type, you code the BEGIN keyword to signal that you are about to begin the code for the function. In this figure, the code begins by declaring a variable of the INT type named vendor_id_var. Then, it uses a SELECT statement to get the vendor ID value that corresponds with the vendor name parameter and to store this value in the variable. Finally, it uses the RETURN statement to return this value to the calling program.

To call a user-defined function, you can use it in an expression as if it's one of MySQL's built-in functions. Then, the value that's returned by the function is substituted for the function. In this figure, the last example shows how to use the get_vendor_id function within a SELECT statement to return the vendor ID value for the vendor with the name of "IBM".

If you find yourself repeatedly coding the same expression within a SQL statement, you may want to create a scalar-valued function for the expression. Then, you can use that function in place of the expression, which can save you coding time and make your code easier to maintain. As a result, you may want to create a set of useful stored functions for your database.

The syntax of the CREATE FUNCTION statement

```
CREATE FUNCTION function_name
(
    [parameter_name_1 data_type]
    [, parameter_name_2 data_type]...
)
RETURNS data_type
sql_block
```

A function that returns the vendor ID that matches a vendor's name

```
DELIMITER //

CREATE FUNCTION get_vendor_id
(
    vendor_name_param VARCHAR(50)
)
RETURNS INT
BEGIN
  DECLARE vendor_id_var INT;

  SELECT vendor_id
  INTO vendor_id_var
  FROM vendors
  WHERE vendor_name = vendor_name_param;

  RETURN(vendor_id_var);
END//
```

A SELECT statement that uses the function

```
SELECT invoice_number, invoice_total
FROM invoices
WHERE vendor_id = get_vendor_id('IBM');
```

The response from the system

invoice_number	invoice_total
QP58872	116.54
Q545443	1083.58

Description

- A *stored function*, which can also be called a *user-defined function* (*UDF*) or just a *function*, is an executable database object that contains a block of procedural SQL code.
- With MySQL, you can only create *scalar functions*, which return a single value.
- To identify the data type that's returned by a function, you use the RETURNS keyword in the declaration for the function. Then, in the body of the function, you use the RETURN keyword to specify the value that's returned.
- A function can accept input parameters that work like the input parameters for a stored procedure.
- A function can't make changes to the database such as executing an INSERT, UPDATE, or DELETE statement.
- To call a stored function, you can use it in any expression just like a built-in function.

Figure 15-9   How to create and call a function

A function that calculates balance due

Figure 15-10 shows a function that calculates the balance due for an invoice. To do that, this function accepts a parameter that contains an invoice ID value. Then, the body of the function calculates the balance due, stores the result of the calculation in a variable named balance_due_var, and uses the RETURN statement to return that value.

The SELECT statement in this figure uses this function to return the balance due for the specified invoice ID value. Note that calling the function like this:

```
get_balance_due(invoice_id) AS balance_due
```

has the same effect as performing a calculation like this:

```
invoice_total - payment_total - credit_total AS balance_due
```

However, using a function has two advantages. First, the code is shorter, which makes it easier to type. Second, the code for calculating the balance due is stored in a single location. As a result, if the formula for calculating the balance due changes, you only need to change it in one location.

A function that calculates balance due

```
DELIMITER //

CREATE FUNCTION get_balance_due
(
    invoice_id_param INT
)
RETURNS DECIMAL(9,2)
BEGIN
  DECLARE balance_due_var DECIMAL(9,2);

  SELECT invoice_total - payment_total - credit_total
  INTO balance_due_var
  FROM invoices
  WHERE invoice_id = invoice_id_param;

  RETURN balance_due_var;
END//
```

A statement that calls the function

```
SELECT vendor_id, invoice_number,
       get_balance_due(invoice_id) AS balance_due
FROM invoices
WHERE vendor_id = 37
```

The response from the system

vendor_id	invoice_number	balance_due
37	547481328	0.00
37	547479217	0.00
37	547480102	224.00

Description

- This function accepts a single parameter that specifies the ID for an invoice, and it returns the balance due for that invoice.

Figure 15-10   A function that calculates balance due

How to drop a function

Figure 15-11 shows how to drop a user-defined function. To do that, you code the DROP FUNCTION keywords followed by the name of the function. This is illustrated by the third example in this figure. In addition, the fourth example illustrates how you can add the IF EXISTS keywords to check if a function exists before dropping it.

To start, though, the first example presents another function named get_sum_balance_due. This function uses the aggregate SUM function described in chapter 5 to return the sum of the total balance due for the specified vendor. What's interesting here is that this function calls the get_balance_due function presented in the previous figure. In other words, this function "depends" on the get_balance_due function.

Then, the second example shows a SELECT statement that uses the get_sum_balance_due function. This statement gets the invoice number and balance due for each invoice for the vendor with an ID of 37. In addition, it gets the total balance due for that vendor.

Like stored procedures, functions depend on underlying database objects such as tables and views as well as other procedures and functions. Because of that, if you drop a database object that a function depends on, the function won't work properly. For example, if you drop the get_balance_due function, the get_sum_balance_due function won't work. As a result, you should avoid dropping any database objects that other database objects depend on.

The syntax of the DROP FUNCTION statement

```
DROP FUNCTION [IF EXISTS] function_name
```

A statement that creates a function

```
DELIMITER //

CREATE FUNCTION get_sum_balance_due
(
    vendor_id_param INT
)
RETURNS DECIMAL(9,2)
BEGIN
  DECLARE sum_balance_due_var DECIMAL(9,2);

  SELECT SUM(get_balance_due(invoice_id))
  INTO sum_balance_due_var
  FROM invoices
  WHERE vendor_id = vendor_id_param;

  RETURN sum_balance_due_var;
END//
```

A statement that calls the function

```
SELECT vendor_id, invoice_number,
       get_balance_due(invoice_id) AS balance_due,
       get_sum_balance_due(vendor_id) AS sum_balance_due
FROM invoices
WHERE vendor_id = 37;
```

The response from the system

vendor_id	invoice_number	balance_due	sum_balance_due
37	547481328	0.00	224.00
37	547479217	0.00	224.00
37	547480102	224.00	224.00

A statement that drops the function

```
DROP FUNCTION get_sum_balance_due
```

A statement that drops the function only if it exists

```
DROP FUNCTION IF EXISTS get_sum_balance_due
```

Description

- To delete a user-defined function from the database, use the DROP FUNCTION statement. If you want to check whether the function exists before you drop it, add the optional IF EXISTS keywords.

- The function in this figure uses the get_balance_due function that's presented in the previous figure. As a result, if you drop the get_balance_due function, the function in this figure won't work.

Figure 15-11   How to drop a function

How to use MySQL Workbench with stored routines

As of press time for this book, MySQL Workbench only provides some basic features for working with stored routines. Figure 15-12 describes these features. If you have a newer release of Workbench, you might want to experiment to see if it provides any additional features. In particular, you should check if it includes tools for creating and debugging stored routines.

How to view stored routines

To start, this figure shows how to use MySQL Workbench to view stored routines. To do that, you can connect to the server and then expand the Routines node for the appropriate database. In this figure, for example, I have expanded the Routines node for the AP database so you can see all of the procedures and functions that were presented in this chapter.

After you display the routines for a database, you can view the code for a procedure or function by right-clicking on its name and selecting the Alter Routine command. Then, MySQL Workbench displays the procedure or function in a tab as shown in this figure. This may come in handy if you need to work with stored routines that were created by other programmers and you don't understand what they do.

How to create stored routines

Although MySQL Workbench doesn't provide any special features for creating stored procedures and functions, you can use it to help you get started writing scripts that create stored procedures and functions. To do that, you can right-click on the Routines node and then select the Create Routine command. When you do, Workbench generates some basic code for the routine that includes a DELIMITER statement, a CREATE PROCEDURE statement, and BEGIN and END keywords. Then, you can modify this code as necessary and add the code that's specific to the stored procedure or function.

After you create a stored procedure or function, it won't appear in the Object Browser right away. To display it, you can refresh the Object Browser. The easiest way to do that is to click the Refresh button near the upper right corner of the Object Browser window.

How to drop stored routines

Once a stored routine is displayed in the Object Browser, you can drop it by right-clicking on it and selecting the Drop Routine command. Then, you can use the resulting dialog box to confirm the drop.

A stored procedure displayed in MySQL Workbench

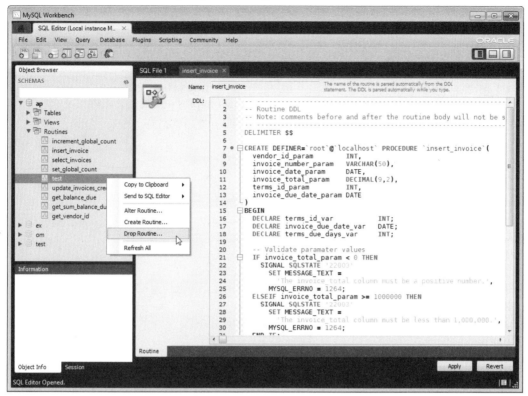

Description

- To view the stored procedures and functions for a database, you can use MySQL Workbench to connect to the database. Then, you can expand the Routines node for the appropriate database in the Object Browser.

- To view the code for an existing procedure or function, right-click on its name and select the Alter Routine command.

- To create a new stored procedure or function, right-click on the Routines node and select the Create Routine command. Then, Workbench generates some basic code, and you can modify this code and add your own code.

- After you create a new procedure, you can refresh the Object Browser to include it in the list of routines. To do that, click the Refresh button near the upper right corner of the Object Browser window.

- To drop a procedure or function, right-click on its name and select the Drop Routine command. Then, use the resulting dialog box to confirm the drop.

- You can use the SHOW PROCEDURE STATUS and SHOW FUNCTION STATUS statements to display information about the stored procedures and functions on a server. For more information, see the MySQL Reference Manual.

Figure 15-12   How to create, view, and drop stored routines

Perspective

In this chapter, you learned how to create two types of stored programs: procedures and functions. The focus of this chapter has been on the skills that SQL developers typically need for working with procedures and functions. However, you should know that there's a lot more to coding procedures and functions than what this chapter has shown. With this chapter as background, though, you should be able to learn whatever else you need on your own.

Terms

stored procedure	user variable
sproc	data validation
procedure	raising an error
parameter	dynamic SQL
compiling a procedure	stored function
calling a procedure	user-defined function (UDF)
passing parameters by position	function
input parameter	scalar function
output parameter	
input/output parameter	

Exercises

1. Write a script that creates and calls a stored procedure named insert_glaccount. First, code a statement that creates a procedure that adds a new row to the General_Ledger_Accounts table in the AP schema. To do that, this procedure should have two parameters, one for each of the two columns in this table. Then, code a CALL statement that tests this procedure. (Note that this table doesn't allow duplicate account descriptions.)

2. Write a script that creates and calls a stored function named test_glaccounts_description. First, create a function that tests whether an account description is already in the General_Ledger_Accounts table. To do that, this function should accept one parameter for the account description, and it should return a value of 1 if the account description is in the table or 0 if it isn't. (Note: If a SELECT statement doesn't return any data, it raises a NOT FOUND condition that your function can handle.)

3. Modify the script that you created in exercise 1 so it creates and calls a stored procedure named insert_glaccount_with_test. This procedure should use the function that you created in exercise 2 to test whether the account description is a duplicate before it issues the INSERT statement. If the account description is a duplicate, this procedure should raise an error with a SQLSTATE code of 23000, a MySQL code of 1062, and a message that says "Duplicate account description."

4. Write a script that creates and calls a stored procedure named insert_terms. First, code a statement that creates a procedure that adds a new row to the Terms table in the AP schema. To do that, this procedure should have two parameters: one for the terms_due_days column and another for the terms_description column.

   If the value for the description column is null, the stored procedure should be able to create a default value for the description column based on the value of the due days column. For example, for a due days column of 120, the description column should have a default value of "Net due 120 days". Then, code a CALL statement that tests this procedure.

16

How to create triggers and events

Now that you've learned how to work with stored procedures and functions, you're ready to learn about two more types of stored programs: triggers and events. Triggers can be executed before or after an INSERT, UPDATE, or DELETE statement is executed on a table. As a result, they provide a powerful way to enforce data consistency, log changes to the database, and implement business rules. Events can be executed at a scheduled time. As a result, they provide a convenient way to automatically perform any task that needs to be run regularly such as scheduled maintenance of tables.

How to work with triggers **446**
How to create a BEFORE trigger 446
How to use a trigger to enforce data consistency 448
How to create an AFTER trigger 450
How to view or drop triggers 452
How to work with events **454**
How to turn on the event scheduler 454
How to create an event 454
How to view, alter, or drop events 456
Perspective **458**

How to work with triggers

A *trigger* is a named block of code that is executed, or *fired*, automatically when a particular type of SQL statement is executed. When using MySQL, a trigger is fired when an INSERT, UPDATE, or DELETE statement is executed on a table. Like stored procedures and functions, triggers were introduced in MySQL 5.0.

How to create a BEFORE trigger

Figure 16-1 presents the syntax for the CREATE TRIGGER statement. To start, you code the CREATE TRIGGER keywords followed by the name of the trigger. In this figure, for instance, the first example creates a trigger named vendors_before_update. This name indicates that the trigger is associated with the Vendors table and that it is fired before an update. This chapter uses a similar naming convention for the other triggers.

After the name of the trigger, you code the BEFORE or AFTER keyword to indicate when the trigger is fired. Then, you identify the statement that causes the trigger to fire. Next, you code an ON clause that identifies the name of the table. In this figure, for instance, the first example creates a trigger that's executed before any UPDATE statements on the Vendors table.

After the ON clause, you code the FOR EACH ROW clause. This clause indicates that the trigger is a *row-level trigger* that fires for each row that's modified. For example, an UPDATE statement that updates five rows would cause the trigger to be executed five times, once for each row. Although some databases support other types of triggers, MySQL only supports row-level triggers.

Within the body of a trigger, you can use the NEW keyword to work with the new values in a row that's being inserted or updated. In this figure, for example, the NEW keyword gets and sets the value for the vendor_state column of the new row. If you try to use this keyword with a row that's being deleted, you'll get an error since this row doesn't have any new values.

You can also use the OLD keyword to work with the old values in a row that's being updated or deleted. You can't use this keyword with a row that's being inserted, though, since a new row doesn't have any old values.

The body of a trigger is identified by the BEGIN and END keywords. In this figure, for example, the body of the trigger contains a single statement that updates the vendor_state column so state codes are always stored with uppercase letters. To accomplish that, this statement uses the UPPER function to convert the new value for the vendor_state column to uppercase.

Since the body of this trigger executes a single statement, it could also be coded without specifying a block of code like this:

```
CREATE TRIGGER vendors_before_update
  BEFORE UPDATE ON vendors
  FOR EACH ROW
  SET NEW.vendor_state = UPPER(NEW.vendor_state);
```

The syntax of the CREATE TRIGGER statement

```
CREATE TRIGGER trigger_name
  {BEFORE|AFTER} {INSERT|UPDATE|DELETE} ON table_name
  FOR EACH ROW
sql_block
```

A CREATE TRIGGER statement that corrects mixed-case state names

```
DELIMITER //

CREATE TRIGGER vendors_before_update
  BEFORE UPDATE ON vendors
  FOR EACH ROW
BEGIN
  SET NEW.vendor_state = UPPER(NEW.vendor_state);
END//
```

An UPDATE statement that fires the trigger

```
UPDATE vendors
SET vendor_state = 'wi'
WHERE vendor_id = 1
```

A SELECT statement that shows the new row

```
SELECT vendor_name, vendor_state
FROM vendors
WHERE vendor_id = 1
```

vendor_name	vendor_state
US Postal Service	WI

Description

- A *trigger* is a named block of code that executes, or *fires*, in response to an INSERT, UPDATE, or DELETE statement.

- You can fire a trigger before or after an INSERT, UPDATE, or DELETE statement is executed on a table.

- You must specify a FOR EACH ROW clause. This creates a *row-level trigger* that fires once for each row that's modified.

- You can use the OLD and NEW keywords to get and set the values for the columns that are stored in the old row and the new row.

- Triggers were introduced in MySQL 5.0.

Figure 16-1   How to create a BEFORE trigger

The advantage of not specifying a block of code is that you don't have to change the delimiter or identify the start and end of the block of code. The disadvantage is that it's more difficult to add statements to the trigger if you later decide that you want the trigger to do more work.

How to use a trigger to enforce data consistency

Triggers are commonly used to enforce data consistency. For example, the sum of line item amounts for an invoice in the Invoice_Line_Items table should always be equal to the corresponding invoice total amount in the Invoices table. Unfortunately, you can't enforce this rule using a constraint on either the Invoices table or the Invoice_Line_Items table. However, you can use a trigger like the one in figure 16-2 to enforce this rule when an invoice amount is updated.

The trigger shown here fires before an UPDATE statement attempts to update the invoice_total column in the Invoices table. When this trigger fires, it checks if the sum of the line items is equal to the invoice total. If it isn't, the trigger raises an error with an SQLSTATE code of "HY000", which indicates a general error. Then, the application that issued the UPDATE statement can handle the error.

Although this example isn't entirely realistic, you can use triggers like this to enforce business rules or to verify data consistency. Since you can program a trigger to accommodate many situations, triggers are more flexible than constraints.

A trigger that validates line item amounts when updating an invoice

```
DELIMITER //

CREATE TRIGGER invoices_before_update
  BEFORE UPDATE ON invoices
  FOR EACH ROW
BEGIN
  DECLARE sum_line_item_amount DECIMAL(9,2);

  SELECT SUM(line_item_amount)
  INTO sum_line_item_amount
  FROM invoice_line_items
  WHERE invoice_id = NEW.invoice_id;

  IF sum_line_item_amount != NEW.invoice_total THEN
    SIGNAL SQLSTATE 'HY000'
      SET MESSAGE_TEXT = 'Line item total must match invoice total.';
  END IF;
END//
```

An UPDATE statement that fires the trigger

```
UPDATE invoices
SET invoice_total = 600
WHERE invoice_id = 100
```

The message from the system

```
Error Code: 1644. Line item total must match invoice total.
```

Description

- Triggers can be used to enforce rules for data consistency that can't be enforced by constraints.

Figure 16-2   How to use a trigger to enforce data consistency

How to create an AFTER trigger

Triggers are commonly used to store information about actions that occur in a database so these actions can be reviewed later. In particular, AFTER triggers are used to store information about a statement after it executes. Figure 16-3 shows how this works.

To start, this figure shows a CREATE TABLE statement that creates a table named Invoices_Audit. This table contains five columns that store information about the action that occurred on the Invoices table. Of these columns, the first three store values from the Invoices table, and the last two store information about the action that caused the statement to execute.

After the CREATE TABLE statement, this figure shows two CREATE TRIGGER statements that add rows to the Invoices_Audit table. The first CREATE TRIGGER statement creates a trigger that executes after an INSERT statement is executed on the Invoices table. This trigger inserts the new values for the vendor_id, invoice_number, and invoice_total columns into the Invoices_Audit table. In addition, it inserts a string value of "Inserted" to indicate that the row has been inserted, and it uses the NOW function to insert the date and time of the action.

The second CREATE TRIGGER statement works similarly, but it executes after a DELETE statement. In addition, it inserts a string value of "Deleted" to indicate that the row has been deleted.

Note that the first trigger inserts the new values for the row that's being inserted since there aren't any old values for this row. However, the second trigger inserts the old values for the row that's being deleted since there aren't any new values for this row.

Although the example that's presented in this figure has been simplified, it presents all of the skills that you need for creating more complex audit tables. For example, if you're having a problem updating rows in a database, you can create an audit table and a trigger to store whatever data you want about each update. Then, the next time the update problem occurs, you can review the data in the audit table to identify the cause of the problem.

A statement that creates an audit table for actions on the invoices table

```
CREATE TABLE invoices_audit
(
  vendor_id            INT              NOT NULL,
  invoice_number       VARCHAR(50)      NOT NULL,
  invoice_total        DECIMAL(9,2)     NOT NULL,
  action_type          VARCHAR(50)      NOT NULL,
  action_date          DATETIME         NOT NULL
)
```

Two AFTER triggers that insert rows into the audit table

```
DELIMITER //

CREATE TRIGGER invoices_after_insert
  AFTER INSERT ON invoices
  FOR EACH ROW
BEGIN
    INSERT INTO invoices_audit VALUES
    (NEW.vendor_id, NEW.invoice_number, NEW.invoice_total,
    'INSERTED', NOW());
END//

CREATE TRIGGER invoices_after_delete
  AFTER DELETE ON invoices
  FOR EACH ROW
BEGIN
    INSERT INTO invoices_audit VALUES
    (OLD.vendor_id, OLD.invoice_number, OLD.invoice_total,
    'DELETED', NOW());
END//
```

An INSERT statement that causes the first trigger to fire

```
INSERT INTO invoices VALUES
(115, 34, 'ZXA-080', '2012-02-01', 14092.59, 0, 0, 3, '2012-03-01', NULL)
```

A DELETE statement that causes the second trigger to fire

```
DELETE FROM invoices WHERE invoice_id = 115
```

A SELECT statement that retrieves the rows in the audit table

```
SELECT * FROM invoices_audit
```

vendor_id	invoice_number	invoice_total	action_type	action_date
34	ZXA-080	14092.59	INSERTED	2012-02-02 10:35:13
34	ZXA-080	14092.59	DELETED	2012-02-02 10:35:13

Description

- You can use an AFTER trigger to insert rows into an audit table.

Figure 16-3   How to create an AFTER trigger

How to view or drop triggers

When you're working with triggers, you often need to view all of the triggers that have been created for a database. Then, you can review information about those triggers, and you can drop them if they are no longer needed.

Figure 16-4 starts by showing how to use the SHOW TRIGGERS statement to view all the triggers in the current database. Usually, that's what you want. In some cases, though, you may want to use the IN clause to specify the database as shown in the second example.

The result set for the second example shows that the AP database contains six triggers, and it provides detailed information about each trigger. First, the Trigger column shows the name of each trigger. Second, the Event column shows the type of statement that causes the trigger to fire. Third, the Table column shows the table for the trigger. Here, five of these triggers are associated with the Invoices table and one with the Vendors table. Finally, the Statement column shows the code for the body of the trigger.

If a database contains a large number of triggers, you may want to use the LIKE clause to display just the triggers with names that match a specified pattern. In this figure, for instance, the third SHOW TRIGGERS statement only shows triggers that start with "ven". As a result, this statement shows just the UPDATE trigger that has been defined for the Vendors table. For more information about using the LIKE clause, please see chapter 3.

Because MySQL doesn't provide a way to alter a trigger, you have to drop it and then create a new trigger to change the way it works. To drop a trigger, you code the DROP TRIGGER keywords followed by the name of the trigger. If you want, you can add the optional IF EXISTS keywords. Since this drops the trigger only if it exists, it prevents an error from occurring if the trigger doesn't exist.

In some cases, you may want to temporarily disable triggers. For example, you may want to disable the triggers for one or more tables before inserting a large number of rows. This can help the INSERT statements run faster, and it lets you insert data that isn't allowed by the triggers. Unfortunately, MySQL doesn't provide a way to disable a trigger. Instead, you have to drop the trigger and then create it again later.

A statement that lists all triggers in the current database

```
SHOW TRIGGERS
```

A statement that lists all triggers in the specified database

```
SHOW TRIGGERS IN ap
```

Trigger	Event	Table	Statement
invoices_before_insert	INSERT	invoices	BEGIN DECLARE terms_id_var INT; DECLARE terms_due_days_var I
invoices_after_insert	INSERT	invoices	BEGIN INSERT INTO invoices_audit VALUES (new.vendor_id, new.invoice_
invoices_before_update_total	UPDATE	invoices	BEGIN DECLARE sum_line_item_amount DECIMAL(9,2); SELECT SUM(line_it
invoices_after_update	UPDATE	invoices	BEGIN INSERT INTO invoices_audit VALUES (old.vendor_id, old.invoice_nu
invoices_after_delete	DELETE	invoices	BEGIN INSERT INTO invoices_audit VALUES (old.vendor_id, old.invoice_nu
vendors_before_update	UPDATE	vendors	BEGIN SET NEW.vendor_state = UPPER(NEW.vendor_state);END

A statement that lists all triggers in a database that begin with "ven"

```
SHOW TRIGGERS IN ap LIKE 'ven%'
```

Trigger	Event	Table	Statement	Timing	C
vendors_before_update	UPDATE	vendors	BEGIN SET NEW.vendor_state = UPPER(NEW.vendor_state);END	BEFORE	NUL

A statement that drops a trigger

```
DROP TRIGGER vendors_before_update
```

A statement that drops a trigger only if it exists

```
DROP TRIGGER IF EXISTS vendors_before_update
```

Description

- To view triggers, use the SHOW TRIGGERS statement. To filter the result set that's returned, include an IN clause or a LIKE clause.
- To drop a trigger, use the DROP TRIGGER statement. To be sure a trigger exists before it's dropped, include the IF EXISTS keywords.

Figure 16-4   How to view or drop triggers

How to work with events

An *event*, or *scheduled event*, is a named block of code that executes, or *fires*, according to the *event scheduler*. By default, the event scheduler is off. As a result, before you begin working with events, you need to turn on the event scheduler. Conversely, if you don't need to use events, you should turn the event scheduler off to save system resources.

Events were introduced in MySQL 5.1. As a result, if you're using MySQL 5.0, you may be able to work with the other types of stored programs (stored procedures, functions, and triggers) but not with events.

How to turn on the event scheduler

Figure 16-5 begins by showing how to check if the event scheduler is on. To do that, you can use the SHOW VARIABLES statement to view the variable named event_scheduler. Then, if the event scheduler isn't on, you'll need to turn it on before you can work with events. To do that, you can use the SET statement to set the value of the event_scheduler variable to ON.

Here, the ON keyword is a synonym for the INT value of 1. Conversely, the OFF keyword is a synonym for the INT value of 0. Since the ON and OFF keywords are easier to read than 1 and 0, this chapter uses these keywords. However, if you're using an older version of MySQL, you may need to use the INT values.

When you use a SET statement to change the event_scheduler variable as shown in this figure, the change only applies until the server is restarted. However, if you want to make this change permanent, you can change this variable in MySQL's configuration file as described in the next chapter.

How to create an event

Figure 16-5 also shows how to use the CREATE EVENT statement to create an event. You can use this statement to create a *one-time event* that occurs only once or a *recurring event* that repeats at a regular interval.

The first CREATE EVENT statement in this figure creates a one-time event named one_time_delete_audit_rows. To do that, this trigger uses the AT keyword to specify that the event should be executed one month from the current date and time. Then, it uses the DO keyword to identify the statements that the event should execute. Here, the statements include the BEGIN and END keywords that identify a block of code. Within that block, a single DELETE statement deletes all rows from the Invoices_Audit table that are more than one month old.

The second CREATE EVENT statement creates a recurring event named monthly_delete_audit_rows. This statement works much like the first statement, except that it uses the EVERY keyword to specify that the event should be executed every month, and it uses the STARTS keyword to specify a starting date of midnight on June 1, 2012. As a result, at the end of every month, this event deletes all audit rows that are more than 1 month old.

A statement that checks if the event scheduler is on

```
SHOW VARIABLES LIKE 'event_scheduler'
```

Variable_name	Value
event_scheduler	OFF

A statement that turns the event scheduler on

```
SET GLOBAL event_scheduler = ON
```

The syntax of the CREATE EVENT statement

```
CREATE EVENT event_name
ON SCHEDULE
   {AT timestamp | EVERY interval [STARTS timestamp] [ENDS timestamp]}
DO sql_block
```

A CREATE EVENT statement that executes only once

```
DELIMITER //

CREATE EVENT one_time_delete_audit_rows
ON SCHEDULE AT NOW() + INTERVAL 1 MONTH
DO BEGIN
  DELETE FROM invoices_audit WHERE action_date < NOW() - INTERVAL 1 MONTH;
END//
```

A CREATE EVENT statement that executes every month

```
CREATE EVENT monthly_delete_audit_rows
ON SCHEDULE EVERY 1 MONTH
STARTS '2012-06-01'
DO BEGIN
  DELETE FROM invoices_audit WHERE action_date < NOW() - INTERVAL 1 MONTH;
END//
```

Description

- An *event*, or *scheduled event*, is a named block of code that executes, or *fires*, according to the *event scheduler*.
- Before you begin working with events, you need to be sure that the event scheduler is on. By default, it's off.
- To check the status of the event scheduler, you can use the SHOW VARIABLES statement to view the variable named event_scheduler.
- To turn the event scheduler on or off, you can use the SET statement to set the value of the event_scheduler variable to ON or OFF. Here, the ON and OFF keywords are synonyms for the INT values of 1 and 0.
- An event can be a *one-time event* that occurs once or a *recurring event* that occurs regularly at a specified interval.
- Events were introduced in MySQL 5.1.

Figure 16-5   How to create an event

The CREATE EVENT statement uses the date/time intervals that work with date functions. As a result, you can use the INTERVAL keyword along with other keywords such as MINUTE, HOUR, DAY, WEEK, MONTH, and YEAR to specify a time. For more information, please see chapter 9.

How to view, alter, or drop events

The skills that you learned for viewing and dropping triggers are similar to the skills that you use to view and drop events. As a result, once you learn how to view and drop triggers, you shouldn't have much trouble viewing and dropping events. For instance, the first three examples in figure 16-6 show how to use the SHOW EVENTS statement to view events, and the last two examples show how to use the DROP EVENT statement to drop an event.

When working with events, you can also use the ALTER EVENT statement to temporarily enable or disable an event or to rename an event. For instance, the fourth example in this figure shows how to use the ALTER EVENT statement to disable an event. To do that, you code the ALTER EVENT keywords, followed by the name of the event and the DISABLE keyword. Then, the fifth example shows how to use the ENABLE keyword to enable an event that has been disabled. Finally, the sixth example shows how to use the RENAME TO keywords to rename an event.

A statement that lists all events on the server

```
SHOW EVENTS
```

A statement that lists all events in a database

```
SHOW EVENTS IN ap
```

	Db	Name	Definer	Time zone	Type	Execute at	Interval value	Interval field
▶	ap	monthly_delete_audit_rows	root@localhost	SYSTEM	RECURRING `NULL`		1	MONTH
	ap	one_time_delete_audit_rows	root@localhost	SYSTEM	ONE TIME	2012-03-24 10:12:18 `NULL`	`NULL`	

A statement that lists all events in a database that begin with "mon"

```
SHOW EVENTS IN ap LIKE 'mon%'
```

	Db	Name	Definer	Time zone	Type	Execute at	Interval value	Interval field	Starts
▶	ap	monthly_delete_audit_rows	root@localhost	SYSTEM	RECURRING `NULL`		1	MONTH	2012-

A statement that disables an event

```
ALTER EVENT monthly_delete_audit_rows DISABLE
```

A statement that enables an event

```
ALTER EVENT monthly_delete_audit_rows ENABLE
```

A statement that renames an event

```
ALTER EVENT one_time_delete_audit_rows RENAME TO one_time_delete_audits
```

A statement that drops an event

```
DROP EVENT monthly_delete_audit_rows
```

A statement that drops an event only if it exists

```
DROP EVENT IF EXISTS monthly_delete_audit_rows
```

Description

- To view events, use the SHOW EVENTS statement. To filter the result set that's returned, include an IN clause or a LIKE clause.
- To enable or disable an event, use the ALTER EVENT statement with the ENABLE or DISABLE keyword.
- To rename an event, use the ALTER EVENT statement with the RENAME TO keywords, followed by the new name.
- To drop an event, use the DROP EVENT statement. To be sure an event exists before it's dropped, include the IF EXISTS keywords.

Figure 16-6   How to view, alter, or drop events

Perspective

In this chapter, you learned how to use triggers to perform tasks that would be difficult or impossible to perform with other features like constraints. At this point, you should be able to create and use triggers that enforce data consistency, implement business rules, and log changes to the database. In addition, you should be able to use events to automatically perform tasks according to a schedule.

Although this is more than the typical SQL developer needs to know, this gives you the perspective that you need when you encounter triggers that have been created by others. This also provides the background that you need for learning more about triggers on your own.

Terms

trigger
fire a trigger
row-level trigger
event
scheduled event
fire an event
event scheduler
one-time event
recurring event

Exercises

1. Open the trigger named invoices_before_update that was shown in figure 16-02. Then, modify it so that it also raises an error whenever the payment total plus the credit total becomes larger than the invoice total in a row. Then, test this trigger with an appropriate UPDATE statement.

2. Create a trigger named invoices_after_update. This trigger should insert the old data about the invoice into the Invoices_Audit table after the row is updated. Then, test this trigger with an appropriate UPDATE statement. If the Invoices_Audit table doesn't exist, you can use the code shown in figure 16-03 to create it.

3. Check whether the event scheduler is turned on. If it isn't, code a statement that turns it on. Then, create an event that inserts a test row that contains test values into the Invoices_Audit table every minute. To make sure that this event has been created, code a SHOW EVENTS statement that views this event and a SELECT statement that views the data that's inserted into the Invoices_Audit table. Once you're sure this event is working correctly, code a DROP EVENT statement that drops the event.

Section 5

Database administration

If you want to become a database administrator, this section should get you started. Although it doesn't show you everything there is to know about database administration, it does get you started by presenting the skills you need to be the database administrator for a MySQL database that runs on a single server. This should be enough for many types of projects, such as a database that's used by a medium-sized web site or a database that's used for a departmental system.

In chapter 17, you'll get an overview of database administration. In addition, you'll learn some practical skills that you can use to monitor and configure a server and work with its logs. In chapter 18, you'll learn how to secure a database and work with user accounts. Finally, in chapter 19, you'll learn how to backup and restore a database. At this point, you should have a solid foundation in database administration.

17

An introduction
to database administration

This chapter begins by presenting an overview of database administration, including the responsibilities of a database administrator and the various types of files that are used by a database. Then, this chapter presents some practical skills that you can use to get started with database administration. These skills include monitoring the server, configuring the server, and working with the server's logs.

Database administration concepts **462**
Database administrator responsibilities 462
Types of database files 464
Types of log files 464
How to monitor the server **466**
How to view and kill processes 466
How to view the status variables 468
How to view the system variables 470
How to configure the server **472**
How to set system variables using MySQL Workbench 472
How to set system variables using a text editor 474
How to set system variables using the SET statement 476
How to work with logging **478**
How to enable and disable logging 478
How to configure logging 480
How to view text-based logs 482
How to view the binary log 484
How to manage logs 486
Perspective **488**

Database administration concepts

Before you learn practical skills for administering a database, it helps to understand some general concepts. To start, you should have a clear understanding of the responsibilities of a database administrator. In addition, you should understand the types of files that are used by MySQL.

Database administrator responsibilities

A *database administrator* (*DBA*) has many responsibilities that vary depending on the database. These responsibilities are summarized in figure 17-1. For most databases, the DBA designs and creates the database as described in chapters 10 through 12. Then, the DBA should secure the database as described in chapter 18. And, of course, the DBA should make sure that the database is backed up regularly so it can be restored up to the current point in time if necessary as described in chapter 19.

When a database goes into production, the DBA is responsible for monitoring the server to make sure it can handle its workload. If necessary, the DBA may need to configure the server to fix a problem or to get it to work more efficiently. To help with these tasks, the DBA may need to review logs to monitor database performance or to identify problems such as queries that run slowly. These skills are described in this chapter.

A database might also be administered by multiple people. For example, large mission-critical databases might be designed and created by a specialist before it's handed over to another DBA who is responsible for monitoring it. Or, if the database is hosted remotely, one DBA at the remote site might be responsible for certain administrative tasks while another DBA might be able to perform other administrative tasks remotely.

This chapter and the next two chapters focus on the skills that a DBA needs to administer a database that's running on a single server. However, it makes sense to run some databases on multiple servers. For example, you can often improve the performance of a large database by running the MySQL server on multiple machines and then running the database on each machine. Then, you can use *database replication* to synchronize the databases so any change made to one database is automatically propagated to the other databases. To do this, you can identify one server as the *master* and the other servers as the *slaves*.

Database administrator responsibilities

Maintenance
- Monitor the server
- Configure the server
- Maintain log files

Design
- Design the database
- Create the database

Security
- Maintain user accounts
- Secure the server and its databases

Backup
- Backup the database regularly
- Restore the database if necessary
- Migrate data to another server if necessary

Miscellaneous
- Start or stop the server when necessary
- Optimize the server
- Update software when necessary
- Enable and manage replication if necessary

Description

- A *database administrator* (*DBA*) has many responsibilities that vary depending on the database.
- Chapter 2 describes how to start and stop the server.
- Chapters 10 through 12 describe the skills that a DBA typically uses to design and create databases.
- Chapters 17 through 19 focus on the skills that a DBA needs to administer a database that's running on a single server.
- *Database replication* involves setting up two or more MySQL servers, usually running on different machines, where one server is the *master* and the other servers are the *slaves*. Then, any changes made to databases on one server are automatically propagated to the databases on the other servers.

Figure 17-1   Database administrator responsibilities

Types of database files

Figure 17-2 summarizes the types of database files used by MySQL server, including configuration files, data files, and log files. To start, MySQL reads a *configuration file* when it starts. For Windows, this file is named my.ini and is usually stored in the base directory. For Mac OS X and Unix, this file is named my.cnf and is usually stored in the /private/etc or /etc directory.

MySQL's data directory contains subdirectories and files that MySQL uses to store the data for its databases. Here, each subdirectory corresponds to a database. For example, the AP database is stored within a directory named AP. Within a subdirectory, the files correspond to the tables and other objects of the database. The table files differ depending on whether the tables are InnoDB or MyISAM. For example, InnoDB uses one file per table (an .frm file). However, MyISAM uses three files per table (.frm, .myd, and .myi). In addition to subdirectories, the data directory may contain *log files* that contain information that's written by the server.

By default, MySQL's data directory is hidden. As a result, you need to be able to view hidden files to see this directory. With Windows, for example, you need to change the settings for the Explorer so it shows hidden files, folders, and drives. With Mac OS X, you can start a Terminal window and execute these two commands:

```
defaults write com.apple.Finder AppleShowAllFiles TRUE
killall Finder
```

To hide these files, you can execute these two commands again but specify a value of FALSE in the first command instead of TRUE.

Types of log files

Figure 17-2 also summarizes the different types of log files that MySQL can create. To start, a *general log* contains a record of client connections, SQL statements received from the clients, and other information. This file is useful for monitoring the server. An *error log* contains messages about server startup and shutdown as well as error messages. This file is useful for troubleshooting problems with starting or stopping the server. And a *slow query log* contains a list of SQL statements that take a long time to execute. This file is useful for identifying queries that need to be rewritten to optimize database performance.

A *binary log* consists of an index file and a series of numbered binary files. The index file contains a list of the binary files, and the binary files contain a record of the changes that have been made to the database. This log can be used with backups to restore a database after a crash. It can also be used to enable replication between a master server and a slave server.

Like a binary log, a *relay log* consists of an index file and a series of numbered binary files. These files are used on a slave server to relay any changes that have been made on the master server to the slave server. This log is only necessary when you're using replication.

Types of database files

File Type	Description
Configuration file	Files that contain configuration options that the MySQL server uses to set its defaults when it starts. For Windows, this file is named my.ini. For Mac OS X and Unix, this file is named my.cnf. For more information, see figures 17-6 and 17-7.
Data file	Files that define the tables, indexes, and other database objects. These files also store any data that's used by the database objects. InnoDB uses one file per table (an .frm file). MyISAM uses three files per table (.frm, .myd, and .myi). Other files are used for other database objects such as views and triggers.
Log file	Files that contain information that's written (logged) by the database server. You can configure your server to turn these files on or off and to control how they work. For more information, see figures 17-9 through 17-13.

Types of log files

Log type	Description
General	A text file that contains a record of client connections, SQL statements received from the clients, and other information.
Error	A text file that contains messages about server startup and shutdown and error messages.
Slow query	A text file that contains SQL statements that take a long time to execute.
Binary	One or more binary files that contain a record of changes that have been made to the database. This log can be used with backups to restore a database after a crash. This log can also be used to enable replication between a master server and a slave server.
Relay	One or more binary files that are used on a slave machine to relay any changes that have been made on the master machine. This log is only necessary when you're using replication.

The base and data directories for Windows

```
C:\Program Files\MySQL\MySQL Server 5.5
C:\ProgramData\MySQL\MySQL Server 5.5\data
```

The base and data directories for Mac OS X and Unix

```
usr/local/mysql/
usr/local/mysql/data
```

Description

- The database server uses several types of files including *configuration files*, *data files*, and *log files*.

- By default, MySQL's data directory is hidden. As a result, you need to be able to view hidden files to see this directory.

Figure 17-2   Types of database and log files

How to monitor the server

When a database is running on a server, you should occasionally monitor the server to make sure that it's running efficiently. That includes making sure the server isn't using too much of the system's CPU and memory, and that the number of connections and traffic aren't too much for the server. To do that, you can view the process list, status variables, and system variables.

How to view and kill processes

A *process* is a connection to the database. To view a list of all the processes that are running, you can open an Admin tab as described in chapter 2. Then, you can select the Server Status option as shown in figure 17-3 to display the Server Status window.

The information at the top of the Server Status window is divided into three sections. The Info section shows the version of the server and indicates whether it's running. The System section shows graphs of the amount of CPU and memory that are being used by the server. Finally, the Server Health section shows graphs of the number of connections to the server, the traffic in KB per second, and so on. By viewing these graphs, you can get an idea of whether the server has enough resources to handle its connections and traffic.

The Connections section of this window shows information about the connections to the database. In this figure, six connections have been established. The first two are the connections for the root user that MySQL Workbench used when it connected to the server to display the SQL Editor tab. Since no processing is currently being performed in this tab, the Command column for these connections indicates that they are sleeping.

The next two connections are also for the root user, but they were used to connect to the server to display the Admin tab. The Command column for the first connection indicates that it is being used to execute a query. Specifically, the SHOW PROCESSLIST statement is being executed on this connection. This is the statement that displays the information in the Server Status window.

Finally, the last two connections are for a user named jim. You'll learn more about working with users other than the root user in the next chapter.

If necessary, you can stop a process by selecting it and clicking on the Kill Connection button. For example, you might want to do that if a process isn't responding. You can also stop a query by selecting it and clicking on the Kill Query button. You might want to do that if a query is stuck or it's taking too long to run. This stops the query, but doesn't stop the process.

Since MySQL Workbench provides a convenient way to view the process list, you'll usually want to use it. However, if you don't have access to MySQL Workbench, you can use the SHOW PROCESSLIST statement to view the list of processes. You can also use the KILL statement to stop a process whenever that's necessary. For more information about these statements, you can look them up in the MySQL Reference Manual.

The process list

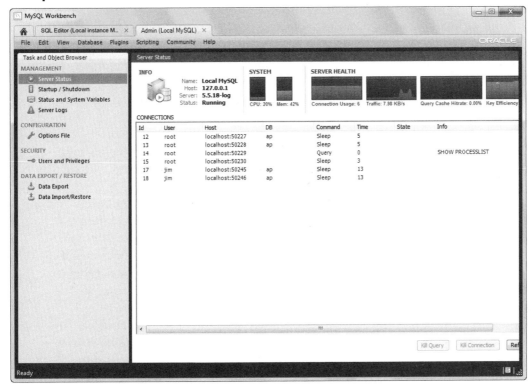

Description

- A *process* is a connection to the database.
- To view the processes that are running, you can start MySQL Workbench and use it to open an Admin tab as described in chapter 2. Then, you can select the Server Status option.
- To stop a query, you can select it and click on the Kill Query button.
- To stop a process, you can select it and click on the Kill Connection button.
- To manually view a list of processes, you can use the SHOW PROCESSLIST statement. To manually stop a process, you can use the KILL statement. For more information about these statements, you can refer to the MySQL Reference Manual.

Figure 17-3   How to view and kill processes

How to view the status variables

Although viewing the process list is often enough to determine whether a server is performing adequately, you can view the *status variables* if you need additional information about the status of the server. To view these variables, you can click on the Status and System Variables option in an Admin tab. Then, if the Status Variables tab isn't displayed, you can click on it to display it. Finally, you can click on one of the groups to display the variables in that group. For example, you can click on the Binlog group to view all status variables that are associated with binary logs. You can click on the Replication group to view all status variables that are associated with replication. And so on. To display all the variables at once, you can click on the All group.

As figure 17-4 shows, the Status Variables tab includes the name of each status variable, along with its current value. In addition, most variables have a description. To learn more about the status of your server, you can read through these variables and their descriptions. Although you probably won't understand the information that all of these variables provide, you should understand some of them. And, you'll learn a lot about the status of your server by reviewing them.

You can also use the Status Variables tab to search for specific variables. To do that, you click on the Search Results group and enter some text in the Search box. Then, only the variables that include the search text are displayed. In this figure, for example, the tab displays only the status variables that include "conn" somewhere in the variable name. As a result, this search displays most status variables that display information about connections to the server.

Status variables

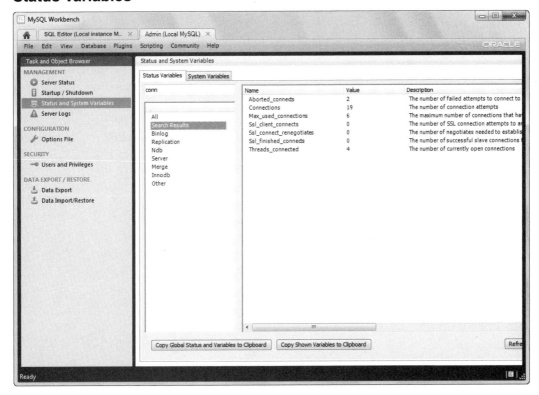

Description

- A *status variable* is a variable that contains information about the status of the MySQL server.

- To view status variables, open an Admin tab and click on the Status and System Variables option. If necessary, click on the Status Variables tab. From that tab, you can click on one of the groups to display different status variables.

- To search for one or more status variables, click on the Search Results group and type a search string in the Search box at the top of the tab. This displays all status variables whose name contains the search string.

- To manually view status variables, you can use the SHOW STATUS statement. For more information about this statement, you can refer to the MySQL Reference Manual.

Figure 17-4   How to view the status variables

How to view the system variables

If you need to check how the MySQL server is currently configured, you can view its *system variables* as shown in figure 17-5. In general, viewing system variables works like viewing status variables. As a result, if you understand how to view status variables, you shouldn't have any trouble viewing system variables.

In the next few figures, you'll learn how to set system variables. As you do, you'll learn more about how these variables work and what they can do.

System variables

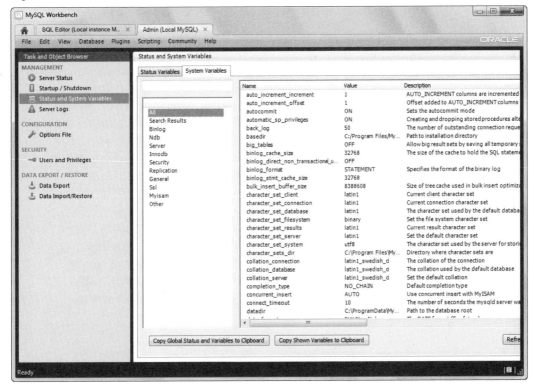

Description

- A *system variable* is a variable that stores a setting for the current configuration of the MySQL server.

- To view server variables, open an Admin tab and click on the Status and System Variables option. If necessary, click on the System Variables tab. From that tab, you can click on one of the groups to display the variables in that group. If you click on the Search Results group, you can enter a search string in the Search box above the group names.

- If you don't have access to MySQL Workbench, you can use the SHOW VARI-ABLES statement to view the system variables. For more information about this statement, you can refer to the MySQL Reference Manual.

Figure 17-5   How to view the system variables

How to configure the server

When you install MySQL, the MySQL Server Instance Configuration Wizard generates a configuration file that's appropriate for your system. For example, if you followed the instructions in the appendixes of this book to install MySQL on your computer, it has been configured appropriately for a developer who is using MySQL for learning and testing. However, if you install MySQL for a production system, you can use this wizard to configure the server so it's appropriate for that system.

If you need to change the server configuration after installing it, you can do that by editing MySQL's configuration file with either MySQL Workbench or a text editor. This sets the system variables for the server. Then, MySQL reads the system variables from the configuration file every time it starts.

You can also use SET statements to set system variables dynamically. When you do that, the settings go into effect immediately and aren't saved in the configuration file. This allows you to change a system variable without having to restart the server. This is sometimes useful if you want to experiment with different settings to see if they work correctly before you change them in the configuration file.

How to set system variables using MySQL Workbench

Figure 17-6 shows how to use MySQL Workbench to set system variables in the configuration file. To do that, you open an Admin tab and click on the Options File option. Then, you click on an appropriate tab and use it to change options.

In this figure, the General tab shows some of the options that you can change. For example, you can use the port variable to change the port number that's used by the server. Similarly, you can use the basedir and datadir variables to change the base directory and the data directory that are used by MySQL.

When you're done making changes, you can click the Apply button to write the changes to the configuration file. However, MySQL won't read the configuration file until it starts. As a result, your changes won't go into effect until you stop and restart the server.

Server configuration options

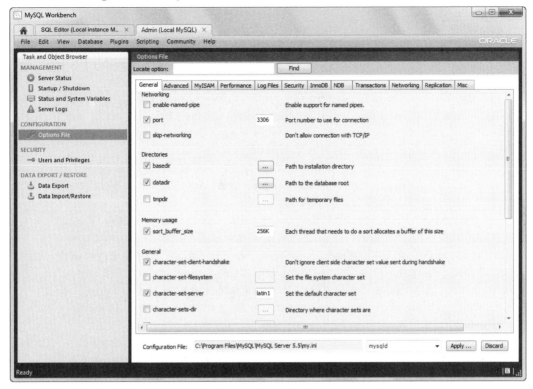

Description

- When MySQL starts, it reads the server configuration file and uses it to set system variables.

- To use MySQL Workbench to change the server configuration file, open an Admin tab and click on the Options File option. Then, click on an appropriate tab and use it to change options. Finally, click the Apply button to write the changes to the configuration file.

- To use MySQL Workbench to change the server configuration file, you may need to run it as an administrator.

- The MySQL server only reads the configuration file when it starts. As a result, your changes won't go into effect until you restart the server.

Figure 17-6   How to set system variables using MySQL Workbench

How to set system variables using a text editor

Another way to set system variables is to use a text editor to edit the configuration file directly. On Windows, the configuration file is named my.ini and is typically stored in MySQL's base directory. On Mac OS X or Unix, this file is named my.cnf and is typically stored in the /private/etc or /etc directory.

Figure 17-7 shows an excerpt from a typical configuration file for a Windows system. Here, I have stripped out the settings for the MySQL clients, and I have stripped out most comments. This makes it easy to see the system variables that are set in a typical MySQL configuration file.

To start, the first line of the configuration file specifies that the following system variables apply to the *mysqld program (*the *MySQL daemon*). This is the MySQL server process that runs in the background.

In the first group of variables, the port variable sets the port to 3306. Then, the basedir and datadir variables set MySQL's base and data directories. These directories are typical for a Windows system. Next, the character-set-server and default-storage-engine variables set the default character set and storage engine for the server. Notice that the names of these variables use dashes instead of underscores. This is acceptable only when you enter a variable name in a configuration file. Because of that, I prefer to use underscores.

The second group of variables begins with a comment that indicates that these variables only apply to MyISAM tables. This shows that you can code a comment by using a pound sign (#) to start the line. In addition, the variable values show that you can use a suffix to specify a number of bytes (K for kilobytes, M for megabytes, or G for gigabytes).

The third group of variables also begins with a comment. This comment indicates that these variables only apply to InnoDB tables.

As you review this code, note that it only sets 23 system variables, even though MySQL provides over 300 system variables. That's because most of the defaults for MySQL are compiled into MySQL. As a result, the configuration file only needs to override the system variables that need to be set.

Although we don't show you how to start the MySQL server from a command line in this book, you should know that you can do that. When you do, you can code system variables on the command line by preceding the variable name with two dashes like this:

```
--port=3307
```

So if you see system variables listed like this in the MySQL Reference Manual, you'll know that it's showing you how to code them on the command line.

A typical installation of MySQL includes alternate configuration files that are appropriate for servers that run small, medium, large, or huge databases. For example, the configuration file named my-huge is appropriate for a server that has 1GB to 2GB of memory and that's mostly dedicated to running MySQL databases. To use one of these files, you can rename the "my" file and then rename the file you want to use to "my". Or, you can view these files in a text editor to see how the system variables are set for various types of servers.

Part of a configuration file for Windows

```
[mysqld]
port=3306
basedir="C:/Program Files/MySQL/MySQL Server 5.5/"
datadir="C:/ProgramData/MySQL/MySQL Server 5.5/Data/"
character-set-server=latin1
default-storage-engine=INNODB
sql-mode="STRICT_TRANS_TABLES,NO_AUTO_CREATE_USER,NO_ENGINE_SUBSTITUTION"
max_connections=100
query_cache_size=0
table_cache=256
tmp_table_size=35M
thread_cache_size=8

#*** MyISAM Specific options
myisam_max_sort_file_size=100G
myisam_sort_buffer_size=69M
key_buffer_size=55M
read_buffer_size=64K
read_rnd_buffer_size=256K
sort_buffer_size=256K

#*** INNODB Specific options ***
innodb_additional_mem_pool_size=3M
innodb_flush_log_at_trx_commit=1
innodb_log_buffer_size=2M
innodb_buffer_pool_size=107M
innodb_log_file_size=54M
innodb_thread_concurrency=10
```

Description

- To edit the configuration file directly, use a text editor. This file is named my.ini (Windows) or my.cnf (Mac OS X or Unix).

- To edit the configuration file, you may need to start your text editor as an administrator. To do that on a Windows system, you can right-click on the icon that starts your text editor and then select the "Run as administrator" command.

- When specifying a number of bytes, you can add a suffix to a number to specify kilobytes (K), megabytes (M), or gigabytes (G).

- A typical installation of MySQL includes alternate configuration files that are appropriate for servers that run small, medium, large, or huge databases. If necessary, you can swap in one of these configuration files by renaming it appropriately.

- To learn more about system variables, you can look up "Server System Variables" in the MySQL Reference Manual. This provides a complete list of all system variables along with detailed descriptions of each variable.

Figure 17-7   How to set system variables using a text editor

How to set system variables using the SET statement

In the previous two figures, you learned how to edit the configuration file so changes to the system variables are stored permanently and read by MySQL when the server starts. Now, figure 17-8 shows how to use the SET statement to set system variables dynamically. When you use this approach, you don't need to restart the server for the changes to take effect. As a result, you can use this approach to experiment with different values for system variables. Then, if you want to make these changes permanent, you can add them to the configuration file as described in the previous two figures.

When you use the SET statement to set system variables, you can set most of them at either the global level or the session level. When you set variables at the global level, any new connections start with these settings. Then, you can override these settings for the session if you need to. However, some variables can only be set at the global level.

The first example in this figure uses a SET statement with the GLOBAL keyword to set the variable named autocommit at the global level. This statement sets this variable to a value of ON, which is a synonym for 1. Then, the second example uses the SESSION keyword to set this variable at the session level to a value of OFF, which is a synonym for 0. If you don't specify the GLOBAL or SESSION keyword, MySQL always attempts to set the session variable. As a result, the SESSION keyword is optional for setting session variables.

When specifying the value of a system variable, you can use the DEFAULT keyword to specify the default value that's compiled into MySQL. For instance, the third example sets the autocommit variable to its default value.

The fourth and fifth examples show how to set the max_connections variable. This variable specifies the maximum number of connections for the server, not the session. As a result, it can only be set at the global level.

When specifying a value that's a number of bytes, you can't use suffixes like you can in a configuration file. However, you can specify the number of bytes as shown in the sixth example or use an expression as shown in the seventh example. Both of these examples specify a value of 35 megabytes.

After you set a system variable, it's often helpful to be able to view it to make sure it's set correctly. To get the value of a system variable, you code two at signs (@@), the GLOBAL or SESSION keyword, a period, and the name of the variable in a SELECT statement as shown in the next to last example. If you don't specify the GLOBAL or SESSION keyword, MySQL returns the session value if it exists as shown in the last example. Otherwise, it returns the global value.

The syntax for setting system variables

Global variables

```
SET GLOBAL var_name = var_value;
```

Session variables

```
SET [SESSION] var_name = var_value;
```

Examples that set system variables

```
SET GLOBAL   autocommit = ON;
SET SESSION autocommit = OFF;
SET GLOBAL   autocommit = DEFAULT;

SET GLOBAL   max_connections = 90;
SET GLOBAL   max_connections = DEFAULT;

SET GLOBAL   tmp_table_size = 36700160;
SET GLOBAL   tmp_table_size = 35 * 1024 * 1024;
```

The syntax for getting system variables

Global variables

```
@@GLOBAL.var_name
```

Session variables

```
@@[SESSION.]var_name
```

Examples that get system variables

Get the global and session values of a variable

```
SELECT @@GLOBAL.autocommit, @@SESSION.autocommit
```

@@GLOBAL.autocommit	@@SESSION.autocommit
1	0

Get the session value if it exists or the global value if it doesn't

```
SELECT @@autocommit
```

@@autocommit
0

Description

- You can use the SET statement to set the values of system variables dynamically.
- If you don't specify the GLOBAL or SESSION keywords when setting the value of a system variable, MySQL always attempts to set the session variable.
- If you don't specify the GLOBAL or SESSION keywords when getting the value of a system variable, MySQL returns the session value if it exists. Otherwise, it returns the global value.
- The LOCAL keyword is a synonym for the SESSION keyword.
- You can use the DEFAULT keyword to set the value of a variable to the default value that's compiled into MySQL.
- When specifying a number of bytes, you can't use suffixes (K, M, G), but you can use expressions.

Figure 17-8   How to set system variables using the SET statement

How to work with logging

Earlier in this chapter, you learned about the types of logs that the MySQL server can create. If these logs aren't enabled on your system, you can enable one or more of them. Then, you can configure them so they work the way you want, and you can view them whenever necessary. Finally, if you use logs, you need to manage them so they don't consume too much disk space.

How to enable and disable logging

When you enable a log, the server does extra work to write data to the log. In addition, the log takes extra disk space. Finally, since logs can contain sensitive data, they can compromise the security of your data if you don't secure the files properly. That's why most logs are disabled by default. As a result, you shouldn't enable a log unless you have a good reason to do so.

For example, if you need help monitoring the server, you can enable the general query log. If you need help finding and fixing errors, you can enable the error log. If you need help restoring data, you can enable the binary log. And, if you need help optimizing a database, you can enable the slow query log.

Figure 17-9 shows how to enable logging. To start, it shows how to use MySQL Workbench to modify the configuration file. Here, the first three options in the Log Files tab enable the general, binary, and error logs. Although you can't see all of the options here, you can use this tab to set all six of the logging options described in this figure.

In addition to enabling the logs, these options allow you to specify a directory and name for the log file. If you don't specify a name, MySQL uses the default names specified in this figure. Similarly, if you don't specify a directory, MySQL stores the log files in its data directory.

If you want to edit the configuration file to set the logging options, you can do that too. In this figure, for instance, the code example shows how to set all six options. Here, the first line enables the general log, and the second line specifies a name and directory for its log file. The third line enables the error log and specifies a name and directory for its log file. The fourth line enables the binary log and specifies a name and directory for its files. And the last two lines enable the slow query log and specify a name and directory for its log file. Note that this code works on a Windows, Mac OS X, or Unix system. Although you typically uses backslashes for Windows, front slashes work as well. So, whenever it makes sense, we've used front slashes in this book.

So, when would you want to store a log file in a directory other than the default directory (the data directory)? Typically, you'd want to do that if you're using binary log files to incrementally back up your data. Then, you can store the log files on a drive other than the drive that's running the MySQL server. That way, if the drive that the server is running on fails, you can still access the binary files and restore the server. To specify a drive on a Windows system, you just code the drive letter at the beginning of the path like this:

```
log_bin="c:/murach/mysql/bin-log"
```

Server configuration options for log files

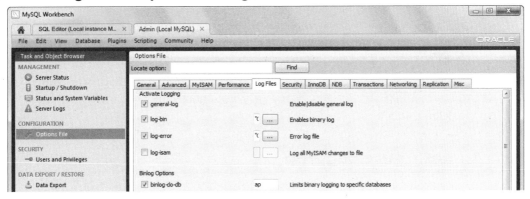

System variables for enabling logging

Variable	Description
general_log	Enables the general log with a default name of HOSTNAME.log.
general_log_file=logname	Specifies the name of the general log file.
log_error[=logname]	Enables the error log. If no name is specified, MySQL uses a name of HOSTNAME.err.
log_bin[=logname]	Enables the binary log. If no name is specified, MySQL uses a name of HOSTNAME. Since MySQL provides its own extensions (.index, .000001, .000002, etc.) for the binary log files, you don't need to specify an extension for the log name.
slow_query_log	Enables the slow query log with a default name of HOSTNAME-slow.log.
slow_query_log_file=logname	Specifies the name of the slow log file.

Logging options set in the server configuration file

```
general_log
general_log_file="/murach/mysql/general.log"

log_error="/murach/mysql/error.log"

log_bin="/murach/mysql/bin-log"

slow_query_log
slow_query_log_file="/murach/mysql/slow.log"
```

Description

- Logs can help you monitor the database, find and fix errors, restore data, and optimize your database.
- Log files can take a significant amount of disk space, and logging can compromise the security of your data if you don't secure the log files properly.
- If you don't specify a directory for a log file, the file is stored in MySQL's data directory.

Figure 17-9   How to enable and disable logging

To specify a drive on a Unix system, you code the Volumes directory and the name of the drive at the beginning of the path like this:

```
log_bin="volumes/archive/murach/mysql/bin-log"
```

In this example, Archive is the name of the drive.

Unfortunately, on a Mac OS X system, MySQL doesn't allow you to specify a directory for the binary log. If you attempt to do that, the server won't start. As a result, if you're using Mac OS X, you must store your binary log files in the default directory.

How to configure logging

If you enable logging, you can configure it so it works the way you want. To do that, you can use any of the techniques shown in this chapter for setting system variables. Figure 17-10 summarizes some of the most commonly used system variables for configuring logging.

The configuration file in this figure shows some examples of how to set these options. To start, the log_output example sends the output of the general and slow query logs to tables instead of to files. This causes these logs to be written to the General_Log and Slow_Log tables of the database named mysql. That way, you can use SELECT statements to view the data that's written to these logs. In addition, you can use events to automatically manage these tables as shown in figure 17-13.

The log_warnings example sets the level of warnings that are logged about connections to the highest level (2). As a result, the server logs errors about both aborted and denied connections.

The expire_logs_days example deletes binary log files that are more than seven days old. This setting is appropriate if you back up your database once a week. That way, if you need to restore your database, you can use the database backup to restore it to somewhere within seven days of the current date. Then, you can use the binary log to apply any changes that have been made since that backup. To do that, you can use the skills described in chapter 19.

The max_binlog_size example sets the maximum size of the binary log file to one megabyte. As a result, when the server reaches this limit, it starts a new binary log file with a new number. However, if MySQL is logging a transaction when it reaches the limit, it finishes the transaction before starting a new file. So, the binary log files may be slightly larger than the size indicated by the max_binlog_size setting.

The long_query_time example causes the server to write queries to the slow query log if they take longer than five seconds. By default, this value is set to ten seconds, but you can set it to a lower value if you want to include queries that take a shorter time to run. Conversely, you can set it to a higher value if you only want to include queries that take a longer time to run.

System variables that apply to multiple types of logs

Variable	Description
`log_output[=target]`	Sends the output for the general log and the slow query log to a file (FILE), a table (TABLE), or nowhere (NONE). If you want to send the output to both a file and a table, you can separate the two targets with a comma (but no spaces).
`log_warnings[=level]`	Determines what errors are logged. The default is 1, which logs aborted connections. To disable this option, set it to 0. To log aborted connections and access-denied errors, set this option to 2.

System variables for the binary log

Variable	Description
`expire_logs_days[=days]`	Deletes binary log files that are more than the specified number of days old. The default is 0, which means files aren't deleted.
`max_binlog_size[=bytes]`	Sets the maximum size of the binary log. The server starts a new log file when the binary log reaches its maximum size. The default is 1073741824 (1GB).

A system variable for the slow query log

Variable	Description
`long_query_time[=seconds]`	Sets the number of seconds that defines a slow query. The default is 10.

Logging options set in the server configuration file

```
# stores the output of the general and slow query logs in a table
log_output=TABLE

# logs warnings about aborted and denied connections
log_warnings=2

# deletes binary log files that are more than 7 days old
expire_logs_days=7

# sets the maximum binary log file size to 1MB
max_binlog_size=1048576

# writes queries to the slow query log if they take longer than 5 seconds
long_query_time=5
```

Description

- You can use any of the techniques for setting global system variables that are described in this chapter to set logging options.

Figure 17-10   How to configure logging

How to view text-based logs

By default, the general, error, and slow query logs are stored in text files. As a result, you can use any text editor to open and view them. Or, you can use MySQL Workbench to view them. To do that, you can open an Admin tab, click on the Server Logs option, and click on the tab for the log you want to view. In figure 17-11, for example, the error log is opened in Workbench. Here, the error log shows some messages that the server logs when it starts and stops.

In this figure, the Server Logs window contains tabs for the error log file and the general log file. However, it doesn't contain a tab for the slow query log file. That's because there aren't any entries in this file. If there were, MySQL Workbench would display a tab for this file as well.

If you configure your system so it stores the general and slow query logs in tables as shown in the previous figure, you can use MySQL Workbench to view these tables, just as you would use it to view a log file. In addition, you can use a SELECT statement to view them. In this figure, for example, the first SELECT statement selects all rows from the General_Log table that's stored in the database named mysql. Of course, if you wanted to, you could easily modify this SELECT statement so it uses the event_time column to display just the most recent rows of this table.

The second SELECT statement selects all rows from the slow_log table of the mysql database. In this figure, this SELECT statement doesn't retrieve any rows because no queries have run slowly enough. As a result, the server hasn't inserted any rows into the table. If the server had written rows to this table, you could use the data in each row to help determine why the query is running so slowly.

The error log displayed in MySQL Workbench

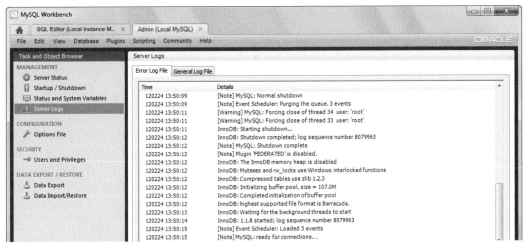

How to view the log files when they are written to tables

The general log

```
SELECT * FROM mysql.general_log
```

event_time	user_host	thread_id	server_id	command_type	argument
2012-02-14 09:05:26	root[root] @ localhost [127.0.0.1]	18	1	Query	SHOW WARNI...
2012-02-14 09:05:26	root[root] @ localhost [127.0.0.1]	18	1	Query	CREATE TABL...
2012-02-14 09:05:27	root[root] @ localhost [127.0.0.1]	18	1	Query	SHOW WARNI...
▶ 2012-02-14 09:05:27	root[root] @ localhost [127.0.0.1]	18	1	Query	CREATE TRIG...

The slow query log

```
SELECT * FROM mysql.slow_log
```

start_time	user_host	query_time	lock_time	rows_sent	rows_examined	db	last_insert_id	insert_id

Description

- By default, the general, error, and slow query logs are stored in text files. As a result, you can use any text editor to open them and view them. Or, you can use MySQL Workbench to view them. To do that, open an Admin tab, click on the Server Logs option, and click on the tab for the log file.

- If you configure your system so it stores the general and slow query logs in tables, you can use MySQL Workbench to view these tables, just as you would use it to view a log file. In addition, you can use a SELECT statement to view them.

Figure 17-11   How to view the text-based logs

How to view the binary log

Figure 17-12 begins by showing the files for a binary log named bin-log. Here, the bin-log.index file is a text file. This file contains a list of all of the numbered files that store the changes that have been made to the database. As a result, you can use a text editor to view and edit it.

However, the numbered log files (bin-log.000001, bin-log.000002, etc.) are binary files. As a result, if you open them with a text editor, you won't be able to read them. To solve this problem, you can start a command line and use the mysqlbinlog program to convert the binary file to a text file. For example, this figure shows how to use the mysqlbinlog program to convert the binary file named bin-log.000001 to a text file named bin-log.000001.sql. Here, the > character indicates that the bin-log.000001.sql file is created as output by the mysqlbinlog program.

If you open the converted text file in a text editor, you'll find that it contains data about the changes that have been made to the database. For example, this figure shows an excerpt from a binary file that shows an INSERT statement that was executed. The binary log file also includes a SET TIMESTAMP statement that identifies the time that the INSERT statement was executed. You can use this information to perform an incremental point-in-time recovery as described in chapter 19.

If you're using Mac OS X, you may wonder why the command for converting the binary file is so different than the command for Windows. To start, you enter the sudo command, which gives you appropriate privileges to execute the mysqlbinlog program successfully. Then, you code a dot and slash (./) before the mysqlbinlog program to show that it's in the current directory (the bin directory). Finally, you code two dots and a slash (../) to navigate down one directory so you can access the data directory. This is the directory where binary files are stored on Mac OS X.

The files for a binary log named bin-log

```
bin-log.index
bin-log.000001
bin-log.000002
bin-log.000003
...
```

How to convert a binary log file to a text file

Using Windows

```
cd /program files/mysql/mysql server 5.5/bin
mysqlbinlog /murach/mysql/bin-log.000001 > /murach/mysql/bin-log.000001.sql
```

Using Mac OS X or Unix

```
cd /usr/local/mysql/bin
sudo ./mysqlbinlog ../data/bin-log.000001 > /murach/mysql/bin-log.000001.sql
```

An excerpt from the bin-log.000001.sql file

```
/*!*/;
# at 181
#120214 14:23:01 server id 1  end_log_pos 349 Query thread_id=6 exec_time=0
error_code=0
use ap/*!*/;
SET TIMESTAMP=1329258181/*!*/;
INSERT INTO invoices VALUES
(115, 97, '456789', '2011-08-01', 8344.50, 0, 0, 1, '2011-08-31', NULL)
/*!*/;
# at 349
#120214 14:23:01 server id 1  end_log_pos 376 Xid = 63
COMMIT/*!*/;
```

Description

- The index file of the binary log is a text file that contains a list of the numbered log files. The numbered log files are binary files.

- To view a binary file, you can use the mysqlbinlog program to convert the file to a text file. Then, you can open the text file in a text editor.

- You can also edit the text file for a binary log. For more information, see chapter 19.

Figure 17-12   How to view the binary log

How to manage logs

Since logs can use a large amount of disk space, you should disable any logs that you don't need. For example, since the general log contains all queries that are sent to the server, it can quickly grow to be very large. As a result, it's common to disable the general log. Then, if you want to monitor all queries sent to the server, you can temporarily enable this log. Similarly, when you're done optimizing the queries on your server, you may want to disable the slow query log.

On the other hand, it's usually a good idea to keep the error log enabled since it contains useful information that can help you troubleshoot problems with the server. In addition, if you're using the binary log to provide for incremental point-in-time recovery, you can't disable it.

If you enable any logs, you need to manage them so they don't consume too much disk space. For the text-based logs (general, error, and slow query), you can use the log rotation strategy described in figure 17-13. With this strategy, you delete any old log files. Then, you rename the current log file. When you do, MySQL server starts a new error log file.

For example, let's say you have an old error log named error.old and the current error log is named error.log. In that case, you can start by deleting the file named error.old. Then, you can rename the current error log (error.log) to error.old. When you do, MySQL starts a new error log named error.log. As a result, you never have more than two error logs on your server at a time.

To get started, you can manage logs by manually deleting and renaming files. Later, you can automate your log management. For example, you can create a batch file for a Windows system or a bash file for a Mac OS X or Unix system. You can also create a timer to execute these files at regular intervals. Since the details for doing this vary depending on the operating system, I won't describe the process here.

If you store the general log or the slow query log in a table, you can use SQL statements to rotate the log tables. You can also create an event that rotates the log tables at a specified interval. For example, this figure shows an event that rotates the general log table once every month.

To start, the DROP TABLE statement drops the table named general_log_old if it exists. Then, the CREATE TABLE statement creates a table named general_log_old that has the same structure and data as the table named general_log. Finally, the TRUNCATE statement deletes all rows from the general_log table. As a result, the general_log_old table now contains the log rows from the previous month, and the general_log table is empty and ready to store the log rows for the current month. Here, you must use a TRUNCATE statement instead of a DELETE statement because the DELETE statement doesn't work with the general_log table.

Since the binary log uses an index file to keep track of its numbered binary files, you can't just delete the old binary files that you no longer want. However, you can use the expire_logs_days system variable that was described in figure 17-10 to delete old binary logs after the specified number of days. This deletes the old binary files and updates the index file.

Strategies for managing logs

Strategy	Description
Log rotation	Applies to text-based logs (general, error, and slow query). To rotate logs, you can save the current log file under a new name and let the server create a new log file. Then, you can delete any old log files when they're no longer needed. If necessary, you can create a series of numbered logs.
Age-based expiration	Applies to the binary log. For this log, you can use the expire_logs_days system variable shown in figure 17-10 to delete the old binary logs after the specified number of days.

An event that rotates the general log every month

```
USE mysql;

DELIMITER //

CREATE EVENT general_log_rotate
ON SCHEDULE EVERY 1 MONTH
DO BEGIN
  DROP TABLE IF EXISTS general_log_old;

  CREATE TABLE general_log_old AS
  SELECT *
  FROM general_log;

  TRUNCATE general_log;
END//
```

Description

- It's generally considered a good practice to disable any logs that you don't need.
- You can manually manage the text-based log files (general, error, and slow query) by deleting and renaming log files.
- You can automatically manage text-based log files (general, error, slow query) by creating batch files (Windows) or bash files (Mac OS X or Unix) that run on a specified schedule.
- If you send the output of the general or slow query logs to a table, you can create an event that uses SQL statements to manage the log tables.
- You can't just delete files from the binary or relay log, since an index is used to keep track of the files in these logs. However, you can set the expire_logs_days system variable to delete files from the binary log after a specified number of days.

Figure 17-13   How to manage logs

Perspective

In this chapter, you were introduced to the responsibilities of a database administrator. In addition, you learned how to perform some of these responsibilities. For example, you learned how to monitor the server, configure the server, and work with log files.

In the next two chapters, you'll learn how to perform two more critical responsibilities of a DBA. First, in chapter 18, you'll learn how to secure a database. Then, in chapter 19, you'll learn how to backup and restore a database.

Although this isn't everything a DBA needs to know, this is enough to get started with the administration of many types of databases. In addition, it provides the background that you need for learning more about database administration on your own.

Terms

database administrator (DBA)
database replication
master
slave
configuration file
data file
log file
general log
error log
slow query log
binary log
relay log
process
status variable
system variable
mysqld program
MySQL daemon

Exercises

1. Start MySQL Workbench and use an Admin tab to view the process list. Then, open four SQL Editor tabs. As you open each one, switch back to the process list and note how the number of processes grows. Next, run some queries and note how they use system resources.

2. Use MySQL Workbench's Admin tab to view these status variables: connections, threads_connected, bytes_received, and bytes_sent. Read the descriptions for these variables to get an idea of what they do.

3. Use MySQL Workbench's Admin tab to view the system variables named basedir and datadir. Note the paths to these directories. Then, view the system variables named log_error and log_bin. Note whether these system variables are set to a value of ON or OFF.

4. Use the Explorer (Windows) or the Finder (Mac) to view MySQL's data directory. To do that, you may have to modify your operating system settings so you can see hidden directories and files. Note that the subdirectories of the data directory correspond with the databases that are running on your system.

5. View the files in the AP subdirectory and note how the names of the files correspond with the tables of this database. To do this on a Mac, you may need to change the permissions for the directory to give yourself the read privilege for the directory. If the data directory contains any log files, note the names of these files.

6. Use the Explorer (Windows) or the Finder (Mac) to find MySQL's configuration file. Note the directory and name of this file on your computer.

7. Use MySQL Workbench's Admin tab to enable the error log and the binary log. Use whatever directories and names you want for the logs. If you get an error indicating that access is denied, you may need to stop Workbench and run it as an administrator. After you enable these logs, restart the server.

8. Use MySQL Workbench's Admin tab to view the error log. Note that it includes messages about the startup and shutdown of the server.

9. Write and execute an INSERT statement that inserts a new row into the Invoices table.

10. Use the mysqlbinlog program to convert the most recent binary file of the binary log to a text file. Next, use a text editor to view that text file. Search for the INSERT statement and view it. Note that the binary log sets a timestamp for the exact time the INSERT statement was executed before it logs the statement.

11. Use a SET statement to temporarily enable the general log. Then, to make sure that this variable was set, use a SELECT statement to view the variable. If you get an error indicating that access is denied, you may need to stop Workbench and run it as an administrator.

12. Use a SELECT statement to select all rows from the Invoices table.

13. Use MySQL Workbench's Admin tab to view the general log. Note that it includes the SELECT statement from the previous step.

14. Use a SET statement to disable the general log. Then, to make sure that this variable was set, use a SELECT statement to view the variable.

15. Use MySQL Workbench's Admin tab to disable the binary log. Then, restart server.

18

How to secure a database

If you have installed MySQL on your own computer and you have only been working with sample databases, security hasn't been a concern. However, when you use MySQL in a production environment, you must configure security to prevent misuse of your data. In this chapter, you'll learn how to do that by writing SQL statements to create users that have restricted access to your database. In addition, you'll learn how to use MySQL Workbench to perform many of the security-related tasks that you can perform with SQL code.

An introduction to user accounts **492**
An introduction to SQL statements for user accounts 492
A summary of privileges 494
The four privilege levels 498
The grant tables in the mysql database 498

How to work with users and privileges **500**
How to create, rename, and drop users 500
How to specify user account names 502
How to grant privileges 504
How to view privileges 506
How to revoke privileges 508
How to change passwords 510
A script that creates users 512

How to use MySQL Workbench **514**
How to use the Admin tab to work with users 514
How to use the SQL Editor tab to connect as a user for testing................ 518

Perspective **522**

An introduction to user accounts

Before you learn the details of managing database security, you should have a general idea of how user accounts work. That's what you'll learn in this topic.

An introduction to SQL statements for user accounts

Figure 18-1 presents a script that contains the SQL statements that are used to create two users and grant them privileges. You'll learn more about how the statements in this script work later in this chapter. For now, we just want to introduce you to the concepts of users and privileges.

This script starts with CREATE USER statements that create two users, named ap_admin and ap_user. Both users can only connect from the local server, and both have a password of "pa55word". Although this password isn't realistic, it illustrates how these statements work.

After the users are created, the GRANT statements set up privileges for each user. Here, the user named ap_admin is granted all the privileges on the AP database. As a result, this user can select, insert, update, and delete data from the tables of the AP database. In addition, this user has many other privileges such as creating or dropping tables, indexes, and views in the AP database. In contrast, the user named ap_user can only select, insert, update, and delete data in the AP database.

If you want to view the privileges for a user, you can use the SHOW GRANTS statement. In this figure, for example, you can see the privileges for the user named ap_admin.

A script that creates two users and grants them privileges

```
CREATE USER ap_admin@localhost IDENTIFIED BY 'pa55word';
CREATE USER ap_user@localhost IDENTIFIED BY 'pa55word';

GRANT ALL
ON ap.*
TO ap_admin@localhost;

GRANT SELECT, INSERT, DELETE, UPDATE
ON ap.*
TO ap_user@localhost;
```

A statement that displays the privileges for the ap_admin user

```
SHOW GRANTS FOR ap_admin@localhost
```

Grants for ap_admin@localhost
GRANT USAGE ON *.* TO 'ap_admin'@'localhost' IDENTIFIED BY PASSWORD '*F71B0AF6B232C58021B6AC63A29FCF13A4E46E59'
GRANT ALL PRIVILEGES ON `ap`.* TO 'ap_admin'@'localhost'

Description

- You use the CREATE USER statement to create a user that has no privileges.
- You use the GRANT statement to grant privileges to a user.
- You use the SHOW GRANTS statement to view the privileges for a user.
- For a partial list of privileges that can be granted, see figure 18-2.

Figure 18-1   An introduction to SQL statements for user accounts

A summary of privileges

Figure 18-2 summarizes some of the common *privileges* that a database user can have. To start, a user can have privileges to work with the data that's stored in a database. These privileges allow a user to execute DML statements, such as the SELECT, UPDATE, INSERT, and DELETE statements. They also allow a user to execute stored procedures and functions. These are the most common types of privileges, since most users need to be able to work with the data that's stored in a database.

A user can also have privileges to modify the definition of a database. These privileges allow a user to execute DDL statements such as the CREATE TABLE, ALTER TABLE, DROP TABLE, CREATE INDEX, and DROP INDEX statements. These privileges are common for administrative users of a database such as database administrators and programmers, but they aren't commonly granted to the end users of a database.

In addition, a user can have privileges to work with the stored programs of a database. These privileges allow a user to execute the statements that you learned about in chapters 15 and 16. For example, the CREATE ROUTINE privilege allows you to execute the CREATE PROCEDURE and CREATE FUNCTION statements.

Object Privileges

Privileges for working with data

Privilege	Description
SELECT	Select data from a table.
INSERT	Insert data into a table.
UPDATE	Update data in a table.
DELETE	Delete data from a table.
EXECUTE	Execute a stored procedure or function.

Privileges for modifying the database structure

Privilege	Description
CREATE	Create a database or a table.
ALTER	Alter a table.
DROP	Drop a database or a table.
INDEX	Create or drop an index.
CREATE VIEWS	Create views.
CREATE ROUTINE	Create a stored procedure or function.
ALTER ROUTINE	Alter or drop a stored procedure or function.
TRIGGER	Create or drop a trigger on a table.
EVENT	Create, alter, drop, or view an event for a database.

Description

- The *privileges* a user has to work with a database control the operations that the user can perform on the database.
- Privileges for working with the data in a database are typically given to all users of the database, include end users.
- Privileges for modifying the structure of a database are typically given to database administrators and programmers.

Figure 18-2   A summary of privileges (part 1 of 2)

The privileges you learned about in part 1 of figure 18-2 are called *object privileges* because they allow the user to create and work with database objects, such as tables, views, and stored procedures. The exact privileges that are available for an object depend on the type of object. In contrast to object privileges, *administrative privileges* allow the user to create new user accounts, show the databases available from the server, shut down the server, and reload the tables that store the privileges for users. These privileges are listed in the first table in part 2 of this figure.

The second table lists some other privileges you'll use frequently. The ALL privilege grants all privileges available at the specified level except the GRANT OPTION privilege. In general, you only grant the ALL privilege to users like database administrators or programmers. In some cases, you may also want to grant these users the GRANT OPTION privilege. If you do, they can grant privileges to other users.

The USAGE privilege doesn't grant any privileges to a user. In most cases, you'll use this privilege when you want to modify other attributes of a user account, such as the password. In that case, this privilege indicates that the existing privileges for the user shouldn't be changed. You'll see an example of how this works later in this chapter.

Before you go on, you should know that MySQL provides many privileges other than the ones shown here. As a result, if the privileges presented in this chapter aren't adequate for your security needs, you can refer to the MySQL Reference Manual for more information. To get started, you can search for "privileges provided" or "privileges". You can also use the SHOW PRIVILEGES statement to view a list of all the privileges that are available.

Administrative privileges

Privilege	Description
CREATE USER	Create new user accounts.
RELOAD	Reload the tables that store the privileges for the users of the database. This refreshes these tables if they have been modified.
SHOW DATABASES	Show the names of all databases on the server.
SHUTDOWN	Shut down the server.

Other privileges

Privilege	Description
ALL [PRIVILEGES]	All privileges available at the specified level except the GRANT OPTION privilege.
GRANT OPTION	Allows a user to grant his or her privileges to other users.
USAGE	No privileges. It can be used to modify existing accounts without changing the privileges for that account.

Description

- *Object privileges* allow the user to create and work with database objects such as tables, views, and stored procedures. The privileges that are available for an object depend on the type of object.

- *Administrative privileges* allow the user to create users, grant privileges, and manage operations on the server. They are not specific to a particular database.

- To see a list of available privileges and their definitions, use the SHOW PRIVILEGES statement.

Figure 18-2   A summary of privileges (part 2 of 2)

The four privilege levels

To understand how privileges work, you need to understand that MySQL grants them at the four different levels shown in the first table in figure 18-3: global, database, table, and column. *Global privileges* provide a user access to all the tables in all the databases. *Database privileges* provide a user access to all tables in a specific database. *Table privileges* provide a user access to all columns on a specified table. And *Column privileges* provide a user access only to specific columns on specific tables. You'll see how to provide privileges at all these levels when you see examples of the GRANT statement in figure 18-6.

The grant tables in the mysql database

To store user and privilege information, MySQL uses the *grant tables* in an internal database named mysql. The second table in figure 18-3 summarizes these tables. To start, the table named User stores the usernames, passwords, and global privileges for all users on the server. Then, the table named DB stores information about the database privileges for each user. Finally, the last three tables store information about table privileges, column privileges, and privileges for accessing stored procedures and functions.

When you grant users access to the databases on a server, you typically want to restrict all users other than administrative users from accessing the mysql database. That's because, if a user has access to the mysql database, he or she can change the user or privilege information directly. For example, the user could insert a row into the User table to create a user with global privileges, or the user could change the privileges of other users. If you restrict access to administrative users, though, this security risk is greatly reduced.

The four privilege levels

Level	Description
Global	All databases and all tables.
Database	All tables in the specified database.
Table	All columns in the specified table.
Column	Only the specified column or columns.

A summary of the grant tables in the mysql database

Table name	Description
user	Stores the usernames and passwords for all users on the server. In addition, stores the global privileges that apply to all databases on the server.
db	Stores the database privileges.
tables_priv	Stores the table privileges.
columns_priv	Stores the column privileges.
procs_priv	Stores the privileges for accessing stored procedures and functions.

Description

- You can use MySQL to grant privileges at four different levels, as shown in the first table above.

- MySQL stores all users for the server and their privileges in *grant tables* in an internal database named mysql.

Figure 18-3   MySQL's privilege levels and grant tables

How to work with users and privileges

Now that you have a basic understanding of users and privileges, you're ready to learn the details for working with users and privileges. This includes creating and dropping users, granting and revoking privileges, and changing the password for an existing user.

How to create, rename, and drop users

Figure 18-4 shows how to work with users. To start, when you use the CREATE USER statement, you typically specify the name of the user, followed by the @ sign, followed by the name of the host that the user can connect from. This is usually followed by the IDENTIFIED BY clause, which specifies a password for the user. This is illustrated in the first example in this figure. Here, the CREATE USER statement creates a user named joel that can connect from the host named localhost with a password of "sesame". In other words, joel can only connect from the same computer where MySQL server is running.

If you don't use the @ sign to specify a host, MySQL uses a percent sign (%) as the name of the host. This indicates that the user can connect from any host. In the second example, for instance, the CREATE USER statement creates a user named jane that can connect from any host with a password of "sesame".

After you use the CREATE USER statement to create a user, the user has no privileges. However, you can use the GRANT statement to assign privileges to the user. You'll learn more about using this statement in figure 18-6.

The third example uses the RENAME USER statement to change the name of the user named joel@localhost to joelmurach@localhost. If this user has privileges, the privileges are transferred to the new name.

The fourth and fifth examples use the DROP USER statement to drop the users named joelmurach@localhost and jane@%. This deletes these user accounts and their privileges from the mysql database. Remember that the users are for all the databases on the server, though. So before you drop a user, you should check with anyone else who is using the server to make sure that the user isn't needed.

How to create a user

The syntax of the CREATE USER statement

```
CREATE USER username IDENTIFIED BY password
```

A statement that creates a user from a specific host

```
CREATE USER joel@localhost IDENTIFIED BY 'sesame'
```

A statement that creates a user from any host

```
CREATE USER jane IDENTIFIED BY 'sesame'     -- creates jane@%
```

How to rename a user

The syntax of the RENAME USER statement

```
RENAME USER username TO new_username
```

A statement that renames a user from a specific host

```
RENAME USER joel@localhost TO joelmurach@localhost
```

How to drop a user

The syntax of the DROP USER statement

```
DROP USER username
```

A statement that drops a user from a specific host

```
DROP USER joelmurach@localhost
```

A statement that drops a user from any host

```
DROP USER jane                                  -- drops jane@%
```

Description

- You use the CREATE USER statement to create a user that has no privileges.
- If you want to specify the host that a user can connect from, you can code the username, followed by the @ character, followed by the hostname.
- If you create a user without specifying a hostname, MySQL uses a percent sign (%) as a wildcard character to indicate that the user can connect from any host.
- You can use the RENAME USER statement to change the name of a user.
- You can use the DROP USER statement to drop a user.

Figure 18-4   How to create, rename, and drop users

How to specify user account names

In the last figure, you saw some examples of user account names. Now, figure 18-5 presents the details for coding these names. Here, the first example shows the account name for a user named john who can connect only from the local host.

The second example shows how to code an account name for the same user using quotation marks. In this example, neither the username nor the hostname contains special characters. As a result, these quotation marks are optional.

In this book, we typically code the quotation marks only when they're necessary. However, some programmers prefer to always code them for consistency. Also, when we use quotes in this book, we typically use single quotation marks ('). However, you can use double quotation marks (") or backticks (`) if you prefer.

The third example shows yet another way to code the same user as the first example. For the host, this example uses an IP address of 127.0.0.1, which is synonymous with the localhost keyword. Although it isn't shown in this figure, you can use an IP address to identify a remote server too if necessary.

The fourth example shows how to create a user that can connect from any host, local or remote. In this example, the account name doesn't use the @ sign to specify a host. As a result, MySQL automatically uses the percent sign (%) wildcard character for the hostname. This indicates that the user can connect from any host.

The fifth example shows how to explicitly code the hostname for a user that can connect from any computer. In this example, the percent sign (%) must be enclosed in quotes because it's a special character.

The sixth and seventh examples show an account name for a user that can connect from a host for a specific domain. Since, the percent sign is coded before the domain name, the user can connect from any computer within a domain name that ends with murach.com. In both examples, the hostname must be enclosed in quotes since it includes the percent sign (%). In addition, the username in the seventh example must be enclosed in quotes since it includes dashes (-).

The syntax of an account name

```
username[@hostname]
```

A user that can only connect from the same server as MySQL

```
john@localhost
```

The same user with optional quotation marks

```
'john'@'localhost'
```

The same user with an IP address instead of the localhost keyword

```
john@127.0.0.1
```

A user that can connect from any computer

```
john
```

The same user but with the wildcard character explicitly coded

```
john@'%'
```

A user that can only connect from the murach.com domain

```
john@'%.murach.com'
```

A username that needs to be coded with quotes

```
'quinn-the-mighty'@'%.murach.com'
```

Description

- If you want to specify the host that a user can connect from, you can code the username, followed by the @ character, followed by the hostname.

- If you specify a user without specifying a hostname, MySQL uses a percent sign (%) as a wildcard character to indicate that the user can connect from any host.

- The username and hostname do not need to be quoted if they are legal as unquoted identifiers. Quotes are necessary to specify a username string containing special characters such as a dash (-), or a hostname string containing special characters or wildcard characters such as a percent sign (%).

- You can use single quotation marks ('), double quotation marks ("), or backticks (`) to enclose a username or hostname.

Figure 18-5   How to specify user account names

How to grant privileges

In general, it's a good practice to use the CREATE USER statement to create users and the GRANT statement to grant privileges. However, MySQL allows you to use the GRANT statement to create users and grant privileges in a single statement. The examples in figure 18-6 illustrate how this statement works.

The first statement creates a user that has no privileges. In other words, the result is the same as using the CREATE USER statement. This user has a name of joel, a host of localhost, and a password of sesame. Because the ON clause is required, it's coded with an asterisk for both the database name and table name. These asterisks are wildcards that indicate that the user has privileges on all databases and all tables, even though no privileges are given. In other words, this user is given a global privilege level.

The second statement creates a user named jim@% and grants all privileges on all databases to that user. To do that, this statement uses the ALL privilege and grants these privileges at the global level (*.*). Finally, this statement includes the WITH GRANT OPTION clause. This grants the GRANT OPTION privilege to the user. As a result, the user can grant privileges to other users.

Although using the ALL keyword makes it easy to grant all privileges to a user, it also makes it easy to grant more privileges than the user needs. And that can make your database less secure. In general, then, it's a good practice to grant a user just the privileges that he or she needs.

To grant all privileges to a user, you must connect as a user such as the root user that has the appropriate privileges. If you connect as another user, that user must have the GRANT OPTION privilege to grant privileges to other users. In that case, though, even if you use the ALL keyword, only the privileges that the current user has are granted to the other users.

The third statement creates a user named ap_user@localhost and grants the SELECT, INSERT, UPDATE, and DELETE privileges on all tables in the AP database to that user. To do that, the ON clause specifies the name of the database, followed by a dot, followed by an asterisk to specify all tables. The fourth statement grants just SELECT, INSERT, and UPDATE privileges to all tables in all databases. The fifth statement grants these privileges on all tables in the AP database. And the sixth statement grants privileges on just the Vendors table in the AP database.

The seventh statement grants privileges to specific columns of a table. Specifically, it grants the SELECT privilege on three columns of the Vendors table, but it only grants the UPDATE privilege on one column. To do that, the column names are listed in parentheses after each privilege. Most of the time, you won't need to grant privileges at the column level, but you can do it if necessary.

The eighth statement assumes that the AP database is the current database. As a result, this statement doesn't specify the database name. Since this makes it easier to work with the privileges of a database, it often makes sense to select the database before working with the privileges of its users.

The syntax of the GRANT statement

```
GRANT privilege_list
ON [db_name.]table
TO user1 [IDENTIFIED BY 'password1'][,
    user2 [IDENTIFIED BY 'password2']]...
[WITH GRANT OPTION]
```

A statement that creates a user with no privileges

```
GRANT USAGE
ON *.*
TO joel@localhost IDENTIFIED BY 'sesame'
```

A statement that creates a user with global privileges

```
GRANT ALL
ON *.*
TO jim IDENTIFIED BY 'supersecret'
WITH GRANT OPTION
```

A statement that creates a user with database privileges

```
GRANT SELECT, INSERT, UPDATE, DELETE
ON ap.*
TO ap_user@localhost IDENTIFIED BY 'pa55word'
```

A statement that grants global privileges to a user

```
GRANT SELECT, INSERT, UPDATE
ON *.* TO ap_user@localhost
```

A statement that grants database privileges to a user

```
GRANT SELECT, INSERT, UPDATE
ON ap.* TO joel@localhost
```

A statement that grants table privileges to a user

```
GRANT SELECT, INSERT, UPDATE
ON ap.vendors TO joel@localhost
```

A statement that grants column privileges to a user

```
GRANT SELECT (vendor_name, vendor_state, vendor_zip_code),
      UPDATE (vendor_address1)
ON ap.vendors TO joel@localhost
```

A statement that uses the current database

```
GRANT SELECT, INSERT, UPDATE, DELETE
ON vendors TO ap_user@localhost
```

Description

- You use the GRANT statement to grant privileges to a user. If the user account doesn't exist, the user is created.

- The ON clause determines the level at which the privileges are granted. You can use the asterisk (*) to specify all databases or tables. If you don't specify a database, MySQL uses the current database.

- The WITH GRANT OPTION clause allows the user to grant their privileges to other users.

Figure 18-6   How to grant privileges

How to view privileges

When you're done granting or revoking privileges, you may want to view the privileges that have been granted to make sure that you have granted the correct privileges to each user. To do that, you can use the techniques described in figure 18-7.

To start, if you want to get a list of users for the current server, you can use a SELECT statement like the one shown in the first example. This statement queries the table named User in the mysql database.

In this figure, the server has six users. Here, the root user is the admin user for MySQL. Note that the Host column for this user specifies localhost. Similarly, the users named joel, ap_user, and ap_admin have a Host value of localhost. In contrast, the users named jim and jane have a Host value of %.

Once you know the names of the users and hosts, you can use the SHOW GRANTS statement to view the privileges for a user. For instance, the second example shows how to view the privileges for a user from any host. In particular, it shows how to view the privileges for the user named jim@%. The result set for this user shows that it has all privileges, including the GRANT OPTION privilege for all tables and databases on the server.

The third example shows how to view the privileges for a user from a specific host. In particular, it shows how to view the privileges for the user named ap_user@localhost. Here, the result set shows that this user has a global USAGE privilege (*.*). By itself, this privilege only allows the user to view the mysql database. It doesn't allow the user to view or work with any other databases. However, this user also has SELECT, INSERT, UPDATE, and DELETE privileges for all tables on the database named AP. As a result, it can work with the data in that database.

The fourth example shows how to view the privileges for the current user. To do that, you can execute a SHOW GRANTS statement without a FOR clause. Here, the result set is for the root user. This user has all privileges, include the GRANT OPTION privilege. This user also has the PROXY privilege, which allows the user to impersonate another user.

A statement that displays a list of users

```
SELECT User, Host FROM mysql.user
```

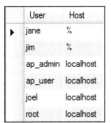

User	Host
jane	%
jim	%
ap_admin	localhost
ap_user	localhost
joel	localhost
root	localhost

The syntax of the SHOW GRANTS statement

```
SHOW GRANTS [FOR user]
```

A statement that shows the privileges for a user from any host

```
SHOW GRANTS FOR jim
```

Grants for jim@%
GRANT ALL PRIVILEGES ON *.* TO 'jim'@'%' IDENTIFIED BY PASSWORD '*90BA3AC0BFDE07AE334CA523CB27167AE33825B9' WITH GRANT O|

A statement that shows the privileges for a user from a specific host

```
SHOW GRANTS FOR ap_user@localhost
```

Grants for ap_user@localhost
GRANT USAGE ON *.* TO 'ap_user'@'localhost' IDENTIFIED BY PASSWORD '*F71B0AF6B232C58021B6AC63A29FCF13A4E46E59'
GRANT SELECT, INSERT, UPDATE, DELETE ON 'ap'.* TO 'ap_user'@'localhost'

A statement that shows the privileges for the current user

```
SHOW GRANTS
```

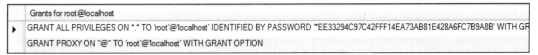

Grants for root@localhost
GRANT ALL PRIVILEGES ON *.* TO 'root'@'localhost' IDENTIFIED BY PASSWORD '*EE33294C97C42FFF14EA73AB81E428A6FC7B9A8B' WITH GR
GRANT PROXY ON ''@'' TO 'root'@'localhost' WITH GRANT OPTION

Description

- You can query the User table in the mysql database to get a list of users for the current MySQL server.
- You can use the SHOW GRANTS statement to display the privileges for a user.

Figure 18-7 How to view privileges

How to revoke privileges

After you've created users and granted privileges to them, you may need to revoke privileges. For example, you may need to revoke some or all of a user's privileges if the user abuses those privileges. To do that, you can use the REVOKE statement as shown in figure 18-8. Since this statement works similarly to the GRANT statement, you shouldn't have much trouble using it.

Here, the first statement shows how to revoke all privileges from a user named jim. To do that, you can code a REVOKE statement that uses the ALL keyword to revoke all privileges. In addition, you must specify GRANT OPTION to revoke the GRANT OPTION privilege. This revokes all privileges from the user on all databases. To be able to use this syntax, you must be logged in as a user that has the CREATE USER privilege. Otherwise, you won't have the privileges you need to execute the REVOKE statement.

The second statement works like the first statement. However, it revokes all privileges from two users. To do that, this statement separates the usernames in the FROM clause with a comma.

The third statement revokes specific privileges from a user. To do that, you separate the privileges with a comma. For example, this statement revokes the UPDATE and DELETE privileges on the Invoices table in the AP database from the user named joel@localhost. To be able to use this syntax, you must be logged in as a user that has the GRANT OPTION privilege and the privilege that you're revoking.

Although the REVOKE statement removes privileges, it doesn't remove the user from the database that MySQL uses to keep track of users. To remove a user account entirely, use the DROP USER statement described in figure 18-4.

The syntax of the REVOKE statement for all privileges

```
REVOKE ALL[ PRIVILEGES], GRANT OPTION
FROM user1[, user2]...
```

A statement that revokes all privileges from a user

```
REVOKE ALL, GRANT OPTION
FROM jim
```

A statement that revokes all privileges from multiple users

```
REVOKE ALL, GRANT OPTION
FROM ap_admin, joel@localhost
```

The syntax of the REVOKE statement for specific privileges

```
REVOKE privilege_list
ON [db_name.]table
FROM user1[, user2]...
```

A statement that revokes specific privileges from a user

```
REVOKE UPDATE, DELETE
ON ap.invoices FROM joel@localhost
```

Description

- You can use the REVOKE statement to revoke privileges from a user.
- To revoke all privileges, you must have the global CREATE USER privilege.
- To revoke specific privileges, you must have the GRANT OPTION privilege and you must have the privileges that you are revoking.

Note

- To completely delete a user account, use the DROP USER statement described in figure 18-4.

Figure 18-8   How to revoke privileges

How to change passwords

To change a password, you can use the SET PASSWORD statement as shown in figure 18-9. To change the password for a user other than the user who's currently logged on, you include the FOR clause on the SET PASSWORD statement to identify the user. For this to work, the current user must have the UPDATE privilege. To change the password for the current user, you can omit the FOR clause.

You can also change a password using a GRANT statement like the one shown in this figure. Here, the USAGE privilege is used so the user's current privileges aren't changed. Then, the IDENTIFIED BY clause is used to specify the new password.

For security reasons, you should always assign a password to each user. To make sure that every user has a password, you can execute a SELECT statement like the one in this figure. This statement retrieves information from the User table of the mysql database for all users who don't have a password. In this case, the SELECT statement returned an empty result set, which indicates that all users have been assigned passwords. However, if this statement returns a result set, you can set a password for each user in the result set. Or, if those users aren't needed, you can drop them.

The syntax of the SET PASSWORD statement

```
SET PASSWORD [FOR user] = PASSWORD('password')
```

A statement that changes a user's password

```
SET PASSWORD FOR john = PASSWORD('pa55word')
```

A statement that changes the current user's password

```
SET PASSWORD = PASSWORD('secret')
```

A GRANT statement that changes a user's password

```
GRANT USAGE ON *.* TO john IDENTIFIED BY 'pa55word'
```

A SELECT statement that selects all users that don't have passwords

```
SELECT Host, User
FROM mysql.user
WHERE Password = ''
```

Description

- To change a user's password, use the SET PASSWORD statement.
- To change the password for another user's account, you must have the UPDATE privilege.
- You can change the current user's password by using the SET PASSWORD statement without a FOR clause.
- You can also change a password using the GRANT statement with the USAGE privilege and an IDENTIFIED BY clause.
- To be sure you've assigned passwords to all users, you can select data from the User table of the mysql database for all users without passwords.

Figure 18-9   How to change passwords

A script that creates users

Figure 18-10 presents a script that creates users and grants privileges for the AP database. This script starts with DROP USER statements that delete the users named john, jane, jim, and joel if they exist. If a user doesn't exist, the statement that deletes that user causes an error. As a result, you should omit these statements if you know that the users don't already exist.

The CREATE USER statements create the users named john, jane, jim, and joel. To make it easy to remember the passwords for these users, this script assigns a password of "sesame" to all four users. Of course, if you really wanted to secure the database, you would need to assign a different, more cryptic password to each user.

After the CREATE USER statements execute, the users exist but they don't have any privileges. Then, the GRANT statements grant specific privileges to each user. Here, because the user named joel is a developer, he is given access to all databases and tables on the server. In addition, he is given the GRANT OPTION privilege. As a result, he can work with the data or structure of any table of any database on the server. However, he can only connect from the local host. This helps prevent hackers from connecting as this user. In general, it's considered a best practice to limit connectivity in this way whenever possible, especially for administrative users.

Unlike the user named joel, the user named jim can only work with data in the AP database. In other words, jim can't modify the structure of the AP database by adding, altering, or dropping objects. That makes sense because jim is a manager, not an administrator. However, jim can grant all of his privileges to other users. For example, he might need to grant privileges to users that he manages. In addition, jim can connect from any host computer. Although this is a security risk, at least a hacker who is able to connect as jim only has access to the AP database.

The users named john and jane have the fewest privileges, since they are end users. These users can work with data in the AP database, but only with the specified tables and privileges. Specifically, they can select, insert, update, and delete data in the Vendors, Invoices, and Invoice_Line_Items tables. However, they can only select data from the General_Ledger_Accounts and Terms tables. Like jim, these users can connect from a computer on any host. Again, this is a security risk, but a hacker who can connect as john or jane has even fewer privileges and can do less damage.

A script that sets up the users and privileges for a database

```
-- drop the users (causes an error if they don't exist yet)
DROP USER john;
DROP USER jane;
DROP USER jim;
DROP USER joel@localhost;

-- create the users
CREATE USER john IDENTIFIED BY 'sesame';
CREATE USER jane IDENTIFIED BY 'sesame';
CREATE USER jim IDENTIFIED BY 'sesame';
CREATE USER joel@localhost IDENTIFIED BY 'sesame';

-- grant privileges to a developer (joel)
GRANT ALL ON *.* TO joel@localhost WITH GRANT OPTION;

-- grant privileges to the ap manager (jim)
GRANT SELECT, INSERT, UPDATE, DELETE ON ap.* TO jim WITH GRANT OPTION;

-- grant privileges to ap users (john, jane)
GRANT SELECT, INSERT, UPDATE, DELETE ON ap.vendors TO john, jane;
GRANT SELECT, INSERT, UPDATE, DELETE ON ap.invoices TO john, jane;
GRANT SELECT, INSERT, UPDATE, DELETE ON ap.invoice_line_items TO john,
jane;
GRANT SELECT ON ap.general_ledger_accounts TO john, jane;
GRANT SELECT ON ap.terms TO john, jane;
```

Figure 18-10   A script that creates users

How to use MySQL Workbench

Since you often use SQL statements to set up the users for a database or to view the privileges that have been granted to a user, it's important to understand the SQL statements presented in this chapter. Once you understand them, you can use MySQL Workbench to work with security. For example, you can use MySQL Workbench to drop or alter an existing user or to grant or revoke the privileges for a user.

How to use the Admin tab to work with users

Figure 18-11 shows how you can work with users using MySQL Workbench. Here, you can see the Users and Privileges window that's displayed when you select the "Manage Security" link from the Server Administration section of the Home tab and then select the Users and Privileges option.

To work with the login information for a user, display the Login tab within the Server Access Management tab as shown in the first screen. Then, you can select a user to display or change the login information for that user. You can also click the Revoke All Privileges button to revoke all the user's privileges. And you can click the Remove button to remove the user. Both of these operations require confirmation.

You can also add an account from the Server Access Management tab. To do that, just click the Add Account button, enter the login information in the Login tab, and click the Apply button.

To view the database privileges for a user, display the Schema Privileges tab, select the user, and select a host and schema combination as shown in the second screen. Then, you can use the check boxes at the bottom of the tab to change the privileges. You can also add a new host/schema combination by clicking the Add Entry button and completing the resulting dialog box. And you can delete a host/schema combination by clicking the Delete Entry button.

As you learned earlier in this chapter, you can also assign privileges to specific tables and columns. However, MySQL Workbench doesn't currently provide a way to view or change privileges at these levels.

The Server Access Management tab

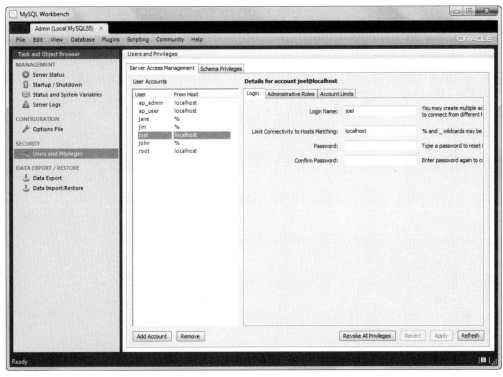

The Schema Privileges tab

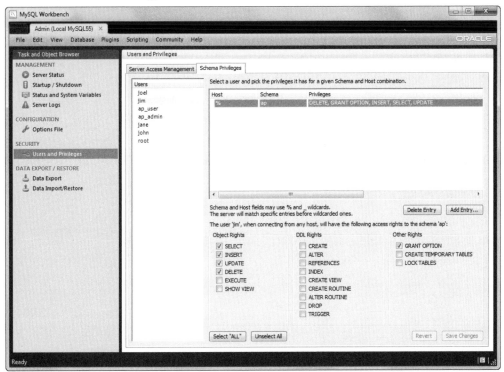

Figure 18-11   How to use the Admin tab to work with users (part 1 of 2)

To view the global privileges for a user, you select the user from the Administrative Roles tab of the Server Access Management tab as shown in the screen in part 2 of figure 18-11. This tab displays a list of pre-defined administrative roles that grant common privileges for those roles. You can use these roles to quickly set up the privileges that are appropriate for different types of database administrators, managers, and designers. In this figure, for example, you can see that the user named joel is assigned to several roles. Then the list to the right of the roles indicates the specific privileges assigned to this user.

The Administrative Roles tab

Description

- To display the Users and Privileges window, click the "Manage Security" link in the Server Management section of the Home page, and then select the Users and Privileges option.

- To add or remove a user account or to revoke all privileges for a user, use the Server Access Management tab.

- To change a user's name, password, or host access options, use the Login tab of the Server Access Management tab.

- To view the database privileges for a user, use the Schema Privileges tab. You can also use this tab to change privileges and to add and remove host/schema access options.

- To view the global privileges for a user, use the Administrative Roles tab of the Server Access Management tab. You can also use the check boxes on this tab to assign privileges that are grouped as pre-defined administrative roles.

Figure 18-11   How to use the Admin tab to work with users (part 2 of 2)

How to use the SQL Editor tab
to connect as a user for testing

To test the username, password, and privileges for a user, you can connect as that user. To do that, you create a new connection for the user as described in figure 18-12.

To start, you display the Home tab and click on the "New Connection" link. Then, you enter the connection information in the resulting dialog box, including a connection name and a username. In this figure, for example, I'm creating a connection named jane for the user with the same name. Here, no hostname is specified because the user can connect from any host. Also, a default schema of AP is specified, so the AP database is used if no other database is selected.

After you create a connection for a user, the connection is added to the list of connections on the Home tab. Then, you can connect as that user by double-clicking on the connection and entering the user's password if necessary.

The Setup New Connection dialog box

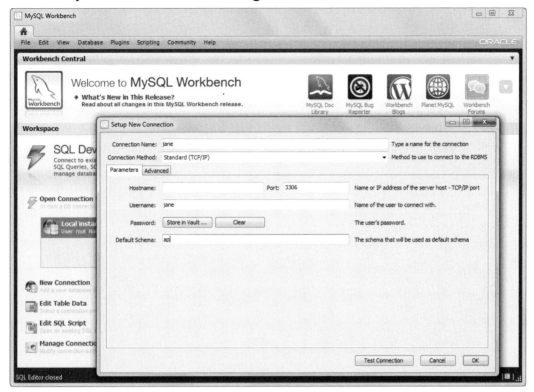

Description

- To create a connection for a user, start MySQL Workbench and display the Home tab if necessary. Then, click on the "New Connection" link in the SQL Development section, and enter the connection information in the resulting dialog box. That includes a name for the connection and a name for the user.

- To connect as a user that has a connection, double-click on the connection for the user in the list of connections, and enter the password for the user if necessary.

Figure 18-12   How to use the SQL Editor tab to connect as a user (part 1 of 2)

When you connect as a user, the name for the connection is displayed in the SQL Editor tab. Then, you can only view the databases and tables that the user has privileges to view. In part 2 of figure 18-12, for example, you can see that the user named jane only has access to five tables in the AP database. In addition, you can only modify the databases and tables that the user has privileges to modify.

To make sure that the user's privileges are working correctly, you can run SQL statements. In this figure, for example, I tried to insert a row into the Terms table. Because the user only has the SELECT privilege on this table, though, MySQL Workbench displayed an error indicating that the command was denied.

MySQL Workbench after connecting as jane

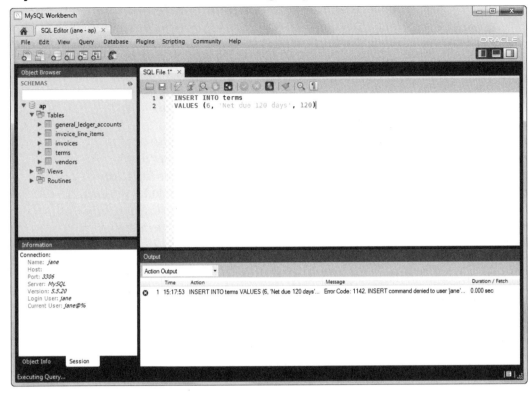

Description

- When you connect as a user, the name for the connection is displayed in the SQL Editor tab.

- When you connect as a user, you can only view the databases and tables that the user has privileges to view, and you can only modify the databases and tables that the user has privileges to modify.

Figure 18-12   How to use the SQL Editor tab to connect as a user (part 2 of 2)

Perspective

Although managing security can be complex, MySQL provides tools to simplify the job. In this chapter, you learned how to manage security by writing SQL statements, and you learned how to use MySQL Workbench to work with users and manage privileges. Once you're familiar with both of these techniques, you can use the one that's easiest for the security task at hand.

In addition to the skills presented in this chapter, you may also need to secure MySQL's file system if the server is running on a computer that has multiple users. That way other users who log in on that computer can't access any of the MySQL files that may contain sensitive data. That includes the data, log, and configuration files you learned about in chapter 17. Because the procedure for securing the file system varies depending on the operating system, this information isn't presented in this book.

You may also need to use SSL to secure the usernames and passwords of users who are allowed to connect remotely. In most cases, users connect locally. For example, a web server often runs on the same machine as the MySQL server. As a result, users of the web site use a local connection to connect to MySQL. If the MySQL server is on a different machine, though, you can learn about providing secure connections by looking up "Using SSL for Secure Connections" in the MySQL Reference Manual.

Terms

privilege
object privileges
administrative privileges
global privileges
database privileges
table privileges
column privileges
grant tables

Exercise

In this exercise, you will start by writing a script that creates a user with specific privileges. Then, you will use MySQL Workbench to connect as that user and test the user's privileges. Finally, you will use the GRANT statement to grant additional privileges to the user and to create a new user.

1. Use MySQL Workbench to connect as the root user.

2. Write a script that creates a user named ray@localhost with a password of "temp". This user should have SELECT, INSERT, and UPDATE privileges for the Vendors table of the AP database; SELECT, INSERT, and UPDATE privileges for the Invoices table; and SELECT and INSERT privileges for the Invoice_Line_Items table. This user should also have the right to grant privileges to other users. Run the script in MySQL Workbench.

3. Check the privileges for ray@localhost by using the SHOW GRANTS statement.

4. Use MySQL Workbench to create a connection for the user named ray@localhost and then connect as that user. Use the Object Browser to see which databases and tables this user can view.

5. Run a SELECT statement that selects the vendor_id column for all rows in the Vendors table. This statement should succeed.

6. Write a DELETE statement that attempts to delete one of the rows in the Vendors table. This statement should fail due to insufficient privileges.

7. Use MySQL Workbench to connect as the root user.

8. Grant the UPDATE privilege for the Invoice_Line_Items table to ray@localhost, and give the user the right to grant the same privilege to other users.

9. Write a GRANT statement that creates a user named dorothy with a password of "sesame", and grant this user privileges to select, insert, and update data from any table in the AP database. However, don't allow this user to delete any data from the database.

10. Check the privileges for dorothy by using the Admin tab of MySQL Workbench.

19

How to back up
and restore a database

When you work with a database that stores important data, you should have a plan for backing up that database regularly. Then, you need to execute that plan. That way, if the hard drive that stores the database fails, you can restore the database and minimize the amount of data that's lost. In this chapter, you'll learn how to backup and restore a database.

You'll also learn some skills that are related to backing up and restoring a database. For example, you'll learn how to import data from a text file and export data to a text file. In addition, you'll learn how to check and repair tables, which can save you from having to restore a table or database.

Strategies for backing up and restoring a database 526
A backup strategy 526
A restore strategy 526

How to back up a database 528
How use mysqldump to back up a database 528
A SQL script file for a database backup 530
How to set advanced options for a database backup 534

How to restore a database 536
How to use a SQL script file to restore a full backup 536
How to execute statements in the binary log 538
How to view and edit statements in the binary log 540

How to import and export data 542
How to export data to a file 542
How to import data from a file 544

How to check and repair tables 546
How to use the CHECK TABLE statement 546
How to use the REPAIR TABLE statement 548
How to repair an InnoDB table 548
How to use the mysqlcheck program 550
How to use the myisamchk program 552

Perspective 554

Strategies for backing up and restoring a database

One important task of a database administrator is to regularly *back up* the database. Then, if the database ever becomes corrupted, the database administrator can use the backup files to *restore* the database.

In this chapter, you'll learn the backup skills that you can use regardless of whether you have the Community Edition or the Enterprise Edition of MySQL. However, you should know that the Enterprise Edition of MySQL includes a backup tool known as MySQL Enterprise Backup that's designed to back up InnoDB tables. As a result, if you're using this edition with InnoDB tables, you may want to use the Enterprise Backup tool instead of the backup strategy presented in this chapter.

A backup strategy

MySQL provides for two types of backups. A *full backup* includes the structure and data of a database. To create a full backup, you can use the mysqldump program as described later in this chapter. This creates a SQL script file that can be used to recreate the database. You should create a full backup at regular intervals. For a medium-size database for a web site, for example, you might want to create a full backup once a week.

When you use the mysqldump program, it locks all tables so other users can't update the database while it's being backed up. As a result, it's a good practice to schedule this backup at a time of low traffic for the database.

An *incremental backup* contains changes that have been made since the last full backup. With the backup strategy shown in this figure, you enable the binary log as described in chapter 17 to create the incremental backups.

When you use this strategy, you shouldn't store your backup files (SQL scripts or log files) on the same hard drive where the MySQL server is running. If you do, those backup files will be lost if that hard drive fails. As a result, when you enable the binary log, it's a good practice to configure it so it writes to a directory on a different hard drive. This has the added benefit of balancing the load between two hard drives.

When you create a backup strategy, don't forget that the database named mysql stores information about the users and privileges for all databases on the server. As a result, you typically want to include this database in your backups.

A restore strategy

The goal of backing up your databases is to allow you to restore them to their exact state at any specified point in time. This is known as a *point-in-time recovery (PITR)*. To restore a database to a point in time, you can use the last full backup. Then, you can use the binary log to restore the database from the time of the last full backup to the specified point in time.

A strategy for backing up databases

1. Use the mysqldump program to regularly create full backups of each database. These backups should be stored in one or more SQL script files.

2. Enable the binary log as described in chapter 17 to create incremental backups.

A strategy for restoring databases

1. Use the mysql program to run the SQL script file for the last full backup. If necessary, you can edit the SQL script file before you execute it.

2. Use the mysqlbinlog program to execute all statements in the binary log that occurred after the last full backup. If necessary, you can edit the binary log before you execute its statements. For example, you can remove any statements that you don't want to execute.

Description

-   It's important for the database administrator to regularly *back up* the database. Then, if the database becomes corrupted, the database administrator can use the backup to *restore* the database.

-   A *full backup* includes the structure and content of a database. You should perform full backups according to a regular schedule.

-   An *incremental backup* only contains changes that have been made to the structure and content of a database since the last full backup.

-   You often want to include the database named mysql in your backups, since this database stores information about the users and privileges for all databases on the server.

-   You shouldn't store your backup files (SQL scripts or log files) on the same hard drive where the MySQL server is running. If you do, those backup files will be lost along with the databases if that hard drive fails.

-   A *point-in-time recovery* (PITR) allows you to restore the data up to any specified point in time.

Figure 19-1   Strategies for backing up and restoring databases

How to back up a database

Now that you understand the basic strategies for backing up and restoring a database, you're ready to learn the details of backing up a database.

How use mysqldump to back up a database

Figure 19-2 shows how to use the mysqldump program to back up, or *dump*, one or more databases into a SQL script file. To start, you display a command prompt and then use the cd command to change to MySQL's bin directory. This is the directory that stores the various MySQL command-line programs, including all of the programs described in this chapter. Just as in chapter 17, I use front slashes in this chapter to separate the directory and file names. However, you typically use backslashes on a Windows system.

After you change the directory, you can run the mysqldump program from the command prompt to perform a backup. To back up a single database using this program, you specify the name of the database on the mysqldump command. To backup multiple databases, you use the --databases or --all-databases option.

After you specify the databases to back up, you code a > character, followed by the path to the SQL script file where you want to store the backup. When you do that, it's generally considered a best practice to add a date to the end of your script file name. In this figure, for instance, all of the examples store the script file in the murach/mysql directory, and all of the SQL file names end with "2012-02-23".

Next, you code the -u option, followed by the name of a user with privileges to back up databases. In this figure, the program connects as the root user. Finally, you code the -p option so the program prompts for a password.

In addition to the --databases and --all-databases options, you often want to use the --single-transaction, --routines, and --events options when you back up a database. That way, your backup works correctly even if you're using transactions, and it includes stored routines and events. In addition, you may want to use the --flush-logs option so the server starts a new binary log file. This makes it easier to find the binary log file or files that you need if you restore the database later.

When you attempt to execute the mysqldump program, you may get an error that indicates that access is denied. To gain access, you can usually start the command prompt as an administrator. In Windows, for example, you can right-click on the icon that you use to start the Command Prompt window and select the "Run as administrator" command.

Similarly, if a firewall is running on your computer, it may attempt to block the mysqldump program. However, if you allow the mysqldump program to access the database, it should work properly.

Before I continue, you should know that you can also use MySQL Workbench to back up one or more databases to a SQL file. To do that, you open an Admin tab, select the Data Export option, select the "Export to Self-Contained File" option on the Object Selection tab, enter the path and name for the backup file, and click the Start Export button. However, as of Workbench 5.2.37, this

How to change to MySQL's bin directory

Using Windows
```
cd /program files/mysql/mysql server 5.5/bin
```

Using Mac OS X or Unix
```
cd /usr/local/mysql/bin
```

How to run the mysqldump program

For a single database
```
mysqldump ap > /murach/mysql/ap-2012-02-23.sql -u root -p
```

For specified databases
```
mysqldump --databases ap ex om mysql > /murach/mysql/backup-2012-02-23.sql
-u root -p
```

For all databases
```
mysqldump --all-databases > /murach/mysql/all-db-2012-02-23.sql -u root -p
```

With additional options
```
mysqldump --databases ap ex om mysql --single-transaction --routines
--events --flush-logs > /murach/mysql/backup-2012-02-23.sql -u root -p
```

Common options for the mysqldump program

Option	Description
`--databases`	Identifies the databases to be backed up.
`--all-databases`	Indicates that all databases should be backed up.
`--single-transaction`	Guarantees that the data seen by mysqldump does not change. This option should be used for databases that use InnoDB tables and transactions.
`--routines`	Include stored procedures and functions.
`--events`	Include events.
`--flush-logs`	Causes MySQL to create a new binary log file using the next number in the sequence.

Description

- You can use the mysqldump program to back up, or *dump*, one or more databases into a SQL script file.

- If you get an error that indicates that access is denied, you may need to start the command prompt as an administrator. In Windows, you can do that by right-clicking on the icon that you use to start the Command Prompt window and selecting the "Run as administrator" command.

- If a firewall is running on your computer, it may attempt to block the mysqldump program. However, if you allow the mysqldump program to access the database, it should work properly.

- On a Mac OS X system, you typically need to code a dot and slash (./) before the name of the mysqldump program to specify that it's in the current directory (the bin directory).

Figure 19-2   How to use mysqldump to back up a database

feature has some bugs that sometime prevent it from working correctly. In particular, the --single-transaction option doesn't work correctly on some systems. As a result, I recommend using the mysqldump program until these issues are resolved.

Another advantage of using the mysqldump program is that it's easier to automate. Although the details for doing this vary depending on the operating system, the same general principles apply to all operating systems. To start, you create a script file that executes the mysqldump command. Then, you use the operating system's task scheduler to execute that script file at a specified interval. For more information on using the task scheduler with your operating system, you can search the Internet.

A SQL script file for a database backup

Figure 19-3 shows an excerpt from a SQL script file for the last database backup you saw in the previous figure. This script starts with some comments that give some general information about this backup. For example, the first line includes information about the mysqldump program. Then, the third line identifies the host (localhost) and the database (AP). Unfortunately, only the first database in the backup is listed, which is probably a bug. Finally, the fifth line identifies the version of the MySQL server.

After the comments, this script includes several lines of code that are surrounded by the /*! and */ characters. These characters identify code that's specific to MySQL. As a result, a MySQL server uses this code, but another type of database server can ignore it. If, for example, you were porting a database from a MySQL server to an Oracle server, this would prevent Oracle from trying to execute these statements.

MySQL uses these statements to set some system variables, which are identified by a double at sign (@@). To do that, it uses some user-defined variables, which are identified by a single at sign (@). In most cases, the script sets these variables the way you want. As a result, you don't usually need to examine this code closely.

Immediately after the /*! characters, this script uses a number to indicate the minimum version of MySQL that's necessary to run the SET statement that follows. For example, 40101 indicates that MySQL 4.01.01 or later can run the statement. Similarly, 40014 indicates that MySQL 4.00.14 or later can run the statement.

After setting the session variables, this script includes a CREATE DATABASE statement that creates the AP database, followed by a USE statement that selects this database. The CREATE DATABASE statement includes an IF NOT EXISTS clause that's used if you're using MySQL 3.23.12 or later. Similarly, this statement includes a DEFAULT CHARACTER SET clause that's used if you're using MySQL 4.01.00 or later. Finally, this script surrounds the name of the database with backticks (`). Although this isn't necessary for the AP database, it's required for names that include spaces or other special characters.

Part of the SQL script file for a database backup   **Page 1**

```
-- MySQL dump 10.13  Distrib 5.5.18, for Win64 (x86)
--
-- Host: localhost    Database: ap
-- -------------------------------------------------------
-- Server version      5.5.18-log

/*!40101 SET @OLD_CHARACTER_SET_CLIENT=@@CHARACTER_SET_CLIENT */;
/*!40101 SET @OLD_CHARACTER_SET_RESULTS=@@CHARACTER_SET_RESULTS */;
/*!40101 SET @OLD_COLLATION_CONNECTION=@@COLLATION_CONNECTION */;
/*!40101 SET NAMES utf8 */;
/*!40103 SET @OLD_TIME_ZONE=@@TIME_ZONE */;
/*!40103 SET TIME_ZONE='+00:00' */;
/*!40014 SET @OLD_UNIQUE_CHECKS=@@UNIQUE_CHECKS, UNIQUE_CHECKS=0 */;
/*!40014 SET @OLD_FOREIGN_KEY_CHECKS=@@FOREIGN_KEY_CHECKS,
FOREIGN_KEY_CHECKS=0 */;
/*!40101 SET @OLD_SQL_MODE=@@SQL_MODE, SQL_MODE='NO_AUTO_VALUE_ON_ZERO' */;
/*!40111 SET @OLD_SQL_NOTES=@@SQL_NOTES, SQL_NOTES=0 */;


--
-- Current Database: `ap`
--

CREATE DATABASE /*!32312 IF NOT EXISTS*/ `ap` /*!40100 DEFAULT CHARACTER SET
latin1 */;

USE `ap`;
```

Description

- These scripts use two dashes (--) to identify comments.
- These scripts surround code in the /*! and */ characters to indicate that the code is specific to MySQL. As a result, a MySQL server can use that code, but another type of database server can ignore it.
- These scripts surround names with backticks (`). This allows for names that include spaces.

Figure 19-3   A SQL script file for a database backup (part 1 of 2)

If you only generate a backup for a single database, the SQL file for that backup won't include the CREATE DATABASE and USE statements. As a result, if you want to recreate the entire database, you need to add these statements to the script.

The script continues with the statements necessary to create the structure and content for the database. That includes the tables of the database, as well as the views, stored procedures, functions, triggers, and events. In part 2 of figure 19-3, you can see the statements for creating the Terms table. To start, a DROP TABLE statement drops the table if it exists. Then, a CREATE TABLE statement recreates the table.

Next, the script uses an INSERT statement to reload all the data into the table. But first, it uses a LOCK TABLES statement to prevent other users from writing data to this table while the script is executing. In addition, it uses an ALTER TABLE statement to disable the indexes for the table. Then, after the data has been inserted into the table, the script enables the indexes for the table. This improves the performance of the insert operations. Finally, the script uses an UNLOCK TABLES statement to allow other users to update this table.

After the SQL statements that create the database and its objects, this script sets some system variables. To do that, it uses some of the user-defined variables that were defined at the beginning of the script. Again, this usually works the way you want, so you don't usually have to examine this code closely.

The last line of this script is a comment that indicates the point in time that the mysqldump program finished creating this SQL file. If you need to restore a database later, you can use this date/time value as the start time for the statements that are stored in your binary log files.

Part of the SQL script file for a database backup   Page 2

```
--
-- Table structure for table `terms`
--

DROP TABLE IF EXISTS `terms`;
/*!40101 SET @saved_cs_client     = @@character_set_client */;
/*!40101 SET character_set_client = utf8 */;
CREATE TABLE `terms` (
  `terms_id` int(11) NOT NULL,
  `terms_description` varchar(50) NOT NULL,
  `terms_due_days` int(11) NOT NULL,
  PRIMARY KEY (`terms_id`)
) ENGINE=InnoDB DEFAULT CHARSET=latin1;
/*!40101 SET character_set_client = @saved_cs_client */;


--
-- Dumping data for table `terms`
--

LOCK TABLES `terms` WRITE;
/*!40000 ALTER TABLE `terms` DISABLE KEYS */;
INSERT INTO `terms` VALUES (1,'Net due 10 days',10),(2,'Net due 20
days',20),(3,'Net due 30 days',30),(4,'Net due 60 days',60),(5,'Net due 90
days',90);
/*!40000 ALTER TABLE `terms` ENABLE KEYS */;
UNLOCK TABLES;


--
-- SQL statement for the table structure and data for all other tables
-- and any triggers associated with those tables
--


--
-- SQL statements for all views, stored procedures, functions, and events
--


/*!40103 SET TIME_ZONE=@OLD_TIME_ZONE */;

/*!40101 SET SQL_MODE=@OLD_SQL_MODE */;
/*!40014 SET FOREIGN_KEY_CHECKS=@OLD_FOREIGN_KEY_CHECKS */;
/*!40014 SET UNIQUE_CHECKS=@OLD_UNIQUE_CHECKS */;
/*!40101 SET CHARACTER_SET_CLIENT=@OLD_CHARACTER_SET_CLIENT */;
/*!40101 SET CHARACTER_SET_RESULTS=@OLD_CHARACTER_SET_RESULTS */;
/*!40101 SET COLLATION_CONNECTION=@OLD_COLLATION_CONNECTION */;
/*!40111 SET SQL_NOTES=@OLD_SQL_NOTES */;
.
.
.
-- Dump completed on 2012-02-23 12:52:15
```

Figure 19-3   A SQL script file for a database backup (part 2 of 2)

How to set advanced options for a database backup

In most cases, the options for the mysqldump program are set the way you want. As a result, you typically only use the options shown in figure 19-2 to create database backups. However, the mysqldump program provides many advanced options, such as the ones shown in figure 19-4 that let you change the way the mysqldump program works. These options let you customize the generated SQL script file so it contains comments and SQL statements that work exactly the way you want.

For example, if you want to delete all old binary log files after the backup is complete, you can specify the --delete-master-logs option. In most cases, you don't want to do this in case there's a problem with the backup file. And you definitely don't want to do this if you're using replication, since it might prevent statements from being relayed to other servers. However, if you're confident in the backup file and you're not using replication, you might want to use this option since it removes old files that are no longer needed.

By default, most of the options in this figure are enabled. For example, the first six options are all enabled by default. As a result, you don't need to use the mysqldump program to specify these options. However, if you want to disable any of these options, you can preface them with "skip-". For example, to disable the --add-locks option, you can use the --skip-add-locks option.

If you want to disable the first four options in this figure, you can specify the --compact option. Then, the SQL script includes only the statements needed to back up the database. This takes less disk space, and it's particularly useful if you're creating a new database and you know that other users won't attempt to access this database as you're creating it.

Some advanced options for the mysqldump program

Option	Description
`--add-drop-table`	For each table, add a statement that drops the table before the statement that creates the table.
`--add-locks`	For each table, surround the INSERT statements with statements that lock and unlock the table.
`--disable-keys`	For each table, surround the INSERT statements with statements that disable and enable keys.
`--comments`	Include comments in the script.
`--quote-names`	Encloses names with backtick (`) characters.
`--create-options`	Includes all MySQL-specific options in CREATE TABLE statements.
`--compact`	Create a more compact SQL script that includes only the statements needed to back up the database. Using this option is the same as specifying the --skip-add-drop-table, --skip-add-locks, --skip-disable-keys, and --skip-comments options.
`--compress`	Use compression in server/client protocol.
`--delete-master-logs`	Deletes all binary log files after performing the dump.
`--force`	Continue even if the program encounters a SQL error.

How to use the "skip" prefix to disable an option

    --skip-add-drop-table

Description

- The mysqldump program contains many advanced options that you can use to control how it works.

- Many options that enable features also include a corresponding option for disabling the option. These options usually begin with "skip-".

- For a complete list of options for the mysqldump program, look up this program in the MySQL Reference Manual.

Figure 19-4   How to set advanced options for a database backup

How to restore a database

A backup of a database is only helpful if you can use it to restore the database in the event of a hardware failure or other problem. So that's what you'll learn to do in this topic.

How to use a SQL script file to restore a full backup

Figure 19-5 shows how to use the mysql program to restore a full backup of one or more databases. To do that, you just use the mysql program to run the SQL script file that contains the full backup.

In this figure, the first example restores the AP database by running the backup file for the AP database that was created by the first example in figure 19-2. Here, the mysql program specifies that you should run this backup file against the AP database. As a result, for this example to work properly, the AP database must exist on the MySQL server. If it doesn't, you must create this database before you run the backup file, or you must edit the backup file so it includes statements to create and select the database. You might edit the backup file, for example, if you're copying the database to another server.

On the other hand, the second example assumes that the backup file includes the statements that create the database or databases that you're restoring. As a result, you don't need to specify the name of the database on the mysql command. This example runs the file that was created by the second example in figure 19-2, which backs up four databases.

Before you restore a database from a script file, it's generally considered a good idea to back up the existing database. That way, if the restore operation doesn't work correctly, you can restore the database back to its previous state. In addition, it's usually a good idea to open the SQL file for the backup and view it to make sure it does what you want. Then, if it doesn't, you can edit this file so it works the way you want it to work. For example, if you only want to restore a single table, you can delete all other statements in the backup file.

You can also use MySQL Workbench to restore databases by running a SQL file that contains a full backup of those databases. To do that, open an Admin tab, select the Data Import/Restore option, select the "Import from Self-Contained File" option on the Import from Disk tab, enter the path and name for the backup file, and click the Start Import button. In most cases, this feature works correctly. If it doesn't, though, you can use the mysql program as described in this figure.

How to use the mysql program to restore databases

A single database
```
mysql ap < /murach/mysql/ap-2012-02-23.sql -u root -p
```

Multiple databases
```
mysql < /murach/mysql/backup-2012-02-23.sql -u root -p
```

Description
- You can use the mysql program to restore one or more databases by running the SQL script file that contains the database backup.
- Before you restore a database from a script file, it's generally considered a good idea to back up the existing database in case the restore operation doesn't work correctly.
- Before you restore a database from a script file, you can open the SQL file and view it to make sure it does what you want. If it doesn't, you can edit this file.
- If you get an error that indicates that access is denied, you may need to start the command prompt as an administrator.
- If a firewall is running on your computer, it may attempt to block the mysql program. However, if you allow the mysql program to access the database, it should work properly.
- On a Mac OS X system, you typically need to code a dot and slash (./) before the name of the mysql program to specify that it's in the current directory (the bin directory).

Figure 19-5   How to use a SQL script file to restore a full backup

How to execute statements in the binary log

Figure 19-6 shows how to use the mysqlbinlog program to execute all or some of the statements in the binary log. To start, the first example shows how to execute all statements stored in a single binary log. Here, the mysqlbinlog program begins by specifying the path and name of the file. Then, it specifies a pipe character (|) followed by "mysql". This indicates that the mysqlbinlog program uses the mysql program to execute the statements in the binary log. Finally, the -u option identifies a user with privileges to restore databases, and the -p option specifies that the program should prompt for a password.

When you restore data using a binary log as shown in the first example, every statement for every database is executed by default. But what if you only need to restore one database from the binary log? In that case, you can use the --database option to specify the name of that database as shown in the second example. Or, what if you only want to execute statements that fall within a specified date/time range? In that case, you can use one or both of the date/time options to specify a starting date/time, an ending date/time, or both a starting and an ending date/time.

Finally, what if your binary log has been split across multiple files due to server restarts or file size limits? In that case, you can specify a list of binary log files as shown in the fourth and fifth examples. In the fourth example, the names of the log files are separated by a space. This works for Windows, Mac OS X, and Unix. For Mac OS X and Unix, you can also use a regular expression to select all binary log files as shown in the fifth example. Although you might expect that you could use a wildcard character to select binary log files with Windows (bin-log.*), this doesn't currently work with the mysqlbinlog program. However, it might work with future versions of this program.

How to use the mysqlbinlog program to execute statements

For all databases
```
mysqlbinlog /murach/mysql/bin-log.000001 | mysql -u root -p
```

For a specific database
```
mysqlbinlog --database=ap /murach/mysql/bin-log.000001 | mysql -u root -p
```

For a specific time range
```
mysqlbinlog --start-datetime="2012-02-01 00:00:00"
/murach/mysql/bin-log.000001 | mysql -u root -p
```

For all databases using multiple binary log files
```
mysqlbinlog /murach/mysql/bin-log.000001 /murach/mysql/bin-log.000002 |
mysql -u root -p
```

For all databases using multiple binary log files (Mac OS and Unix only)
```
mysqlbinlog /murach/mysql/bin-log.[0-9]* | mysql -u root -p
```

Common options for the mysqlbinlog program

Option	Description
--database=db_name	Identifies the database.
--start-datetime=datetime	Identifies the starting date/time.
--stop-datetime=datetime	Identifies the ending date/time.

Description

- You can use the mysqlbinlog program to execute statements in the log file for all databases or for a specified database. You can also execute statements that fall within a specified date/time range.

- If the statements you want to execute are stored in multiple binary logs, you should specify all of them on the command prompt in sequence from the lowest numbered log file to the highest numbered log file.

- On a Mac OS X system, you typically need to (1) begin by coding the sudo command, (2) code a dot and slash before the name of the mysqlbinlog program and the mysql program, and (3) specify a path to the data directory. For example, you can execute the first example shown above like this:

```
sudo ./mysqlbinlog ../data/bin-log.000001 | ./mysql -u root -p
```

Figure 19-6   How to execute statements in the binary log

How to view and edit statements in the binary log

In most cases, you can use the technique shown in the previous figure to execute the statements you need from the binary log without viewing or editing those statements. In some cases, though, you may need to view the binary log to examine the statements you want to execute. Or, you may need to delete some statements from the binary log so they're not executed.

For example, suppose that a user accidentally issued a DROP DATABASE command. In that case, using the mysqlbinlog program to execute the statements in the binary log would just execute this statement again, which wouldn't restore the database. To solve this problem, you can use the mysqlbinlog program to convert the binary log file to a text file so you can display and edit it.

Figure 19-7 shows how to use this program. Here, the example at the top of the figure creates a text file named bin-log.000001.sql from a binary file named bin-log.000001. In other words, the name of the text file is the same as the name of the binary file, but with a .sql extension. This makes it easy to keep track of how your binary files correspond with your text files. It also makes it easy to use MySQL Workbench's SQL Editor to open the text file. However, you can use any text editor you want to open this file.

Once you've opened the text file, you can search it to find the statement you want. In this figure, for example, the DROP DATABASE statement is highlighted. Here, the second line is a comment that shows that this statement was executed at this time

```
120228 13:04:14
```

which can be expanded out to

```
2012-02-28 13:04:14
```

At this point, you have two options for solving the problem. If you don't need to execute any statements in the log file that come after this statement, you can use the --stop-datetime option shown in the previous figure to stop executing statements one second before the DROP DATABASE statement was executed. However, if you need to execute statements that come both before and after this statement, you can delete the DROP DATABASE statement from the text file. This statement begins with a comment that identifies the position number (# at 433) and it ends with the semi-colon (;) that ends the statement. Once you've edited this text, you can use the mysql program to execute it as shown in this figure. Or, you can use MySQL Workbench to execute it just as you would any other SQL script.

If you study the statements in this log file, you'll see that the INSERT and DROP DATABASE statements are both preceded by a SET TIMESTAMP statement. These statements set the timestamp system variable, which identifies the time that each statement was executed. Then, if the statement uses the NOW function, the value of the timestamp variable is used instead of the system's current date and time.

How to convert a binary log file to a SQL file

```
mysqlbinlog /murach/mysql/bin-log.000001 > /murach/mysql/bin-log.000001.sql
```

An excerpt from the converted file

```
BEGIN
/*!*/;
# at 173
#120228 13:02:45 server id 1  end_log_pos 201      Intvar
SET INSERT_ID=126/*!*/;
# at 201
#120228 13:02:45 server id 1  end_log_pos 406      Query      thread_id=144
exec_time=0      error_code=0
use ap/*!*/;
SET TIMESTAMP=1330462965/*!*/;
INSERT INTO vendors VALUES
(DEFAULT, 'Eagle Networks', '1289 Olive Ave.', NULL, 'Fresno', 'CA',
'93711', '559-431-7283', 'Shaw', 'Doug', 3, 527)
/*!*/;
# at 406
#120228 13:02:45 server id 1  end_log_pos 433      Xid = 94239
COMMIT/*!*/;
# at 433
#120228 13:04:14 server id 1  end_log_pos 510      Query      thread_id=144
exec_time=0      error_code=0
SET TIMESTAMP=1330463054/*!*/;
DROP DATABASE ex
/*!*/;
# at 510
#120228 13:04:58 server id 1  end_log_pos 551      Rotate to bin-log.000003
pos: 4
DELIMITER ;
# End of log file
ROLLBACK /* added by mysqlbinlog */;
/*!50003 SET COMPLETION_TYPE=@OLD_COMPLETION_TYPE*/;
```

How to use the mysql program to execute the converted file

```
mysql < /murach/mysql/bin-log.000001.sql -u root -p
```

Description

- If a binary log contains statements that you don't want to execute, you can convert the binary file for the log to a text file. Then, you can edit the text file.

- After you edit the text file for the binary log, you can use MySQL Workbench or the mysql program to execute the text file just as you would execute any SQL script.

- On a Mac OS X system, you typically need to (1) begin by coding the sudo command, (2) code a dot and slash before the name of the mysqlbinlog program, and (3) specify a path to the data directory. For example, you can execute the first example shown above like this:

```
sudo ./mysqlbinlog ../data/bin-log.000001 > /murach/mysql/bin-log.000001.sql
```

Figure 19-7   How to view and edit statements in the binary log

How to import and export data

When you back up a database as shown earlier in this chapter, you can use the backup script file to copy the database to another server. In that case, backing up the database can be referred to as *exporting a database*. Similarly, when you restore a database from a backup that was performed on another server, it can be referred to as *importing a database*.

In addition to exporting and importing an entire database, you may sometimes need to export data from a database to a file or import data from a file to a database. For example, you may need to load shipping rates that are stored in a text file into a table. Or, you may need to export data so it can be used by a spreadsheet program or imported by another database. Fortunately, MySQL makes it easy to import and export data.

How to export data to a file

Figure 19-8 shows how to export data to a file. To do that, you can add an INTO OUTFILE clause to a SELECT statement to save the result set in an output file. By default, this clause uses a tab character (\t) to separate, or *delimit*, columns. And it uses a new line character (\n) to separate, or delimit, rows. When you store this type of data in a file, the file is known as a *tab-delimited file*. This type of file is commonly used to store and transfer data.

The first example in this figure exports all data from the Vendor_Contacts table and stores it in a tab-delimited file named vendor_contacts.txt. Since this is a small table with just three columns and eight rows, the SELECT statement exports the entire table. If necessary, though, you can limit the amount of data by including a column list and a WHERE clause.

Since it's easy to export data to a tab-delimited file, and since this format can be read by most other programs, this is the type of file that you usually want to use. However, if you need to export your data to another format, you can include the optional FIELDS clause to specify the delimiters for the columns and rows. For example, it's also common to store data in a *comma-delimited file*. To export data to a comma-delimited file, you can include a FIELDS clause with a TERMINATED BY clause that indicates that every column should be terminated by a comma (,) and an ENCLOSED BY clause that indicates that each column should be enclosed by double quotes ("). In this figure, for instance, the second example exports the data in the Vendor_Contacts table to a comma-delimited file.

In addition, if your data might contain a double quote character ("), you also need to include an ESCAPED BY clause to specify an *escape character*. Then, MySQL uses the escape character to identify any double quote characters that are part of the data. In this figure, for instance, the second example uses a backslash character as the escape character. Since the backslash character is used to escape special characters such as tabs (\t), new lines (\n), and single quotes (\'), though, you must code two backslashes (\\) to use a backslash character as the escape character.

The syntax of the SELECT for exporting data to a file

```
SELECT column_list
INTO OUTFILE file_path
[FIELDS [TERMINATED BY string]
        [ENCLOSED BY char]
        [ESCAPED BY char]
FROM table name
[WHERE search_condition]
[ORDER BY order_by_list]
```

A tab-delimited file

The statement

```
SELECT *
INTO OUTFILE '/murach/mysql/vendor_contacts.txt'
FROM vendor_contacts
```

The file contents

```
5       Davison     Michelle
12      Mayteh      Kendall
17      Onandonga   Bruce
44      Antavius    Anthony
76      Bradlee     Danny
94      Suscipe     Reynaldo
101     O'Sullivan  Geraldine
123     Bucket      Charles
```

A comma-delimited file

The statement

```
SELECT *
INTO OUTFILE '/murach/mysql/vendor_contacts.txt'
FIELDS TERMINATED BY ',' ENCLOSED BY '"' ESCAPED BY '\\'
FROM vendor_contacts
```

The file contents

```
"5","Davison","Michelle"
"12","Mayteh","Kendall"
"17","Onandonga","Bruce"
"44","Antavius","Anthony"
"76","Bradlee","Danny"
"94","Suscipe","Reynaldo"
"101","O'Sullivan","Geraldine"
"123","Bucket","Charles"
```

Description

- You can add an INTO OUTFILE clause to a SELECT statement to save the result set in an output file.

- You can use the FIELDS clause to identify the character that's used to *delimit* columns, the character that's used to delimit rows, and an *escape character*.

- On a Mac OS X system, you may get an error that indicates that you don't have permissions to write to the /murach/mysql directory. To get around this issue, you can write the file to the /tmp directory. Then, you can copy the file from this directory to the /murach/mysql directory.

Figure 19-8   How to export data to a file

How to import data from a file

Figure 19-9 begins by showing how to use the LOAD DATA statement to load data from an input file into a table. Specifically, it shows how to use this statement to import the data that was exported by the examples in the previous figure.

To start, you code a LOAD DATA clause that identifies the path and name of the file. Then, you code an INTO TABLE clause that identifies the table that you want to import the data into as shown in the first example in this figure. If you're working with a tab-delimited file, that's all you need to do. If you're working with a comma-delimited file, though, you need to include a FIELDS clause that identifies the delimiters and the escape character. In this figure, for instance, the second example includes the correct delimiters and escape character for the comma-delimited file that was created in the previous figure.

For an import to work successfully, the columns in the input file must match the columns in the table. In this figure, for example, the Vendor_Contacts table has three required columns: an INT column followed by two VARCHAR(50) columns. As a result, MySQL must be able to convert the data that's stored in the vendor_contacts.txt file to the data types specified by the Vendor_Contacts table.

In addition, the data in the input file must not conflict with the values of any unique keys that are already stored in the rows of the table. If that happens, you'll get an error that indicates that you were attempting to make a duplicate entry. Usually, that's what you want. If it isn't, you can delete any duplicate entries from the table.

How to use the LOAD DATA statement to import data from a file

The syntax

```
LOAD DATA INFILE file_path
INTO TABLE table_name
[FIELDS [TERMINATED BY string]
        [ENCLOSED BY char]
        [ESCAPED BY char]]
```

A tab-delimited file

```
LOAD DATA INFILE '/murach/mysql/vendor_contacts.txt'
INTO TABLE vendor_contacts
```

A comma-delimited file

```
LOAD DATA INFILE '/murach/mysql/vendor_contacts.txt'
INTO TABLE vendor_contacts
FIELDS TERMINATED BY ','
       ENCLOSED BY '"'
       ESCAPED BY '\\'
```

Description

- You can use the LOAD DATA statement to load data from an input file into a table.

- The columns in the input file must match the columns in the table.

- The data in the input file must not conflict with the values of any unique keys that are already stored in the rows of the table.

- You can also use the mysqlimport program to load data from an input file into a table. For more information, see the MySQL Reference Manual.

Figure 19-9   How to import data from a file

How to check and repair tables

When the server or operating system shuts down unexpectedly, the tables in a database can become corrupted. When that happens, the users of the database won't be able to access the table data. Then, you can use the tools MySQL provides to determine which tables need to be repaired. In addition, you can use MySQL tools to repair MyISAM tables. However, since the InnoDB engine is typically able to recover from unexpected shutdowns on its own, MySQL doesn't provide tools for repairing InnoDB tables. If it can't recover, though, you can use the technique you'll learn in just a minute to restore the corrupted tables.

How to use the CHECK TABLE statement

Figure 19-10 shows how to use the CHECK TABLE statement to check tables. This statement works for both InnoDB and MyISAM tables. In addition, with MySQL 5.0 and later, this statement works for views.

If the CHECK TABLE statement finds no problems with a table, it will mark the table as OK as shown in the Msg_text column in all three examples in this figure. This allows MySQL to begin using the table again. The CHECK TABLE statement might also give you a message of "Table is already up to date" if it wasn't necessary to check the table. If it doesn't return either of these messages, you should repair the table as described in the next figure.

In most cases, you'll use the CHECK TABLE statement to check a single table or view using the default options as shown in the first example. However, if you need to check multiple tables or views, you can separate the names of the tables or views with commas as shown in the second example.

If you don't specify any options, the CHECK TABLE statement uses the MEDIUM option to do its check. However, if you need to change the default options, you can specify them after the list of tables or views. For example, you can specify the EXTENDED option to perform a more thorough check that takes longer. Or, you can specify the QUICK option to perform a less thorough check that runs faster. To speed this check even further, you can specify the FAST or CHANGED options. These options automatically include the QUICK option, which is usually what you want. In this figure, for instance, the third example specifies the FAST option.

Before you specify any of these options, you should know that they are ignored by the InnoDB engine. As a result, if you're checking an InnoDB table, you don't need to code these options. The exception is the FOR UPGRADE option, which is used by both the InnoDB and MyISAM storage engines.

The syntax of the CHECK TABLE statement

```
CHECK TABLE table_list option_list
```

Options for the CHECK TABLE statement

Option	Description
EXTENDED	Does a full scan of each row. This ensures that the table is 100% consistent, but takes a long time.
MEDIUM	Does an average scan of each row. This is the default for a MyISAM table.
QUICK	Does a quick scan of the rows.
FAST	Checks only tables that have not been closed properly. Uses the QUICK option.
CHANGED	Checks only tables that have been changed since the last check or that have not been closed properly. Uses the QUICK option.
FOR UPGRADE	Checks whether the tables are compatible with the current version of MySQL.

A statement that checks a single table

```
CHECK TABLE vendors
```

Table	Op	Msg_type	Msg_text
ap.vendors	check	status	OK

A statement that checks multiple tables and views

```
CHECK TABLE vendors, invoices, terms, invoices_outstanding
```

Table	Op	Msg_type	Msg_text
ap.vendors	check	status	OK
ap.invoices	check	status	OK
ap.terms	check	status	OK
ap.invoic...	check	status	OK

A statement that uses an option

```
CHECK TABLE vendors, invoices FAST
```

Table	Op	Msg_type	Msg_text
ap.vendors	check	status	OK
ap.invoices	check	status	OK

Description

- The CHECK TABLE statement works for InnoDB and MyISAM tables. With MySQL 5.0 and later, this statement also works for views.
- All of the options except for FOR UPGRADE are ignored by the InnoDB engine. This engine automatically performs a thorough check that detects most problems. If it finds a problem, the server shuts down to prevent the problem from getting worse.
- The FOR UPGRADE option is useful if you upgrade to a newer version of MySQL. In that case, a change in the new version might make data from the old version incompatible with the new version.
- The CHECK TABLE statement works only when the server is running.

Figure 19-10   How to use the CHECK TABLE statement

How to use the REPAIR TABLE statement

Figure 19-11 shows how to use the REPAIR TABLE statement to repair corrupted MyISAM tables. This statement works much like the CHECK TABLE statement. However, it has fewer options, so it's easier to use. In addition, the CHECK TABLE statement doesn't work for InnoDB tables.

When you use the REPAIR TABLE statement, the repair operation can sometimes cause the table to lose data. As a result, it's generally considered a best practice to make a backup of a table before performing a repair. That's especially true if it's critical to retain all data.

As it repairs a table, the REPAIR TABLE statement checks whether an upgrade is required. If so, it automatically performs the same upgrade operation that's performed by the FOR UPGRADE option of the CHECK TABLE statement.

How to repair an InnoDB table

If the CHECK TABLE statement finds a problem with an InnoDB table, the server shuts down to prevent the problem from getting worse. Because of that, you have to use the procedure shown in figure 19-11 to repair an InnoDB table.

To start, you add the innodb_force_recovery system variable to the MySQL configuration file. Although you can code different values for this variable, a value of 4 is typically sufficient. To learn more about this value and the other values you can code, see the MySQL Reference Manual.

Once you've added the innodb_force_recovery system variable, you can restart the server. Then, you should be able to back up the database that contains the corrupted tables as described earlier in this chapter. Next, you remove the innodb_force_recovery variable from the configuration file and restart the server. Finally, you can restore the database from the backup you just created.

In most cases, this procedure will fix the corrupted tables and restore most of the data. If it doesn't, you can use your last full backup and your incremental backups to restore the database.

How to repair a MyISAM table

The syntax of the REPAIR TABLE statement

```
REPAIR TABLE table_list option_list
```

Common options for the REPAIR TABLE statement

Option	Description
QUICK	Performs a standard repair that fixes most common problems.
EXTENDED	Performs a more extended repair.

A statement that repairs a single table

```
REPAIR TABLE vendors
```

A statement that repairs two tables and uses an option

```
REPAIR TABLE vendors, invoices QUICK
```

How to repair an InnoDB table

1. Use a text editor as described in chapter 17 to add this system variable to the configuration file:

   ```
   innodb_force_recovery=4
   ```

2. Restart the server, and then use the mysqldump program to back up the database.

3. Remove the innodb_force_recovery variable from the configuration file, restart the server, and restore the database to fix the corrupted tables and restore as much data as possible.

Description

- To repair a MyISAM table, you can use the REPAIR TABLE statement. This statement works only when the server is running.

- The REPAIR TABLE statement checks the table to see whether an upgrade is required. If so, it automatically performs the same upgrade operation that's provided by the FOR UPGRADE option of the CHECK TABLE statement.

- It's generally considered a best practice to make a backup of a table before performing a table repair operation, since a table repair operation can sometimes cause you to lose data.

- To repair an InnoDB table, you use the procedure shown above. The innodb_force_recovery system variable allows the server to restart so you can back up and then restore the database that contains the corrupt tables.

- If restoring the database doesn't fix the corrupted tables, you can use your last full backup and your incremental backups to restore the database.

Figure 19-11   How to repair tables

How to use the mysqlcheck program

Figure 19-12 shows how to use the mysqlcheck program to perform the same kinds of checks and repairs that you can perform with the CHECK TABLE and REPAIR TABLE statements. If you understand how these statements work, you shouldn't have much trouble understanding how to use the mysqlcheck program. The advantage of using the mysqlcheck program is that it allows you to check all tables in a database without having to specify the name of each table.

As usual, if you're using a Mac OS X system, you typically need to code a dot and slash (./) before the name of the mysqlcheck program. This indicates that this program is in the current directory (the bin directory).

How to use the mysqlcheck program to check tables

For a single database
```
mysqlcheck ap -u root -p
```

For multiple databases
```
mysqlcheck --databases ap ex om -u root -p
```

For all databases
```
mysqlcheck --all-databases -u root -p
```

For specified tables within a database
```
mysqlcheck ap vendors invoices -u root -p
```

For a quick check
```
mysqlcheck ap --quick -u root -p
```

For an extended check
```
mysqlcheck ap --extended -u root -p
```

Common options for checking tables

Option	Corresponding CHECK TABLE option
--extended	EXTENDED
--medium-check	MEDIUM
--quick	QUICK
--fast	FAST
--check-only-changed	CHANGED
--check-upgrade	FOR UPGRADE

How to use the mysqlcheck program to repair tables

For a standard repair
```
mysqlcheck ap --repair -u root -p
```

For an extended repair
```
mysqlcheck ap --repair --extended -u root -p
```

Common options for repairing tables

Option	Description
--repair	Performs a repair that fixes most common problems.
--extended	A more extended repair than the standard repair.
--quick	A faster repair than the standard repair.

Description

- The mysqlcheck program uses the CHECK TABLE and REPAIR TABLE statements to check and repair one or more tables.
- Most of the check and repair options are ignored by the InnoDB engine.
- You can only use the mysqlcheck program when the server is running.

Figure 19-12   How to use the mysqlcheck program

How to use the myisamchk program

Figure 19-13 shows how to use the myisamchk program to check and repair MyISAM tables. If you understand how to use the mysqlcheck program described in the previous figure, you shouldn't have much trouble understanding how this program works.

The advantage of the myisamchk program is that you can use it while the server is stopped. If, for example, the server won't start due to corrupted tables, you can use the myisamchk program to attempt to repair those tables. However, you should not attempt to use the myisamchk program if the server is running. That's because this program won't work if another program is using the same table. In that case, you should use one of the other techniques presented in this chapter.

When you use the myisamchk program, you need to point to the table in the file system. To do that, you begin by coding the path to the MySQL data directory. Then, you code the name of the database followed by the name of the table. In this figure, for instance, all examples specify a path to the Engine_Sample table for the EX database. The MySQL data directory shown in these examples is the default path on a Windows system. However, this path will be different on a Mac OS·X or Unix system.

Unlike the CHECK TABLE statement and the mysqlcheck program, you can both check a table and repair it using a single myisamchk command. To do that, you use the --force option as shown in the last example in this figure. Then, if the program finds a problem with the table, it automatically repairs it.

If you're using a Mac OS X system, you typically need to begin with the sudo command, code a dot and slash (./) before the name of the myisamchk program, and specify the data directory. For example, you can execute the first example in this figure like this:

```
sudo ./myisamchk "../data/ex/engine_sample"
```

How to use the myisamchk program to check a table

For a standard check

```
myisamchk "/ProgramData/MySQL/MySQL Server 5.5/data/ex/engine_sample"
```

For a medium check

```
myisamchk --medium-check
"/ProgramData/MySQL/MySQL Server 5.5/data/ex/engine_sample"
```

For an extended check

```
myisamchk --extend-check
"/ProgramData/MySQL/MySQL Server 5.5/data/ex/engine_sample"
```

Common options for checking a table

Option	Corresponding CHECK TABLE option
--extend-check	EXTENDED
--medium-check	MEDIUM
--check	QUICK
--fast	FAST
--check-only-changed	CHANGED
--force	None. Automatically repairs the table if errors are found. Uses the --recover option.

How to use the myisamchk program to repair a table

For a standard repair

```
myisamchk --recover
"/ProgramData/MySQL/MySQL Server 5.5/data/ex/engine_sample"
```

For a quick repair

```
myisamchk --recover --quick
"/ProgramData/MySQL/MySQL Server 5.5/data/ex/engine_sample"
```

For an extended repair

```
myisamchk --safe-recover
"/ProgramData/MySQL/MySQL Server 5.5/data/ex/engine_sample"
```

Common options for repairing a table

Option	Description
--recover	Performs a standard repair that fixes most common problems.
--quick	A faster repair than the standard repair.
--safe-recover	A more extended repair than the standard repair.

A command that checks a table and repairs it if necessary

```
myisamchk --force
"/ProgramData/MySQL/MySQL Server 5.5/data/ex/engine_sample"
```

Description

- The myisamchk program can check and repair MyISAM tables.
- You should only use the myisamchk program when the server is stopped.

Figure 19-13   How to use the myisamchk program

Perspective

In this chapter, you learned how to back up your databases and how to restore them if necessary. If you combine these skills with the skills you learned in the previous chapter for securing a database and working with user accounts, you are on your way to becoming a successful database administrator. Of course, there's much more to learn than what's presented here. If you're interested in learning more, I recommend *High Performance MySQL* from O'Reilly. This book presents an in-depth look at database security and backup, and it presents other important topics such as optimization and replication that can take your DBA skills to the next level.

Terms

back up a database
restore a database
full backup
incremental backup
point-in-time recovery (PITR)
dump a database
export a database
import a database
delimit columns or rows
tab-delimited file
comma-delimited file
escape character

Excercise

In this exercise, you back up a database to create a backup script file. Then, you make some changes to the database and delete it. Finally, you restore the database from the backup script and the binary log file.

Back up a database

1. Enable binary logging as described in chapter 17.

2. Start a command prompt and use the mysqldump program to create a full backup of the AP database. This backup should include the structure and data for the database, as well as any stored routines, functions, and events for the database. After the dump, leave the command prompt open.

3. Start MySQL Workbench and open the backup script that was created by the mysqldump program. Make sure that this script contains all the SQL statements needed to restore the structure and data of the database. If necessary, add the CREATE DATABASE statement that creates the AP database and the USE statement that selects it.

4. Use MySQL Workbench to execute an INSERT statement that inserts one row into the Vendors table of the AP database.

5. Use MySQL Workbench to execute a DROP DATABASE statement that drops the entire AP database.

Restore a database

6. Switch back to the command prompt and use the mysql program to run the backup script. This should restore the entire AP database.

7. From the command prompt, use the mysqlbinlog program to convert the highest numbered file for the binary log to a text file.

8. Use MySQL Workbench to open the text file for the binary log and review its contents. Make a note of the time that the DROP DATABASE statement was executed.

9. Switch back to the command prompt and use the mysqlbinlog program to execute all the statements in the binary log for the AP database that come after the time of the last full backup but before the time of the DROP DATABASE file. To do that, you may need to view the last line of the backup script to get the exact time that this backup was completed.

Appendix A

How to install the software for this book on Windows

Before you begin reading this book, we recommend that you install two products: (1) the MySQL Community Server and (2) MySQL Workbench. Both of these products are available for free from the MySQL web site, and you can download and install them on your computer as described in this appendix.

After you install these products, we recommend that you download the source files for this book that are available from the Murach web site (www.murach.com). Then, we recommend that you run the SQL script that creates the databases that are used throughout this book.

When you've installed all of the products described in this appendix, you're ready to gain valuable hands-on experience by doing the exercises that are presented at the end of each chapter. To start, chapter 2 shows how to use MySQL Workbench to run SQL statements against a MySQL database. Then, as you progress through the rest of the book, you can use MySQL Workbench to open the SQL statements that are installed on your computer and run them against the databases that are installed on your computer.

This appendix assumes that you're using Microsoft Windows as your operating system. If you want to install the software for this book on a Mac OS X system, please see appendix B. Or, if you want to install the software for this book on another operating system such as Unix, the MySQL web site provides instructions for installing the MySQL Community Server and MySQL Workbench on most modern operating systems.

How to install the software from mysql.com **558**
How to install the MySQL Community Server 558
How to install MySQL Workbench 558
How to install the software from murach.com **560**
How to install the source files for this book 560
How to create the databases for this book 562
How to restore the databases 562

How to install the software from mysql.com

This topic shows how to install the MySQL Community Server and MySQL Workbench. Both of these software products are available for free from the MySQL web site. The procedures for installing these products were tested against MySQL Community Server 5.5 and MySQL Workbench 5.2. However, you should be able to use similar procedures to install earlier and later versions of these products.

How to install the MySQL Community Server

MySQL Community Server is a database server that's free and easy to use. Since it's designed to run on most modern computers, it's ideal for developers who want to install it on their own computer so they can learn how to work with a MySQL database. That's why this book assumes that you have installed the Community Server on your computer as shown in figure A-1.

When you install MySQL on your computer, you need to specify a password for the root user. When you do, *make sure to remember the password that you enter.* If security isn't a concern for you as you're learning, *we recommend using "sesame" as the password.* That way, the password will be easy to remember.

All of the SQL statements presented in this book have been tested against MySQL Community Server 5.5. As a result, you can use the statements presented in this book to work with this version of the database. Since MySQL is backwards compatible, these statements should also work with future versions of MySQL. In addition, most statements presented in this book work with earlier versions of MySQL, and we have done our best to identify any statements that don't.

How to install MySQL Workbench

MySQL Workbench is a free graphical tool that makes it easier to work with MySQL databases. Since MySQL Workbench is an ideal tool for learning how to work with MySQL, it is bundled with the Community Server in one convenient installation package. As a result, if you use the MySQL Installer to install the Community Server as described in figure A-1, you also get MySQL Workbench. However, if you want to install MySQL Workbench separately, you can do that too. For more information, visit the Downloads page of the MySQL web site.

All of the skills for working with MySQL Workbench that are presented in this book were tested against version 5.2.38. As a result, if you're using this version of MySQL Workbench, these skills should work exactly as described. However, MySQL Workbench is being actively developed and is changing quickly. As a result, if you're using a later version of MySQL Workbench, these skills may not work exactly as described, but they should work similarly.

The URL for the MySQL Installer

`http://dev.mysql.com/downloads/installer/`

How to install MySQL Community Server and MySQL Workbench

1. Find the download page for the MySQL Installer for Windows. This page is currently available at the URL shown above. If necessary, you can search the Internet for "MySQL Installer for Windows".

2. Follow the instructions provided on that web page to download the installer file to your hard drive.

3. Find the installer file on your hard drive and run it.

4. Respond to the resulting dialog boxes. You can accept most of the default options, but you should specify a password for the root user. *Make sure to remember the password that you enter.* If security isn't a concern for you as you're learning, *we recommend using "sesame" as the password.*

5. To make sure that the database has been installed correctly, start MySQL Workbench when the installation is finished. To do that, double-click on the stored connection named "Local instance MySQL55" and enter the password you specified in the previous step to log in to the database server as the root user.

Notes

- You can also install MySQL Server and MySQL Workbench separately. For more information about that, you can visit the Downloads page of the MySQL web site.

- To make it easy to start MySQL Workbench, you may want to pin the program to your taskbar or add a shortcut to your desktop.

Figure A-1   How to install MySQL Community Server and MySQL Workbench

How to install the software from murach.com

Once you have installed the MySQL software products, we recommend that you install the source files for this book. In addition, we recommend that you create the databases that are used throughout this book.

How to install the source files for this book

Figure A-2 shows how to install the source files for this book. This includes a SQL script that you can use to create the databases that are used throughout this book as described in the next figure. It includes SQL scripts that contain the SQL code for all of the examples in this book. And it includes the SQL scripts that contain the solutions to the exercises that are at the end of each chapter.

The source files for this book are contained in a self-extracting zip file (an exe file) that you can download from www.murach.com. When you download and execute this file, it will unzip the SQL script files for the book into the C:\murach\mysql directory. Within this directory, you can find the subdirectories that contain the source files as shown in this figure.

The default installation directory for the source files

```
C:\murach\mysql
```

How to download and install these files

1. Go to www.murach.com and navigate to the page for *Murach's MySQL*.
2. Click the link for "FREE download of the book examples."
3. Select the "All book files" link for the self-extracting zip file, and respond to the resulting pages and dialog boxes to download a setup file named msql_allfiles.exe onto your hard drive.
4. Use Windows Explorer to find the setup file on your hard drive.
5. Double-click this file and respond to the dialog boxes that follow. If you accept the defaults, this installs the source files into the directory shown above.

The directories that contain the source files

Directory	Contains
db_setup	The SQL script that's used to create the three databases for this book.
book_scripts	The SQL scripts for all of the examples presented in this book.
ex_solutions	The SQL scripts for the solutions to the exercises that are at the end of each chapter.
diagrams	The MySQL Workbench file for the diagram that's presented in chapter 10.
java	The source code for the Java application that's presented in chapter 1.
php	The source code for the PHP application that's presented in chapter 1.

The databases

Database	Description
ap	The AP (Accounts Payable) database. This is the primary database that's used in this book.
om	The OM (Order Management) database. This database is used in some of the examples in this book.
ex	The EX (Examples) database. This database contains several tables that are used for short examples.

Description

- All of the source files described in this book are in a self-extracting zip file (an exe file) that can be downloaded from www.murach.com.

Figure A-2   How to install the source files for this book

How to create the databases for this book

Before you can run the SQL statements presented in this book, you need to create the three databases described in the previous figure. The easiest way to do that is to use MySQL Workbench to run the SQL script that's stored in the create_databases.sql file. The procedure for doing this is described in figure A-3.

To determine if the SQL script ran successfully, you can review the results in the Output window. In this figure, for example, the Output window shows a series of statements that have executed successfully. In addition, the Object Browser window shows that the three databases have been created. The other database, named Test, is a database that comes with MySQL.

If the script encounters problems, MySQL Workbench displays one or more errors in the Output window. Then, you can read these errors to figure out why the script isn't executing correctly.

Before you can run the create_databases.sql script, the database server must be running. By default the database server is automatically started when you start your computer, so this usually isn't a problem. However, if it isn't running on your system, you can start it as described in chapter 2.

How to restore the databases

As you work with the code that's presented in this book, you may make changes to the databases or tables that you don't intend to make. In that case, you may want to restore the databases to their original state so your results match the results shown in this book. To do that, you can run the create_databases.sql file again. This drops the three databases described in this appendix and recreates them.

The directory that contains the create_databases.sql file

`C:\murach\mysql\db_setup`

MySQL Workbench after executing the create_databases.sql file

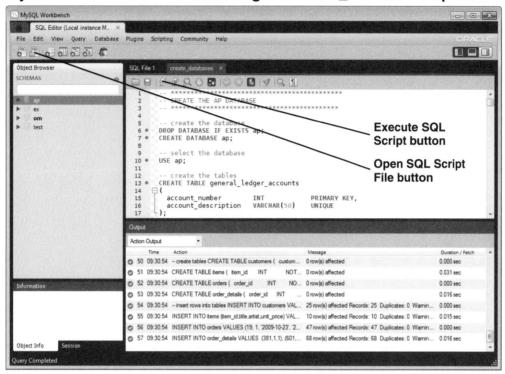

How to create the databases

1. Start MySQL Workbench.

2. Connect as the root user to an instance of MySQL that's running on the localhost computer. To do that, double-click on the stored connection named "Local instance MySQL55" and enter the password for the root user if prompted.

3. Open the script file by clicking the Open SQL Script File button in the SQL Editor toolbar. Then, use the resulting dialog box to locate and open the create_databases.sql file. When you do, MySQL Workbench displays this script in a code editor tab.

4. Execute the script by clicking the Execute SQL Script button in the code editor toolbar. When you do, the Output window displays messages that indicate whether the script executed successfully.

How to restore the databases

- Run the create_databases.sql script again to drop the databases and recreate them.

Description

- For the create_databases.sql file to run, the database server must be running. By default, the database server is automatically started when your start your computer. If it isn't running on your system, you can start it as described in chapter 2.

Figure A-3   How to create and restore the databases for this book

Appendix B

How to install the software for this book on Mac OS X

Before you begin reading this book, we recommend that you install two products: (1) the MySQL Community Server and (2) MySQL Workbench. Both of these products are available for free from the MySQL web site, and you can download and install them on your computer as described in this appendix.

After you install these products, we recommend that you download the source files for this book that are available from the Murach web site (www.murach.com). Then, we recommend that you run the SQL script that creates the databases that are used throughout this book.

When you've installed all of the products described in this appendix, you're ready to gain valuable hands-on experience by doing the exercises that are presented at the end of each chapter. To start, chapter 2 shows how to use MySQL Workbench to run SQL statements against a MySQL database. Then, as you progress through the rest of the book, you can use MySQL Workbench to open the SQL statements that are installed on your computer and run them against the databases that are installed on your computer.

This appendix assumes that you're using Mac OS X as your operating system. If you want to install the software for this book on a Microsoft Windows system, please see appendix A. Or, if you want to install the software for this book on another operating system such as Unix, the MySQL web site provides instructions for installing the MySQL Community Server and MySQL Workbench on most modern operating systems.

How to install the software from mysql.com **566**

How to install the MySQL Community Server 566

How to install MySQL Workbench 568

How to install the software from murach.com **570**

How to install the source files for this book 570

How to create the databases for this book 572

How to restore the databases 572

How to install the software from mysql.com

This topic shows how to install the MySQL Community Server and MySQL Workbench. Both of these software products are available for free from the MySQL web site. The procedures for installing these products were tested against MySQL Community Server 5.5 and MySQL Workbench 5.2. However, you should be able to use similar procedures to install earlier and later versions of these products.

How to install the MySQL Community Server

MySQL Community Server is a database server that's free and easy to use. Since it's designed to run on most modern computers, it's ideal for developers who want to install it on their own computer so they can learn how to work with a MySQL database. That's why this book assumes that you have installed the Community Server on your computer as shown in figure B-1.

When you install the Community Server on your computer, the root user is created automatically so you can log in to the server. However, a password isn't assigned to this user by default. In other words, the server is not secure. If you want to secure the server, you can assign passwords to all users of the server as described in chapter 18.

In addition to the server itself, the download for MySQL Community Server includes the MySQL Startup Item and the MySQL preference pane. You can use the Startup Item to start and stop the server by entering commands in a terminal window. You can use the MySQL preference pane shown in this figure to start and stop the server and to control whether the MySQL server starts automatically when you start your computer.

All of the SQL statements presented in this book have been tested against the MySQL Community Server 5.5. As a result, you can use the statements presented in this book to work with this version of the database. Since MySQL is backwards compatible, these statements should also work with future versions of MySQL. In addition, most statements presented in this book work with earlier versions of MySQL, and we have done our best to identify any statements that don't.

The URL for downloading the MySQL Community Server

http://dev.mysql.com/downloads/mysql/

How to download and install the MySQL Community Server

1. Find the download page for the MySQL Community Server. This page is currently available at the URL shown above. If necessary, you can search the Internet for "MySQL Community Server download".

2. Follow the instructions provided on that web page to download the appropriate disk image (DMG) file for your operating system to your hard drive.

3. Find the DMG file on your hard drive and double-click it. This opens a window with two package (PKG) files and a preference pane (prefPane) file in it.

4. Double-click the PKG file for MySQL, and respond to the resulting dialog boxes to install it.

5. Double-click the PKG file for the MySQL Startup Item, and respond to the resulting dialog boxes to install it.

6. Double-click the MySQL.prefPane file and respond to the resulting dialog box to install the MySQL preference pane.

7. Make sure MySQL has been installed correctly by going to System Preferences under the Apple menu and double-clicking on MySQL in the Other section of the preference pane. If the MySQL preference pane indicates that the server is running or if you can start the server, MySQL is installed correctly.

The MySQL preference pane

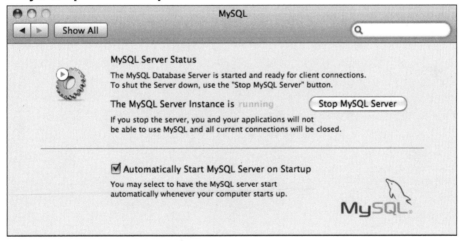

Description

- The MySQL Startup Item allows you to start and stop the server by entering commands in a terminal window.

- You can use the MySQL preference pane to start and stop MySQL and to control whether MySQL starts automatically when you start your computer.

- To display the MySQL preference pane, use the Apple menu to display the System Preferences dialog box. Then, double-click the MySQL icon in the Other category.

Figure B-1 How to install the MySQL Community Server

How to install MySQL Workbench

MySQL Workbench is a free graphical tool that makes it easier to work with MySQL databases. To install MySQL Workbench, you can use the first procedure in figure B-2.

After you install MySQL Workbench, you should make sure that it's configured for use with this book. To do that, you may need to add two connections as described in the second procedure in this figure. The first one lets you connect to the server so you can code and run SQL statements. The second one lets you connect to the server so you can manage it.

All of the skills for working with MySQL Workbench that are presented in this book were tested against version 5.2.38. As a result, if you're using this version of MySQL Workbench, these skills should work exactly as described. However, MySQL Workbench is being actively developed and is changing quickly. As a result, if you're using a later version of MySQL Workbench, these skills may not work exactly as described, but they should work similarly.

The URL for downloading MySQL Workbench

`http://dev.mysql.com/downloads/workbench/`

How to download and install MySQL Workbench

1. Find the download page for MySQL Workbench. This page is currently available at the URL shown above. If necessary, you can search the Internet for "MySQL Workbench download".

2. Follow the instructions provided on that web page to download the disk image (DMG) file for MySQL Workbench.

3. Find the DMG file on your hard drive and double-click on it. Then, respond to the resulting dialog boxes.

How to configure MySQL Workbench for this book

1. Start MySQL Workbench.

2. If the list box in the SQL Development section of the Home tab doesn't include a connection, you'll need to create one so you can use it to code and run SQL statements. To do that, click the "New Connection" link. Then, enter "Local instance MySQL55" for the connection name in the resulting dialog box and click the OK button.

3. If the list box in the Server Administration section of the Home tab doesn't include a connection, you'll need to create one so you can use it to manage the server. To do that, click the "New Server Instance" link and respond to the resulting dialog boxes. You should be able to accept the default values for most steps. In the last step, enter "Local MySQL55" for the name of the instance.

Notes

- Although you can use any names you want for the two connections you create in MySQL Workbench, "Local instance MySQL55" and "Local MySQL55 are the names of the default connections that are created on a Windows system for MySQL version 5.5, and they're the names we use in this book.

- To make it easy to start MySQL Workbench, you may want to keep this application in your dock.

Figure B-2   How to install MySQL Workbench

How to install the software from murach.com

Once you have installed the MySQL software products, we recommend that you install the source files for this book. In addition, we recommend that you create the databases that are used throughout this book.

How to install the source files for this book

Figure B-3 shows how to install the source files for this book. This includes a SQL script that you can use to create the databases that are used throughout this book as described in the next figure. It includes SQL scripts that contain the SQL code for all of the examples in this book. And it includes the SQL scripts that contain the solutions to the exercises that are at the end of each chapter.

The source files for this book are contained in a zip file that you can download from www.murach.com. When you download this file and unzip it, it stores the SQL script files for this book in a directory named mysql. Within this directory, you can find the subdirectories that contain the source files as shown in this figure. After unzipping these files into the mysql directory, we recommend moving this directory into another directory named murach that's directly on your hard drive. That way, the paths on your computer will match the paths specified in this book.

The installation directory for the source files

`/murach/mysql`

How to download and install these files

1. Go to www.murach.com, and navigate to the page for *Murach's MySQL*.

2. Click the link for "FREE download of the book examples."

3. Select the "All book files" link for the regular zip file, and respond to the resulting pages and dialog boxes to download a file named msql_allfiles.zip onto your hard drive.

4. Use the Finder to locate the zip file on your hard drive, and double-click on it to unzip it. This creates the mysql directory and its subdirectories.

5. If necessary, use the Finder to create the murach directory directly on your hard drive.

6. Use the Finder to move the mysql directory into the murach directory.

The directories that contain the source files

Directory	Description
db_setup	The SQL script that's used to create the three databases for this book.
book_scripts	The SQL scripts for all of the examples presented in this book.
ex_solutions	The SQL scripts for the solutions to the exercises that are at the end of each chapter.
diagrams	The MySQL Workbench file for the diagram that's presented in chapter 10.
java	The source code for the Java application that's presented in chapter 1.
php	The source code for the PHP application that's presented in chapter 1.

The databases

Database	Description
ap	The AP (Accounts Payable) database. This is the primary database that's used in this book.
om	The OM (Order Management) database. This database is used in some of the examples in this book.
ex	The EX (Examples) database. This database contains several tables that are used for short examples.

Description

- All of the source files described in this book are in a zip file that can be downloaded from www.murach.com.

A note about right-clicking

- This book often instructs you to right-click, because that's common on PCs. On a Mac, right-clicking is not enabled by default. Instead, you can use the Ctrl-click instead of the right-click. Or, if you prefer, you can enable right-clicking by editing the system preferences for your mouse.

Figure B-3   How to install the source files for this book

How to create the databases for this book

Before you can run the SQL statements presented in this book, you need to create the three databases described in the previous figure. The easiest way to do that is to use MySQL Workbench to run the SQL script that's stored in the create_databases.sql file. The procedure for doing this is described in figure B-4.

To determine if the SQL script ran successfully, you can review the results in the Output window. In this figure, for example, the Output window shows a series of statements that have executed successfully. In addition, the Object Browser window shows that the three databases have been created. The other database, named Test, is a database that comes with MySQL.

If the script encounters problems, MySQL Workbench displays one or more errors in the Output window. Then, you can read these errors to figure out why the script isn't executing correctly.

Before you can run the create_databases.sql script, the database server must be running. By default, the database server is automatically started when you start your computer, so this usually isn't a problem. However, if it isn't running on your system, you can start it as described in figure B-1.

How to restore the databases

As you work with the code that's presented in this book, you may make changes to the databases or tables that you don't intend to make. In that case, you may want to restore the databases to their original state so your results match the results shown in this book. To do that, you can run the create_databases.sql file again. This drops the three databases described in this appendix and recreates them.

The directory that contains the create_databases.sql file

`/murach/mysql/db_setup`

MySQL Workbench after executing the create_databases.sql file

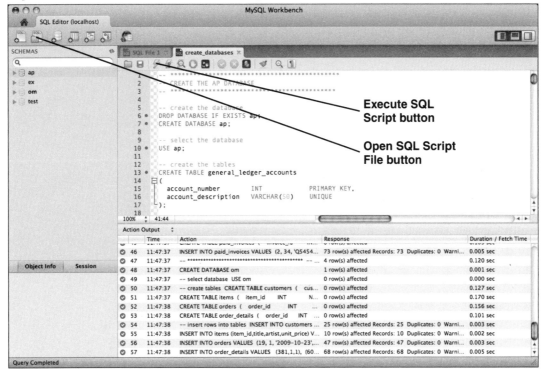

How to create the databases

1. Start MySQL Workbench.

2. Double-click on a stored connection for the root user to connect to an instance of MySQL that's running on the localhost computer. If you created the connection named "Local instance MySQL55" in figure B-2, you can use this connection.

3. Open the create_databases.sql file by clicking the Open SQL Script File button in the SQL Editor toolbar. Then, use the resulting dialog box to locate and open the file. When you do, MySQL Workbench displays this script in a code editor tab.

4. Execute the script by clicking the Execute SQL Script button in the code editor toolbar. When you do, the Output window displays messages that indicate whether the script executed successfully.

How to restore the databases

- Run the create_databases.sql script again to drop the databases and recreate them.

Description

- For the create_databases.sql file to run, the database server must be running. By default, the database server is automatically started when your start your computer. If it isn't running on your system, you can start it as described in figure B-1.

Figure B-4   How to create and restore the databases for this book

Index

- operator, subtraction, 85
--characters (comment), 32, 33
!= operator, 95
% operator (modulo) 85
* operator
    all columns, 80, 81
    multiplication, 85
.NET, 34, 35
/ operator (division), 85
/*...*/ characters (block comment), 32, 33
+ operator (addition), 85
< operator, 94, 95
<= operator, 94, 95
<> operator, 94, 95
= operator, 94, 95
> operator, 94, 95
>= operator, 94, 95

A

ABS function, 250, 251
Account name, 502, 503
Ad hoc relationship, 116, 117
ADD PRIMARY KEY, 324, 325
Addition operator, 85
Admin tab (MySQL Workbench), 44, 45, 514, 515
Administrative privileges, 496, 497
Administrative Roles tab (MySQL Workbench), 516, 517
ADO.NET, 34, 35
AFTER keyword (trigger), 446, 447
AFTER trigger, 450, 451
Aggregate function, 152-155
Aggregate query, 152-155
Alias
    column, 82, 83
    in ORDER BY, 108, 109
    table, 118, 119
ALL keyword
    aggregate function, 152, 153
    SELECT, 81, 93
    subquery, 178, 179
    UNION, 142, 143
ALTER EVENT statement, 456, 457
ALTER INDEX statement, 23
Alter Table command (MySQL Workbench), 53
ALTER TABLE statement, 23, 322-325
ALTER VIEW statement, 368, 369
Ambiguous column name, 116, 117

American National Standards Institute (ANSI), 18, 19
American standard code for information interchange,
    see ASCII
AND operator, 96, 97, 122, 123
ANSI (American National Standards Institute), 18, 19
ANSI/ISO SQL, 19
ANSI-standard SQL, 18, 19
ANY keyword, 176, 177, 180, 181
AP database
    script that creates, 331-333
    tables available, 48, 49
API (Application Programming Interface), 6, 7, 34, 35
Apostrophes in literal values, 87
Application
    server, 8, 9
    software, 6, 7
    web, 8, 9
Application programming interface (API), 6, 7, 34, 35
Approximate numeric type, 222, 223
Approximate value, 252, 253
Argument, 86, 87
Arithmetic expression, 84, 85
Arithmetic operator, 84, 85
AS keyword (SELECT), 82, 83
ASC keyword, 106, 107, 328, 329
Ascending sequence, 106, 107
ASCII, 218, 219
    control characters, 236, 237
Assign columns, 284, 285
Associate table, 286, 287
Attribute, 278, 279, 316, 317
Auto increment column, 15
AUTO_INCREMENT attribute, 316, 317
AVG function, 152-155

B

Back end, 7
Back up a database, 526, 527
    script, 530-533
Base table, 26, 27, 76, 77, 354, 355
BCNF (Boyce-Codd normal form), 294, 295
BEFORE keyword (trigger), 446, 447
BEGIN keyword, 374, 375, 394, 395
BETWEEN operator, 100, 101
BIGINT data type, 221
Bin directory, 484, 485, 528, 529
Binary log, 464, 465, 484, 485, 540, 541
    convert to text, 484, 485, 540, 541
Bit, 218, 219
BLOB (Binary Large Object) data type, 230, 231
Block comment, 32, 33
Block of code, 374, 375

BOOL data type, 220, 221
BOOLEAN data type, 220, 221
Boolean expression, 76, 77, 382, 383
Boyce-Codd normal form (BCNF), 294, 295
Browser (web), 8, 9
Business components, 8, 9
By position (parameters), 416, 417
Byte, 218, 219

C

C#, 34, 35
Calculated value, 26, 27, 80, 81
    assigning name, 82, 83
Call a procedure, 416, 417
CALL statement, 375, 376, 416, 417
Cartesian product, 140, 141
CASCADE option, 320, 321
Cascading delete, 320, 321
CASE (computer-aided software engineering), 284, 285
CASE function, 268, 269
CASE statement, 384, 385
Cast, 234, 235
CAST function, 234, 235, 246, 247
CEILING function, 250, 251
Cell, 10, 11
CHANGED option, 546, 547
CHAR data type, 15, 216-219, 234, 235
CHAR function, 236, 237
Character set
    specify, 344, 345
    view, 342, 343
CHARACTER SET keyword, 344, 345
CHARSET clause, 344, 345
CHECK TABLE statement, 546, 547, 550, 551
Client, 4, 5
    software, 6, 7
Client/server system
    architectures, 8
    hardware components, 5
    implementations, 5
    versus file-handling system, 7
CLOB (Character Large Object) data type, 230, 231
COALESCE function, 270, 271
Codd, E.F., 10, 18, 19
Code
    block of, 374, 375
    procedural, 378, 379
Code editor tab (MySQL Workbench), 55
Codes for date/time format strings, 261
Coding guidelines, 32, 33
COLLATE clause, 344, 345
Collation, 340-345
    specifying, 344, 345

viewing, 342, 343
Column, 10, 11
    alias, 82, 83
    altering, 322, 323
    ambiguous name, 116, 117
    attribute, 316, 317
    definition, 52, 53
    function, 152, 153
    identical values, 92, 93
    identifying indexes, 292, 293
    list (INSERT), 200, 201
    naming, 82, 83
    position (ORDER BY), 108, 109
    privileges, 498, 499
    qualified name, 116, 117
    specification, 80, 81, 83, 86
    table (MySQL Workbench), 334, 335
Column-level
    constraint, 318, 319
    foreign key constraint, 320, 321
    primary key constraint, 318, 319
Comma-delimited file, 542, 543
Comment, 32, 33, 190, 530, 531
Commit, 402, 403
COMMIT statement, 402, 403
Comparison operator, 94, 95, 176, 177
Complex query, 190-193
Composite
    index, 292, 293
    primary key, 10, 11
Compound condition, 96, 97
    join, 122, 123
    search, 162, 163
CONCAT function, 80, 81, 86, 87, 242-245
CONCAT_WS function, 242-245
Concatenate, 80, 81, 86, 87
Concatenation operator, 86, 87
Concurrency, 406-411
Concurrency problems, 408, 409
Condition
    compound join, 122, 123
    compound search, 96, 97
    join, 116, 117
Condition handler
    declare, 390, 391
    multiple, 396, 397
    use, 392, 393
Configuration file, 464, 465, 474, 475
Configure
    logging, 480, 481
    server, 472, 473
Connecting as a user (MySQL Workbench), 520, 521
Connecting table, 286, 287

Connection object (Java), 38, 39
Connector/J driver, 34, 35, 38
Connector/Net driver, 34, 35
Constraint, 24, 25, 318, 319
    altering, 324, 325
    foreign key, 288, 289
CONSTRAINT keyword, 318, 319, 324, 325
CONTINUE handler, 390-395
Conversion (implicit), 94
Convert binary log to SQL file, 540, 541
CONVERT function, 234, 235
Converting data types, 232, 233
Correlated subquery, 182, 183
Correlation identifiers, 446, 447
COUNT function, 152-155
Counter, 386, 387
CREATE DATABASE statement, 23, 314, 315, 330, 331
CREATE FUNCTION statement, 434, 435
CREATE INDEX statement, 23, 328, 329
CREATE OR REPLACE VIEW statement, 368, 369
CREATE PROCEDURE statement, 374, 375, 416, 417
CREATE TABLE AS statement, 199
CREATE TABLE statement, 23, 198, 199, 316, 317
CREATE TRIGGER statement, 446, 447
CREATE USER statement, 492, 493, 500, 501, 508, 509, 512, 513
CREATE VIEW statement, 354, 355, 358, 359
CROSS JOIN keywords, 140, 141
CURDATE function, 254, 255
CURRENT_DATE function, 90, 91, 254, 255
CURRENT_TIMESTAMP function, 254, 255
Cursor, 388, 389
CURSOR variable type, 388, 389
CURTIME function, 254, 255

D

Data
    display, 378, 379
    import from a file, 544, 545
Data access API, 6, 7
Data access model, 34, 35
Data consistency (triggers), 448, 449
Data definition language (DDL), 22, 23
Data elements
    identify, 280, 281
    subdivide, 282, 283
Data file, 464, 465
Data manipulation language (DML), 22, 23
Data redundancy, 290, 291
Data structure
    denormalize, 302, 303
    design, 278, 279

    normalized, 290, 291, 294, 295
    unnormalized, 290, 291
Data type, 14, 15, 216-237
    converting, 232-237
Data validation, 422, 423
Database
    back up, 526, 527
    create, 314, 315
    drop, 314, 315
    relational, 10, 11
    restore, 526, 527, 536, 537
    script that sets up privileges for, 512, 513
    server, 4, 5
Database administrator (DBA), 22, 23, 462, 463
Database backup script, 530-533
Database diagram, 16
Database engine, 44, 45
Database files, 464, 465
Database management system (DBMS), 6, 7
Database objects, 22-24, 48, 49
Database privileges, 498, 499
Database replication, 462, 463
Database server, 9
    start and stop, 44, 45
Date (search for), 264, 265
DATE column, 226, 227
DATE data type, 15, 216, 217, 225, 234, 235
DATE function, 260, 261
Date literal, 94, 95
Date values, 266, 267
Date data types, *see date/time data types*
Date/time data types, 216, 217, 224, 225, 254-257
Date/time format, 260, 261
Date/time functions, 256, 257
Date/time literal values, 226, 227
Date/time perform calculations, 262, 263
Date/time units, 258, 259
DATE_ADD function, 262, 263
DATE_FORMAT function, 88, 89, 260, 261
DATE_SUB function, 262, 263
DATEDIFF function, 262, 263
DATETIME column, 264-267
DATETIME data type, 216, 217, 224, 225, 234, 235, 264, 265
DATETIME function, 260, 261
DATETIME value, 266, 267
DAYNAME function, 256, 257
DAYOFMONTH function, 257
DAYOFWEEK function, 256, 257
DAYOFYEAR function, 257
DB2 database system, 18, 19
    compared to other databases, 20, 21
DBA (database administrator), 22, 23, 462, 463

DBMS (database management system), 6, 7, 9
DDL (Data Definition Language), 22-24
Deadlock, 412, 413
DEALLOCATE statement, 430, 431
DEC data type, 222, 223
DECIMAL data type, 222, 223, 234, 235
Declarative referential integrity (DRI), 288, 289
Declare condition handler, 390, 391
DECLARE keyword, 380, 381
DECLARE statement, 374, 375
DECLARE...CONDITION statement, 390, 391
DECLARE...HANDLER statement, 390, 391
Declaring a variable, 380, 381
DEFAULT attribute, 316, 317, 331-333
DEFAULT keyword, 380, 381, 476, 477
    with INSERT, 202, 203
Default sequence (sort order), 106, 107
Default value
    column, 14, 15
    parameter, 420, 421
DELETE statement, 23, 30, 31
    subquery, 210, 211
    syntax, 210, 211
    through view, 366, 367
DELIMITER statement, 374, 375
Denormalize, 302, 303
DESC keyword, 328, 329
    in ORDER BY, 106, 107
Descending sequence, 106, 107
Design a data structure, 278, 279
Dialect (SQL), 18, 19
Dirty read, 408, 409
DISABLE keyword, 456, 457
Disable logging, 478, 479
DISTINCT keyword
    aggregate function, 152-155
    SELECT, 80, 81, 92, 93
    self-joins, 124, 125
DISTINCTROW keyword, 93
DIV function, 84, 85
Division operator, 85
DKNF (domain-key normal form), 294, 295
DML (Data Manipulation Language), 22, 23
Domain, 294, 295
Domain-key normal form (DKNF), 294, 295
DOUBLE data type, 222, 223, 252, 253
DOUBLE PRECISION data type, 222, 223
Double quotes
    alias, 82, 83
    literal value, 86, 87
    string literal, 86, 87
Double-precision number, 222, 223
DRI (declarative referential integrity), 288, 289

Drivers (database), 34, 35
Drop a table, 326, 327
DROP DATABASE statement, 23, 314, 315, 330, 331
DROP EVENT statement, 456, 457
DROP FOREIGN KEY keywords, 324, 325
DROP FUNCTION statement, 438, 439
DROP INDEX statement, 23, 328, 329
DROP PRIMARY KEY keywords, 324, 325
DROP PROCEDURE statement, 432, 433, 374, 375
DROP TABLE statement, 23, 198, 199, 326, 327
DROP TRIGGER statement, 452, 453
DROP USER statement, 500, 501, 508, 509
DROP VIEW statement, 368, 369
Dump, 528, 529
Duplicate rows (eliminating), 92, 93
Dynamic SQL, 430, 431

E

EER (enhanced entity-relationship), 42
EER diagram, 16, 17, 42, 304, 305, 308, 309
EER model, 304-307
Ellipsis, 80
ELSE clause, 382, 383
ELSEIF clause, 382, 383
ENABLE keyword, 456, 457
Enable logging, 478, 479
END keyword, 374, 375, 394, 395
ENGINE clause, 348, 349
Enhanced entity-relationship (EER), 42
    diagram, 16, 17
    model, 304, 305
Enterprise system, 4, 5
Entity, 278, 279
Entity-relationship diagram, 16, 17
Entity-relationship model, 278, 279, 304, 305
ENUM data type, 227, 228
Equal operator, 94, 95
Equijoin, 136, 137
ER (entity-relationship) model, 278, 279
Error codes (MySQL), 390, 391
Error handler, 390, 391
Error log, 464, 465, 482, 483
Errors
    common causes, 58, 59
    raise, 422, 423
Event, 374, 375, 454-457, 528, 529
Event scheduler, 454, 455
Exact numeric type, 222, 223
Execute Current Statement button (MySQL Workbench), 55
Execute SQL script button (MySQL Workbench), 63
EXECUTE statement, 430, 431

EXISTS operator, 184, 185
EXIT handler, 390, 391, 394, 395
Explicit conversion, 232-235
Explicit syntax, 116, 117
    for outer join, 131
Export data to a file, 542, 543
Expression, 80, 81
    arithmetic, 84, 85
    comparing two, 94, 95
    ORDER BY, 108, 109
    string, 86, 87
    testing, 90, 91
EXTENDED option (CHECK TABLE), 546-551
Extension (SQL), 18, 19
EXTRACT function, 258, 259

F

FALSE keyword, 220, 221, 388, 389
FAST option (CHECK TABLE), 546, 547, 550, 551
FETCH statement, 388, 389
Field, 10, 11
FIELDS clause, 542, 543
Fifth normal form, 302, 303
File
    comma-delimited, 542, 543
    tab-delimited, 542, 543
File-handling system vs. client/server system, 7
Filter, 76, 77
Fire a trigger, 446, 447
Fire an event, 454, 455
First normal form, 296, 297
FIXED data type, 222, 223
Fixed-length string, 218, 219
Fixed-point data type, 222, 223
FLOAT data type, 15, 222, 223, 252, 253
Floating-point data type, 222, 223
    search, 252, 253
FLOOR function, 250, 251
Flow of execution (controlling), 376, 377
Flush-logs option (mysqldump), 528, 529
FOR clause, 510, 511
FOR EACH ROW clause, 446, 447
FOR UPGRADE option, 546, 547
Foreign key, 12, 13, 116, 117, 286, 287
    coding, 320, 321
    in MySQL Workbench, 338, 339
FOREIGN KEY keywords, 320, 321, 324, 325
Form (normal), 294-303
FORMAT function, 236, 237
Formatting dates and times, 260, 261
Fourth normal form, 302, 303
FROM clause, 26, 27, 76, 77, 116, 117
    subquery, 188, 189

Front end, 7
Front-end processing, 7
Full backup, 526, 527
FULL keyword, 130, 131
Full outer join, 130-135, 146, 147
FULLTEXT index, 346, 347
Function, 86-89, 242-271, *see also stored function*

G

General log, 464, 465, 482, 483
GLOBAL keyword, 410, 411, 476, 477
Global positioning system (GPS), 216, 217
Global privileges, 498, 499, 516, 517
GMT (Greenwich Mean Time), 254, 255
GRANT OPTION, 508, 509
Grant privileges, 504, 505
GRANT statement, 492, 493, 504, 505, 510, 511
    syntax, 504, 505
Grant tables (mysql database), 498, 499
Greater than operator, 94, 95
Greater than or equal to operator, 94, 95
Greenwich Mean Time (GMT), 254, 255
GROUP BY clause, 156-161
    CREATE VIEW, 358, 359
Guidelines (coding), 32, 33

H

HAVING clause, 156-161
    compared to WHERE clause, 160, 161
    subquery, 186, 187
History (SQL), 18, 19
Home tab (MySQL Workbench), 42, 43, 304, 305
HOUR function, 256, 257
HOUR_SECOND function, 258, 259
HTML tags, 36

I

IBM (DB2), 18, 19
IDENTIFIED BY clause, 500, 501
Identify data elements, 280, 281
Identify tables, 284, 285
IF EXISTS keywords, 314, 315
IF function, 270, 271
IF NOT EXISTS keywords, 314, 315
IF statement, 375, 376, 382, 383
IFNULL function, 270, 271
Ignore date values, 266, 267
Implicit conversion, 94, 232, 233
Implicit syntax (join), 128, 129
Import data from file, 544, 545
IN keyword (parameter), 418, 419

IN operator, 98, 99, 174, 175
Incremental backup, 526, 527
INDENTIFIED BY clause, 510, 511
Index, 10, 11
    columns, 292, 293
    composite, 292, 293
    create, 328, 329
    drop, 328, 329
    FULLTEXT, 346, 347
    in MySQL Workbench, 336, 337
Informix, 20
Inline view, 188, 189
Inner join, 28, 29
    combined with outer join, 134, 135
    explicit syntax, 116, 117
    implicit syntax, 128, 129
    SQL-92 syntax, 116, 117
INNER keyword, 116, 117
InnoDB storage engine, 346, 347
INOUT keyword (parameter), 418, 419
Input parameter, 418, 419
Input/output parameter, 418, 419
INSERT function, 242-245
INSERT statement, 23, 30, 31, 200, 201
    default value, 202, 203
    multiple rows from subquery, 204, 205
    null value, 202, 203
    through view, 366, 367
Instance, 278, 279
INT data type, 15, 220, 221
Integer data type, 15, 220, 221
INTEGER data type, 220, 221
Integer division, 85
Integers, 216, 217
Integrity (referential), 12, 13
INTO clause, 375, 376
INTO keyword, 380, 381
    and INSERT, 200, 201
INTO OUTFILE clause (SELECT), 542, 543
IS NULL clause, 104, 105
Isolation level, 410, 411
ITERATE statement, 386, 387

J

Java application, 34, 35, 38, 39
Java Database Connectivity (JDBC), 6, 7, 34, 35
Java driver, 35
java.sql package, 39
JDBC (Java Database Connectivity), 6, 7, 34, 35, 38-39
Join
    between databases, 120, 121
    compound condition, 122, 123
    condition, 116, 117
    cross, 140, 141
    implicit syntax, 128, 129
    inner, 28, 29, 116-119
    more than two tables, 126, 127
    multi-table, 126, 127
    natural, 138, 139
    outer, 28, 29, 130-135
    self, 124, 125
JOIN keyword, 116-141

K

Key
    column, 13
    composite primary, 10, 11
    foreign, 12, 13, 286, 287
    non-primary, 10, 11
    primary, 10, 11, 286, 287
    unique, 10, 11
Keywords, 76, 77
Kill a process, 466, 467
KILL statement, 466, 467

L

LAN (local area network), 4, 5
Large object (LOB) data type, 216, 217
LARGETEXT data type, 231
LAST_DAY function, 257
Latin1 character set, 218, 219, 341
LEAVE statement, 386, 387
LEFT function, 88, 89
LEFT keyword, 130, 131
Left outer join, 130-135
LENGTH function, 242-245
Less than operator, 94, 95
Less than or equal to operator, 94, 95
LIKE
    clause, 342, 343
    operator, 102, 103
    wildcards, 102, 103
LIMIT clause, 76, 77, 110, 111
    CREATE VIEW, 358, 359
    expanded syntax, 110, 111
Linking table, 286, 287
List of users, 506, 507
Literal,
    date, 94, 95
    numeric, 94, 95
    string, 86, 87, 94, 95
Literal date/time values, 226, 227
Literal value, 84, 86, 87

LOAD DATA statement, 544, 545
LOB (Large Object) data type, 230, 231
Local area network (LAN), 4, 5
Local instance MySQL (MySQL Workbench), 46, 47
LOCAL keyword, 476, 477
LOCATE function, 242-245, 248, 249
Lock-tables (mysqldump), 534, 535
Locking, 406-411
    preventing concurrency problems, 408, 409
Log, 478, 479
    binary, 484, 485
    managing, 486, 487
    text-based, 482, 483
    types, 464, 465
    written to tables, 482, 483
Logging
    configure, 480, 481
    disable, 478, 479
    enable, 478, 479
Logical operator, 96, 97
LONGBLOB data type, 231
Loop, 386, 387
Lost update, 408, 409
LOWER function, 242, 243
    in ORDER BY clause, 106, 107
LPAD function, 242, 243
LTRIM function, 242-245

M

Many-to-many relationship, 12, 13, 286, 287
Mask, 102, 103
Master, 462, 463
MAX function, 152-155
MEDIUM option, 546, 547
MEDIUMBLOB data type, 231
MEDIUMINT data type, 221
MEDIUMTEXT data type, 231
MIN function, 152-155 ·
MINUTE function, 257
MOD function, 84, 85
Modulo operator, 85
Monitoring (server), 466, 467
MONTH function, 257
MONTHNAME, 256, 257
Multi-table join, 126, 127
Multiple condition handlers, 396, 397
Multiple-byte character set, 218, 219
Multiplication operator, 85
Multivalued dependencies, 294, 295
my.cnf, 464, 465
my.ini, 464, 465
MyISAM storage engine, 346, 347

myisamchk program, 552, 553
MySQL
    command line, 66, 67
    compared to other databases, 20, 21
    daemon, 474, 475
    database system, 20, 21
    driver, 35
    error codes, 390, 391
    improved extension (mysqli), 34 , 35
MySQL monitor
    start and stop, 66, 67
    use, 66-69
MySQL Reference Manual, 64, 65
MySQL Workbench, 334-339, 514, 521
    Admin tab, 44, 45, 514, 515
    database design, 304, 305
    Home tab, 42, 43, 304, 305
    local instance MySQL, 46, 47
    Objective Browser, 48, 49, 51, 53
    open database connections, 46, 47
    Server Administration, 42-45
    SQL Development, 42, 43
    SQL statements, 54, 55
    Task and Object Browser, 44, 45
    work with a database, 46, 47
mysqlbinlog program, 538, 539
mysqlcheck program, 550, 551
mysqld program, 474, 475
    advanced options, 534, 535
mysqldump, 528, 529
mysqli (MySQL improved extension), 34 , 35

N

Name (column), 82, 83,
Named condition, 394, 395
    built-in, 391
Natural join, 138, 139
NATURAL keyword, 138, 139
NCLOB (National Character Large Object) data type,
    230, 231
Nest, 382, 383
Nested, 360, 361
    sort, 106, 107
    subqueries, 170, 171
    view, 360, 361
Network, 4, 5
New connection (MySQL Workbench), 518, 519
NEW keyword, 446, 447
New rows (inserting), 200, 201
Non-primary key, 10, 11
Nonrepeatable read, 408, 409
Normal form, 290, 291, 294, 295
    domain-key, 294, 295

fifth, 302, 303
first, 296, 297
fourth, 302, 303
second, 298, 299
third, 300, 301
Normalize data structure, 294, 295
Normalized, 290, 291
Not equal operator, 94, 95
NOT EXISTS operator, 184, 185
NOT FOUND condition, 390, 391, 396, 397
NOT IN operator, 174, 175
NOT NULL attribute, 316, 317-319, 331-333
NOT operator, 96-99
NOW function, 254, 255
Null
    aggregate function, 152, 153
    defined, 14
    INSERT, 202, 203
    search for, 104, 105
    UPDATE, 206, 207
NUMBER data type, 15
NumberFormat class, 38, 39
Numeric
    data, 250, 251
    data type, 216, 217
    function, 250, 251
    literal, 94, 95
NUMERIC data type, 222, 223

O

Object browser (MySQL Workbench) 48, 49, 51, 53
Object privileges, 496, 497
Offset, 110, 111
OLD keyword, 446, 447
ON clause, 136-139, 328, 329, 504, 505
ON DELETE clause, 320, 321
ON phrase, 116, 117
One-time event, 454, 455
One-to-many relationship, 12, 13, 286, 287
One-to-one relationship, 12, 13, 286, 287
Open source database system, 20, 21
Open SQL script (MySQL Workbench), 61
OPEN statement, 388, 389
Operating systems, 20, 21
OR operator, 96, 97, 122, 123
OR REPLACE keywords, 354-357
Oracle
    compared to other databases, 20, 21
    database system, 18, 19
ORDER BY clause, 26, 27, 76, 77, 106-109
    alias, 108, 109
    coding, 156, 157
    column position, 108, 109
    expanded syntax, 107
    expression, 108, 109
Order of precedence, 84, 85, 96, 97
Orphaned, 288, 289
OUT keyword (parameter), 418, 419
Outer join, 28, 29, 130-135
    combined with inner join, 134, 135
    examples, 132, 133
    explicit syntax, 131
OUTER keyword, 130, 131
Output parameter, 418, 419

P

Packages, 18, 19
Parameter, 86, 87
    default value, 420, 421
    input, 418, 419
    input/output, 418, 419
    output, 418, 419
    passing by position, 416, 417
Parentheses, 96, 97
Parse
    dates and times, 256, 257
    strings, 248, 249
Password (change), 510, 511
PDO (PHP Data Objects), 34
    API, 36, 37
    object, 36
Phantom read, 408, 409
PHP, 34-37
Pipe, 80
Point-in-time recovery (PITR), 526, 527
PostgreSQL, 20
POWER function, 250, 251
Precedence, 84, 85
Precision, 222, 223
Predicate, 76, 77
PREPARE statement, 430, 431
Primary key, 10-13, 116, 117, 286, 287, 318, 319
    composite, 10, 11
PRIMARY KEY keywords, 318, 319
Privileges, 492-509
    administrative, 496, 497
    four levels, 498, 499
    grant, 504, 505
    modify database structure, 494, 495
    object, 496, 497
    revoke, 508, 509
    script that sets, 512, 513
    view, 506, 507
    working with data, 494, 495

Procedural code, 378, 379
Procedure, *see stored procedure*
Process (view or kill), 466, 467
Process list, 467
PROXY privileges, 506, 507
Pseudocode, 192, 193

Q

Qualified column name, 116, 117
QUARTER function, 257
Query, 26, 27
    aggregate, 152-155
    results, 7
    SQL, 6, 7
    summary, 152-155
QUICK option, 546-553
Quotes (string literal), 86, 87

R

Raise an error, 422, 423
RAND function, 250, 251
RDBMS (relational database management system), 18,
    19
READ COMMITTED isolation level, 410, 411
READ UNCOMMITTED isolation level, 410, 411
Read-only view, 362, 363
REAL data type, 222, 223
Real number, 216, 217, 222, 223
Real-world system, 278, 279
Recommendations (coding), 32, 33
Record, 10, 11
Recover option, 552, 553
Recurring event, 454, 455
Redundant data, 290, 291
Reference constraint, 320, 321
Reference Manual (MySQL), 64, 65
REFERENCES clause, 324, 325
REFERENCES keyword, 320, 321
Referential integrity, 12, 13, 288, 289
REGEXP, 102, 103
Related tables, 12, 13
Relational database, 10, 11
Relational database management system (RDBMS), 18,
    19
Relationship
    ad hoc, 116, 117
    between tables, 12, 13,
Relay log, 464, 465
Rename column (SELECT), 82, 83
RENAME TABLE statement, 326, 327
RENAME TO keywords, 456, 457
RENAME USER statement, 500, 501

REPAIR TABLE statement, 548, 551
REPEAT loop, 386, 387
REPEATABLE READ isolation level, 410, 411
Repeating columns, 290, 291, 296, 297
REPLACE function, 242, 243
Restore database, 526, 527, 536, 537
Result set, 26, 27
    MySQL Workbench, 55
    sorted by column name, 106, 107
Result table, 26, 27
Results (query), 7
ResultSet object (Java), 38, 39
RETURN keyword, 434, 435
RETURNS keyword, 434, 435
REVERSE function, 242-245
REVOKE statement, 508, 509
RIGHT keyword, 130, 131
Right outer join, 130-135
Roll back, 402, 403
ROLLBACK statement, 402, 403
ROLLBACK TO SAVEPOINT statement, 405, 406
ROLLUP operator, 164, 165
ROUND function, 88, 89, 250, 251
Rounded value, 252, 253
Routines, 528, 529
Row, 10, 11
    delete, 210, 211
    duplicate, 92, 93
Row-level trigger, 446, 447
RPAD function, 242, 243
RTRIM function, 242-245

S

Save point, 405, 406
SAVEPOINT statement, 405, 406
Scalar function, 152, 153, 434, 435
Scalar-valued function, 434, 435
Scale, 222, 223
Scheduled event, 454, 455
Schema, 48, 49, 120, 121
Schema privileges tab (MySQL Workbench), 514, 515
Schemas list (MySQL Workbench), 55
Scientific notation, 222, 223
Script, 60, 61, 330, 331
    backup database, 530-533
    create database, 331-333
    create users, 512, 513
    PHP, 36
Search condition, 76, 77
    compound, 96, 97, 162, 163
    subquery, 170, 171
Search for null, 104, 105

Searched CASE function, 268, 269
Searched CASE statement, 384, 385
SECOND function, 257
Second normal form, 298, 299
SELECT clause, 26, 27, 76, 77
    code, 80, 81
        expanded syntax, 81
        subquery, 186, 187
SELECT statement, 23, 55, 76, 77
    basic syntax, 77
    display data, 378, 379
    examples, 78, 79
    four clauses of, 77
    GROUP BY clause, 157
    HAVING clause, 157
SELECT subquery, 170, 171
Self-join, 124, 125
SERIALIZABLE isolation level, 410, 411
Server, 4, 5
    application, 8, 9
    configure, 472, 473
    monitoring, 466, 467
    software, 6, 7
    web, 8, 9
Server configuration (log files), 479
Server management (MySQL Workbench), 514-517
SESSION keyword, 410, 411, 476, 477
SET clause (UPDATE), 206, 207
SET data type, 227, 228
SET NULL keywords, 320, 321
SET PASSWORD statement, 510, 511
SET SESSION statement, 348, 349
SET statement, 380, 381, 388, 389, 428, 429, 476, 477
SET TIMESTAMP statement, 484, 485
SET TRANSACTION ISOLATION LEVEL statement,
    410, 411
Seven normal forms, 294, 295
SHOW CHARSET statement, 342, 343
SHOW COLLATION statement, 342, 343
SHOW DATABASES statement, 68, 69
SHOW ENGINES statement, 346, 347
SHOW ERRORS statement, 390, 391
SHOW EVENTS statement, 456, 457
SHOW FUNCTION STATUS, 441
SHOW GRANTS statement, 492, 493, 506, 507
SHOW PRIVILEGES statement, 496, 497
SHOW PROCEDURE STATUS, 441
SHOW PROCESSLIST statement, 466, 467
SHOW STATUS statement, 468, 469
SHOW TRIGGERS statement, 452, 453
SHOW VARIABLES statement, 342, 343, 346, 347,
    454, 455, 470, 471
SHOW WARNINGS statement, 390, 391

SIGN function, 250, 251
SIGNAL statement, 422, 423
SIGNED data type, 234, 235
Significant digits, 222, 223
Simple CASE function, 268, 269
Simple CASE statement, 384, 385
Simple loop, 386, 387
Single quotes
    alias, 82, 83
    literal value, 86, 87
Single-byte character set, 218, 219
Single-line comment, 32, 33
Single-precision number, 222, 223
Slave, 462, 463
Slow query log, 464, 465, 482, 483
SMALL INT data type, 221
Snippets tab (MySQL Workbench), 56, 57
Software, 6, 7
SOME keyword, 176, 177, 180, 181
Sort, *see ORDER BY clause*
Sort order, 106, 107
SPACE function, 242, 243
Spatial data type, 216, 217
Specification (column), 80, 81
Sproc, 416, 417
SQL, 6, 7
    ANSI-standards, 18, 19
    coding guidelines, 32, 33
    dialect, 18, 19
    dynamic, 430, 431
    extensions, 18
    history, 18, 19
    query, 6, 7
    standards, 18, 19
    syntax, 56, 57
    variant, 18, 19
SQL editor tab (MySQL Workbench), 518, 519
SQL script
    create AP database, 331-333
    enter and execute, 62, 63
    open and save, 60, 61
SQL Server, 18, 19
    compared to other databases, 20, 21
SQL standards, 18, 19
SQL statement, 22, 23
    control flow of execution, 376, 377
    enter and execute, 54, 55
SQL/Data System, (SQL/DS), 18, 19
SQL-92 standards, 116, 117
SQLEXCEPTION condition, 390, 391, 396, 397
SQLSTATE code, 390, 391, 396, 397, 422, 423
SQLWARNING condition, 390, 391, 396, 397
SQRT function, 250, 251

Standard SQL, 19
Standards (SQL-92), 117
Start Server button (MySQL Workbench), 44, 45
START TRANSACTION statement, 402, 403
Status variable, 468, 469
Stop Server button (MySQL Workbench), 44, 45
Storage engine (view and specify), 346, 347
Stored function, 374, 375, 434-439
Stored procedure, 374, 375, 416-433
    drop, 432, 433
    insert a row, 424-427
Stored programs, 374-397
Stored routine, 374, 375
    with MySQL Workbench, 440, 441
String, 86, 87, 242-249
    concatenate, 86, 87
    data type, 216, 217
    format, 86, 87
    parse, 248, 249
    sort, 246, 247
String expression, 86, 87
String functions, 242-249
    examples, 244, 245
String literal, 86, 87, 94, 95
String pattern, 102, 103
Structured Query Language (SQL), *see SQL*
Subdivide data elements, 282, 283
Subquery, 98, 99, 170-193
    ALL keyword, 178, 179
    ANY keyword, 180, 181
    comparison operator, 176, 177
    correlated, 182, 183
    DELETE statement, 210, 211
    EXISTS keyword, 184, 185
    FROM clause, 188, 189
    HAVING clause, 186, 187
    IN operator, 174, 175
    in search condition, 170, 171, 174, 175
    insert multiple rows, 204, 205
    INSERT statement, 204, 205
    introduce in SELECT, 170, 171
    NOT EXISTS keyword, 184, 185
    NOT IN operator, 174, 175
    SELECT clause, 186, 187
    SOME keyword, 180, 181
    uncorrelated, 182, 183
    UPDATE statement, 208, 209
SUBSTRING function, 242-245, 248, 249
SUBSTRING_INDEX function, 242-245, 248, 249
Subtraction operator, 85
SUM function, 152-155
Summary query, 152-155, 164, 165
Sybase, 20

Syntax conventions, 76, 77
Syntax errors (handling), 58, 59
SYSDATE function, 254, 255
System variable, 470, 471
    enable logging, 479
    log files, 480, 481
    set using a SET statement, 476, 477
    set using a text editor, 474, 475
    set with MySQL Workbench, 472, 473

T

Tab-delimited file, 542, 543
Table, 10, 11, 316, 317
    alias, 118, 119
    alter, 322, 323
    base, 26, 27
    drop, 326, 327
    in MySQL Workbench, 334, 335
    relationships between, 12, 13
    rename, 326, 327
    truncate, 326, 327
Table constraints, 324, 325
Table data (view and edit), 50, 51
Table name (qualify), 121
Table privileges, 498, 499
Table scan, 292, 293
Table-level constraint, 318, 319
    foreign key, 320, 321
    primary key, 318, 319
Tables (identify), 284, 285
Task and Object Browser (MySQL Workbench), 44, 45
Temporal data types, *see date/time data types*
Teradata, 20,
Test expressions, 90
TEXT data type, 216, 217, 230, 231
Text-based logs, 482, 483
THEN clause, 375, 376
Thin client, 8
Third normal form, 300, 301
TIME data type, 224, 225, 234, 235
Time values
    ignore, 264, 265
    search for, 266, 267
TIME_FORMAT function, 260, 261
TIME_TO_SEC function, 262, 263
TIMESTAMP data type, 224, 225
TINYBLOB data type, 231
TINYINT data type, 221
TINYTEXT data type, 231
TO_DAYS function, 262, 263
Transaction, 402-413
Transaction isolation level, 410-413

Transitive dependencies, 294, 295
Trigger, 374, 375, 446-453
    AFTER, 450, 451
    drop, 452, 453
    enforcing data consistency, 448, 449
    row-level, 446, 447
    view, 452, 453
TRIM function, 242-245
TRUE keyword, 220, 221, 388, 389
TRUNCATE function, 250, 251
TRUNCATE TABLE statement, 326, 327
Type, *see Data type*

U

UDF (user-defined function), 374, 375, 434-439
Uncorrelated subquery, 182, 183
Unicode standard, 218, 219
Union
    simulate full outer join, 146, 147
    syntax, 142, 143
UNION keyword, 142-147
UNIQUE attribute, 316, 317
Unique constraint, 318, 319
Unique key, 10, 11,
UNIQUE keyword, 328, 329
Universal time coordinate (UTC), 254, 255
Unix Millennium bug, 224, 225
Unix operating system, 20
Unnormalized data structure, 290, 291
UNSIGNED attribute, 220-223
UNSIGNED data type, 234, 235
Updatable view, 362, 363, 365
Update (lost), 408, 409
Update existing rows, 206, 207
UPDATE privilege, 510, 511
UPDATE statement, 23, 30, 31, 206, 207
    through view, 364, 365
    with subquery, 208, 209
UPPER function, 242, 243
USAGE privilege, 510, 511
USE statement, 314, 315, 330, 331
User accounts, 492, 493, 500, 501
    connect as, 520, 521
    create, 512, 513
    list, 506, 507
    specify name, 502, 503
User variable, 418, 419, 428, 429
User-defined function (UDF), 374, 375, 434-439
Username, 502, 503
Users and Privileges (MySQL Workbench), 516, 517
USING clause, 136-139
UTC (Universal Time Coordinate), 254, 255

UTC_DATE function, 254, 255
UTC_TIME function, 254, 255
UTF-8 character set, 218, 219
utf8, 341

V

Value, 10, 11
    approximate, 252, 253
    literal, 84, 86, 87
    null, 104, 105
    rounded, 252, 253
VALUE ERROR exception, 422, 423
VALUES clause, 200, 201
VARCHAR data type, 15, 218, 219
Variable
    declare, 380, 381
    set, 380, 381
    status, 468, 469
    system, 470, 471, 472, 473
    user, 418, 419, 428, 429
Variable length string, 218, 219
Variant, 19
VB.NET application, 34, 35
View
    benefits, 356, 357
    creating, 354, 355
    deleting through, 366, 367
    inserting through, 366, 367
    nested, 360, 361
    read-only, 362, 363
    updatable, 362, 363
    updating through, 364, 365
Viewed table, 355
Visual Basic, 34, 35

W

WAN (wide-area network), 4, 5
Web, 8, 9
Web-based system, 8, 9
WEEK function, 257
WHEN clause, 268, 269
WHERE clause, 26, 27, 76, 77, 94, 95
    BETWEEN phrase, 100, 101
    compared to HAVING clause, 160, 161
    DELETE, 210, 211
    IN phrase, 98, 99, 174, 175
    IS NULL clause, 104, 105
    join condition, 128, 129
    LIKE phrase, 102, 103
    logical operators, 96, 97
    REGEXP phrase, 102, 103

subquery, 170-193
UPDATE, 206, 207
WHILE loop, 386-389
Wide-area network (WAN), 4, 5
Wildcard, 102, 103
Windows, 20, 21
WITH CHECK OPTION clause, 364, 365
WITH GRANT OPTION, 504, 505
WITH ROLLUP operator, 164, 165

XYZ

Y2K38 problem, 224, 225
Year 2038 problem, 224, 225
YEAR data type, 225
YEAR function, 257
yyyy-mm-dd format, 226, 227
z/OS operating system, 20, 21
ZEROFILL attribute, 220-223

The software that you need for this book

- MySQL Community Server (a free download).
- MySQL Workbench (a free download).

The source code that you can download

- The script file that creates the three databases used in this book.
- The source code for all of the examples in this book.
- The solutions to the exercises that are at the end of each chapter.

How to download the software

1. Go to www.mysql.com.
2. Use the pages on that site to download and install the MySQL Community Server and MySQL Workbench.
- For more details, see appendix A (Windows) or appendix B (Mac OS X).

How to download the source code

1. Go to www.murach.com and navigate to the page for *Murach's MySQL*.
2. Use the links on that page to download the source code. For Windows, download the self-extracting zip file (an exe file). For Mac OS X, download the regular zip file.
3. Double-click the downloaded file and respond to the dialog boxes that follow.
- For more details, see appendix A (Windows) or appendix B (Mac OS X).

How to create the databases

1. Start MySQL Workbench as described in chapter 2.
2. Run the script named create_databases.sql in the murach/mysql/db_setup directory.
- For more details, see appendix A (Windows) or appendix B (Mac OS X).

www.murach.com